NEW VOICES IN ARAB CI'

NEW VOICES IN ARAB CINEMA

Roy Armes

Indiana University Press

Bloomington and Indianapolis

This book is a publication of

Indiana University Press
Office of Scholarly Publishing
Herman B Wells Library 350
1320 East 10th Street
Bloomington, Indiana 47405 USA

iupress.indiana.edu

Telephone   800-842-6796
Fax   812-855-7931

Manufactured in the United States of America

Cataloging information is available from the Library of Congress.

ISBN 978-0-253-01516-7 (cloth)
ISBN 978-0-253-01522-8 (paperback)
ISBN 978-0-253-01528-0 (ebook)

1 2 3 4 5 20 19 18 17 16 15

For Helen, Philip, and Alison

Arab cultural modernity in the twentieth century was probably even more far-reaching than during the nineteenth-century renaissance, since it went beyond the written word. Other forms of cultural creation presented themselves, different ways in which Arab artistic expression could reflect its time—in the visual arts, theatre, music and in particular the cinema.

Samir Kassir, *Being Arab*

Contents

Acknowledgments

Many people have helped me with the compilation of this book, and I thank those, among them festival organizers and film distributors, who have guided me to new sources of material: Masoud Amrall Al Ali of the Gulf Film Festival, Marie-Claude Behna of the Association de Cinéma Arabe, Stéphanie Boring of Films d'Ici, Catherine Chicot, Jaqueline Dallmair of trigon-film, Mona Deeley of Zenith Films, Nick Denes of the Palestinian Film Foundation, Alberto Elena of the Carlos III University in Madrid, Haithem El-Zabri of the Palestine On-line Store, Yael Friedman, May Hossam of Misr International Films, Rose Issa, Tarik Khalami of the Centre Cinématographique Marocain, Thierry Lenouvel of Ciné-Sud Promotion, Nicole Mackey of Fortissimo Films, Diran Mardirian of Video Chico in Beirut, Leïla Mourad of Aramis Films, Egil Odegard of the Norwegian Film Institute, Anne-Cécile Pavaux of 3B Productions, Éliane Raheb of the Beirut Film Festival, Michel Riachi of Nadilekolnass in Beirut, John Sinno of Typecast Films in Seattle, Annabel Thomas, Suzanne Widmer of trigon-film, and Abdellah Zerguine of Regard Sud.

I am especially grateful to those filmmakers who provided, or helped provide, access to DVD or on-line copies of their own films: Ahmad Abdalla, Layth Abdulamir, Mohamed Alatar, Kamal Aljafari, Khaled al-Haggar, Koutaïba al-Janabi, Ayda Ben Aleya, Nigol Bezjian, Nadia Cherabi-Labidi, Dima El-Horr, Abbas Fahdel, Dalia Fathallah, Nasri Hajjaj, Moktar Ladjimi, Najwa Najjar, Éliane Raheb, Ahmed Rashwan, Djamila Sahraoui, Leila Sansour, Hany Tamba, Tariq Teguia, and Hady Zaccak.

Last, but by no means least, I must thank the Leverhulme Trust for the award of a further Emeritus Fellowship which helped to finance the research for this book.

Abbreviations

ACCT	Agence de Coopération Culturelle et Technique (France)
AIF	Agence Intergouvernementale de la Francophonie (France)
ALBA	Académie Libanaise des Beaux Arts (Lebanon)
ANAF	Agence Nationale des Actualités Filmées (Algeria)
AUB	American University of Beirut (Lebanon)
CAAIC	Centre Algérien pour l'Art et Industrie Cinématographiques (Algeria)
CAV	Centre Audio-Visuel (Algeria)
CBA	Centre Bruxellois de l'Audiovisuel (Belgium)
CCM	Centre Cinématographique Marocain (Morocco)
CLCF	Conservatoire Libre du Cinéma Français (France)
CNC	Centre National Cinématographique (France)
CNCA	Centre National du Cinéma Algérien (Algeria)
CPC	Cinema Production Centre (Palestine)
DAMS	Département d'Art, de Musique et du Spectacle (part of the University of Bologna, Italy)
ENADEC	Entreprise Nationale de Distribution et d'Exploitation Cinématographiques (Algeria)
ENATT	École Nationale des Arts et Techniques du Théâtre (France
ENAPROC	Entreprise Nationale de Production Cinématographique (Algeria)
ENPA	Entreprise Nationale de Productions Audiovisuelles (Algeria)
ESAD	École Supérieure d'Art Dramatique (part of the University of Geneva, Switzerland)
ESEC	École Supérieure des Études Cinématographiques (France)
ESRA	École Supérieure de Réalisation Audiovisuelle (France)
FAS	Fonds d'Action Sociale (France)
FED	Fonds Européen de Développement (Brussels, Belgium)
FEMIS	Fondation Européenne des Métiers de l'Image et du Son (France)
FEPACI	Fédération Panafricaine des Cinéastes (Burkina Faso)

FESPACO	Festival Panafricain du Cinéma de Ougadougou (Burkina Faso)
FIS	Front Islamique du Salut (Algeria)
FLN	Front de Libération Nationale (Algeria)
FTCA	Fédération Tunisiennes des Cinéastes Amateurs (Tunisia)
IDHEC	Institut des Hautes Études Cinématographiques (France)
IESAV	Institut d'Études Scéniques et Audiovisuelles (part of the Université Saint-Joseph in Beirut, Lebanon)
IKON	Interkerkelijke Omroep Nederland (Netherlands)
INSAS	Institut National des Arts et du Spectacle et Techniques de Diffusion (Belgium)
ISADAC	Institut d'Art Dramatique et Animation Culturelle (Morocco)
ISM	International Solidarity Movement (United Kingdom)
JCC	Journées Cinématographiques de Carthage (Tunisia)
LAU	Lebanese American University (Lebanon)
NGO	Non-governmental organization
NTFS	National Film and Television School (United Kingdom)
OAA	Office des Actualités Algériennes (Algeria)
OFC	Office Fédéral de la Culture (Switzerland)
OIF	Organisation Internationale de la Francophonie (France)
ONCIC	Office National du Commerce et de l'Industrie Cinématographiques (Algeria)
PARC	Palestine Agricultural Relief Committee (Switzerland)
PCL	Partie Communiste Libanaise (Lebanon)
PLO	Palestine Liberation Organization (Palestine)
RTA	Radiodiffusion Télévision Algérienne (Algeria)
RTBF	Radio-Télévision Belge de la Communauté Française (Belgium)
SATPEC	Société Anonyme Tunisienne de Production et d'Expansion Cinématographiques (Tunisia)
USJ	Université Saint Joseph (Beirut, Lebanon)
VGIK	Vsesoyuznyi Gosudarstvennyi Institut Kinematografii (All-Union Cinema Institute)
ZDF	Zweites Deutsches Fernsehen (Germany)
ZSP	Zone de Solidarité Prioritaire (France)

NEW VOICES IN ARAB CINEMA

Introduction

THIS BOOK is a personal journey through aspects of contemporary Arab film-making, dealing essentially with feature-length documentary films and fictional features made by filmmakers who began their careers in the 2000s. It has been an enjoyable and very revealing journey. The hundreds of films I have viewed basically adopt a single perspective: they are for understanding, liberty, equality, tolerance, and greater freedom for women. Not a single film I have seen—or even heard of—advocates jihad, war, violence, or oppression. According to Wissam Mouawad (currently a student at the Sorbonne) in a curious little article, my pleasure is a form of "neo-Orientalism," worse than the original, because we in the West are now employing local "manufacturers" (he refuses to call them artists) to produce the vision we wish to receive of the Arab world.[1] He chooses a predictably easy target for his wrath (Nadine Labaki's *Where Do We Go Next?*—a film clearly aimed at a popular audience). His argument would have been much more difficult to sustain had he chosen, for example, Haifaa al-Mansour's even more widely distributed and universally admired debut feature, *Wadjda*.

The reasons for the uniformity of approach shared by so many of the new Arab filmmakers is easily explained. It lies largely in the situation of the film-makers themselves. For independent filmmakers working in the Maghreb and the Middle East, the norm is European/US education and film training, foreign (mostly French) co-production funding, and in many cases, expatriate, usually European, residence (Nadine Labaki is almost unique in not having received a foreign education and/or training). Their films are all designed, at least in part, to please European funding organizations and potential coproduction collaborators and (for documentaries) international television corporations and NGO (non-governmental organization) sponsors, without whose continuing support the filmmaker's career is unlikely to progress. It will be fascinating to see if the increasing availability of Gulf funding—through the Doha festival, for example—changes the nature of Arab filmmaking.

One result of this double identity is certainly an ambiguity, which is not restricted to the Arab world. Writing elsewhere about filmmaking in sub-Saharan Africa, I quoted a telling observation by Moussa Sene Absa:

> African intellectuals live a duality, which they suppress most of the time. However, they speak French among themselves, they eat in French at the table at home, and often, they live in France; but when they shoot a film, they shoot it in their own language![2]

The same is true of Western-trained filmmakers in the Arab world. The reason why their work is so important and revealing is that they so often use their unique insider/outsider position, combined with acute intellectual insight and artistic ability, to clarify the issues confronting the modern-day citizens of both African and Arab worlds. This book sets out to show that, far from peddling clichés, as Mouawad asserts, modern Arab filmmakers offer truly probing insights into the complex world in which they find themselves.

Though touching on the work of a small number of independent directors who have made their feature debuts in Egypt in the 2000s, this book ignores the continuing force of the Egyptian film industry, which still largely operates, with great commercial success, in traditional ways and which calls for a separate study. This book also largely ignores the emerging cinemas of the Gulf, since the basis of production there (plentiful local financing, a well-endowed festival structure, limited international distribution, often local training) is so different from the situation which is prevalent elsewhere in the Arab world. Films from the Gulf remain largely unknown in the West. The three-day "Festival des Films du Golfe" held at the Institut du Monde Arabe in Paris (March 23–26, 2014) was, it seems, the first of its kind in Europe and comprised just four features and a dozen shorts. A couple of new voices among the three dozen or so feature filmmakers who have made a feature film in the Gulf are, however, briefly dealt with. The main focus here was intended to be on all the new independent voices emerging in Arab cinemas in the 2000s, dealing extensively with seven leading filmmaking countries of the Arab world, three in the Maghreb—Algeria, Morocco, and Tunisia—and four in the Middle East—Lebanon, Palestine, Iraq, and Syria. Although many filmmakers have been incredibly generous in sharing with me copies of their personal DVDs, certain films have, inevitably, eluded me. In such cases I have provided, wherever possible, factual information about the films, alongside the filmmakers' own synopses, statements of intent, and responses to interviews.

On a wider level, it has proved impossible to access enough new Syrian films to make a personal assessment of film production there. I include, therefore, a brief outline of developments, largely names and dates. Moroccan cinema has burgeoned during the decade—overall some 125 films in the years 2000–2010 and no less than 23 in 2011 alone. Almost all of these have been sponsored and partly financed by the Moroccan Film Centre (CCM) and aimed largely, it would seem, at the local market. The bulk of this production has also proved inaccessible to me, but almost all the Moroccan films which meet my criteria (i.e., being co-produced with an intended international audience in mind and hence available in subtitled DVD format) have proved accessible, and these films are discussed here at length.

I make this journey of discovery as someone who has fifty years' experience of writing about cinema, but who is not an Arabic-speaker. The films dealt with in detail here are therefore, by definition, those for which subtitled copies exist. This limitation in fact defines precisely the body of work which I wish to examine here: Arab films which, unlike mainstream Egyptian cinema, are not directed primarily at local filmgoers but have a wider intended audience outside the immediate Arab world. The Lebanese director Danielle Arbid speaks for many of these filmmakers when she says of her first feature:

> I don't make films to show them only in the Arab world, or Lebanon. I live in France, and my film was financed by French, Belgian and German companies. I feel the freedom to say what I want to say and film what I want to film. No one tells me what to film.[3]

Arbid's approach is echoed by that of Annemarie Jacir:

> I don't think women make different kinds of films to men. . . . You just want to be a filmmaker. Yes, I am Palestinian, yes, I am a woman—but I am so many other things too. . . . It does box you in at times.[4]

In a similar vein, Elia Suleiman says with regard to his film *The Time That Remains*:

> I'm saying it's an experience that can be identified with everywhere in the world. We live in a place called "the globe" today that has a multiplicity of experiences in it. My films do not talk about Palestine necessarily. They are Palestinian because I am from that place—I reflect my experience.[5]

Djamila Sahraoui is of the same opinion:

> I don't make films for the market. But I am very happy that my film is seen worldwide. And that confirms for me that people are the same everywhere. When I see the Swedes, Spanish and Italians talk to me about my work, they talk to me in the same way, they are all aware of the same issues.[6]

In effect, this book is concerned, to a large extent, with a kind of "art house" Arab cinema. There are many ways in which these films could be approached. My concern throughout has been with narrative structure, how facts and arguments are combined and how stories and fictional characters are woven together, so as to give both a firsthand insight into immediate developments in the contemporary Arab world and, very often, to reflect on how these developments have been shaped by the past.

For local audiences, potential access to these films through conventional commercial Arab distribution circuits will often be very limited. Few if any of them draw on the assumptions of traditional (Egyptian) film genres or directly seek out the same audience. This is not to say that many of them have not in fact enjoyed the support of a large local audience, precisely because they are unconventional. But whether banned at home (as a few of them are) or emerging as unexpected box office hits, their achievements are always fascinating.

My original intention was to limit this volume to a consideration of the hundred or so filmmakers who were born after 1960 and have begun their feature film careers since 2000. At the outset of writing, dealing with these filmmakers alone seemed a coherent and logical plan. But it soon became apparent that the cut-off points of 1960 (birth) and 2000 (feature debut) were too rigid and did not allow a reflection of the real scope of new and contemporary Arab cinema. For one thing, there were, in addition, around forty older filmmakers who had not been able to begin their feature careers till after 2000. Their films are among those which define the decade and it seemed impossible to exclude them from the body of work to be examined.

The year 2000 also proved problematic. A number of those whose feature film debuts came after 2000 have a history of significant feature-length documentary filmmaking in the 1990s, and a consideration of this work is clearly necessary for a proper appreciation of their fictional output. Another problem which presented itself was the fact that twenty or so members of the 1960s generation, spread across the Maghreb and the Middle East, managed to make their debuts in the late 1990s, though the bulk of their work is, in most cases, in the 2000s. These filmmakers are, in many cases, among the most talented of their generation—authentic new voices that could not be excluded.

I did not initially have a cut-off point for this study, but history has provided me with one: the Arab Spring of 2011. Some of the films discussed in detail here were released after 2011, but few reflect the potentially momentous events of that year, though several point clearly to the need for popular explosion. At the time of writing, there are a number of insightful documentary reflections on the immediate events of 2010–2011, such as Mourad Ben Cheikh's Tunisian *No More Fear / Plus jamais peur* (2011) and Ahmed Rashwan's Egyptian *Born on the 25th of January / Moloud fi khamsa we aishreen yanair* (2011). These vivid immediate responses have, of course, been overtaken by subsequent events, and though they offer unique insights, their conclusions will inevitably need to be reshaped in the light of history. There have also been some fictional films which reflect the immediate impact of the political upheaval. Key here are the fictional features produced by two members of an earlier generation: *Millefeuille* (2013) by the Tunisian Nouri Bouzid and *After the Battle / Après la bataille* (2012) by the Egyptian Yousry Nasrallah. Immediate fictional responses have also been made by two of the younger Egyptian independents: Ibrahim El Batout's *Winter of Discontent / El sheita elli fat* (2012) and Ahmad Abdalla's *Rags and Tatters / Farsh wa ghata* (2013) both capture vividly the upheavals in the lives of some of those on the periphery of the events in Tahrir Square.

The eventual outcomes of the popular uprisings of 2011 are still unclear, but this set of events will inevitably shape the aims and ambitions of Arab filmmakers in the years to come, just as the fifteen-year civil war in Lebanon has dominated the work of virtually every contemporary Lebanese filmmaker. Arab cinema has always been shaped by wider historical events and upheavals. The founding generation of modern Arab filmmaking in the 1960s personally experienced independence from colonial rule, and their films reflect the hopes and dreams of those savoring the promise of national freedom. A later generation, coming to maturity in the 1980s, was shaped, as Nouri Bouzid has observed, by the trauma of the 1967 Arab defeat and a growing disillusionment with Arab post-colonial societies. This present volume deals in essence with those who constitute the first generation born after independence (in the Maghreb) or the dissolution of the structures of government bequeathed by mandatory powers (in the Middle East). These filmmakers are faced with a world shaped by new global forces, including American cultural dominance, and, in their personal lives, the reality or threat of exile. A feature film normally takes three years or more from initial concept to realized project, so it will be several years before the full outlines of the new filmic sensibility shaped by the Arab Spring will become clear. But a new focus, mood, and sensibility there will undoubtedly be.

Even the extensions to the original rigid plan for this book do not mean, however, that it covers the full richness of Arab cinema in the 2000s. It is undeniable that some fascinating films have been made in the 2000s by filmmakers who are by no means "new voices." There are, for example, the veterans (most notably Youssef Chahine and Merzak Allouache), whose careers date back to the state film production organizations so prevalent in the 1970s or before (in Chahine's case) and have continued into the 2000s. Other members of this generation, who personally experienced national independence, have offered isolated new films, often after a gap of ten years or so. There are also those who established a so-called *beur* cinema in France in the mid-1980s and have continued to explore new relationships with the Maghreb. In addition, there are those who pioneered new styles of independent feature filmmaking in the Arab world as early as the

1980s—away from the concerns and constraints of the state. Most of these film-makers continue to produce prolifically in the 2000s. Many of those who strove to establish Arab documentary in the 1980s have also continued their work well into the 2000s. The films by individual members of these groups of filmmakers offer fascinating insights, even if they fall outside the scope of the present project, focused on the new voices in contemporary Arab cinema.

1   Characteristics of the New Cinema

Egypt continues to dominate Arab cinema in the 2000s, as it has always done, with the vast majority of its filmmakers based at home, and many of its most talented directors trained at the Cairo Higher Cinema Institute and expected to spend a year or two working in an assistant role before beginning a first feature. Cinema in Egypt has an impressive history, with well over 3,000 feature films made since the mid-1920s by around 400 directors.[1] Its films get by far the widest release throughout the Arab world, on both cinema and television screens. In the 2000s, some 330 feature films have been made by over 120 directors. But production elsewhere in the Arab world can match this in terms of output, if not in terms of audience figures. During the same period of the 2000s, over 200 feature films were made in the Maghreb and the Middle East by new filmmakers alone. There are, overall, just as many Arab feature filmmakers outside Egypt who have directed at least one feature film. These are divided fairly equally between the Maghreb and the Middle East, but they have made far fewer films, with only a tiny handful of filmmakers having had to opportunity to direct, say, three films in a decade. Yet the figures in the 2000s are impressive. For example, Egyptian filmmakers released just 35 fictional features in 2007, whereas some 22 were produced in the Maghreb and a further 10 in the Middle East.

Like their predecessors, the new filmmakers of the 2000s in both the Maghreb and the Mashreq keep their distance from Egyptian mainstream cinema, though it continues to dominate television screens throughout the Arab world. In one sense they have no choice, given the lack of any industrial infrastructure outside Egypt, which is the only Arab country to have a national cinema in the traditional sense in which the term is used in the West. Nowhere outside Egypt is there sufficient popular support for locally produced films to make them commercially viable without state aid, foreign co-production, or external funding.

What is perhaps more surprising, since the two areas have such very different histories (in terms of colonialization and the path to independence, for example) and such diverse systems of government (though virtually all are repressive in some way), is that filmmakers in both areas have chosen to adopt much the same approach to filmmaking. The basic characteristics of Maghrebian cinema, which Denise Brahimi picks out in the introduction to her book *Cinquante ans de cinéma maghrébin* are common as well to the cinemas of the Middle East.

In both areas, cinemas "essentially develop not through heroic gestures, but with a critical intent, unequivocally expressing a disillusionment, indeed a dissatisfaction"[2]—what Hélé Béji has called "national disenchantment."[3] The 2000s have seen the emergence of a generation with no firsthand experience of colonization or the governmental structures bequeathed by colonialism. For these filmmakers, the faults of contemporary society do not lie in a colonial past but in a maladministration occurring in the present. In so far as they use the past, it is frequently as a means of offering a critique of the present, which censorship restrictions prevent them from confronting directly. We find cinemas which may be socially critical but where political confrontation is never permitted. Comparatively few films are banned (though some have very restricted home distribution), but that is because filmmakers cannot fail to be aware of the constraints within which they must work.

Rather than being shaped by post-colonialism, the views of the 2000s generation are defined by the pressures and possibilities of globalization. The crucial role played by the United States—rather than by France, the former colonizer—for contemporary Arab filmmakers is well captured by Dalia Fathallah in her statement of intent concerning her documentary *Beirut Cowboy:*

> Even if I do not wish to admit it to myself, like so many Arabs, I still dream of America, this new world where I would be able to reinvent and recreate myself. . . . How is our dream of America confronted today with the US policy towards the Arab World? In Beirut, the capital which has always incarnated both the American dream of capitalism and modernity and that of Arab unity, I go searching for these two dreams.[4]

The filmmakers' approach is as much a product of their own social position as it is of their age. Although their films so often deal with the poor, with downtrodden women, outcast children, and exploited would-be migrants, their own personal situations are very different. They are typically members of a bi- or tri-lingual elite, often educated at some of the most prestigious universities in the West and trained at the foremost film schools in Europe, the United States, and Russia. Many of them live, by choice or necessity, in exile. Although they frequently are totally involved with the issues confronting the modern Arab world—particularly the role and status of women—they must of necessity approach these issues, to some extent at least, as outsiders. Their particular situation, however, allows them to be in the forefront of efforts for change. Indeed, some of the younger women directors, from both the Maghreb and the Middle East, who have lived and studied abroad for many years and are not held in check by local censorship or financing, often express in their films attitudes which would have been inconceivable to their mothers' generation.

Brahimi's comment that Maghrebian filmmakers ignore not only the model of the Egyptian commercial film but also the possibilities offered by Western genres is also a characteristic of Middle Eastern cinemas. The opportunities for social critique offered by the thriller are underexploited, and though comedies have proved themselves to be the most popular type of film with audiences at home and abroad, this genre too has been largely ignored—to the extent that Kevin Dwyer was able write an article about Moroccan cinema titled "One Country, One Decade, Two Comedies."[5] Has there been a single Arab horror film—in either the Maghreb or the Mashreq—since Hafsa Zinaï-Koudil's Algerian *Woman as the Devil* in 1993? Is there any real Arab forerunner for Scandar Copti and Yaron Shani's film noir–style thriller, *Ajami?*

A further area of popular cinema totally ignored is, as Brahimi observes, the pornographic film. As she notes, although "everyone knows that pornographic DVDs circulate widely in the Maghreb, as in other Muslim countries,"[6] Arab films show an extreme reticence in the depiction of any aspect of overt sexuality, the only exception to this being a handful of mostly Western-trained and European-based women directors. Representations of sexual frustration, on the other hand, are to be found in abundance. This cannot be explained simply in terms of constraints imposed by Islam. As Brahimi again observes, with reference to the fifty films she is analyzing, "Islam is present in a certain number of films, negatively or positively," but "it is only exceptionally that the Muslim religion plays a fundamental role."[7] There is a constant critique of Islamic fundamentalism, but this is from a standpoint analogous to that adopted in the West, not from any position rooted in alternative traditional Muslim values.

At the same time, in neither the Maghreb nor the Middle East has there been any parallel to the situation in the Egyptian film industry, where "a growing number of filmmakers, actors, and actresses, veiled and unveiled, refuse to visually portray sexually explicit scenes, appear in immodest clothing, or depict immoral characters."[8] Outside Egypt, there has been no sign of this "new regime of morally disciplined representations in the 'clean cinema' trend," as Egyptian critics have dubbed it. Equally, there is no sign of "a shift in the Islamic Revival towards regarding the entertainment industry as an arena for refashioning religio-ethical norms, particularly ones surrounding the female body and sexuality."[9] On the contrary, there has been a tendency for younger filmmakers, and women directors in particular, to take a more open approach to female sexuality (though this step generally remains modest by Western standards).

To the extent that the contemporary cinemas of the Maghreb and the Middle East are "art house" cinemas, in conventional critical parlance, the film directors are by definition film authors (or *auteurs*). But equally if not more significant in terms of actual production financing is the fact that France has adopted for its funding of films from the South the very same criteria which were developed for the funding of its own domestic cinema. These criteria are followed by virtually all other European funding bodies which deal with Arab filmmaking. In the French system, as Martin Dale points out, funds are allocated not to producers but formally to the director (legally recognized as the film's author), and subsidies are granted to those projects with the greatest "cultural merit."

This gives the *auteur,* whether in France or from abroad, "a significant bargaining tool in negotiating with producers and distributors."[10] The combination of foreign funding and the lack of a local production infrastructure also adds to the Arab filmmaker's responsibility. He or she must usually, of necessity, combine the roles of scriptwriter, producer, and director. If the film does achieve international festival screening, it will be the filmmaker who has to take on the tasks of promotion and publicity. Despite these constraints, contemporary Arab filmmakers remain, typically, independent and thoughtful critics of their own societies, with their values rooted in the more liberal traditions of both East and West. Their films, whether documentaries or features, give us a fascinating insight into how they wish to present, to as wide an audience as possible, the issues which they see as crucial to their societies in a constantly changing world.

2 The Filmmakers

NOURI BOUZID has pointed out the significance of the June 1967 Arab defeat for his own generation of filmmakers, who were born in the 1940s and made their breakthrough in the 1980s.[1] The generation born since 1960 and making its breakthrough in the 2000s is very differently placed. These filmmakers were either small children or not yet born in 1967. The shared political experiences shaping their lives have been the Yom Kippur War in 1973; the outbreak of the fifteen-year civil war in Lebanon in 1975; the eight-year Iran-Iraq War, which began in 1980; the successive assaults by Israeli forces on both Palestine and Lebanon; and the two Palestinian intifadas. As a result of the upheavals caused by these wars, many of the filmmakers have shared the experience of voluntary or enforced exile, often beginning in childhood or adolescence.

Their individual national experiences differ greatly, however. In the Maghreb, the new filmmakers constitute the first generation born after independence, but they have also experienced the rise of Islamic fundamentalism and life under often brutal dictatorships. In Lebanon, they grew up in the midst of seemingly interminable civil conflict and constant repetitions of foreign invasion and occupation, extending up to the 33-Day War of 2007. In Palestine, they experienced the continual tightening of Israeli rule, the Palestinian response to this (the two intifadas), and more recently, the blockade of Gaza and its bombardment in 2008. In Syria and Iraq, those whose parents had not been driven into exile grew up under Baath party rule and experienced at first hand the constraints imposed by the tyrannies of Hafez al-Assad and Saddam Hussein.

There are also cultural distinctions separating this new generation from the previous one. The world has changed since the mid-1980s. Talking of her sense of the difference between her own work and that of Nouri Bouzid and Ferid Boughedir (fourteen and fifteen years older than she is, respectively), the Tunisian filmmaker Nadia El Fani has said: "This difference is based on the fact that I belong to a generation that listened to rock and roll; we experienced the 1970s. There is a small gap between their generation and mine; there was no smooth transition between the two."[2]

There is work of real distinction to be found in the films of the 2000s new-comers, but much of the output is, in stylistic terms, fairly conservative. Only a few of the filmmakers have adopted styles that compare with the narrative inno-vation to be found, for example, in the work of their Francophone West African contemporaries, such as Jean-Pierre Bekolo, Mahamat Saleh Haroun, or Abder-rahmane Sissako. At the same time, though a number of the younger directors have made telefilms for broadcast transmission, there has been no breakthrough to truly popular forms of the kind exemplified by the "Nollywood" home video dramas of Nigeria. Equally, none of the younger filmmakers outside of Egypt has followed the example of Jocelyne Saab and made a mainstream Egyptian movie. The French notion of the individual filmmaker, seen legally as the author (*auteur*) of the film, seeking acclaim and establishing a reputation at international film festivals, remains the norm, as do foreign funding and co-production.

The New Importance of Women Filmmakers

Until the mid-1990s women made up little more than 6 percent of the total num-ber of feature filmmakers in the Maghreb, and there were even fewer women feature directors active in the Middle East. After the very real contributions of Arab women to the (expatriate dominated) beginnings of Egyptian filmmaking,[3] very few women were given the opportunity to direct a feature film. Sometimes the exclusions are staggering. No woman was given employment as a director within any of the successive Algerian state film production organizations. The two Algerian women pioneers, the prize-winning novelist Assia Djebar (elected to the Académie Française in 2004) and her fellow writer Hafsa Zinaï-Koudil each made just a single feature, in 1978 and 1993, respectively. But both Djebar's *La nouba* and Zinaï-Koudil's *Woman as the Devil* were 16mm works produced by Algerian television (RTA). Yamina Bachir-Chouikh's *Rachida* in 2002 was therefore the first 35mm feature film for cinema release to be directed by an Al-gerian woman, and though the filmmaker herself is resident in Algeria, all the production financing for this work came from France. The three other Algerian-born women to make a breakthrough in the 2000s, Yamina Benguigui, Djamila Sahraoui, and Nadia Cherabi-Labidi, are all French based and French funded. A similar pioneering role has been filled in Syrian documentary production by another Paris-based woman filmmaker, Hala al-Abdallah Yakoub.

But in Morocco, Tunisia, and Lebanon, conditions in the 2000s have been more favorable, and women make up about a quarter of all new directors. Sev-eral of these have already shown striking originality of tone and subject matter. Most focus largely on aspects of women's lives in the Arab world, and they often bring to this subject matter a quite novel perspective. But they by no means form a unified group, and indeed, their principal characteristic is perhaps their very diversity.

Virtually all the women born in the 1960s and 1970s who have made a fictional feature have lived, worked, and/or trained abroad. There is no single pattern of entry to filmmaking, but it is notable that none of them has had the conventional, sheltered upbringing reserved for so many women in the Arab world. Among those from the Middle East, for example, the Palestinians Annemarie Jacir, Najwa Najjar, and Cherien Dabis and the Lebanese Dahna Abourahme, all learned their filmmaking in the United States, where they were brought up. The Lebanese feature director Danielle Arbid has lived all her adult life in Paris. Her compatriots, Sabine El Gemayel and Dima El-Horr, both studied in Canada and worked initially in the United States before completing a first feature. Among the Syrian women filmmakers, the Canadian-born Ruba Nadda studied in New York. Waha al-Raheb may have had a conventional European-style film training, studying at the Université de Paris VIII, but as the daughter of a diplomat, she was born in Cairo and went to school in cities as varied as Moscow and Khartoum. Nadine Labaki is the only 2000s Middle Eastern woman feature filmmaker to have studied exclusively at home, in her case at IESAV in Beirut.

The Maghrebian women filmmakers born since 1960 belong to the first generation born since their countries achieved independence, yet a remarkable number of them live in France or were trained there. The key exception is the first to begin a feature film, Imane Mesbahi, who was born in 1964. The daughter of the pioneer Moroccan director Ahmed Mesbahi, in two of whose features she appeared as a child, she is the only Maghrebian woman filmmaker to have studied at the Cairo Higher Cinema Institute. She began her first feature, *The Paradise of the Poor / Le paradis des pauvres* in 1994, but it was not released until 2002 and had little success. Two other Maghrebian women filmmakers, who were born in France to immigrant families, Nadia El Fani and Zakia Tahiri, went straight into the film industry, El Fani as assistant director and Tahiri initially as an actress. Others born in France, among them Karin Albou and two lesser-known Moroccan-born filmmakers, Stéphanie Duvivier and Aicham Losri, followed the more usual pattern for future feature filmmakers, of formal film study in Paris.

Training in France or Belgium was also the preparation sought by the four women feature filmmakers, all born to middle-class families in the Maghreb, who went on to make the greatest impact on Maghrebian audiences (and, in some instances, on the censors as well). The Tunisian Raja Amari and three Moroccans, Yasmine Kassari, Narjiss Nejjar, and Laïla Marrakchi, have all used to the full the new perspective on Arab women's lives which living in Europe has given them. In some cases, their approaches to issues such as class and sexuality are closer to their French contemporaries (with whom they had, in some cases, studied) than to traditional attitudes in the Maghreb. The result in Tunisia and Morocco has been uproar, especially from male critics, notoriety for the filmmakers, and often, considerable commercial success for their films.

Of the fifteen or so women filmmakers who have made feature-length documentaries, mostly in video, only the Moroccan Dalila Ennadre lacks a university
education and learned her skills working as a production assistant in various
countries. Otherwise the new women documentarists tend to be university-
educated but to lack formal film training, though a handful did pursue formal
film studies. Dalia Fathallah followed her academic studies in Beirut and Tours
with a period at FEMIS in Paris. Dahna Abourahme trained in documentary production in New York, while Annemarie Jacir studied film at Columbia University. Rima Essa studied filmmaking in Jerusalem, while Éliane Raheb and Zeina
Daccache both followed courses at IESAV in Beirut. But many of the new women
documentary filmmakers have had a very different prelude to filmmaking. The
Moroccan Leila Kilani studied sociology in Paris. Ula Tabari studied theatre and
the visual arts before appearing as an actress in several films and working as assistant director on Samir's *Forget Baghdad*. The United States–based Jackie Reem
Salloum studied fine art at Eastern Michigan and New York Universities. Maryse
Gargour obtained a doctorate in information sciences in Paris and worked as a
journalist there and in Beirut. May Oday and Suha Arraf also worked initially as
journalists.

This mass of educated and articulate women has changed the way in which
a whole array of aspects of Arab society are experienced and depicted. Often the changes are subtle, and in no case is there an attempt to romanticize
women's lives or to avoid criticism where this is due. But there is a new perspective, which is most evident in the treatment of women's sexuality. Here,
the closer a filmmaker is to France, the more openness tends to be displayed.
Those who were born in France (such as Nadia El Fani or Karin Albou) or have
lived in Paris since their teens (Danielle Arbid) are quite unself-conscious in
depicting women's desires and portraying their naked bodies. Often even those
who have merely studied in France (such as Raja Amari and Laïla Marrakchi)
develop ways of depicting women's lives which are troubling to local censors.
This is a far cry from the traditional Arab male approach of equating sexuality
and frustration.

Questions of Identity

Outside Egypt, contemporary Arab cinema as a whole can be broadly characterized as a nomadic cinema, and it is no longer possible to make any kind of simple
equation between a filmmaker's place of birth, his or her place of residence, and
the sources of production financing. Since exile, permanent or temporary, voluntary or enforced, plays such a large part in the lives of these filmmakers, the issue
of nationality is complex. This is particularly so with respect to those belonging
to the second generation of exiles, who have been born abroad.

The documentary filmmaker Omar al-Qattan, who was born in 1964, considers these issues in an article titled "The Challenges of Palestinian Filmmaking (1990–2003)." He is frank about his own background:

> I was born into a wealthy family, to Palestinian parents, in Beirut. I came to the UK at the age of 11 and have been here ever since. I think and write in three languages. More importantly, I have never lived in a refugee camp, have never been hungry, have never personally been dispossessed, have never suffered physical injury as a result of military oppression and so on.[4]

So what, he asks, makes him a Palestinian filmmaker: "my family origins, nostalgia, political commitment?" The answer he gives is one which could apply (with respect to their own countries) to many other filmmakers—Lebanese, Syrian, or Iraqi—living in the Arab diaspora:

> Being Palestinian or engaging with the Palestinian cause has been and continues to be a process, not an absolute given, where I as an individual am constantly reviewing and revisiting my relationship with the Palestinian people, their struggle, their land, their memories, and so on. This relationship is always problematic.[5]

For those Palestinians whose parents were not forced into exile, who were born within Israeli borders and are therefore Israeli citizens, there are other problems of identity. As Elia Suleiman has said,

> We Palestinians living in Israel are the shy ones. The inhibited. We act as if we were closet-case Palestinians. Our Palestinian sisters and brothers in the West Bank and Gaza generally ignite uprisings first and then we join in. . . . It is our sisters and brothers who keep reminding us of our silent and tragic existence.[6]

There are often tensions with Palestinians living outside Israel's borders, with occasional accusations of "collaboration" if they seek funding from Israeli state film-support organizations (which, as Israeli citizens, they are perfectly entitled to do).

At the same time, for many Jewish citizens of Israel, Palestinian Arabs are not regarded as "real Israelis." This attitude is reflected in a dictionary of Israeli cinema published in Paris as recently as 2012. Although dozens of trivial Israeli films are dealt with, the only Palestinian given his own entry is Mohamed Bakri (listed, of course, as an actor). The author, Hélène Schoumann, devotes just two and a half pages to the whole Palestinian film output, writing dismissively:

> Palestinian cinema struggles to make its voice heard, despite its lack of resources. . . . it would need only little to grow and finally find its true place. Already a few prizes awarded at international festivals have encouraged it.[7]

Similarly, a two-DVD history of Israeli cinema, published in the Arte Éditions series "Voyage à travers le cinéma," makes no mention of Palestinian filmmaking in its introduction, includes only Mohamed Bakri (again as an actor) in the list of "film personalities," and includes an extract from only one Palestinian film, Tawfik Abu Wael's *Thirst*.[8] These are attitudes this current study sets out to refute absolutely.

European and US film festivals also exacerbate issues relating to identity. As far as African and Arab festivals (such as FESPACO and the JCC) go, a claimed Palestinian identity is unproblematic. But in Europe and the United States, there are often problems. Nizar Hassan tells the story of the difficulties which arose after his film, *Invasion,* was selected for an INPUT conference to be held in Barcelona. He defined himself as Palestinian, but this caused the organizers huge problems because Palestine is not a country. First, Hassan was categorized as a representative of "the Rest of the World," but this did not offer a way to provide the funding necessary for him to attend. He was then redefined simply as an Israeli (an identity which he strenuously denied), and then, quite bizarrely, he was listed as an Afghan. Only after weeks of email correspondence was he able to get himself defined formally as a Palestinian.[9] In a similar vein, in the United States the film *Divine Intervention,* directed by Elia Suleiman (who similarly defines himself as Palestinian), "provoked opposition to its submission for the entry as the Foreign Language Oscar, since Palestine was not a country."[10]

Another area in which there are parallel—if somewhat different—concerns about identity is Iraq. Because of the violent political upheavals in the South, most of the Iraqi film production in the 2000s has occurred in the relatively more tranquil area of Iraqi Kurdistan, and much of this has been produced by ethnic Kurdish directors. In talking about Iraqi film production, it is impossible to ignore filmmakers as significant as Hiner Saleem or Shawkat Amin Korki, though they are, by definition, not Arabs. Here, as elsewhere in this book—in dealing with second-generation Arab exiles, for example—I have tried to be as liberal as possible. For me, the dual identity—Kurd in terms of allegiance, yet Iraqi in terms of state identity—is simply another example of the multiple, often conflicting identities so common in the Middle East. I am heartened by the fact that there is no overt hostility in the films I have seen. Saleem's *Kilometer Zero,* for example, is built around the gulf in mutual understanding between an Arab and a Kurd, but the Arab taxi driver is by no means caricatured or belittled.

The relationship between filmmaker and homeland will clearly vary from individual to individual, from country to country, and it is difficult to make clearcut decisions on specific nationality. But wherever they live, the filmmakers dealt with here retain deep ties with the place they identify as their homeland. The situation is well captured by a quotation (from Anton Shammas) which Kamal Aljafari includes in *The Roof:* "And you know perfectly well that we don't ever leave home—we simply drag it behind us wherever we go, walls, roof and all." The link between filmmaker and country, whether shaped by personal memories, passed-down parental recollections, or simply the workings of the filmmaker's own imagination, is often one of the most important keys to the work produced.

Similar kinds of questions haunt both those born abroad to immigrant or exile parents and those who have themselves chosen, or been driven into, exile. Nabil Ayouch, who was born and brought up in Paris of mixed Maghrebian descent, has explained:

> France gave me a culture, an education, principles and values, but not an identity and certainly no roots. Morocco gave me the beginnings of an identity and roots, some replies to my questioning, but in a society which I could neither understand nor grasp, and in which I felt myself to be a stranger.[11]

Abbas Fahdel, who left Iraq to study abroad at the age of eighteen, makes the parallel situation very clear in the opening voice-over of *Return to Babylon*. Ostensibly designed so that he could meet up with family and friends, the purpose of his journey is actually "to make peace with that part of myself that remains for ever attached to my homeland."

In defining nationality I have relied here largely on the filmmakers' own assertions and on the (admittedly very liberal) criteria of the various Arab film festivals. Arab cinema, as it is presented here, is largely the product of Arabs living locally or in exile, but a number of the most interesting filmmakers are the children of mixed marriages—having a French mother and a Maghrebian father, for example. In addition, there are fascinating contributions by Kurds and by the occasional Armenian or Arabic-speaking Jew, born, brought up, or living in the confines of the wider Arab world.

Training

The training these filmmakers have received has been largely international, not at all focused on specific Arab issues and priorities. Two future Lebanese directors actually managed to work for their Hollywood heroes. Samir Habchi trained under Francis Ford Coppola in Hollywood, and Ziad Doueiri followed his studies at UCLA with work in Hollywood, most notably as camera assistant to Quentin Tarantino. But most potential filmmakers have had to rely on formal training.

About half of the new 2000s filmmakers are film school trained, but only half a dozen or so received their training in an Arab or Middle Eastern context. Arab filmmakers from outside Egypt continue to turn their backs on the Cairo Higher Cinema Institute. As has been noted, only one Arab woman filmmaker of this generation, the Moroccan Imane Mesbahi, trained there. Five other filmmakers who did not to go to Europe, the former Soviet Union, or North America for their training are Nadine Labaki, Zeina Daccache, and Simon El Habre, who all studied in Beirut; Massoud Arif Salih, who trained in Kurdistan; and Tawfik Abu Wael, who studied at Tel Aviv University.

The most favored training location in Europe has been Paris. Among those who have studied there are the Algerian Malek Bensmaïl; the Moroccans Faouzi Bensaïdi, Omar Chraïbi, Souad El Bouhati, Stéphanie Duvivier, Mohamed Ali El Mejoub, Hicham Alhayat, Kamal Kamal, Ismaïl Ferroukhi, Laïla Marrakchi, Narjiss Nejjar, Mohamed Chrif Tribeck, and Nour-Eddine Lakhmari (who also studied in Norway); the Tunisians Karin Albou, Raja Amari, Elyes Baccar, Moktar Ladjimi, and Moez Kamoun; the Lebanese documentarists Maher Abi Samra and Hady Zaccak; and the Syrian Waha al-Raheb. Another Syrian, Joud Saeed, also studied in France, but at the Université Louis Lumière in Lyon.

Two Moroccans, Hassan Legzouli and Yasmine Kassari, studied at the Belgian film school, INSAS. The Moroccan Mohamed Zineddaine studied in Bologna and his compatriot Hicham Alhayat in Geneva. Mohamed al-Daradji trained in Holland and the United Kingdom, and Kamal Aljafari in Cologne. Josef Fares learned filmmaking in Sweden, where he began his career with a comedy about the local Lebanese community. Koutaïba al-Janabi studied in Budapest. Among graduates from the Moscow film school, the VGIK, in the former Soviet Union, are two Syrians (following the national tradition), Nidal al-Dibs and Khatib El Bassel; one Iraqi, Zahavi Sanjavi; and one Lebanese, Samir Habchi. Those trained in the United States include the Moroccans Hakim Belabbes and Saïd Nouri; the Palestinian trio of Annemarie Jacir, Najwa Najjar, and Cherien Dabis; two Lebanese, Ziad Doueiri and Assad Fouladkar; and the Paris-based Algerian, Nadir Moknèche. The Tunisian Nawfel Saheb-Ettaba and three Lebanese directors, Sabine El Gemayel, Dima El-Horr, and Mahmoud Kaabour, received their training in Canada. The Moroccan Mohamed Ahed Bensouda also trained there, after completing his studies at the Sorbonne.

Of the remainder, a number studied drama: the *beurs* Chad Chenouga, Azize Kabouche, and Lyèce Boukhitine; the Tunis-born Abdellatif Kechiche and Néjib Belkadhi; the Algerian Lyes Salem; the Moroccans Yassine Fenane and Zakia Tahiri; and the Lebanese Wajdi Mouawad. A very few of the others avoided film school and followed the traditional film industry pattern of working initially as production assistants, assistant directors, or editors. Among these are the Palestinian Hany Abu Assad, the Moroccan Jérôme Cohen Olivar, and the French-based Tunisian Nadia El Fani. Others adopted less conventional paths: the Lebanese Danielle Arbid and the Moroccan Hamid Faridi came from journalism, the Algerian Rabah Ameur-Zaïmèche and Moroccan Leila Kilani studied sociology, and Mourad Boucif was engaged in community work; Abdelilah Badr was a martial arts specialist in Belgium, where Ismaël Saidi worked as a police inspector.

Funding

The kinds of funding enjoyed by Arab directors in the 1980s and 1990s have continued into the new millennium, with the French Fonds Sud in the forefront, supporting over thirty of the younger filmmakers. Particularly for documentary, European television organizations continue to play an important role, as do a variety of regional funding bodies and charitable organizations concerned with the issues of the developing world. More recently, an increasing amount of money has come from the Gulf, where interest in media production is on the increase. The complexity of the package of one million euros needed to finance a Palestinian feature is very clear from the credits of Annemarie Jacir's *Salt of This Sea*. This film was co-financed by production companies from eight different countries, plus one television network: JBA Production (France) as the lead producer, Philistine Films (Palestine—Jacir's own company), Thelma Film AG (Switzerland), Tarantual (Belgium), Louverture Films (USA), Clarity World Films (UK), Augustus Film (Netherlands), and Mediapro (Spain), as well as Swiss Romand Television. In addition, the credits acknowledge the support of the Office Fédéral de la Culture (OFC, Switzerland), the Centre du Cinéma et de l'Audiovisuel de la Communauté Française de Belgique et des Télédistributeurs Wallons, the Nederlands Fond Voor de Film, the Instituto de Cine y de las Artes Audiovisuales, the Institut Català de les Indústries Culturals, Catalan Films & TV, the Fondation Groupama Gan pour le Cinéma, the French General Consulate in Jerusalem, the Hubert Bals Fund of the International Film Festival of Rotterdam, Procirep and l'Angoa-Agicoa, the Fonds Sud Cinéma, the French Ministry of Culture and Communication, the Centre National Cinématographique (CNC), and the French Ministry of Foreign Affairs, as well as Cinéma en Mouvement 3 Festival de San Sébastien.[12]

This predominance of largely foreign funding adds to the complexity of defining precisely a film's "national" identity. Filmmakers living in exile feel themselves attached to their country of origin, but with only the occasional film able to recover its costs in the domestic market, the notion of a "national cinema" in the sense that the term would be applied to European, Asian, or Latin American cinemas is inappropriate here. Even in Morocco, which has consistently produced a dozen or more features a year (with levels reaching two dozen by 2011), investment in local production amounts to barely a tenth of that invested annually by foreign production companies using Morocco as a location for films or television productions with quite alien values.

To obtain European funding, a film normally requires a fully worked-out script in French or some other European language, even if it is intended to be shot with Arabic dialogue. For this reason, the various possibilities for funding and developing scriptwriting, often attached to those festivals which support cinema from the South, have been particularly important for the development of Arab cinema. Nadine Labaki, for example, profited from a Cannes Film Festival project, which allowed her to spend six months in Paris, scripting *Caramel,* while Najwa Najjar received funding from the Amiens Scriptwriting Award and participated in the Sundance Screenwriters Lab while preparing *Pomegranates and Myrrh.* Danielle Arbid obtained a bursary from the Montpellier festival to help her script *In the Battlefields.* Just like Heiny Srour in 1984, Nadir Moknèche's success in setting up his first feature, *Madame Osmane's Harem,* in 2000, was aided by winning a French scriptwriting contest. In the credits for *Salt of This Sea,* Annemarie Jacir acknowledges the aid of no less than four organizations funding or tutoring scriptwriting: the Paul Robeson Foundation, Sundance Screenwriters Lab, Paris Cinema Project, and Berlinale Co-Production & Talent Project Market.

A Cosmopolitan Generation

The filmmakers born since 1960 constitute, by any criterion, a cosmopolitan generation. Dima El-Horr's self-definition, "I dream in Arabic, speak English and write and read in French," encapsulates their shared existence.[13] Nadia El Fani has elaborated this in terms of Tunisian intellectuals:

> In the Tunis that I know, people speak Arabic and French; that's how we are. . . . We experience things differently because we are just as much at home there as we are here. . . . We have assimilated both cultures and ultimately I see it as a blessing.[14]

Malek Bensmaïl has speculated on whether the use, by members of the younger generation, of titles with wider connotations (Teguia's *Rome Rather than You* or his own *China Is Still a Long Way Away,* for example) for films whose content is exclusively Algerian, is a reflection of foreign financing or simply "reflects a population which wants to leave."[15]

Although many of them speak admiringly of Youssef Chahine, in his later years very much an outsider in relation to mainstream Egyptian cinema, there is no sense in which these filmmakers are shaped by the history of Arab cinema. Asked about which filmmakers had influenced him most, Tawfik Abu Wael, for example, named François Truffaut, Andrei Tarkovsky, Bernardo Bertolucci, Ingmar Bergman, and Martin Scorsese. Jilani Saadi, asked about his film tastes, replied with references to neorealism, Pasolini, Tarkovsky, and Ettore Scola.[16] Responding to a 2012 *Sight and Sound* poll of "best directors," Mohamed Souweid listed Tarkovsky, Bresson, Fassbinder, Pasolini, Ford, Cassavetes, Antonioni, Sirk, Hitchcock, and Bergman. The Egyptian independent Ibrahim El Batout refused to concede that he had been influenced by any other director, but offered a thoroughly eclectic list of his favorites: Krzysztof Kieslowski, Alejandro Iñárritu,

Wim Wenders, Emir Kusturica, Youssef Chahine, and Shadi Abdel Salam.[17] This was matched by his contemporary Ahmad Abdalla, who named Theo Angelopoulos, Paul Thomas Anderson, Nuri Bilge Ceylan, Kim Ki-duk, and Mike Leigh as the key filmmakers for him.[18]

The Lebanese Nadine Labaki is one of the few Arab filmmakers of her generation not to be trained abroad, but asked about the sources of the style of *Where Do We Go Next?* she said it was influenced by *Grease* and also by films she saw as a child, such as *Snow White* and *Cinderella*.[19] The Syrian Khatib El Bassel has translated the autobiographies of Andrei Tarkovsky and Ingmar Bergman. Laïla Marrakchi has referred to a range of (largely recent) Hollywood films as influences on her first feature: 'Seeing over and over the teen movies of my childhood, like *American Graffiti*, *The Breakfast Club*, *Rebel without a Cause*, *The Outsiders*, and *Rumblefish*, gave me the courage to start writing on this subject.[20] Likewise, Raja Amari has spoken of her closeness to the new French cinema of François Ozon and Arnaud Despleschin—filmmakers who attended the same courses at FEMIS in Paris.

As far as the Maghreb is concerned, the bulk of the filmmakers—even those regarded as part of the *beur* community—were born in the countries whose nationality they claim. But a number of the Maghrebians (Karin Albou, Nadia El Fani, Zakia Tahiri, Nabil and Hichem Ayouch among them) were born in Paris, though in some cases they lived there only for a short period of time (sometimes just a matter of months). The birthplaces of a number of the new Middle Eastern filmmakers reflect the realities of the Arab diaspora. Of the Syrians, Waha al-Raheb was born in Cairo, Ruba Nadda in Montreal, Soudade Kaadan in Paris, and Khatib El Bassel in the Netherlands. Among the Lebanese, Dahna Abourahme was born in Jordan, Michel Kammoun in Sierra Leone, and Chadi Zeneddine in Gabon. The Egyptian Atef Hetata was born in New York. In addition, as we have seen, several leading Palestinian women directors were born abroad: Annemarie Jacir in Saudi Arabia and Cherien Dabis and Najwa Najjar in the United States. An extreme case is Yahya Alabdallah: though generally described as a Palestinian-Jordanian, he was born in Libya, brought up initially in Saudi Arabia, established his production base in Jordan, and received co-production funding from Dubai for his first feature.

3 Documentary

Many important documentary filmmakers of the 1990s, such as the Palestinians Mohamed Bakri, Samir Abdallah, and Maï Masri (usually working with her husband Jean Chamoun), as well as the exiled Iraqis Mysoon Pachachi, Samir, and Saad Salman, continued their exclusively documentary careers into the new decade, but they are not "new voices" and their output falls outside the scope of this study. They are responsible for many of the most striking documentaries of the past decade. While there has been a widening of interest in documentary in both Palestine and Lebanon, with many of the newcomers being female directors, there has been far less development of documentary filmmaking in the Maghreb, with just a couple of substantial debuts by filmmakers focused exclusively on documentary. A number of directors have, however, interspersed their fictional and documentary productions. Among these are the Moroccan Nabil Ayouch and the Tunisians Moktar Ladjimi, Nadia El Fani, and Raja Amari. Their documentaries are discussed alongside their feature films in the relevant section of this book. Iraqi documentary production still lags behind feature filmmaking in its international identity; and in Syria there is just one major figure of note, Hala al-Abdallah Yakoub, who lives and works as a filmmaker and producer in Paris.

Many of the newer documentarists making their debuts after 2000 follow the patterns of production and presentation established by their predecessors, and the standard television length of fifty-two minutes (accepted by Arab film festivals as constituting a documentary feature) remains the norm. But there has been one significant shift in the 2000s. As the new digital technology—with its lower costs and minimal crewing requirements—has become ever more available, new styles of documentary work have begun to be produced, particularly in the Middle East. We find increasing numbers of documentaries with a distinctly personal tone and approach. The autobiography or family portrait has become much more popular with filmmakers, though comparatively few of such works have found a wide distribution. The new technology allows the filmmakers to deal directly with their own personal experiences, or those of their immediate family, focusing on these topics not because of any wider historical or political importance, but for the insights these lives give into the lived Arab experience of the present. Even within this new genre, there is a wide range of approaches. As we shall see when we turn to consider Palestinian documentary in the 2000s, there is a huge gulf between Juliano Mer-Khamis celebrating the work of his mother, a renowned activist famous throughout Palestine and Israel, and Raed Andoni devoting a whole feature-length documentary to his own encounters with a psychotherapist, seeking a cure for his persistent headaches.

Although the autobiographical documentary is new to the Arab world, it has been an acknowledged form in the United States since the 1960s. A useful definition of the form is offered by Jim Lane. The documentary image and sound, he tells us, "evoke an immediately recognizable view of the real world, but because of the complex, mitigating circumstances of the autobiographical subject, the viewer is also aware of the everpresent filter of the filmmaker."[1] The viewing experience is thereby subtly changed: "Moving back and forth through the temporal unfolding of the work, the viewer understands the work as views of the subjectively delimited world of the autobiographical subject. Such a world is full of assurances and directness and obliquity—the things that make up a life."[2]

Initial explorations of the form are already to be found in the Arab world during the 1990s, in works by the women directors Izza Genina and Fatima Jebli Ouazzani in Morocco, for example. Among those adopting the form in the 2000s are male directors such as Kamal Aljafari and Raed Andoni in Palestine, Mohamed Souweid and Mahmoud Kaabour in Lebanon, and the Iraqi Abbas Fahdel in his two documentaries about return to Baghdad. There are perhaps even more women who adopt this form, including Ula Tabari in Palestine, Éliane Raheb in Lebanon, Hala al-Abdallah Yakoub in Syria, and the French-based Tunisian feature filmmaker Nadia El Fani. Each of these voices is distinctive and personal, and none aims for the detached, objective stance characteristic of much conventional documentary.

Palestine

Four filmmakers, all born before 1960 but making their debut in the 2000s, have played a key role in shaping Palestinian documentary: Juliano Mer-Khamis, Nasri Hajjaj, Mahmoud al-Massad (also sometimes referred to as Mahmoud Massad), and Maryse Gargour. They come from very different backgrounds and have very different filmic objectives. Their diverse backgrounds show the extent of the Palestinian diaspora, and the range of their subject matter largely defines that of Palestinian documentary during the decade.

Juliano Mer-Khamis, who was born in 1958 in Nazareth, was of Israeli nationality and acted in a number of Israeli and foreign films. His sole documentary, *Arna's Children / Les enfants d'Arna / Atfal Arna* (2004) is a complex look at his own personal history. Dutch-produced and co-directed by Danniel Danniel, *Arna's Children* is about the children taught at the drama school in the Jenin refugee camp run by his mother, a noted Israeli activist for Palestinian rights. Mer-Khamis himself was an activist and an actor, who continued his mother's work by running the Freedom Theatre, a community theatre for children, in the same refugee camp. He once described himself as a "Hebrew-speaking Palestinian with Communist views,"[3] and sensed that his liberal attitudes risked alienating those in the Palestinian community with fundamentalist views. Indeed, on April 4, 2011, Mer-Khamis was shot dead by masked gunmen outside the theatre he had founded and which had earlier been subjected to firebomb attacks. Commenting on the murder, Kadura Musa, governor of Jenin, said: "He was a Palestinian citizen of Israeli origin. An actor and an artist, but most of all, a true human being. We don't know why this happened, but all the people of the camp condemn the death of this son of ours whose mother also did so much for the people of Jenin."[4]

Arna's Children subtly intercuts and interrelates footage from three periods of Mer-Khamis's life: 1992, when he began assisting his mother in her children's theatre project at the Jenin refugee camp; 1995, around the time of his mother's death; and 2002, when he returned to Jenin to see what had happened to her protégés. Much changed over the course of these ten years, as the children developed into young adults, some now with children of their own.

The film begins with the indefatigable Arna Mer, seriously ill from cancer and just out of the hospital, campaigning against the Israeli occupation and the blockade of Jenin. Although in 1948, at the age of eighteen, she had fought for the foundation of Israel, she subsequently married Saliba Khamis, a Palestinian who was one of the founders of the Israeli Communist Party, and became an activist for Palestinian rights. Her son films her triumphant return to the theatre and recalls the exercises he devised for the children and the methods his mother used to allow them to express, through performance and painting, their anger at the Israeli army's destruction of their homes. We later see an increasingly frail Arna make her final return to her "children," expressing no regrets for her eventful and tempestuous life. She and her son were greeted warily at first because of their Jewish origins, but within a few years they had come to be seen as part of the family—Arna as a mother to her young charges.

Among the children from the project, four boys are picked out: Nidal, the youngest in the group; Yosef, his older brother; Ashraf, Yosef's best friend; and Ala, a neighbor of Nidal and Ashraf. There are scenes of the four of them acting on stage at the age of eight or nine, getting immense pleasure from the experience, several even thinking of acting as a career (though they have never actually seen a play). Ala is seen painting to express his feelings about the destruction of his home. There also disturbing scenes of some of them appearing in front of an Israeli television crew, Nidal acting out a scene of brutal Israeli interrogation and

Ashraf describing acting as giving him a sense of power, like throwing a Molotov cocktail.

Returning in 2002 to find out what has happened to them in the meantime, Mer-Khamis finds himself warmly welcomed—as a brother—by many of his former pupils. Cutting back and forth across ten years, he charts the changes in their lives. All four boys have been caught up in the Israeli-Palestinian conflict, but their fates have been very different. Yosef and Nidal died when they carried out a suicide bombing in Israel in October 2001, killing four women and injuring many others (we see their martyr video and footage of the aftermath). Ashraf was killed in the battle of Jenin in 2002 (we see his body loaded onto a truck to be buried in a mass grave with fifty others).

Mer-Khamis talks to their parents and contemporaries to find out their motivation. The reticent Ala, who always preferred painting to acting, has become the head of an Al-Aqsa group in the camp, where they fight Israeli tanks with hand weapons and improvised explosives during the 2002 assault. The devastation is widespread and Arna's theatre in ruins. The tone darkens, as we see the Palestinian resistance groups in action, and seemingly inevitably, Ala is killed, two weeks after the birth of his first child. His martyr poster joins those of Nidal, Yosef, and Ashraf on the walls of Jenin, and the film concludes with a chant of defiance from the new generation of Jenin's children.

Arna's Children is a powerful work, exhibiting great skill as it weaves together scenes of past and present. It provides a revealing insight into the Israeli-Palestinian situation. It shows poignantly—through the actions of Arna and her son—the possibilities of creative Jewish-Arab cooperation. At the same time, it makes the audience understand the pressures—feeling trapped and helpless, needing to defend one's own space—which drive young Palestinians to resist. It is tragic that Juliano Mer-Khamis was himself murdered while carrying on his mother's work.

Nasri Hajjaj was born in 1951 in the Ein El Hilweh refugee camp in Lebanon and worked for twenty years as a journalist before turning to film. His two feature-length documentaries focus on the experience of exile. *Shadow of Absence / L'ombre de l'absence / Dhil al-gheyab* (2007) opens with a personal perspective: a visit by the director to Naameh, a Palestinian village occupied by the Israelis in 1948 and now obliterated. This was the birthplace of his father, who always dreamed of being buried there, and the sight of it reduces him to tears. *Shadow of Absence* is a wide-ranging, loosely organized documentary on the Palestinian diaspora, focusing on the burial of those who have died in exile. There are world-famous figures, such as the writer Emile Habibi, the academic Edward Said, and the political cartoonist Naji al-Ali, who have been denied burial in their birthplaces by the Israeli law of no return. While Jews from anywhere in the world, even those who have never even visited the country, are positively encouraged to be buried in Israel, Palestinians who have left the country (often forced into exile) have no right whatsoever to be buried there. At least they now have graves, tended by those close to them, outside Israeli borders. But other Palestinians have been less fortunate. Many of those murdered in Israeli assaults on refugee camps, for example, were given an improvised anonymous mass burial, of which few traces now remain. Others have been buried and personally commemorated in formal cemetery sites around the Arab world, but often at inappropriate locations because of tensions between various Arab factions. Palestinians victimized during their lives are, in many cases, penalized after death as well. The film maintains a personal note throughout (the voice-over is both written and spoken by the filmmaker) and is aided greatly by the sensitive use of music and quotations from the poetry of the great Palestinian poet Mahmoud Darwish.

Hajjaj's second documentary, *As the Poet Said / Kama kkal ashair* (2009), offers a portrait of Darwish. Again the film is loosely structured. It contains no voice-over commentary to trace Darwish's life or to locate his death. There is no explicit evaluation of his work, and we never see the poet himself in person. But his image recurs throughout the film in photographs, book covers, and even images drawn on a wall. Instead of following conventional documentary techniques, the film relies solely on Darwish's own poetry. *As the Poet Said* opens with a piano improvisation (by Hiba al Kawa) inspired by a Darwish poem, and from then on the film is shaped by readings of his poetry, some by the poet himself in sound recordings, others by fellow poets, filmed on location. Most of these readings are in Arabic, by the poet himself and other Arab poets, but we also hear the poet's words read in English, French, Portuguese, and Kurdish. None of the readers' comments on Darwish's life or work—the readings themselves are left to testify to Darwish's widespread importance to his fellow poets: José Saramago from Portugal, the Nigerian Nobel Prize winner Wole Soyinka, the Israeli poet Yitzhak Laor, the French poet-politician Dominique de Villepin, the Lebanese Joumana Haddad, and the American Michael Palmer, as well as the Palestinian poets Ahmad Dahbour and Dalia Taha. There is also a reading by children at the school in the Ein El Hilweh refugee camp where the director was born.

The carefully composed images reflect the filmmaker's wide research into Darwish's life: shots of his mother's house in Palestine (where his own image "gazes tenderly" from photos hung on the walls) and also his favorite room at the Madison Hotel in Paris, from his time in exile there. Other images reflect the surroundings of the poets who read his words or illustrate themes from the poems themselves (most notably, a horse "exiled" in the desert). Some images are enigmatic to those unfamiliar with Darwish's life, for example, shots of the Texas Medical Center in Houston. But the overall impression made by the images is that of loss, particularly evident in shots of the empty theatres and auditoriums where Darwish had once given readings. This is a portrait in which, as the title suggests, the director lets the poet speak for himself through his poetry.

Mahmoud al-Massad was born in 1959 in Zarqa, Jordan, to exiled Palestinian parents and studied at Yarmouk University in Jordan. He subsequently traveled widely in Europe, working in various assistant roles and making his own short films. Since 2003 he has been based in Jordan, where he has pioneered documentary filmmaking. He made several short documentaries there before completing his first feature-length documentary.

Recycle / Recyclage / Ea'adat khalk (2007) is set in the director's birthplace, Zarqa, Jordan's second-largest city, and the action is framed by reference to its best-known former resident, Osama bin Laden's lieutenant and notorious al-Qaeda terrorist, Abu Musab al-Zarqawi (real name Ahmad Fadiel). The film opens with one of al-Zarqawi's inflammatory speeches on television and, toward the end of the film, George W. Bush is shown announcing al-Zarqawi's death to the world in 2005. But the film's focus is on another Zarqa resident, Abu Ammar, who grew up alongside al-Zarqawi and is acquainted with his cousins, who still live in the city. Filmed close up by al-Massad himself with a handheld digital camera, *Recycle* is focused almost exclusively on Abu Ammar, who is seen mostly in the company of his young son, Abu Bakr. We do not see or hear from his father, with whom he has quarreled, with disastrous consequences for the family business, nor from Abu Ammar's first wife, who has borne him eight children. His second wife is shown only on the occasion when, clad in a full burka, she visits a clinic to find out why she cannot conceive.

Despite being a subject of the camera's intense scrutiny for an hour or so, Abu Ammar remains an enigma. How can one reconcile his mujahedeen past in Afghanistan with his present non-aggressive stance toward life? When all his business efforts, such as a scheme to sell cars in Iraq, fail, how can he think that he can support a second wife (and second potential family) when he already has eight children by his first wife? Why does an intelligent man (as he evidently is) try to make a living collecting scrap cardboard from the streets of Zarqa? Interwoven with Abu Ammar's daily struggles are evening discussions with his friends and contemporaries: How did the non-religious boy they all knew, Ahmad Fadiel, become a world-renowned fanatical terrorist? How are the precepts of Islamic jihad to be reconciled with everyday existence? How is one to make a life for oneself in Jordan? At the end, having had to move out to a tenement apartment and to recognize that his planned book on Islam will never be written, Abu Assad needs an extreme solution. We last see him, against his most cherished beliefs, newly shaven and in a business suit, setting out to try to create a new life in the United States. *Recycle* offers a vivid portrayal of life for ordinary people in Jordan, a typical Arab country in so many ways, where there is no form of democracy allowing the expression of an individual voice and no national prosperity sufficient to make a local life economically viable.

Al-Massad followed this with *This Is My Picture When I Was Dead* (2010), which tells the remarkable story of Bashir Mraish, whose father was a leading PLO militant, responsible for an ambitious but failed bomb attack in Israel. Pursued by the Israeli secret service, he was eventually assassinated in Athens in 1983. The young Bashir, then four years old, who was also in the car where his father was assassinated, was reported dead by the world's media. In fact he survived, and the film follows his investigation of the past, through conversations with his family and his own doctor, an old acquaintance of his father. The film, which includes scenes reconstructing the assassination as well as contemporary footage shot in Jordan, is a somewhat disillusioned portrayal of the Palestinian struggle, with Bashir's mother lamenting the passing of the days when the revolution was clean and noble and Bashir dismissing contemporary political leaders, who, he says, are squabbling over the rewards of a victory they have not even won. *This Is My Picture When I Was Dead* offers a sympathetic portrait of Bashir, though it gives remarkably little insight into his contribution to the ongoing cause for which his father died, or his own role as one of Jordan's leading political cartoonists.

Maryse Gargour, the only woman in this group, is concerned with using film to probe the past and its impact on the present. She was born in Jaffa and brought up in Lebanon. Later, she studied at the Université de Paris II and worked as a journalist in Beirut and for UNESCO. She has dual French and Lebanese nationality. Beginning in 1988, she made four short documentaries before embarking on her first sixty-one-minute work, *The Land Speaks Arabic / La terre parle arabe* (2008). The film covers the period from the roots of Zionism in the late nineteenth century to the expulsion of the Palestinians from their land in 1948. It is remarkable for a number of reasons one of which is newly discovered footage of rural Palestine before 1948, "footage of how people in these villages were living, with women wearing their traditional dresses going about their daily business." Gargour has observed that, without these, "it would have been impossible for me to make this movie, for all this footage allowed me to recreate the Palestinian space, and this is very precious for me."[5]

The Land Speaks Arabic sets out to confront the Israeli myth that "Palestine was a land without people, destined for a people without land." It opens with the argument by the British-based Palestinian academic Nur Masalha that the foundation of Israel can best be understood in the context of the ideology of nineteenth-century European colonization, when settlers saw themselves as totally superior to the peoples they colonized. In the case of Israel, this intrusion was further justified by the false assertion of a blood link between contemporary European Jews (in fact descended largely from converts) and the Israelite peoples of Palestine two thousand years ago.[6] Even if, as Chaim Weizmann asserted, this was a land promised by God to Abraham in the Old Testament, the claims to it by the European settlers, who flooded into Palestine in ever-increasing numbers, were extremely dubious. With meticulous detail and constant reference to archival material, the film probes the contradictions of Zionist thought and the gradually more explicit assertion of the need to expel the existing population to make space for a Jewish homeland. None of these concepts had any connection with the thinking of the so-called Arab Jews, who had been living alongside their Arab neighbors in Palestine for centuries. As there was no support from the ruler of the Ottoman Empire for the establishment of a Jewish state, the Zionists turned to the British, when the mandate was established. The Balfour Declaration sealed the fate of the Palestinians.

The third strength of the film, along with the pre-1948 footage and the meticulous documentation, is the testimony of those who recall life before the intrusion of the settlers, a time when Arabs, Jews, and Christians lived side by side without tensions. There are also the memories of those who recall the British Mandate and of those who participated in the 1930s Arab revolt. The crushing of this by the British left a situation where Arabs were prohibited from even carrying knives, while the Jewish settlers were permitted to organize their settlements as military garrisons. By 1948, there existed a disarmed Palestinian majority and a 100,000-strong Jewish militia (including women alongside the men). Elements of this settler militia turned to terrorism in the years before the establishment of Israel, attacking Palestinians in urban communities and eventually striking at British targets as well, most notoriously the King David Hotel. Inevitably, at the point of the establishment of Israel, hundreds of thousands of Palestinians were expelled from their homes (the Nakba), and Gargour has obtained vivid testimony from those who were driven into exile. As an ironic afterpiece, Gargour cites Weizmann again: "We Jews are borne on the wings of peace. We are brought up in the sign of peace. Not a hair of the native population has been touched. Not a hair!" *The Land Speaks Arabic* is a forceful piece of filmmaking, lucidly demonstrating the clash between a peaceful rural community and the outsiders who burst upon them and seized their land, as well as the disastrous role of the British as they exercised their mandate powers. This is documentary filmmaking of the highest quality.

The work of these four slightly older filmmakers can be seen as setting the parameters for much of the 2000s work of the generation born after 1960. One concern of many of the new filmmakers is to engage with the past and to document it through interviews and newsreel material—creating valuable archives of past experience. They also wish to examine the way in which contemporary life is shaped by this past—even by struggles which, because of changed circumstances, no longer have the same immediate relevancy. At the same time, the new filmmakers are also concerned to probe immediate issues, again making much use of interview techniques and also drawing much more on their own personal experiences, to expose the struggles in the present, in response to new and increasing Israeli pressure and aggression.

* * *

One of the first Arab filmmakers of the 1960s generation to make a breakthrough into feature-length documentary filmmaking in the 1990s was **Nizar Hassan**, who is described by Gertz and Khleifi as "the paramount Palestinian documentary film director of our time."[7] Born in 1960 in the village of Mashhad in the Nazareth area, he is a self-taught Palestinian-Israeli filmmaker who began his career as early as 1991 with the first of a number of short documentaries. He has since made a number of feature-length works. *Independence / Indépendance / Istiqlal* (1994) is a very personal debut, with Hassan returning to his native village to talk directly, sometimes with himself on camera, to his mother and to people he knows intimately (his teacher and school colleagues) about Israeli Independence Day. For his mother's generation, in the 1950s and early 1960s, there was a lack of real political awareness, despite family members having been forced into exile. At that time, the Israeli celebrations were basically accepted by Arab citizens. The Israeli state was bringing modernizing programs in education and building roads, for example, in what had been a poor rural community. Some of Hassan's contemporaries are politically articulate about the situation of Arabs in 1990s Israel, but the most fascinating of his probing interviews are with those who have chosen to come to terms with the Israeli state. One of these is his friend Muhamed, who now runs a construction company and who drives a truck with yellow number plates (normally reserved for Jews). He accepts that he is therefore stoned by Palestinian activist demonstrators. Another central figure among Hassan's contemporaries is Hussein Suliman, who is mayor of Mashhad and who has photographs of Israeli military leaders on his office wall. On his election poster, however, he is pictured with Yasser Arafat, whom he met in Tunis at a conference which he attended not as a Palestinian but as "an Arab Israeli representing the Labour Party." He delights in demonstrating his ability to ring the president's residence and engage in dialogue with a presidential aide. His stated aim is election to the Knesset.

Hassan's second feature, *Jasmine / Yasmin* (1996), deals with the position of women and the question of so-called honor killings in Arab society, focusing on a woman "who is incarcerated for being an accomplice to the murder of her younger sister, a woman who has 'disgraced the family.'" Again, Hassan involves himself directly in his subject matter, with Gertz and Khleifi noting that, at the end of the film, he "entraps himself in a web of his own design, when his sister, a university student, turns the tables, accusing him of maltreating the women in the family."[8] *Myth* aka *Fable / Ustura* (1998) traces the ambiguities—as well as the injustices—stemming from the expulsion of a Palestinian family in 1948 from the town of Saffouri (now renamed Zipouri). The family were scattered in exile between Jordan and Lebanon, with only some of them able to negotiate a return to Palestine. With the passing of time, even the details of their dispersal are disputed, but the major clash is between the fates of two of the brothers. Salim, whom the family did manage to get back to Israel, was educated in Jewish schools and is suspected of collaboration because of the contacts he has developed with key authority figures. Meanwhile Mahmoud, who has ended up as a filmmaker in Germany, may (or may not) have been a PLO activist and associate of Arafat. As usual, it is the tensions and contradictions within family relationships which fascinate Hassan, who is always happy to probe and ask awkward questions.

After *Cut / Coupure / Tarady* (2000), described by Gertz and Khleifi as "the first work by a Palestinian director that deals exclusively with Jewish people,"[9] Hassan made a shorter piece, *Challenge / Le défi / Tahaddi* (2001). This records the impossibility for both Hassan and his producer Raed Andoni to respond to a commission from the producer Mohamed Makhlouf to make a short (two- to four-minute) work, commemorating the Gazan schoolboy Mohammad al-Durra and intended to open a Gulf film festival. Mohammad al-Durra is the Palestinian child whose death in his father's arms on September 30, 2000, during crossfire between Israelis and Palestinians, was recorded live by French television cameras and broadcast worldwide.

From the way *Challenge* is shot, it is clear that the filmmakers were aware from the outset that the project was likely to fail. First, there are the Israeli travel restrictions and checkpoints, which make it almost impossible for Hassan and Andoni even to meet up (Gertz and Khleifi devote a whole chapter of their book on Palestinian cinema to "roadblock movies"). Then there is the added and insoluble problem of the filmmakers being unable to enter Gaza in order to supplement the existing newsreel footage. The same problem exists with another potential subject for the proposed film, Faris Anda. Also a ten-year-old, he was photographed, in a widely distributed image, confronting an Israeli tank with a stone in his hand—but was killed two days later. Perhaps the most telling scene is that in which the various filmmakers and technicians involved in the project compare their identity papers (all differently bound and inscribed), to confirm on camera what they certainly already knew: that wherever they were born and whatever their personal allegiance, they belong to a country, Palestine, which, in the eyes of the Israeli bureaucracy, simply does not exist. Hassan's examination of mundane issues around the failure of the original commission makes fascinating viewing, in a way that any recycling of a well-known (if harrowing) television sequence might not have done.

Hassan's next feature-length work, *Invasion / Envahissement / Ijtiyah* (2003), deals with what the Israelis dubbed "Operation Defensive Shield," their March

2003 invasion of the West Bank, where the only significant resistance came from the Palestinians who attempted to defend their homes in the Jenin refugee camp. As usual, Hassan's approach to his subject is distinctive. He does not concentrate on interviewing Palestinian survivors or celebrating Palestinian martyrs, but instead converses with a very different witness. This, it soon emerges, is Yuval, one of the Israeli military drivers of the massive D9 bulldozers, who helped to raze Jenin to the ground, often under Palestinian sniper fire, during the fighting. The two men sit side by side (with Hassan a little to the rear) in an editing suite, looking at and discussing the images to be used in the film, here projected on a monitor screen. The discussion is without blame or animosity, an examination of the evidence rather than a confrontation. Yuval is offered the opportunity to delete from the film any sequence which he deems false or inappropriate.

This discussion—how many buildings were destroyed, how long did each one take, which homes had Yuval personally knocked down—forms the narrative core of the film. Interwoven are shots of the devastated streets, with small children playing amid the ruins, and also a series of individually titled interview sequences with Palestinians, ranging from "The Dream" (a shattered home) to "The Kid" (a newly orphaned child). Through these tales of vanished dreams and lost loved ones, connections are made and the picture of the Jenin siege is gradually pieced together, with its impact on the Palestinian victims made clear. The callousness of the occupiers is clear in the slogans which the returning Palestinians find in their willfully smashed-up homes ("Thanks for the hospitality—see you at the peace conference"). The last images Hassan shows on the monitor are of Yuval back home in Israel (shot by Hassan's assistant Oleg Peckowitz). Yuval emerges as a fairly typical Israeli conscript. Israel just had to win, though he himself has no personal sense of superiority toward Arabs. His abiding memory is not of Arab deaths but of his own situation: trapped in his bulldozer for up to forty-eight hours at a time, unable to open the door because of possible snipers and therefore engulfed in the stench of his own excrement. The film's final titles give a somber account of the cost of the confrontation: two hundred homes destroyed and a further three hundred damaged; thirty Palestinian fighters and twenty-six civilians killed, along with twenty-three Israeli soldiers.

Abou Khalil's Grove / Karm Abu Khalil (2005), co-funded by ZDF and Arte, is an example of a genre which has become increasingly common in Arab filmmaking in the 2000s: the personal, autobiographical documentary. Here, Hassan probes the identity of his grandfather, discovering a man who was, in many ways, different from the rest of his family and his village. A shopkeeper-cum-trader rather than a farmer, Saud Abdel Kader (born in 1890 and dying in 1988) made a modest fortune, which was reflected in the fact that he owned a vineyard, that he bought his own elegant clothes in Haifa, that his wife did not have to toil throughout the year in the fields, and that his children were better dressed than other villagers. A key source, alluded to in the credit sequence, is a tape recording describing his own life made by Hassan's grandfather. This historical material forms an audio counterpoint to the recurrent visual record of Hassan helping his cousins each day during the harvest in the olive grove, which his grandfather acquired and which gives the film its title. The film ends when the harvest is complete.

The bulk of the film is made up of interviews with members of Hassan's immediate family, especially his uncles, but also with a member of the local Israeli community, who had arrived at the age of fourteen at the local kibbutz, which had been founded by fellow eastern European migrants in the mid-1930s. The picture that emerges is one of continuous alien dominance over this rural Palestinian community—by the Ottomans, the British protectorate, and finally the Israelis—in which only the brutality of the Israeli onslaught in 1948 stands out. These were life experiences which deprived Hassan's uncles of even the dream of a better future.

The film presents itself openly as a construct. Hassan appears in shot as the interviewer, we see him and his assistant conducting archival research, and there is even a clip of the failed interview material when the sound recorder was discovered not to be working. The film's action is divided into four "days," though there is little evidence that (apart from the harvesting sequences) this was the actual order of shooting. But this manner of shaping the narrative shows clearly that the film is a record of immediate responses, even if they are half-remembered recollections rather than a formal investigation of the village of Mashhad during the period covered by the film. Instead of attempting to put his family's memories into any kind of wider historical context, Hassan becomes quixotically obsessed with a single family image. His mother was the only school-girl in the village to wear shoes and socks (the rest went barefoot) and, as such, was chosen to meet Golda Meir when she came to inaugurate an Israeli-built link road to the village. The image of this meeting (and the sight of his mother's socks) becomes the driving force for Hassan in the latter part of the film.

South / Janoub (2008), made in collaboration with the same foreign producers, has a wider perspective, namely, the situation in contemporary Lebanon. It opens with a street sign, "Cité de la Moskowa," which, Hassan makes clear, is the name of a district in Paris which no longer exists. The sign, however, recurs as the seemingly ironic background to the film's rather limited inputs of factual information. This includes an explanation of the significance of the Ashura, a definition of "the last war" (that of July–August 2006, between Israeli forces and Hezbollah), and the distinction between the Hezbollah demonstration on March 8 and that of Moustaqbal on March 14). The film's title, *South,* refers to two very real existing sites: the Lebanese South and the southern area of Beirut. The two geographic spaces are significantly linked: the (largely Shiite) South of

Lebanon had traditional links with Palestine, but Israeli invasion and occupation have sent many of its inhabitants into local exile in the North, transforming the traditionally upper-class village of Haret Hreit into a lower-class Shiite suburb of Beirut, Dahieh.

As usual, Hassan acts as in-shot interviewer and makes no attempt to hide the mechanics of production. He offers no personal perspective on the subject of the film—"What does it mean to be a Shiite today?"—and the wider significance of the subject is hardly explored. What interests Hassan are the personal stories of those he interviews, principally Lokman, an archivist who has staged an exhibition about Harat Hreik; two female Lebanese journalists who have written about the topic of being a Shiite; and an ex-communist activist, Anouar Badr el Din, who is now a committed Shiite. The recurrent newsreel-style footage of the Ashura ceremonies in Beirut culminates in the totally personal image of Anouar introducing his young son to the self-mutilation ritual fundamental to the Shiite sect. One key to the film is the sectarianism that pervades all aspects of Lebanese life, shaping and defining, through the identity papers everyone is required to carry, even those who reject such divisions. A second is the overwhelming weight of the past in Lebanon, particularly the events of the civil war. As one of the journalists, Mona, puts it: "There is such a divide in this country that it's even forbidden to bring back memories."

Nizar Hassan's work is particularly fascinating not only for its insights and constant originality but for the way in which he confronts one of the central problems of Palestinian documentary. How can the filmmaker say something fresh when the imagery is always the same: an Israeli helicopter (secure in the absence of anti-aircraft missiles) raiding a built-up area full of women and children, survivors digging out the dead after a heavy Israeli artillery or tank barrage, a row of Palestinian homes bulldozed by drivers unconcerned about the consequences, a small boy armed with a pebble confronting an Israeli tank? One of Hassan's answers is always to probe the evidence. He is totally committed to personal testimony, but he asks whether things are really true just because witnesses say them to the camera. Is an Arab to be condemned because (somehow) he was admitted to a posh Israeli school and met future Israeli political leaders? Is someone really a PLO militant when people who should know him do not recognize him from a key photograph? How does war look from inside an Israeli bulldozer? The key characteristic of Nizar Hassan's cinema is its immediacy. He always probes and never offers glib answers. He does not attempt simply to impart information but rather provokes thought and debate through his intense interrogation of his interviewees.

* * *

There are a surprising number of younger women filmmakers, all born since 1960 and with very varied backgrounds, who have been engaged in Palestinian documentary in the 2000s. Two of these have strong United States connections: Dahna Abourahme and Jackie Reem Salloum (sometimes referred to as Jacqueline Salloum).

Dahna Abourahme is a key exponent of both contemporary and historical approaches. Born in Amman, she studied at the New School of Social Research in New York (specializing in editing and sound design). She worked in New York on several youth projects with the future feature filmmaker Annemarie Jacir, and is currently based in Jordan. Her first feature-length documentary, *Until When . . .* (2004), shot at the time of the Second Intifada, is set firmly in the present and looks at the lives of four Palestinian families who are living in the Dheisheh refugee camp, founded in 1949. These are rural people forced to live in cramped urban communities (over eleven thousand people from forty-five villages crowded into half a square mile), and the first voices we hear are those of older people recalling a very different way of life: houses surrounded by trees (olive, fig, apricot, apple, plum), which, having been planted by the villagers themselves, were harvested annually. There are no trees in the camp. This memory of village life and its rituals, recounted by the older members of the community and picked up by their grandchildren, is a constant thread in the film. The past—the 1948 expulsion of 750,000 Palestinians and its aftermath—is captured in an excellent array of black-and-white still photographs. But the strength of the film is the vivid testimony of the present, especially the words of the young people, who have never known any sort of freedom but who dream of a better life. The villages where their families once lived are less than ten kilometers away, but now they are destroyed—left desolate or replaced by new Jewish communities—and impossible even to visit because of Israeli restrictions.

The difficulties of the present are revealed—restricted water and electricity, the difficulties of travel to work when the main roads are available only to Jewish drivers, Arabs left to the mercy of soldiers' whims and aggressions at the frequent checkpoints. Past struggles against an all-powerful occupier are touched upon, but the general tone of the film—as its title implies—is one in which a positive outcome is hard to imagine. The dream of a Palestinian return is alive and real, but the Oslo agreements have provided nothing concrete. The young have their aspirations, but there is no way of seeing how they can ever be realized. Having explored this one camp for three-quarters of an hour, *Until When . . .* ends with images of five other camps and a reinforced sense of the uncertainty implied by the film's title. Twenty years later, Dahna Abourahme's apprehensions cannot be faulted.

The director's second feature, *The Kingdom of Women: Ein El Hilweh* (2010), is a highly sophisticated examination of the Palestinian past, specifically the consequences of the Israeli bulldozing of the Ein El Hilweh refugee camp in Southern Lebanon and the arrest and imprisonment of all men between fourteen and sixty years of age living in the camp. Instead of concentrating on the purely negative aspects of the atrocity, Abourahme interviews seven women who lived through it and found themselves forced to take on new and unexpected roles. The result is an invigorating account of women discovering new resources within themselves when faced with the challenges of tackling male roles (physically rebuilding and refurbishing the camp), taking on political activity (organizing women's protests and replanning the community), and supporting each other when they themselves are imprisoned. The film shows the tiny amount of treasured possessions saved from the destruction and its aftermath (beads, embroidery, letters) and recalls a host of imaginative responses from the women, such as Um Muhammad turning her father's battered old taxi into a fruit-and-vegetable stall in order to support her family.

As one would expect from someone with Abourahme's professional experience, there is an imaginative use of sound throughout the film, but what gives the film its particular strength and richness is the black-and-white animation by Lena Merhej which punctuates it, drawing on the published political cartoons of Naji al-Ali and depicting the women's possessions, faces, and attitudes. Abourahme used animation because "it can get to the heart of the feeling, the raw simplicity of it. . . . It goes towards imagination because it has a playful element to it. . . . The play between reality and imagination is important because it is like imagining a kingdom of women and the possibilities that can exist for them."[10] As Rania Jawad rightly notes, the film "plays on a dialogue between reality and imagination, not an imagination that is unrealizable but specifically one that has been enacted and can be reconfigured and learned from."[11]

Jackie Reem Salloum was born in Beit Jala and studied fine art at Eastern Michigan and New York Universities; she is now based in New York. She made *Slingshot Hip Hop* (2008), a ninety-four-minute study of the first Palestinian groups to discover hip-hop and use it to express Palestinian concerns in quite a new way. From the opening credit sequence, which uses animation as well as live action, the film's jagged editing matches perfectly the rhythms of the music it deals with. The Palestinian young people involved—in Lyd and Akka within Israel, in Gaza and the West Bank—are very much cut off from the outside world. The pioneering group DAM (Tamar, Suhell, and Mahmoud) reveal the very diverse influences—from filmmaker Spike Lee and Edward Said, to the American rapper Tupac Shakur—that helped shape their initial ideas. But the greatest influence on them and on their successors is what happens around them, on the streets. For them, the Intifada was "a reality check," giving them, as Israeli Arabs, a new connection and involvement with the Palestinian cause. From the start, one is led to sense the connection between the rhythms of hip-hop (adopted from Black American protest) and the lives of Palestinian children on the streets. Visits to schools show how easily they can connect with the young to spread a message of self-respect but non-violence, and this is reinforced by the close rapport between the group and the youthful audiences at their performances. The lyrics, too, capture perfectly the defiance of those confronting overwhelming force while armed only with stones. DAM's song "Who's the Terrorist" became a huge hit and led to other rappers taking up the cause, such as Mohamed Shalabi in Akka. The difficulties of his life are exemplified by the problem he has in traveling by bus, since he is so often viewed as a potential terrorist by Jewish travelers if he speaks Arabic. He also acknowledges the tensions within Arab society, when he tries to help a first women's rap group, Arapaya (Safaa and Nahwa).

Also among those who have followed in the steps of DAM is a group based in Gaza, PR (DR, Mezo, and Kan'aan). Their situation is even bleaker than that of Israeli Arabs, trapped all their lives in Gaza and able to travel only with extreme difficulty the fourteen miles from one end of Gaza to the other, often being held up for seven or eight hours at an Israeli checkpoint. They do eventually manage to meet up with another isolated Gaza rapper, Ibrahim Abu Rahala, but there seems no possibility of escaping the Gaza prison to meet other rappers or to hear performances by foreign groups. Their first public performance is a huge event for them.

The Israeli-based groups have greater mobility, and so DAM is able to stage a number of performances, including one illegal show at the Dheisheh refugee camp. They make friends there with other would-be rappers, only to discover months later that the boys have been imprisoned for resisting an Israeli incursion into the camp. When they encounter a would-be woman rapper, Abeer El Zinati, the inevitable Arab family problems with the very idea of a woman performing on stage recur. Abeer does, however, fulfil her dream by secretly singing on stage with another emerging group, WEH (Alaa, Adi, and Anan). DAM and PR's great dream of meeting up and performing together seems about to be realized when they are scheduled to perform together, with the US group Patriarch, in Ramallah. But at the last moment PR, who have all the necessary visas and paperwork, are stopped at the Israeli checkpoint. An addendum to the film does show the eventual meeting of the two groups, when weeks later PR are allowed out of Gaza, though just for three days.

The last words in *Slingshot Hip Hop* show the positive spirit with which Salloum manages to fill her film: "There is still good in the world, my friend." This is a Palestinian documentary with a unique tone and structure. While hiding nothing of the horrors of Israeli occupation and Israel's double standards as far as its own Arab citizens are concerned, it captures perfectly the essential optimism of young musicians whose lives might otherwise be overwhelmed by drugs and despair.

* * *

There are three more notable new Palestinian women documentary filmmakers, Rima Essa, Suha Arraf, and May Oday, who all live and work in Palestine and whose films look unflinchingly at the present.

Rima Essa studied in Jerusalem and made a number of shorter documentaries before completing her first feature-length work. A passion to document the present rather than to make a conventional documentary is the impulse behind her *My Name Is Ahlam* (2010). This film traces unflinchingly the slow, seemingly inexorable passage toward death of a Palestinian child, Ahlam, suffering from leukemia. Full emphasis is given to the struggles of her mother, Aisha, to get proper treatment for her daughter. But there is no comment from her, or explicit voice-over narration by the filmmaker, to draw attention to the obstacles Aisha faces even to reach the hospital: the need to travel in four successive taxis because of roadblocks, her eventual prohibition from making the crossing because of her brother's conviction for armed combat with the Israelis, the shortages of essential drugs at the hospital itself. We, the audience, are left free to draw our own conclusions as to who is to be blamed for the child's steady decline.

Suha Arraf was born in 1969 in the Galilee and now lives in Jerusalem, where she works as a journalist and filmmaker. She has made a dozen or so shorter documentary films, beginning in 1997, and has also worked as co-scriptwriter on two Israeli features directed by Eran Riklis, *The Syrian Bride* (2005) and *The Lemon Tree* (2009). Her feature-length documentary, *Women of Gaza* (2010), offers a very close-in, non-judgmental study of its female protagonists. The making of this film has a complex, contradictory history, beginning with interviews Arraf conducted, as a journalist, with male members of Hamas. In 2005 she was drawn to look at the role of women in the movement, but a lack of funds and the outbreak of hostilities between Hamas and Fatah interrupted production. When Arraf began again in 2009, she was, according to the opening credits, refused access to Gaza but at the same time given funding for the project by one of the Israeli government's film-funding bodies. This is a documentary directed, it seems, by a video link connecting the director/producer (located elsewhere) to the production manager (on the ground in Gaza). Like Essa's work, *Women of Gaza* has no organizing voice-over narration and emerges as a profoundly ambiguous statement about life for women under Hamas rule. This is a totally closed patriarchal society, in which women who accept the society's views on the fundamental role of women—to breed sons and rejoice in their eventual martyrdom—can feel themselves empowered. This is the situation of the film's dominant figure, a woman with a history of family involvement in the Palestinian liberation struggle dating back to the British Mandate. But the power she possesses can be exercised only in terms of authority over other women and from behind an all-enveloping burka. There is no space in this authoritarian society for the voice of a mother who simply mourns her son and feels no sense of joy at his death as a martyr.

May Oday made just one personal short, *When Walls Speak* (2008), which looks back on her own childhood in Ramallah, before turning to the present to make her first feature-length debut. *Diaries* (2010) presents a perceptive view of young women's lives in Gaza. The film begins with the filmmaker's own first impressions of Gaza a year after the horrific Israeli assault—that despite the devastation this is an attractive city, where people carry on an apparently normal sort of life. But through interviews with three young women of her own age (mid-twenties) she learns how women in particular are doubly trapped, first and most obviously, by the Israeli forces, which shut them off from the outside world and inflict physical deprivation on them (arbitrarily cutting off the electricity, for example). But there are also the less tangible but equally real pressures exerted on young women by the Islamic fundamentalist Hamas administration, most obviously by imposing on them the requirement to keep their heads covered at all times, but also by implementing a whole range of social prohibitions. At the end of her shooting, Oday experiences the deprivations of Gaza at first hand, when she finds that the authorities refuse for some time to allow her to leave.

* * *

Two other young Palestinian filmmakers, Ula Tabari and Leila Sansour, both living abroad, adopt very different perspectives, each of which offers a specific and novel insight into the ongoing problems of Israeli-Palestinian relations.

Ula Tabari, who defines herself as possessing an Israeli ID and a Palestinian dream, was born in 1970 in Nazareth and established her career as an actress in Paris. She has appeared in several films, most notably in two made in the 1990s by Elia Suleiman, *Chronicle of a Disappearance* and *The Arab Dream*. She directed her first feature-length video documentary, the ninety-minute *Private Investigation / Enquête personnelle / 'Alaqna wa khalaqna* in 2002. It looks directly at her own past experience and how it shapes the present. The opening caption makes clear her concerns:

> Like many other Palestinian kids in Israeli schools, I raised the Israeli flag, sang and danced to glorify the state of Israel on its Independence Day. But the next day, which is the official Independence Day, when people were supposed to go out, either to a picnic or to the beach, my father was constantly sick, and we never left the house.

The opening sequence establishes both the theme of identity and the director's own present personal circumstances, living a very modern life in her apartment in the 19th arrondissement in Paris. The US pop song overlaying her walk to her apartment contrasts strongly with the plaintive Arab song about love and separation which accompanies the images bringing her back home at the film's conclusion. Although she includes images of her own Israeli childhood, the film lacks the constant personal voice-over one might expect from such a personal film, though a close-up of her eyes is a recurring motif. Instead Tabari allows her interviewees to tell their own stories and make their own comments.

The bulk of the film is set in Nazareth, where Tabari's parents still live. Her mother emerges as an Israeli Arab who has come to terms with the restrictions imposed on her and has worked within Israeli society as a teacher. At one point, she sits at the piano to play and sing the Israeli national anthem with gusto and no apparent unease. She is shocked at the end of the film by an Al Jazeera documentary which disparages the attitudes of Israeli Arabs like herself. For most of the film Tabari's father remains a silent figure in the background. But eventually his very different views emerge. He is coaxed into reciting a half-remembered poem about lost identity, and we hear a voice-over comment: "The pain, my daughter, the repressed pain, sometimes stops you, sometimes makes you talk, and at other times stops you talking." Whereas his wife refuses to leave what she feels is her own home and country, he does not concede that he lives in his own home or his own country. He wishes to die among his family—but this would mean becoming, like them, a refugee.

This difference of viewpoint regarding the ambiguous situation of Israeli Arabs in a Jewish state is reflected in the various interviews Tabari conducts in Nazareth. She finds Arabs who celebrate the Israeli Independence Day (the Palestinian Nakba) and shopkeepers who are happy selling Israeli flags. She finds an English-speaking politician who explains the working of the Israeli equivalent of South African apartheid (land confiscation which has left the Arab 20 percent of the population owning 2.5 percent of the land, and an official view that sees them not as citizens but as a threat to security). One old friend, who was once politically involved, explains why such activity is simply not practical anymore; another tells her with a wry smile that Arab citizenship "is their lie that we believe in more than they do." A couple who have founded their own school talk about their experiences, and their young pupils show an astonishing awareness of the world in which they live. Perhaps there is real hope for a new generation? Tabari's *Private Investigation* is in no way dogmatic. Instead it offers real insight into the complexities of the situation of Israeli Arabs, who are, on the one hand, deprived of true democratic citizenship but, on the other, enjoy freedoms of expression that are rare elsewhere in the Arab world.

Leila Sansour, who was born in Moscow to a Palestinian father and Russian mother, is currently based in London, where she works as a journalist and producer. She has made several short films, documentaries for Al Jazeera, and the low-budget feature-length *Jeremy Hardy versus the Israeli Army* (2002) from a production base in London. The latter film was made in support of the International Solidarity Movement (ISM), which organizes non-violent campaigns by foreign activists against Israeli occupation, some of which involve the foreigners acting as human shields against the Israeli army. It is dedicated to Rachel Corrie, the young US student killed in 2003 by an Israeli bulldozer while trying to protect Palestinian homes from destruction.

Jeremy Hardy, an English stand-up comedian, is persuaded by Sansour to join an ISM group and to participate in a documentary, but his arrival on Good Friday 2002 coincides with Ariel Sharon's decision to invade and occupy the West Bank. In an article in the newspaper *The Guardian,* Hardy described the result as "four days in hell." His unarmed group's first outing was met by Israeli troops firing live ammunition, resulting in several injuries, one of them serious. Hardy felt compelled to accept the offer by the British consul to evacuate him from Bethlehem. When he returned in July, "the contrast with Easter was stunning. For all the menace in the air before the incursion, there had been a frenzy of human activity. Now everyone seemed to have vanished and nothing moved but armoured cars."[12] This time, however, he was able to take part in a successful group effort to deliver medical supplies.

Sansour found no media support for her project in the United Kingdom and had to pay the full production costs herself, but, as she says, "independent production is a luxury that you can only afford once, but what a luxury it is. I would not have missed it for the world."[13] The film does not attempt to put the Israeli incursion into a political context or tackle any of the wider issues. Its strength is the way in which it captures firsthand the bewilderment, fear, and frustration of a committed outsider, faced with the might of the Israeli military. *Jeremy Hardy versus the Israeli Army* allows this basic situation to speak for itself.

*   *   *

In addition to these seven women, there are five male documentarists born after 1960, three with foreign connections and two with strong roots in the occupied territories, who adopt very different approaches to the issues involving Palestine: Mohamed Alatar, Hany Abu Assad, Sobhi al-Zobaïdi, Emad Burnat, and the much younger Khaled Jarrar. The work of Alatar, al-Zobaïdi, Burnat, and Jarrar is discussed in detail here, and that of Hany Abu Assad alongside his fictional features in the section on feature filmmaking.

Mohamed Alatar was born in Jordan but is now resident in the United States. His work, which takes the form of polemical, fact-driven documentary, reflects both his professional experience of working in the film industry and his involvement as a political activist and co-founder of the organization Palestinians for Peace and Democracy. His fifty-two-minute documentary *The Iron Wall* (2006) begins with a 1923 quotation from a pioneer Zionist, Vladimir Jabotinsky, which is still very relevant today:

> Zionist colonization must either stop, or else proceed regardless of the native population. . . . It can proceed and develop only under the protection of a power that is independent of the native population—behind an iron wall, which the native population cannot breach.

The Iron Wall is a passionate and committed work, which was produced by the Palestinian Agricultural Relief Committee (PARC). Though dedicated "To all the people of the Holy Land," it sets out the case against Israeli settlements and the building of the Wall, which was nearing completion when the film was shot. No Zionists are interviewed, only those—Palestinians, Jewish peace activists, and former Israeli soldiers—who can contribute to the film's argument, namely, that despite the participation of Israel in the 1991 Madrid Conference and the 1993 Oslo Declaration of Principles (involving the exchange of land for peace), the unchanging policy of the Israeli government, since the founding of the state, has been a steady (and increasing) encroachment on Palestinian land. This has two aspects: the creation of "facts on the ground" (i.e., physical Israeli structures on confiscated land) and the permanent foreclosure of the establishment of a Palestinian state.

The film traces the various escalating stages of the Israeli occupation, beginning with the intrusions of Zionist fundamentalist settlers in the mid-1970s. Their creation of settlements was supported by the government—the film quotes Yitzak Shamir's assertion that "the settlement of the Land of Israel is the essence of Zionism." But there were never enough fundamentalist settlers to satisfy the government's ambitions; thus Ariel Sharon is quoted as saying, "Everybody has to move, run and grab as many hilltops as they can to enlarge the settlements because everything we take now will stay ours. . . . Everything we don't grab will go to them." As a result of this thinking, a new type of settler was created: "economic" settlers (calculated as now comprising 80 percent of the total), who were attracted by low housing costs and various state subsidies. Residing in protected enclaves and traveling on roads reserved solely for Jews, they can move about freely and live their daily lives while hardly encountering any Arabs or even seeing Arab settlements. At the time the film was made, such roads and settlements encompassed 42 percent of the land intended for the future Palestinian state and fragmented it in a way intended to deny any Palestinian unity.

The Iron Wall also looks at the present. The 150,000 Palestinian settlers in Hebron (the burial place of Abraham) live under such constant curfew that the city is now virtually a ghost town. They are at the mercy of 450 well-armed Israeli fundamentalist settlers, who are totally above the law. As vivid footage shows, these Israeli settlers can fire at random at Palestinians with no army intervention and beat up Palestinians in front of a police force which will then arrest the victims. The same brutality is shown during the construction of the Wall: Palestinian dwellings are torn down, vineyards destroyed, and Palestinians separated from their land. Perhaps the most informative section of the film is the graphic sequence depicting the path of the Wall. Instead of following the 315-kilometer path of the Green Line (the border between Israel and the West Bank), it snakes and weaves for 670 kilometers through Palestinian land, making dozens of illegal settlements effectively part of Israel and fragmenting what is left of the Palestinian territory. The film is an intelligent, lucid, and closely argued indictment of Israeli occupation policies, and the DVD quotes the opinion of President Jimmy Carter: "The best description of the barrier, its routing and impact, is shown in the film *The Iron Wall*."

Alatar has since directed *Jerusalem . . . The East Side Story* (2008), a work of fifty-seven minutes, also produced by PARC and available through the French NGO for Palestine. The approach is the same as that in the earlier film. There is a well-structured argument, backed up by telling statistics and illustrated with well-chosen images. There are interviews with Palestinians, Israeli peace activists, and concerned Americans, as well as with a Palestinian Christian leader, but no space is given to any advocate for Israeli government policy. The film opens with a well-edited collage of scenes depicting the diversity of a very vibrant city— showing Jerusalem as it could potentially be. This is followed, after the credits, by a brief historical overview of Palestinian history: the British Mandate, the Balfour Declaration, and the 1948 UN partition of the land into two states, with Israel being given 56 percent of the land despite the Jews making up only 33 percent of the population and actually owning only 6 percent of the land. A similar division of Jerusalem itself also occurred. After footage of the first wave of refugees driven from their homes, the film's core argument begins with the almost obligatory scene of an elderly Palestinian woman, clasping her deeds of ownership, as she revisits her former home.

Like its predecessor, *Jerusalem . . . The East Side Story* (2008) is structured as an indictment of Israeli policy, backed up with a mass of supporting statistics and emotional interviews with numerous victims who have lost everything. The fatal turning point for the Palestinians was, of course, the 1967 war, when a triumphant Israel occupied the whole of Palestine and Jerusalem and began what the film describes as a policy of ethnic cleansing. This policy involved the enactment of laws clearly differentiating between the rights of Jews and Arabs. Jerusalem itself was expanded by appropriating Palestinian farmland, while excluding the villages in which the farmers themselves lived. Limited citizenship was offered to those actually resident on the day a census was held (with tests including some knowledge of Hebrew). Those absent for whatever reason—all refugees, for example—were excluded from citizenship.

The Ministry of the Interior has adopted a variety of ways to exclude or expel Arab residents of Jerusalem. Those leaving Jerusalem without valid Israeli travel permits are prevented from returning, even those married to Palestinians living on the West Bank. Mothers of West Bank children seeking specialist hospital treatment in Jerusalem are often not allowed to travel with their children, even if these are just five or six years old. Existing houses owned by Palestinians are systematically destroyed, and any new ones built by them are deemed illegal and subject to demolition. Land is routinely confiscated, and checkpoints have been established to restrict and even to prevent movement within Palestinian territory. One key effort has been to establish exclusive control of the Old City—the location of many of the most sacred sites of Judaism, Islam, and Christianity: successive Jewish temples, the Al-Aqsa mosque and the Dome of the Rock, and the Church of the Holy Sepulchre. The physical space of Jerusalem, like that of the rest of Palestine, has been fragmented by the Wall, which has been built on Palestinian territory.

As the film points out, all of these Israeli incursions are illegal under international law, but nothing is being done to prevent them despite their evident racist nature. Israel is concerned only with appropriating the occupied territory and expelling the local inhabitants. One might have thought that, thanks to all these pressures, the Jewish population would feel secure, but in fact, as the film points out, they still feel threatened by the demographic challenge posed by the much higher Arab birth rate: within a few decades Arabs may outnumber Jews in what is intended to be a "Jewish" democratic state. These two films, driven by forcefully expressed and well-documented commentaries, are among the most telling critiques in Palestinian cinema of current Israeli policies.

Sobhi al-Zobaïdi, who was born in 1961 in Jerusalem, went on to study economics at the University of Bir Zeit and film at New York University. He has worked extensively as an actor. The best known of his early films is the twenty-six-minute *My Very Private Map / Ma carte géographique à moi / Kharitati-l-khassa jiddan,* which looks at life for Palestinians living under virtual siege in Ramallah. His approach to the documentary form is quite different from that of Mohamed Alatar.

Al-Zobaïdi has been quoted as saying in 2003 that "the contemporary filmmaker understands that the personal story is missing from our collective narrative,"[14] and the opening title of his digitally shot fifty-two-minute documentary describes *Crossing Kalandia / Ubur Kalandia* (2002) as a video diary. The film begins in the most personal of ways, with shots of his newborn daughter Kenza breast feeding; a key decision he has to make early on is whether to move the family out of their apartment, since it is situated just opposite Yasser Arafat's office. Standing in the way of any movement is the Kalandia roadblock separating Ramallah from Jerusalem—at one point his wife, who has taken Kenza to see her grandmother in Jerusalem, is trapped on the other side of the roadblock, refused permission to pass through and return home. This, as al-Zobaïdi makes clear, is the way the roadblock is designed to operate, with arbitrary, unannounced closures and irrational decisions as to which individuals may or may not pass through at any time. This is not a security post but a means of making life as difficult as possible for ordinary Palestinians.

Although *Crossing Kalandia* is a personal video, it is not introspective. Al-Zobaïdi's main concern is a professional one: what should he film? When he first ventures onto the streets, he films the most obvious signs of a people under siege: roadblocks, devastation, funerals, popular demonstrations. He also does a few interviews—with a sympathetic Israeli woman reporter, a Palestinian sociologist, an English-speaking Palestinian settler. Al-Zobaïdi wants to capture some of Palestine's cultural life under siege—a book reading, a concert, the visit of the foreign writers chronicled in Samir Abdallah's *Writers on the Borders*. But he is driven back to the pessimistic conclusion that the Israelis want to treat the Palestinians just as the Americans treated the native Americans: by eradicating their culture, with the "compensation" of a possible identity as villains in future movies, akin to "red Indians" in Hollywood westerns. *Crossing Kalandia* is an admirable firsthand account of life under Israeli bombardment: lucid, directly personal, and scrupulously honest.

Emad Burnat is not a professional filmmaker but a Palestinian farmer, who bought his first camera to record the birth of his youngest son, Jibril, in 2005. He subsequently used it (and its successors) to record the impact of the Israeli government's decision to build a wall through his West Bank village of Biln, to separate it from the ever-growing Jewish settlement, Modiin Illit, on the surrounding hills. With financing from a wide variety of international television organizations, Burnat developed this material into a feature-length documentary in collaboration with the Israeli activist and filmmaker Guy Davidi, to whom he had supplied footage for his own feature-length documentary, *Interrupted Streams*. In 2012 the resulting film, *Five Broken Cameras / Cinq caméras brisées*, was nominated for an Academy Award. There were the usual disputes about the film's national identity: both filmmakers were, on occasion, accused in their local press of collaborating with "the enemy," and Burnat was initially refused entry to the United States at Los Angeles airport by immigration officials who refused to believe that a Palestinian could possibly have an official invitation to the Academy Awards ceremony.

The strength of *Five Broken Cameras* is its simplicity. It is made up largely of footage shot by Burnat over five years of protests (with some additional footage of Burnat himself shot by Davidi and other cameramen). It is a tribute to the tenacity of Burnat, his brothers, and his friends, who faced years of constant harassment and arbitrary arrest by Israeli soldiers without giving up. The opening shot of the film shows us the five successive cameras used by Burnat, each in turn smashed by an Israeli soldier in a face-to-face encounter or hit by an Israeli bullet. Burnat's need to document is obsessive—at one point even his wife urges him to give up. Certainly the pattern of events is always the same: unarmed Palestinians—often men, women, and children—set off on a peaceful protest, only to be met with tear gas and live bullets by Israeli soldiers who are clearly under orders to conduct no sort of dialogue. Meanwhile the Israeli settlement grows inexorably, and the settlers are allowed to burn down the Palestinian olive groves with no fear of punishment. Understated but painfully clear to any spectator is the experience of Burnat's son, Jibril, who grows up amid this oppression and whose first words are "wall," "bullet," and "army." The threat to children only a little older than himself is very real, as the Israelis conduct raids on the village in the middle of the night, specifically to arrest children and thereby cow their parents into submission. But the Palestinian community, including its young people, remain defiant, and at the end of the film we learn that Burnat has bought his sixth camera.

Khaled Jarrar, who was born in Jenin in 1976 and is currently based in Ramallah, has a background as a visual artist, which distinguishes him from other Palestinian documentarists. He studied first at the Palestine Polytechnic University and then at the Palestine International Academy of Art and made his initial reputation as a photographer (staging exhibitions at various Israeli checkpoints in 2004, for example). His first short films and videos received screenings at international festivals, but he is best known for his design project "Live and Work in Palestine," which aims to assert a Palestinian identity—to proclaim Palestine as a nation-state (which legally it is not): "I was thinking—how come the Israelis decide who is welcome in our country? We would like to welcome everybody! So I said I would make a 'Green Card' for my friends; a kind of ironic permit which says they can live and work in Palestine."[15] The next stage was to develop postage stamps, featuring the beautiful Palestine Sunbird and a jasmine flower, which he sold at art fairs for the stated price of 750 fils (the old Palestinian currency, equivalent to about 75 cents). More daring still, he designed a "State of Palestine" passport stamp, organizing presentations to stamp people's actual passports in Ramallah, as well as in Berlin and Paris. These caused the Israeli officials who saw them some concern and bewilderment (they look like authentic passport stamps), and a few tourists reportedly had their journeys delayed.

It was inevitable that Jarrar would become concerned with the Wall and all it stands for; his first video short, *Journey 110,* is about people who used a sewage tunnel to try to reach Jerusalem. His first seventy-minute feature, *Infiltrators / Mutasalilun* (2012), took some four years to complete. It contains the obligatory shots of Palestinian women queuing in their dozens, penned up, at the official crossing points. Even when their papers are in order, the Israeli conscript guards hold them back for no apparent reason. They permit only a handful to pass, seemingly taking particular delight in separating couples (a mother and a daughter, say) by allowing one through and delaying the other. But most of the film is concerned with Palestinians trying to evade the Israeli controls and outwit the border police. These are ordinary people, mostly young men, not terrorists or suicide bombers, who daily are prevented from getting to work, going to a hospital, or visiting relatives. Guided by people smugglers, who may or may not be honest, they pay for transport and try in ever more ingenious ways to scale the wall, helping each other and using improvised ladders and ropes. They knowingly risk broken limbs as they leap from the top of the wall. Where there is a gap, they stream through it, even if this means wading through garbage. The sheer numbers of those making this attempt and the determination they display are astonishing.

Their efforts are filmed by Jarrar himself, using a DigiBeta camera. The images, some shot while he is running with the crowd, are jarring, jagged, and disrupting. At times we see tight close-ups of the action; at others—particularly at night—we are not well placed and have difficulty in making out what exactly is going on in the distance. Jarrar himself is sometimes blocked, unable to get a clear sight of the action, let alone compose a well-framed image. The style gives a visceral quality to the imagery, drawing us tightly into these people's actions; as a spectator you can feel the immediacy of the struggle and effort. There is no commentary or explanation of precise locations, and only the most sparse use is made of music. Since everything is filmed from the Palestinian side of the Wall, we are left with no idea of what happens to those who do get across. Are the women actually allowed to pray at the Al-Aqsa mosque, or are there other impediments put in their way? What happens to the young men who run across the border road on the Israeli side and vanish out of sight? What is the outcome for Ali, whom we see caught, beaten, and arrested by Israeli guards? This is a game of cat-and-mouse in which we are unsure whether any of the Palestinians have actually succeeded.

Jarrar is a committed artist. As he told an interviewer: "I believe that art can create reality. I don't believe in this kind of art that tries to separate itself from politics and reality—they can't be separated." In his view, "art should make a difference and we should use art to send our message loudly to shake and provoke the system."[16] In *Infiltrators* he gives a wonderfully vivid portrayal of the impact of the Wall on Palestinian citizens who resist being cooped up like animals. It is a tribute to their tenacity and determination.

* * *

Two more male Palestinian documentarists—Kamal Aljafari and Raed Andoni—are key participants in the kind of personal documentary style that became increasingly prevalent in the later 2000s.

Kamal Aljafari was born in 1972 in Ramallah and studied media production in Cologne, where he is now based. He adopts a very personal tone in his reflections on the issues of exile and exclusion, in two feature-length documentaries. Both are German funded but shot during periods of return to Palestine. The settings of *The Roof / Le toit / Al-sateh* (2006), shot in October and November 2004, are Ramle (where his parents live), Jaffa (the home of his grandmother and uncle), and Jerusalem (where he meets up with a young woman (a relative or friend—the credits do not clarify). The opening pre-credit sequence (a conversation occurring, we later discover, in Jerusalem) is the only occasion in which Aljafari tells us about his own experiences (his imprisonment for six and a half months during the Intifada). Later, we see other portions of this conversation, in which his companion reveals her own ambitions—to become a lawyer, perhaps even a judge. This is the only moment in the film in which a Palestinian reveals ambition and drive.

The Roof, like Aljafari's subsequent feature, is a totally controlled work, with immaculate camera work, marked by slow pans and long-held immobile long shots. There is never the intrusion of the unexpected, of a chance or random event. This is unmistakably a single, personal vision, but perhaps the most significant aspect of the film is what is lacking. Uniquely in a film chronicling a return from exile, there are no scenes of welcome, no overflow of emotion, no outpouring of reminiscence. There are, it is true, a couple of sequences in which his relatives speak briefly of the past, and one tiny scrap of voice-over talks of when it all began—1948—when families, like the Aljafaris, were blocked for days in Jaffa harbor. They returned inland to find themselves exiles in their own land, their own homes destroyed, housed instead in homes vacated by others, those who had managed to escape (the film tells us that the Arab population of Jaffa declined from 120,000 to 3,000).

In Aljafari's sharply defined vision, the Palestinians—his own extended family included—are a defeated people, silent, marginalized, and passive. Their living conditions are poor compared to those of the "Russians and Iraqi Jews" now claimed to be dominating Ramle. The embodiment of their oppression is the Israeli bulldozer, responsible for the rubble from destroyed Arab houses piled up on a once-pleasant beach, protected by armed soldiers while blocking a needed throughway, and "accidentally" tearing off the whole front wall of a family home in a peaceful Arab quarter.

Port of Memory / Port du souvenir (2009), Aljafari's second film, follows a similar stylistic pattern: no voice-over commentary, little dialogue or interaction between characters, numerous enigmatic scenes, frequent repetitions of identical long shots and pans. The new work is even more fragmented than its predecessor. No coherent geography of Jaffa is established, and the relationships between Aljafari's family and the other characters are not clarified. The Christian family (grandmother and daughter) are presumably neighbors, but there is no indication of how either family relates to other people in the film. There is no sense of a unity, of a community, which might provide a focus for action. Aljafari's uncle regularly takes food to a neighbor, but we never see who this is (just as the lawyer in the opening scene, when Salim asserts his ownership of their home, remains invisible).

Jaffa is depicted as a desolate, shrinking Arab ghetto, steadily being oblit-erated by the Israelis, who have already destroyed thirty thousand houses so as to remove all trace of what was once a thriving Palestinian community. The streets are empty, with none of the normal bustle and movement of a port or city. The repeated actions shown are enigmatic: women washing their hands, a man prowling on his Vespa, unexplained tensions in a café, Aljafari's uncle delivering food to an unseen neighbor. The later sequences of the city are interspersed with unexplained shots of an Israeli sentimental pop singer and brief action sequences from two Menahem Golan films (including *Delta Force*). These sequences, shot, it seems, by Israeli crews on location in Jaffa, presumably connote the creeping Israeli cultural invasion (to match the physical incursion of the bulldozers); but nothing is spelled out, and no protest is voiced.

The films of Kamal Aljafari are significant because of their particular auto-biographical tone in relation to the treatment of Palestinian issues. Both films are intimate, personal studies of members of the filmmaker's own immediate family and their domestic living situation. In the interior shots there is a concentration on small gestures and on sentimental objects and images. Conversations are im-precise, and a general air of passivity prevails. Silence and ambient sound (such as that emanating from the television set, which is constantly turned on in interior scenes) play a crucial role in establishing the atmosphere.

The narratives, in so far as they exist, are minimal: the inability/failure to repair a roof in *The Roof* and the muted attempt to resist seizure of the house by the Israeli authorities in *Port of Memory*. Every shot seems marked by the am-biguous status of the filmmaker, an Israeli passport holder, bilingual in Arabic and Hebrew, but sensing himself to be an outsider in his homeland: he does not participate, express opinions, or attempt to effect change. Little factual informa-tion is given, and there is no overt political argument. Rather, the sense is that of a dream or nightmare: we hear in *Port of Memory,* for example, words on the telephone saying the house has been saved, but the phone did not ring and this is no more than an expression of the uncle's deepest longing.

Raed Andoni, who was born in 1967 in Transjordan, is a self-taught film-maker with ten years' experience of producing documentaries through his com-panies, Dar Films in Ramallah and Les Films de Zayna in Paris. Among the films he has produced are documentaries by Nizar Hassan and Rashid Masharawi. He has also directed a documentary, *Improvisation, Samir and His Brothers / Improvisation, Samir et ses frères* (2005), shot in digital beta. His first feature, *Fix Me* (2010), partly financed by Fonds Sud in 2010, is one of the most strikingly personal and autobiographical of all Palestinian documentaries. This ninety-eight-minute work traces the filmmaker's progress through twenty weekly psy-chotherapy sessions, as he seeks a cure for the crippling persistent headache which impedes his working life. *Fix Me* is an intimate work, which evidently helped the filmmaker come to terms with himself and his lifestyle (he confides that he was not the same person after completing both the therapy and the film).[17] The political factors in a life led under Israeli occupation—creating conditions where migraine might be considered a normal response—are not dwelt upon. Instead the film, which displays an agreeable wit and self-deprecating humor, is a purely personal statement. In its treatment of those around him, it is marked by Andoni's stated individual documentary ethic: "to preserve, whatever happens, a form of respect towards the other people I was filming, since this is necessary if any relationship is to flourish."[18]

So that he would not unduly influence the personal events being filmed, the sequences in the hospital where he was treated were shot by a Swiss camera team who did not speak Arabic (the film is a Palestinian/Swiss/French co-production). In addition, the rules of his therapy meant that Andoni was not allowed to see the material shot in the hospital until he had completed his treatment, with the result that he had over twenty hours of unseen material at the editing stage. Andoni also includes footage of his family's responses (including that of his mother, who clearly thinks he's mad, and a nephew who, Andoni feels, represents much of his own personality at the age of twenty. There are also two characters who, for Andoni, are outwardly stronger—Omar, his electrician, who has successfully fought cancer for years, and Bashir, the man with whom Andoni shared a prison cell some twenty years earlier (and whose memories do not coincide at all with his own). While he resists the classification of his film as a comedy, Andoni does stress that humor is a necessity when one is faced with the Palestinian situation. For him the film poses a universal question: how to participate in society while at the same time constructing your own personality. What is distinctive is that "this is a question asked more in Palestine than anywhere else."[19]

Lebanon

One older director, resettled in Beirut and making his first Lebanese feature-length documentary in 2003, is included in some listings of Lebanese filmmakers, though he is of Armenian descent and many of his films treat aspects of exile and (more recently) Armenian traditional culture.[20] **Nigol Bezjian** was born in 1955 in Aleppo (Syria), but brought up in Beirut. At the age of seventeen he left for the United States, where he studied filmmaking and made his first films—including the feature-length *Chickpeas* (1994). Of the three films he has made since his return to Beirut in 1997, two are short films. The thirty-five-minute *Roads Full of Apricots* (2001) is a slow-moving (often soft-focus) English-language meditation on return from exile, spoken by a woman, but bearing a remarkable similarity to Bezjian's own personal trajectory. *Verve* (2002) is a virtually abstract fifteen-minute piece, without dialogue or commentary, featuring a renowned

Armenian folk dancer, edited from the five hours of video footage shot during the dancer's visit to Beirut.

The feature-length *Muron* (2003) is an excellent example of the rich diversity of Lebanese culture, which embraces a variety of Christian cultures alongside the majority Muslim faith. The film is a full feature-length documentary, which takes as its subject the preparation of the traditional holy oil (Muron), used in the Armenian Church to baptize children, to ordain priests, and to consecrate churches. Bezjian follows in meticulous detail the obtaining of the forty-four necessary ingredients—oils, spices, incenses, and even wine. This is followed by the elaborate preparation (mixing, cooking, and filtering over a long period), in which women and children are allowed to participate. The eventual installation of the purified oil on the church altar for forty days is, however, the task of priests alone.

This meticulous, ritualized, and intensely serious work permits Bezjian to construct a slow-paced narrative, with a minimum of explanatory titles and voice-over, and at the same time allows plenty of scope for his favored digitally remastered imagery. Throughout, a background of chanted and sung holy music serves to remind the viewer of the intense religious meaning of these actions. The climax, attended by the head of the church and his bishops in full ritual regalia, before a congregation of thousands, is the ceremony of blending the new Muron (brewed every seven years) with the remnants of the Muron previously prepared and used, symbolizing the 1,700-year history and continuity of the Church. The film ends with the ritual which embodies this: the baptism of a child.

* * *

Like Palestine, Lebanon has seen the emergence of a new generation of younger filmmakers in the 2000s. Outstanding is the work of four Lebanese women filmmakers, all born in Beirut in the 1970s, but from very different backgrounds: Dalia Fathallah, Danielle Arbid, Éliane Raheb, and Zeina Daccache. All were children when the fifteen-year civil war, which would shape their adolescence, began in 1980. The work of Arbid will be discussed, along with her feature work, in the section on feature filmmaking.

Dalia Fathallah was born in 1972. After receiving a degree from the American University of Beirut, she studied economics and urban planning, first at ALBA in Beirut, then at the François Rabelais University in Tours, before working on various developmental projects. She subsequently took courses in filmmaking both in Beirut and at FEMIS in Paris. She has also written a French-language novel, *Balcons et abris* (Balconies and Shelters), published in Paris in 2003. Her first documentary, *Chronicle of a Return to South Lebanon / Chronique d'un retour au Sud Liban / Mabrouk at-tahrir* (2002), a French-Lebanese co-production, takes as its subject an aspect of the doctorate in political science, which she completed at Tours in 1999 and which dealt with the Israeli occupation in Southern Lebanon.

As the text preceding the film indicates, the Israelis invaded Southern Lebanon in 1978. Although there was a partial withdrawal in 1985, the Israelis retained control of a buffer zone until 2000. The film is concerned with what is happening in this newly liberated zone—from which 89 percent of its pre-1978 population of 600,000 were, over time, expelled by the Israelis.

Anxious to record a moment of history, on May 24, 2000, the day on which the final Israeli withdrawal was completed after twenty-two years of occupation, Fathallah accompanies the Chahrour family on their return to their home in the village of Kfarhamam. The initial response is euphoric as they drive south, banners waving and car horns blaring, past cheering crowds at the roadside. Their family home is undamaged, though dilapidated after twelve years of neglect, and they are able to make a triumphant return to the Khiam prison as well, where they were held and ill-treated by the Israelis as punishment for their support of their son Jamal, who was part of the armed Lebanese (largely communist) resistance. The family, returning after twelve years of exile from their native village, immediately set about restoring their home and their land. Their situation is very different from the family with whom they share a courtyard and who were once family friends. The aged Oum and Abu Kassem stayed behind during the occupation, and, needing a way to support his four children, their son joined the Israeli-organized militia, the South Lebanese Army. He is now under arrest as a collaborator and they are ostracized.

The Chahrour family are hostile to their neighbors, feeling that the penalties for collaboration are too light (compared to the punishments they themselves suffered under Israeli rule) and react badly to rumors of early release. They also complain about the central government, which offers them no compensation and no protection against possible further intrusions by the Israelis. At the May 2001 celebrations of the liberation of Kfarhamam (from which "collaborators" are excluded), a new tension becomes apparent between the communists, who began the resistance to the Israelis, and the newly emergent Islamic force of Hezbollah. A year later, there is still a shortage of water and a lack of government projects. The first releases from prison occur, and the head of the Israeli-controlled Civil Administration justifies his role: "We were slaves taking orders." The tensions persist but there have been no serious incidents, and Abu Kassem can gradually begin to participate in the community again.

The final words are left to Jamal, the communist resistance fighter who has now been elected to the new administration. Talking of his children he says, "I'll try to make them forget the horrors of war, but naturally I'll teach them their history. . . . I'll teach them to love their country, nothing more. I'll try to keep them away from feelings of hatred and rancor." But the optimism of these words is undercut by the film's final caption, which records that Israeli shelling resumed in April 2002, forcing many who had returned to Kfarhamam to leave once more.

Perhaps, Fathallah concludes, the two years following the liberation of the South were no more than a time of fragile truce for Kfarhamam.

As might be expected given Fathallah's academic background and sociological studies, *Chronicle of a Return to South Lebanon* is a meticulously structured documentary, rooted in observation and interview. Fathallah offers no interpretation or judgment of her own, preferring to allow people's actions and interviews speak for themselves. This is not only a highly informative communication for present-day audiences but also an invaluable contribution to the future archival record of contemporary Lebanon.

Fathallah received Fonds Sud support for *Beirut Cowboy / Le cowboy de Beyrouth* (2005), which was known during the production process by the more descriptive title *Beirut between New York and Baghdad / Beyrouth entre New York et Bagdad*. This second documentary is much more personal in its origins, as the filmmaker herself has explained: "As a child I grew up with the intonation of Arab language and music. I watched the Chinese Sinbad cartoons, and his flying carpet took me from one Arab city to another, I flew towards Baghdad, the land of palm groves and water, of the pure Arab language." Her father, a Sunni Muslim from Beirut, was an ardent follower of Nasser, but he also "spoke of America, a strong and fascinating America." As a result, she still dreams of America, "this new world where I would be able to reinvent and recreate myself."[21] The French-produced, ninety-minute *Beirut Cowboy* is an exploration of both how America is seen by the Lebanese in today's Beirut and how the dream of an Arab nation has gradually dissolved.

The film is, once again, narrated by Fathallah herself; the key figure is her father, Toufic, whose comments open and close the film, which is in one sense the story of his growing disillusionment. As a child, he was fascinated by Hollywood movies, so that he shared the common dream of traveling to America and making his fortune. People of his generation began to give up French and learn English. Study at the American University of Beirut (which Fathallah did in fact attend) was the highest aspiration for one's daughter's education. Then came disillusionment with the United States. He witnessed the bombing of the American embassy, which brought direct intervention to an end, but became increasingly aware of the consequences of US support for Israel. At the end of the film, even the election of President Obama provokes little optimism. Parallel to this is the collapse of the dream symbolized by Nasser's nationalization of the Suez Canal, replaced by the horrors of the seemingly unending civil war, and now the thirty-three-day Israeli invasion.

Fathallah also interviews people of her own generation: Pierre, who remembers the atrocities he witnessed during the civil war; Malak, a Palestinian who campaigns on the streets against US support of Israel; and Khaled, who participates in the Democratic Left Movement. Their views, a mixture of fascination and revulsion toward the United States, are very similar to those of Fathallah's father and of the director herself. She keeps her own dream of America alive through correspondence with her friend Katia, who actually realized hers, emigrating and putting Lebanon in the back of her mind—even to the extent of marrying an American Jew. Despite everything, the fascination with foreign countries remains strong in Beirut, with American goods proliferating and cheaper imitations being made locally (the jeans labeled "Elvis" instead of Levis). But it is only a dream, and the words and attitudes of Ismaïl, a young man who is actually leaving, seem only to diminish rather than strengthen it. Fathallah's progression from documentation to self-analysis is typical of the shift that occurs during the 2000s. Her work offers few answers but her probing questions are acute, and the variety of insights she gathers make her work an admirable portrait of her time.

Éliane Raheb was born in 1972 and studied at IESAV, where she now teaches. She has been very active in Beirut cultural organizations, curating the Beirut International Film Festival and participating in the film cooperative Beirut DC. She made a number of short fictional and documentary works before completing the first of her three feature-length documentaries in 2001. These show a marked personal approach. The tone of her first hour-long video documentary, *So Near, Yet So Far / Si proche, si loin / Qarib wa Baidi* (2001), is captured in the pre-credit sequence, which juxtaposes a clip from Charlie Chaplin's *The Kid* (the first film she ever saw) with the unforgettable television image of the Palestinian child, Mohammad al-Durra who is gunned down by Israeli troops, in the arms of his father, who is trying to shelter him. In a manner that would become common in the course of the decade, Raheb begins her film by introducing herself to us, showing family photographs, and talking openly about her upbringing. Born in Beirut into a Christian Maronite family originally from Southern Lebanon, she spent the period of the civil war, which began when she was three, constantly moving from place to place, mostly in Lebanon but briefly in Cyprus, too, as her father struggled to keep his family safe. She admits her childhood naiveté, growing up believing that all Lebanese were Christians, all Syrians were Muslims, and all Palestinians were monsters and troublemakers. She records her disbelief on discovering that her favorite neighbors in Brumana were in fact members of a Palestinian refugee family. This moment, a child proclaiming "I am a Palestinian" to her friends, is at the heart of the film.

To make *So Near, Yet So Far* Raheb traveled to Southern Lebanon, Egypt, Palestine, Jordan, and Paris, and this film is, in a very real sense, her own journey of self-discovery. She records, for example, her astonishment at her first sight of the Lebanese-Israeli border. In order to trace the impact of Israeli aggression—and especially the Palestinian response, the Intifada—on Arab children, she does not look at the acts of violence suffered but picks out small instances of instinctive childish resistance: a group of Lebanese children who steal an Israeli cow in response to the soldiers' confiscation of a hundred of the family's goats, a Jordanian schoolgirl who speaks out and creates a protest at her school, an eleven-year-old who runs away from home to try to join the Intifada.

Raheb's journey takes her on to Paris, where she learns something of the experience of Arab exiles—children told in school that Palestine doesn't exist, a young man beaten up when he inadvertently wanders into a Jewish rally. Most importantly, Raheb meets up with her former Palestinian neighbor, Danielle Abyad, now well integrated into French society. Having lived all her life in exile, Danielle feels increasingly distanced from Palestine and its people. She no longer remembers that first little act of defiance in the garden at Brumana, which is at the origin of this film. The film ends with Raheb's return to the old family home and her belief that, if only Danielle were there, she too would remember. *So Near, Yet So Far* is a delicately made film, which captures perfectly the children's need to do something in response to happenings they cannot fully comprehend. This is a war which concerns these children deeply, though their own situations are very different from those immediately caught up in the fighting in, say, Beirut or Gaza.

Raheb's second feature, *That's Lebanon / C'est ça le Liban / Haydha Lubnan* (2008), co-produced by the German television station ZDF, is if anything even more personal, beginning in home video style with Raheb summoned on her cell phone by her mother, to spend her thirty-fourth birthday (August 6, 2006) at the family home outside Beirut. She agrees, and ominously the day coincides with a series of Israeli air raids on southern Beirut. Her parents, like other parents talking to their offspring later in the film, advise Raheb to leave Beirut and, if possible, create a life abroad, even if this means separation from the family.

The film itself deals with Lebanon in the immediate present, in the aftermath of the assassination, on February 14, 2005, of Rafiq Hariri, the president who had held Lebanon together and worked tirelessly to rebuild Beirut during the first fifteen years after the end of the civil war. *That's Lebanon,* like its predecessor, is structured as a personal inquiry rather than an explanatory analysis. It explores, from Raheb's personal perspective as a member of a younger generation of Maronite Christians, the events leading up to the new elections, the elections themselves, and their aftermath, in Southern Lebanon, in Beirut, and in the North. The full complexity of Lebanon's electoral system emerges from Raheb's inquiries. There are the carefully balanced (for their time) structures devised by the French under the protectorate, which no one has ever had the courage or authority to change. For example, electors can only register and vote in the towns and villages where their families lived thirty-five years ago (even if these are villages obliterated by Israeli bombing), and whatever the outcome, the president will always be a Maronite and the prime minister a Sunni.

The rules, in other words, take no account of the new political forces which emerged during and after the civil war, which itself fragmented Lebanese society, breaking up mixed communities and increasing sectarianism. Divided community structures, combined with the continued power of family and patronage, mean that the outcome is often known well before the vote even takes place. Raheb's film captures vividly the resulting confusion: what other society would hold celebrations to mark the thirtieth anniversary of the *outbreak* of the civil war? Her style reflects the contradictions she finds in her own society, as she lays tracks of popular traditional songs—such as "O Lebanon, You Are a Piece of Paradise" and "O Beirut, Queen of the World"—over images of a society in chaos, mixes political posters with underwear advertisements, and juxtaposes Saad Hariri's celebration of victory (*before* the elections) with images of Méliès-style early film trickery (shown coincidentally at the same time at the French Cultural Centre).

Raheb draws on the views of two outsiders from her own generation: Fadi, who has just returned from exile and is rapidly disillusioned, and Afif, who is a communist sympathizer and who denies belonging to any sect. But Raheb is working from within a Maronite perspective, and the film's sharpest insights come from interviews with her own parents and those of her colleague and sound recordist, Zeina Sfeir. Raheb's mother has to admit that she now has no Muslim friends, and the gathering of her women friends to celebrate the month of the Virgin Mary breaks up angrily when Raheb tries to ask probing questions. Her father refuses to say who shelled and destroyed the family house in Beirut (because it was fellow Maronites). Most powerful is the film's final confrontation between Raheb and her father, where he tries to put forward the traditional Maronite view of Lebanon ("without the Maronites, there would be no Lebanon"). But it is clear from his words here, as from those of other Maronites earlier in the film, that the community has been shattered by the loss of what it had assumed was its natural authority. He tells his daughter she is talking nonsense and is lost in her ideas. He hopes she will eventually see things as he does, and quotes the parable of the prodigal son.

Sleepless Nights / Layali bala noom (2012) is less immediately personal, but it is an even more penetrating and raw expression of Lebanon's current situation. In 1991 an amnesty was pronounced, exonerating all those who had participated in political killings—including, of course, the politicians who passed it into law. But, it would seem, it solved nothing. Over twenty years later, *Sleepless Nights* explores the lives of two of those who experienced the civil war at first hand. It is a film which bears all the marks of the more abrasive approach of Rehab's partner, the Palestinian documentarist Nizar Hassan, who worked as producer, writer, and editor on the film. A British psychotherapist, Alexandra Asseily, married to a Lebanese, has set up a "Garden of Forgiveness" in the spirit of the amnesty, but this seems as remote as the amnesty itself from the real, lived-out problems of the two contrasting figures on whom the film focuses.

The first is a figure from Rehab's own community, Assaad Shaftari, a committed Maronite Christian, who participated in the amnesty, admitting to being an intelligence officer and to participating in five hundred killings. But perhaps there were more—certainly there are details he does not wish to discuss. Although he has no doubts about the validity of fighting for a Christian Lebanon—and collaborating with the Israelis in this cause—he has not found peace as a result of the amnesty. He is a disturbed figure, still despising Muslims, still certain about his own motives for torturing and killing hundreds of opponents during the civil war, but constantly troubled by the immunity he has been given. He is ill at ease with himself, seemingly craving punishment. He allows himself to be filmed, in one of the film's most disturbing sequences, participating in a clown workshop (complete with a taped-on red nose). For him, amnesty and (at least partial) admission of guilt has brought no closure.

Equally troubled is Maryam Saiidi, whose fifteen-year-old son Mahir was, it would seem, killed while fighting alongside communist forces at a university in Beirut in 1982. She knows her son is dead but will not allow him to be listed among the martyrs of the war. She has spent two decades seeking her son's grave. Her confrontation, at an exhibition of photographs of the Lebanese dead, with Shaftari, who she assumes knows the answer to her quest, is electric. But at the end of film, when the filmmakers point out the almost certain resting place of her son, this resolves nothing. She does not pause to pray or speak or cry, just turns away and walks out of shot.

In 2009 this group of female filmmakers—Fathallah, Raheb, and Arbid—was joined by another woman filmmaker, who brings a unique background to her documentary work. **Zeina Daccache** began her studies at IESAV in Beirut, before turning to drama (with Philippe Gaulier) in London, drama therapy at Kansas State University, and clinical psychology at the Haigazian University in Beirut. Since then she has worked both as an actress in television and as a drama therapist concerned with the disadvantaged and traumatized.

Twelve Angry Lebanese / Douze Libanais en colère (2009) is an account of the staging of her own reworking of Reginald Rose's play *Twelve Angry Men* (on which Sidney Lumet's film with Henry Fonda is based). This "Theatre in Prison" project was funded by the European Union in 2007 and realized in 2008. Daccache's drama workshops take place in Lebanon's Roumieh Prison, where murderers, rapists, and drug dealers are held.

In the opening sequences, we see prisoners briefly act out the core of the play, when one juror stands up against his eleven co-jurers, saying that they must talk before they condemn a man to death. We then see Daccache explaining the play and the motivations of the characters, as well as the prisoners' initial incomprehension of the situation in which they are being invited to participate. Rehearsals begin, and some prisoners, who lose control of themselves, have to be discarded. The numbers are reduced from the initial 150 applicants, and the real preparations are undertaken. Eventually about 45 prisoners are involved: the actors and musicians, but also the backstage crew.

Daccache mixes the normal preparation of the play (learning the text, for example, which at first some cannot be bothered with) with challenges to the cast to use the play as a way of understanding themselves and how they ended up in prison. One of her starting points is a relaxation class for the cast, where they lie flat on their backs and are invited to think about themselves and whether they have ever proved themselves in life. After a brief intermission—a song of loss, regret, and grief—Daccache resumes her work with the prisoners, talking about the easiest defense mechanism—denial—and pointing out that they must open themselves up if they hope to communicate to an audience. Later she observes how attitudes are shaped by childhood experiences: they all still behave at times like demanding children or domineering parents, but what of their roles as adults? Later, they all agree that they must learn to trust each other, but the three responses we see to Daccache's challenge—"Decide what you want to share with us"—show how difficult this is for them. There are exercises in movement and in speaking a text, and gradually the incidental music, inspired by the text but composed and sung by the prisoners themselves, begins to take on a more important role. When Daccache harangues them about the need for commitment, there is some dissent and (unhappy with being bossed by a woman) they nickname her Abu Ali. As the date of the opening approaches, there are normal setbacks (for example, one of the actors is released a few days before the first performance).

Interspersed with these sequences related directly to the production of the play are a series of totally involving scenes, mostly shot with the prisoners talking directly to the camera. Some of these capture the prisoners' feelings about being in prison, while others trace their unfolding relationship with the project and the way in which this gradually gives them fresh insight into themselves. Early on, there is an amazing sequence in which ten prisoners speak of their crimes, their punishment, and (usually) the amount of time served, mostly direct-to-camera in close-up. Interestingly, not one of them claims innocence: rape (five years); murder (fifteen years, eight to go); drug dealing (eight years to go); murder (death sentence); murder (fifteen years at age seventeen, one year to go); murder (life sentence, fourteen years served); murder (four years served and still no judgment); drug dealing (five years); and murder (life sentence, eighteen years served). The final prisoner, who plays to the crowd, names himself Youssef (Grandpa) Chankar and explains that he has a life sentence, of which the 18 years already served = 216 months = 6,570 days = 157,440 hours = 9,446,400 minutes = 566,784,000 seconds.

The prisoners talk of the difficulty of indefinite prison sentences and of the miserable routine of prison life, where thinking and building relationships are forbidden. But most of those speaking to camera now show a steadily increasing self-awareness: Zeina Daccache's ways of thinking are coming to be part of each of them. They begin to envision a life after prison which does not involve returning to crime; they are beginning to think about the rest of their lives with the sort of commitment and responsibility Dacccache demands of them as actors.

The opening night is attended by a host of dignitaries, led by the minister of the interior, and parts of this evening's performance are targeted directly at them. All the actors admit to having been terrified; many of them cried. In all, there are eight performances, of which the most moving—followed by hugs, holding, and tears—is that staged on Mother's Day, when their families are allowed to attend.

This is a remarkable documentary directed by the young woman who found backing for the project and organized the prison performance, Zeina Daccache. Although this is her debut feature as a director (the film runs to seventy-eight minutes), it is remarkably assured and has a an immensely involving rhythm. It gives remarkable insight into ways of getting solitary and often embittered prisoners involved in a joint, collaborative project and shows at the same time how this experience can benefit them by giving them a space in which to think and to commit. The end titles give encouraging information: the minister of the interior has finally implemented a long-delayed law enabling the early release of prisoners, and funding has been made available for Zeina Daccache to continue her work at Roumieh prison.

* * *

More recently, toward the end of the decade, a further wave of very diverse filmmakers has emerged. These include Simon El Habre, Mahmoud Hojeij, Akram Zaatari, Hady Zaccak, and Maher Abi Samra. The range of approaches is very varied, from observational documentary to post-Godardian deconstruction.

Simon El Habre studied at ALBA in Beirut, where he was born, and at FEMIS in Paris. He subsequently directed commercials and television reports for various channels and also worked as an editor on short and documentary films, including those of Ghassan Salhab, before completing his first full feature-length documentary, *The One Man Village / Le village d'un seul homme / Samaan bildayaa,* in 2008. It is an observational documentary—a portrait of his uncle Semaan El Habre, who is now the sole inhabitant of the village of the Ain El Halazoun. This Christian mountain village, which at one time housed forty-five families, was totally destroyed during the civil war, when the inhabitants fled to neighboring areas or to the capital, Beirut. The film follows Semaan through his solitary daily routines, caring for his cows, horse, dogs, and chickens, over a period of some eighteen months. It also records the occasional return of other villagers to tend their land or harvest their crops, though none chooses to stay the night. Semaan himself seems a natural loner, admitting "I am one who likes to suffer. Suffering is good in order to live life fully,"[22] but the film does not probe his attitudes in a serious way, taking him at his own self-estimation and producing a very sympathetic portrait.

Though clearly a low-budget production, *The One Man Village* is crisply shot and nicely paced. There is strong sense that this is very personal project—the director treated a similar subject in his diploma film at ALBA. He has claimed that this is a film about memory, but in fact it is about the collective refusal, by the former inhabitants of the village, to confront and come to terms with what happened in the civil war. No one, neither Semaan nor his occasional visitors, talks about the past, and no one, apart from Semaan, contemplates a return, though Semaan's experience shows that this is economically possible. The ending has more than a touch of melancholy: a shot through the rear window of a car leaving the village, accompanied by a popular song singing the praise of "my village."

Mahmoud Hojeij was born in Lebanon in 1975. He began his studies at the American University of Beirut (AUB), then went on to study film at Sheffield Hallam University and to complete a doctorate in Switzerland. He began making short documentaries in 1997. *Wish You Were Here* (2006), which was produced by the Center for Behavioral Research at AUB (where he now works), is a slight, nostalgic portrait of the Ras Beirut district, where AUB is located. Hojeij interviews academics at the university and the local lighthouse keeper, barber, and florist, as well as writers and a Palestinian ambassador who was born there. There is also a selection of old black-and-white photographs to support the view of this part of Beirut as a cultural center where racial tensions were never allowed to dominate an open and tolerant way of life.

Akram Zaatari was born in 1966 and grew up in Saïda in Southern Lebanon. He subsequently studied architecture at the American University of Beirut, graduating in 1989. Two years later he went to New York, where he studied communication sciences and media and discovered the medium of video. On his return to Beirut, he began his career making short films and documentaries for Future Television until 1997. As he has said, he made numerous videos there: "These did not belong to any precise genre; they included short films, documentaries, video essays and formal explorations."[23] Although he taught photography at the American University of Beirut, he does not consider himself a photographer, being fascinated instead by the processes and uses of photography. He has always been concerned with "how and why people make images, how they feel linked to them, why, for example, they throw away one but keep another in their wallets or, nowadays, on their mobiles."[24]

Since he helped found the Arab Image Foundation in 1997, he has worked extensively as a curator and archivist, staging photographic exhibitions and installations across the world, including at such prestigious locations as MoMA in New York, the Tate Gallery in London, and the Venice Biennale. His curiosity about photography has also extended into film, and he has organized numerous film programs and events. In a sense, his work in video production can be seen as a by-product of his archival concerns. His interests are very apparent in the series of seven short films which make up the series *Image+Son* (1995–1996), the best known of which are *Red Chewing Gum / El-elkeh al-hamra* and *Crazy for You / Majnounak*. Here and in his later feature-length video work, the influence of Jean-Luc Godard's later works and writings is very evident.

One fascinating early example of his work is *All Is Well on the Border Front / Tout va bien à la frontière / Al-shareet bi khayr* (1997). This has the typical in-gredients of a forty-three-minute documentary: interviews to camera by three Southern Lebanese combatants who were caught and imprisoned, with a voice-over narration provided by the letters to his mother of a Palestinian prisoner of the Israelis. There are passages from traditional songs by a couple of old men, the obligatory words of defiance spoken by a very young child, and fragments of television war footage.

But instead of being edited together as seamlessly as possible, *All Is Well on the Border Front* constantly makes clear that this documentary discourse is a con-struct. At the beginning of the film, the cameraman explains some of the tricks and devices that a camera allows. He appears with his own views at other points in the film. At the end, we see the interviewees rehearsing and being coached in the delivery of what had seemed to be spontaneous testimony. Although there is nothing to indicate unequivocally that these testimonies are fictitious, the inter-viewees are presented against bright yellow, red, and blue backgrounds, which wrench them out of context and hence problematize their words. The film pro-vides insight into life in Saïda, which at the time of shooting was in the Israeli "Occupied Security Zone." *All Is Well on the Border Front* continually makes the audience stop and think, to question the assertions it puts forward and to be aware of how they are communicated.

Zaatari's subsequent video work is linked even more closely to his archival practice. His full feature-length documentary, *Today / Aujourd'hui / Al-yaoum* (2003), made after a succession of shorts, has been described as "an elegant medi-tation on the photography of the Middle East—from exotic portraits of nomadic Bedouins in the Syrian desert to television clips of Beirut today."[25] At its New York premiere, a reviewer wrote:

> In a thoughtful, dreamlike montage, the Beirut-based video artist and New School graduate Akram Zaatari examines archival photos, from portraits of Bedouins in the desert to the bomb-rent sky over the Lebanese capital. The imagery moves from an exotic rural past, when the central conflict was between camel and car, to the strife-ridden present of propaganda and urban

alienation. From his perch at the editing station, where he assembles these layers of history, Zaatari wonders what truths are ultimately captured in these photographs.[26]

Saïda, June 6 1982 (2004) is a more personal reflection on the photographs that a 16-year-old Zaatari took as he watched the Israeli invasion and bombing of his birthplace. He has returned to the same subject in his most recent video, *Letter to a Refusing Pilot* (2013), his meditation on a story which Zaatari first heard in 1982 (and which turned out to be true) that an Israeli pilot, given the task of bombing the local school (founded, incidentally, by the director's father) refused and dropped his bombs into the sea. As Zaatari has observed: "The importance of the story is that it gives the pilot a human face. It gives what he is about to bomb, which is considered terrorist ground; it also gives that a human face. I think it's important in times of war that everyone is a human being."[27]

Another, earlier example of the filmmaker as archivist is *In This House / Fi hatha al-bayt* (2005). This tells the story of a Lebanese resistance fighter who occupied an abandoned house for some six years during the struggle against the Israeli occupation of Southern Lebanon. When ordered to leave, Ali Hahsisho wrote a letter to the owners and buried it in a mortar shell in their garden. Zaatari resolves to unearth it.

A fascinating insight into Zaatari's approach can be obtained from his curious little book *A Conversation with an Imagined Israeli Filmmaker Named Avi Mograbi*.[28] Avi Mograbi is, of course, a real revisionist Israeli filmmaker, whose best-known feature is *Happy Birthday, Mr Mograbi* (1999). This, Ella Shohat tells us, "interweaves stories about his commissions to make fiftieth anniversary films about both Israeli independence and the Palestinian *Nakba*. . . . In a sardonic tone and within a diary-like video journal, *Happy Birthday, Mr Mograbi* stages a counterpoint between two clashing film projects."[29] This is the work which, it seems, prompted Zaatari's *Conversation*. The back cover of the book, usually a source of firm factual information, prefaces each statement about the project with the disclaimer "It is said that. . . ." Apparently, the pair met twice in Aubervilliers in 2010, spent more than a week together sharing experiences, watched Godard's *Notre musique*, and disagreed over Roman Polanski's personal life. Zaatari concluded by inviting Mograbi to leave Israel and come to live in Lebanon.

Zaatari begins the book by stating "I, Akram Zaatari, a documentary filmmaker from Lebanon, address Avi Mograbi, a documentary filmmaker from Israel," then immediately modifies this: "My name is not Akram Zaatari. And the person I am addressing is not Avi Mograbi. We have simply decided to name ourselves as such, playing roles that have been prescribed for us by a situation, like characters in a play or film, and like two individuals born in two enemy states." There is no way of knowing what is real and what is invented in this "conversation," which basically is told from Zaatari's point of view but into which Mograbi intervenes "by Skype" and in red type. What is clear is that the book is full of reminiscences and speculations, provoked by the exchange of old photographs of their two families.

Hady Zaccak, who was born in 1974 in Beirut, studied at IESAV, at the Université Saint Joseph in Beirut, and then at FEMIS in Paris. He is the author of a history of Lebanese cinema, *Le cinéma libanais: Itinéraire d'un cinéma vers l'inconnu (1929–1996)*. Lebanese film history is also the subject of several of his first short films. *The Pioneers of Lebanese Cinema / Les pionniers libanais du cinéma* (1995), made at IESAV, looks back at the "golden era" of Lebanese filmgoing and deals with those who established Lebanese filmmaking with isolated, individual works from the 1930s through to the 1960s: Jordano Pidutti, Ali al-Ariss, Georges Kahi, Michel Haroun, and Georges Nasser among them. *Lebanon through Its Cinema / Le Liban à travers le cinéma / Loubnan min khilal es cinema* (2003) is a more complexly structured work, which draws on clips from some fifty feature films, mostly those made by Lebanese directors but including a few made in Lebanon by foreign filmmakers as well. The film has a loose thematic structure focusing on specific locations that recur (the airport, the village, Beirut at night) and on film genres (with gangster films giving way to those dealing with militants during the civil war). The documentary ignores issues of chronology and quality, using processes of crosscutting, to enable films to "dialogue" across the decades (a 1930s actor in a black-and-white film seemingly watching a 1960s color song sequence; a question in a 1950s film answered by characters from the 1970s; etc). *The Cinema of War in Lebanon / Cinéma de guerre au Liban / Cinema el-harb fi Loubnan* (2003) is a more conventionally structured documentary, using interviews and film extracts to cover the whole range of films shot in Lebanon which deal with the war: committed documentaries, action films inspired more by James Bond than by reality, works actually shot during the fighting, and more reflective fictional works taking their inspiration from the ruins of Beirut immediately after the end of the war.

Zaccak has since made a number of other documentaries, most of them funded by or with Gulf producers. *Refugees for Life / Laji'oun mada el hayat* (2006) is a characteristically uncompromising look at the situation of Palestinian refugees in Southern Lebanon. As always, Zaccak is keen to set out clearly the roots of the current situation and to locate precisely by name those whose testimony he calls upon. In 1948, 700,000–800,000 Palestinians were expelled from their homeland, and about 100,000 of these settled (temporarily, they assumed) in Lebanon. Sixty years later, their number has risen to 400,000, variously settled in refugee camps and so called groupings. Many of those born in the camps are now themselves parents, but they have no rights over the ramshackle (state-owned) properties in which they live (to repair a damaged roof or shattered windowpane is a criminal offense). Even for those with Lebanese IDs, there are few jobs they are permitted to do and no path to citizenship. Educational and medical facilities for the young and elderly are extremely limited. Those who have managed to emigrate often have better lives, but Zaccak's inquiries among those settled in Germany found few who felt confident enough to talk on camera, and their children increasingly see themselves simply as Germans. For those in the camps, there is the technical possibility of a "right to return" contained in UN Resolution 194, adopted on December 11, 1948, but never implemented. Zaccak's key interviewees see this as no more than a dream, which will never be realized.

Subsequent films by Zaccak explore the divisions within mainstream contemporary Lebanese society, focusing particularly on the country's fragile national identity. *The War of Peace: Voices from Lebanon / Harb el salam* (2007) looks at a group of students and former students of the American University of Beirut, all in their twenties, and contains statements from various political leaders as well. The year is 2006, after the assassination of Rafiq Hariri, the withdrawal of the Syrians after thirty years of occupation, and the July 2006 Israeli war. Initially, the students are introduced very formally (as isolated individuals talking in studio-based profile), giving their own views as to whether they think a further civil war is imminent. Later, they are filmed less formally in their particular living contexts, talking freely about themselves and their backgrounds. Subsequently, when they are shown talking together, we see that there is less dialogue than argument among them. Differences are exacerbated by elections at AUB, which draw them into hostile groups of chanting students, some of which (predictably) object to the election results when they are announced. Tensions increase even more as other political events intrude. After the assassination of Pierre Gemayel, the streets of Beirut, which are already full of political posters and slogans, are lined by police and soldiers dealing with the wider demonstrations which inevitably ensue. The film captures extremely graphically the problems of these young people in a society in which the national Lebanese identity is always threatened by underlying sectarian divisions. Not surprisingly, the students' last discussions are of their personal situations, particularly whether or not to emigrate.

Zaccak's subsequent two films offer a matching pair of studies of the sectarian divide in Lebanon: *Shi'a Echoes from Lebanon / Asda' a shi'a min Loubnan* (2007) and *Sunni Echoes from Lebanon / Asda' a sunnia min Loubnan* (2008). Both fifty-two-minute documentaries follow the same pattern, choosing as the lead figure an artistically engaged but politically ambivalent young man, while also focusing on two or three other young people who have deep political commitments. Both films have significant interventions by a major religious or political figure. In the Shiite film, the key figure is Marwan Hamdan, an aspiring filmmaker (and Zaccak's assistant director), who is flanked by an Amal supporter and fervent, burka-clad follower of Hezbollah. Here the clerical interventions come from Sheikh Sayyed Hani Fahs. In the Sunni film, the musician Khaled Soubeih argues against sectarianism, but his tolerant attitude is set against views of the supporters of the Future Movement, the Islamic Jamaa, and the Nasseri Popular Organisation. The politician Saad Hariri (son of Rafiq) is the authority figure interviewed here. What is fascinating is the way in which, despite the sectarian divide, these young people have the same preoccupations: the role of the father and family loyalties, the relationship between religious and secular beliefs, and the importance of physical space (such as the various districts of a Beirut divided on sectarian lines) in their lives.

In *A History Lesson / Darson fel tareekh* (2009), Zaccak looks at the question of national identity in so far as it affects younger Lebanese students. The film opens with a typically lengthy (but very appropriate) quotation from the French poet Paul Valéry:

> History produces dreams and drunkenness. It fills people's hearts with
> false memories, it exaggerates their reactions, exacerbates old grievances,
> torments them in their repose and encourages a delirium of grandeur or a
> delusion of persecution. It makes whole nations bitter, arrogant, insufferable
> and vainglorious.

Zaccak looks at the teaching of history in five Beirut schools with differing faith or secular affiliations, which are made clear by the contrasting ceremonies with which they begin the school day. Although there is supposed to be a standard history curriculum, there can be no single textbook, as there is no unified view of Lebanese history itself (particularly with regard to the civil war, which is, perhaps inevitably, not included in the curriculum). The film probes the very different views of Lebanese history held by five very articulate young schoolchildren, the attitudes of their parents, and the kinds of history lessons they receive, based on one or another of the twenty or so available (differently oriented) textbooks. Perhaps the most revealing sequence comes at the end, when we are shown that only one of the children can recite or sing the words of the Lebanese national anthem. Although in this way it questions the limits of the young people's perceptions, the film is always respectful toward its subjects, caught in the multiple paradoxes of Lebanese national identity.

Taxi Beirut (2011), also produced by Al Jazeera, is a slighter work, a look at three Beirut taxi drivers and the different ways in which they cope for many hours a day with the problems of traffic in a very crowded city. Their musings about their cars, their customers, and their lives are intercut with lyrically shot sequences of the city itself, being rebuilt yet again.

In the course of *Taxi Beirut,* one of the drivers, Fouad, talks of flying to Germany in 1961 to buy a Mercedes 180, which he drove back to Beirut to use as a taxi serving the top hotels. Perhaps this inspired Zaccak to undertake his next project, *Marcedes* (2011), an unexpectedly quirky account of sixty years of Lebanese history employing that same car, the Mercedes Pontin (known locally as the Marcedes). Here described as a "family," the cars were introduced into Lebanon at the end of the 1950s and are used as a link across the decades.

The film begins, in typical Zaccak manner, with a long quotation on the problems of sectarianism, but then uses less familiar material (animated sequences, archival footage, and radio recordings) to trace the Marcedes's integration into Lebanese tradition. It participates in the pre–civil war boom years and then becomes a working tool for taxi drivers. During the civil war, it is both a favored mode of transport for armed militants and a war victim (images of shot-up and burnt-out cars by the roadside). Now in postwar Beirut, its newly imported younger "cousins" ferry politicians to conferences as well as to assassination assaults. It survives, somehow, into the present, ending up as a pop icon.

Zaccak's best work is a model of informational documentary: always setting out its terms of reference, detached in its approach, respectful to its wide range of interviewees, and always illuminating on the director's favorite topic—the problems of Lebanese national identity.

Maher Abi Samra was born in 1965 in Beirut and studied at FEMIS in Paris, where he lived from 1990 to 2004, working as an assistant director and making a number of short films. Since then he has lived between Beirut and Paris. In *Women of Hezbollah / Femmes du Hezbollah* (2004), Abi Samra returns to Ramel el Ali, the district of southern Beirut which became home to the Shiites driven from Southern Lebanon during the Israeli war. It offers portraits of two formidable women, Zeinab and Khadije, both activists with Hezbollah, which over the years has established itself there. Abi Samra, who describes himself as a secular liberal, offers a helpful commentary, putting his interviewees' comments and revelations into the context of recent Lebanese history.

The younger of the two, Zeinab, has very firm views on the direction her life should take, namely, to please God and do what is expected of her. She expects her husband to do his duty, too, even if this means martyrdom, and will bring up her three small children to follow his example. The much older Khadije has a history of political activism predating the emergence of Hezbollah, back to a time when being an activist meant supporting Yasser Arafat's PLO, and she has a wide-spread reputation as the first woman to be imprisoned by the Israelis. Her initial political beliefs came easily to her. She did not know there were any Christians in Lebanon, and when she was naughty as a child, her mother always warned her, "Be careful, the Jews are coming." As Hezbollah grew in reputation, owing to its opposition to the Israeli invaders and its provision of services which normally would be the responsibility of the government, it was natural that Khadije would align herself with it. She also accepts the importance of mar-tyrdom in the struggle for freedom. Rather chillingly she says, "God is not satis-fied with me, because none of my sons has died as a martyr."

Neither woman has the slightest doubt about her religious identity or po-litical allegiance—their ideal state is Iran, the principal source of Hezbollah funding. Toward the end of the film, however, both express concern with the situation of women in Lebanon. Both were denied an education by their parents, and Khadije, who was married at fourteen, had to surrender her six children when she chose to divorce. Both long for greater equality for women, though this will have to come after the struggle for liberation has been won. Neither blames Islam for the situation, Khadije expressing the view that "it has nothing to do with religion" and everything to do with Lebanon's being "a traditional Eastern society"—as if the two were unrelated. Abi Samra, who has proved himself an excellent guide to the complexities of Lebanese politics, is revealed, in retrospect, as being as poor as anyone else at foretelling Lebanon's future. Here he suggests that Hezbollah is now in retreat—but then who, in 2004, could have anticipated Hezbollah's successful confrontation of the latest Israeli incursion or its role in the struggle for power in Syria?

Abi Samra's second (fifty-minute) documentary, *Shatila Roundabout / Rond-point Chatila* (2004), is focused on 150 meters of the main road going through the camp. He does not dwell on the horrors that occurred there in the past but on the day-to-day lives of the present inhabitants, waiting for something to happen but basically aware that they have absolutely nothing to look forward to.

Abi Samra's first full feature-length (eighty-five-minute) documentary is *We Were Communists / Nous étions communistes / Sheoeyin kenna* (2009). This is an intensely personal film. Along with Hussein, Bachar, and Ibrahim, he is one of four friends whose lives the film follows, and he includes extracts from his own earlier work in this film. All four face the camera in close-up to present themselves, giving name, religion, place of birth, and reason for joining the PCL (Partie Communiste Libanaise), as well as the date of this,1982, when Beirut was besieged by the Israeli army). Later they meet together in Abi Samra's apartment to discuss their past activism and native villages. As the introduction to the film at the Venice Biennale notes:

> Four men recount their stories from the battlefield, their broken dreams
> and their eventual disillusionment at the height of the country's ongoing
> unsettled crisis. At once artistically and politically audacious, incisive and
> tender, *Sheoeyin kenna* travels the chimerical and daunting reality of Leba-
> non's post-war landscape.[30]

Interviewed about the film, Abi Samra has explained its significance for him:

All my films are actually about Lebanon. I heard that "once you leave a place, when you come back you search for the memories you left, the things that you left." I left the country in 1990 and came back in 2004, so it is as if the present doesn't belong to me; what belongs to me is the past, and the past is my friends, my neighborhood.[31]

He has also made clear how this new film follows the pattern set by his earlier work:

As always in my films, I go from the general to the individual, to show a person, not a piece of something bigger. Like in *Women of Hezbollah,* where I focus only on two characters, what I am interested in is how they live their everyday lives. In *Shatila Roundabout* I did the same. This singling out of the characters is because I don't like anybody to consider me as just part of a whole thing. Any individual, even belonging to a certain group or ideology, should be considered for what he is himself. He continues to be an individual, to practice and face things from a personal and unique approach.[32]

* * *

One filmmaker who has chosen to turn to the autobiographical documentary genre is Mahmoud Kaabour, who offers an affectionate study of his grandmother.

Mahmoud Kaabour, who was born in 1978, studied in Canada, and is currently based in Dubai, is a key example of the filmmaker as chronicler of his own personal family story. He returned to Lebanon to make *Teta a Thousand Times / Teta mille fois / Teta alf marra* (2010), a forty-seven-minute work, which was shown as a feature-length documentary in competition at the JCC in Tunis. This is an affectionate and light-hearted study of the filmmaker's eighty-three-year-old grandmother, who still lives in the big old apartment where she brought up her children and many grandchildren. She spends her life alone now, drinking coffee and, against medical advice, smoking her *argileh.* She looks out over the neighborhood from her balcony and makes her presence felt, even if she is now largely house-bound. The director is her favorite grandchild because he resembles her beloved violinist husband and bears his name. He has brought back from Canada a remastered version of the seven emotional, improvised violin solos his grandfather recorded in old age in this very apartment, which he plays to her. Mahmoud has also brought back to Beirut his Canadian bride, whom he marries there (allowing his grandmother full scope for her wicked tongue and also a few sincere tears). The film ends irreverently with an enactment of her death (from which she emerges smiling). The film is a perfect example of the personal autobiographical documentary now so popular in Arab cinema.

Egypt and the Maghreb

Although the area lacks the strong documentary traditions of Palestine and Lebanon, a great deal of documentary work, much of it made for local television, has been produced in Egypt and throughout the Maghreb, though very little of it gets an international cinema release. This section of the book cannot claim, therefore, to amount to any sort of critical history; it contains just a handful of isolated works by dedicated documentary filmmakers born since 1960 whose films offer fascinating specific insights. In addition to the documentaries discussed here, there are also other, equally significant contributions in the 2000s from those pioneers who, alongside their Middle Eastern colleagues, had helped establish Maghrebian documentary in earlier decades, such as Jean-Pierre Lledo in Algeria and Simone Bitton in Morocco. There is also a striking body of work produced by filmmakers better known as feature directors. Among those who have interspersed documentary and fictional films in the 2000s are the Algerians Yamina Benguigui and Djamila Sahraoui, the Moroccans Nabil Ayouch and Leila Kilani, and the Tunisians Moktar Ladjimi, Nadia El Fani, and Raja Amari. Their collective fictional and documentary works are discussed together in the section on feature filmmaking.

* * *

In **EGYPT** a fascinating figure is **Nadia Kamel**. Born in 1961 in Cairo, she abandoned her initial studies of microbiology and chemistry to devote herself to filmmaking. Since then her career has followed a pattern akin to that of her feature-film contemporaries Khaled El Hagar and Atef Hetata: years of working as an assistant director, on occasion for such key figures as Youssef Chahine and Yousry Nasrallah. For her major documentary, the Egyptian-French co-production *An Egyptian Salad / Salade nature / Salata baladi* (2008), she chose a form that has become increasingly popular among Arab filmmakers in the 2000s—the personal, autobiographical family chronicle. She has said that "the original inspiration for this film was simple enough: a love of my family's stories and a wish to share them. It was a story-telling project." But as the project got underway, she discovered that this adventure was more complicated: "A mixture of hope and fear overtook me." The reason for this initial anxiety was the realization that, because of the national and religious issues it raised, her family story could hardly fail to be controversial: "In my family, religions and cultures get married, when they seem to be divorcing in the global arena. In a world where my family's identities are being squeezed into irreconcilable positions, I needed to document my history."[33]

Kamel's mother, Naila Kamel, also known as Mary Rosenthal, in her eighties at the time of shooting, could hardly have a more complex background. Naila is a half-Jewish, half-Italian Christian, who converted to Islam when she married her half-Turkish, half-Ukrainian husband (another translation of the title would be "a mixed salad'). The couple were politically active members of the Egyptian communist party, and Naila at one time spent seven years in jail in Cairo. The political upheavals of the mid-twentieth century (the founding of Israel in 1948 and the advent of Nasser in Egypt) dislocated Naila's extended family. While Naila stayed in Cairo, her Jewish cousins, Sarina and Peppo, moved to Israel, and her parents emigrated to Italy, where other family members still live.

The film is triggered by an intolerant sermon by an imam in a Cairo mosque, in effect calling for a holy war. This raises Nadia's concern for her ten-year-old nephew Nabeel, and she devises a project to take him and his grandmother to Italy and Israel so that he can meet his wider family and her mother be reunited with the cousins she has not seen for over half a century. Nadia does not hide the fact that the trip arouses real hostility in her family, especially on the part of her father and her sister Dina (Nabeel's mother), while the nervous grandmother has to be bullied into participating. The project is also impracticable, since Nabeel has no real passport, just a travel document, and would be barred from Israel. Confronted by identity complications even more serious than his grandmother's (he is "half Egyptian, a quarter Palestinian, one eighth Italian, one sixteenth East European Jewish, one sixteenth Turkish Jewish"),[34] Nabeel responds by speaking English whenever he can. *An Egyptian Salad* is a raw film, not a politically correct statement. People say what first comes into their heads, and this is far from constituting a nostalgic plea for Egypt's mythical cosmopolitan past. But it is a true portrait of a (remarkable) family, with all the tensions and intimacies that this implies.

* * *

Another Egyptian documentary filmmaker, this time with no links at all to the Egyptian film industry, is **Hanan Abdalla**. She was born in London in 1988 to activist parents who were forced to leave Egypt and eventually settled in England. She studied politics and philosophy at Oxford University, graduating in 2010, and took various short courses in filmmaking before moving to Cairo to undertake her first documentary project, the feature-length *In the Shadow of a Man / Zoll Ragel* (2011). The film ends with footage of the Egyptian Arab Spring, but its main focus is on the past experiences of four women—Wafaa, Suzanne, Shahinda, and Badreya—who come from very different backgrounds and have had very different experiences. What they all have in common is the situation of living in a totally male-dominated society. From their frank and often intimate personal testimonies, the film offers a revealing portrait of a whole range of aspects of women's lives—courtship, marriage and divorce, work, family life, and domestic violence. Abdalla, who constantly keeps herself in the background, has drawn moving and revealing testimony from a very well chosen range of women from different social and age groups. The plea for change post-2011 is palpable. Abdalla herself quotes one of her interviewees, Shahinda: "A woman cannot be independent in a country that is not independent. . . . She cannot be free in a country that is enslaved. You can't limit women's demands based on their gender. . . . You can't separate women's demands from the reality of society itself."[35] This is a very impressive documentary debut.

* * *

In **ALGERIA**, the key figure to challenge the pre-eminence of the documentary filmmakers established in the 1990s is **Malek Bensmaïl**. Born in 1966 in Constantine, he is in the forefront of contemporary Algerian documentary filmmaking. He began as a schoolboy, making little films in Super 8 and participating in Algerian amateur filmmaking. In 1988 he left for Paris, where he studied at ESEC. He also underwent a brief training period at Lenfilm Studios in St. Petersburg. He began making documentaries in the early 1990s, but the first of his works to deal with Algeria was the thirty-minute documentary *Territory (Territories) / Territoire(s),* made in 1996. Since then, through his documentary work, he has kept a close eye on a whole range of aspects of Algerian society. He is one of the few Maghrebian documentarists not to have been tempted to produce a fictional feature; his sole ventures into this area are two short fictional films, *Algerian TV Show* (1996) and *Dêmokratia* (2002).

Dêmokratia, an ambitious work shot in 35mm film, is a somewhat awkwardly structured work, attempting to combine both real and imagined or remembered elements. The real situation—the ritual surrounding the execution of a brutal dictator (unnamed), whose body is dragged off ignominiously at the end—is handled with convincing detail. The dictator's voice-over commentary reveals the full extent of his ignomi025y, his contempt for freedom, and his delight in humiliating his adversaries. Some of the images injected into this sequence— such as the striking scene where advisors at a cabinet meeting are forced to sit on toilets rather than chairs—reveal a gruesome imagination. There are also fantasy images, of the bullets simply failing to pierce his body and of his former subordinates being overwhelmed by the thought of his death, which clearly belong to the dictator's consciousness. But other images—such as archival recordings of real-life dictators (Mussolini, Ceaușescu, etc.) who met a similar end—seem inserted by the filmmaker to make his own points. Crucially, the status of the beautiful young woman who emerges from an empty landscape at the beginning at the film and speaks of lost love and the need of trust is uncertain. Is she the dictator's actual mistress, abused by him and toyed with by his successors? Or is she a symbolic figure—democracy, even?

Bensmaïl went on to make two 52-minute television documentaries at the end of the decade. *Decibled* (1998) is a look at recent developments in Maghrebian music, at the artists involved in the fusion of African and Western sources and the resulting music's impact on audiences in Algeria and within the immigrant community in France. *Boudiaf: An Extinguished Hope / Boudiaf, un espoir assassiné* (1999) is very different, dealing with the brief (180-day) presidency of Mohamed Boudiaf, who had founded the FLN but was forced into exile by Ahmed Ben Bella in 1963, soon after independence had been achieved. Summoned to return after the upheavals of 1988, he brought order to the country by confronting the Islamists. But he also attacked the corruption he found within the contemporary ranks of the FLN and was assassinated by one of his bodyguards on January 29, 1992. Bensmaïl constructs his film largely out of archival footage, as well as interviews with Boudiaf's widow and those who had worked with him or followed his career as journalists.

In the 2000s, Bensmaïl established his reputation as a keen observer of Algeria today with a sequence of varied documentaries, most of them of full (ninety minutes) feature length. *A Holiday All the Same / Des vacances malgré tout* (2001) tells the story of Kader Kabouche, who left Algeria as a young electrician in 1964 to work and settle in France, where he has five children, all French citizens. For the past twenty years he has been having a house built for him by his brother in the small town near Algiers, where he was born. This is his first visit home in fifteen years, intended specifically to supervise the completion of the installation work and to introduce two of his grown-up children to what he can achieve and what he will be leaving to them.

Although the film opens with a sequence of 1960s archival footage—a newsreel hailing the arrival of hundreds of new workers from abroad—this is a film focused entirely on a single family. From the start, Kader's project generates problems with paperwork and visas, anticipating the film's central concern with identity. But eventually, despite hours of delay, the Kabouche family forms part of a mass of passengers arriving, like many others, in a car piled high with belongings and presents in the port of Algiers. There are the inevitable exchanges of hugs and photographs, a boat trip, and a visit to a tourist beach, but no immediate culture shock: the relatives, like the Kabouche family, converse naturally in French. The initial problems are practical: the house is not finished, there is no proper piped water supply, the furniture is unreliable, and the locally purchased food is not of an acceptable quality.

Despite the fact that *A Holiday All the Same* has a simple and conventional narrative shape (departure, holiday, return), however, it is not merely an observational documentary. Instead, it is a work filmed intimately within the family. Bensmaïl personally operates the digital camera, as well as directing the film, and he also involves the son, Amar Kabouche, as his assistant. As a result, the restrictions on the family's self-expression are minimal; their reactions are consistently immediate and spontaneous. We do not have merely a simple set of contrasts between France and Algeria—for example, the daughter's inability to accept the constraints on women, seen as unquestionable by her cousins, or Kader's horror (as a person who was born there) at the pollution of the local beach. What Bensmaïl conveys most strongly is the way in which this cross-cultural encounter challenges the Kabouche family's assumptions that they can unquestionably be French citizens and passport holders while at the same time maintaining an untroubled secondary Algerian identity. The family's sense of its own identity—as well as its Algerian home—remains in some doubt at the end of the film.

In *Algeria(s)* / *Algérie(s)* (2003), Bensmaïl collaborated with Thierry Leclère and Patrice Barrat on a Canal+ project comprising two 80-minute conventional informative documentaries on Algerian history. The first part, *A People without a Voice / Un peuple sans voix,* looks at the events leading up to the crisis of 1992. It opens with a forceful and eloquent plea—direct to camera—by a mother who is just burying her daughter for the Algerian people to stand up against the violence tearing the country apart. It ends with dramatic footage of the assassination of President Mohamed Boudiaf at a rally in Annaba, where he had begun his political career decades earlier. He begins his speech: "Other countries have outpaced us through science and technology. Islam . . . ," only to be cut off at that point by a hail of bullets.

Between these two dramatic high points, *A People without a Voice* is a somber, carefully researched account of the successive failures of the Algerian state both to reflect the instincts of its people and to give Algeria the prosperity (particularly in terms of youth employment) which its physical resources should merit. Combining a range of interviews with both participants and observers and well-chosen extracts of archival material, the film traces the combination of army coups and failure of FLN political awareness which led to the situation in 1988. At that point, street disorders, involving mostly young people, were allowed to escalate in mass demonstrations organized by the Front Islamique du Salut (FIS) which claimed to speak in the name of the people. The FLN response—to offer democratic elections to a totally unprepared people, who had known only autocratic rule since independence—led inevitably to the electoral triumph in the initial municipal elections of FIS, the only organized group opposing the FLN. One fascinating outcome of this electoral victory was the (temporary) closure of the Cinémathèque Algérienne because it showed foreign films that did not reflect Islamic values. In the subsequent parliamentary elections, the FIS made its own strategic mistake, provoking the army to intervene, cancel the elections, and call in Mohamed Boudiaf as a replacement president.

The second part of *Algeria(s), A Land in Mourning / Une terre en deuil,* begins with Boudiaf's death, the circumstances of which remain contentious, since no postmortem was carried out. The focus switches to the emerging civil war in Algeria, as the FIS turned to terrorism (assassinating dozens of military personnel and a range of intellectuals and artists) and the army responded with summary arrests, torture, and executions. Despite the violence, there were tentative negotiations between the two sides, which have only come to light recently. In 1999, after years of stalemate, the army's sole candidate, Mohamed Bouteflika, was elected president (the other six candidates mysteriously withdrew on the eve of the ballot). An experienced politician, he set in motion the process by which the Islamist militants were granted amnesty and reintegrated into normal life, despite the angry protests of relatives of those who had been assassinated. No mention was made, of course, of the crimes committed by the military, who retained real power in Algeria and found themselves in the international limelight—as opponents of Islamic terrorism—after September 9, 2011.

Algeria(s) is a consummately professional work, seeking to piece together the actual history of Algeria, which the regime, in power for forty years, has been keen to keep hidden (Bensmaïl admits that, as a child, he had never heard of Boudiaf's role in founding the FLN). The central thread of the story is clear, however: that of a regime which provoked the rise of Islamism through corruption and economic failure, turned it toward violence, and then both fought it and exploited the battle against it in order to keep other truths hidden. The visual material is spares—the team had limited cooperation from the state television service and no access to the army's own archives—but the interviews are revealing. Most striking, perhaps, is the fact that none of the politicians, generals, or militants interviewed admits to even the slightest personal responsibility for the ten years of civil war and the death of 100,000 Algerian citizens.

Alienations / Aliénations (2004) is described by its producer Gérard Collas as the "director's cut" of a television production, *Algerian Therapies / Thérapies algériennes*. Its length (1 hour 45 minutes) indicates the significance for Bensmaïl of the material he has captured. Set in the psychiatric hospital at Constantine, the film has a very personal dimension: the director's father, Belkacem Bensmaïl, was a pioneer of Algerian psychiatry and one of the hospital's founders.[36] The film opens with shots of his grave at Aïn Makhlouf and a personal dedication to his father, in voice-over, by the director. *Alienations* is a difficult film for the viewer. Bensmaïl, who photographed the film with a minimal crew as well as directing it, clearly wants the voices of these damaged patients to be heard, and the film shows clearly that he has won their trust, as well as that of the medical staff. The range of problems faced by the patients is extremely wide—political and religious issues, family and social concerns—and some of the accounts given are plausible, while others seem delusional. The mixture of languages in which they express themselves gives a clear indication of their disorientation.

The film opens with a visit to a cave site, where traditional forms of exorcism, involving sacrificial offerings, incense, bathing, dance, and induced trance states, continue to be practiced. Later we meet an imam who regards possession by a jinn as part of normal Muslim belief. But because there is no questioning from behind the camera nor any organizing voice-over commentary to orient the viewer, these views are given the same weight as those advocating the modern therapies pursued in the psychiatric hospital. In similar fashion, the patients' accounts of their illnesses are put on the same level as those of the medical staff treating them. *Alienations* gives us plenty of evidence as to the pressure which Algerian society puts on its citizens, but because of his concern to listen rather than to probe or explain, Bensmaïl gives no indication of the extent to which modern psychiatric techniques are contributing to a cure.

The Great Game / Le grand jeu (2005) is another purely observational documentary, with Bensmaïl again in charge of the camera. The opening of the film reveals the outcome of President Bouteflika's campaign for re-election and sets out (but does not examine) the key event leading up to polling day: the firing of the prime minister, Ali Benflis, secretary general of the FLN, which has ruled Algeria as a one-party state since independence. As Benflis emerges as the rival candidate in the election, Bouteflika, who already controls the state media (including the sole television station), acts to annul the outcomes of the last FLN congress, limit the party's activities, and freeze its assets. Benflis, whose campaign Bensmaïl follows day by day across the whole country, clearly believes he has the support of the people, as his various rallies seem to show. He emerges as an energetic and committed candidate, untroubled by the problems (obvious to an outsider) of running as an independent, a new voice, when he has been both head of the FLN and a member of Bouteflika's cabinet. He is totally unprepared for the declaration of the result of the election on Friday, April 9th—Boutiflika: 83.49 percent; Benflis: 7.93 percent.

The enigmatic title of Bensmaïl's subsequent documentary, *China Is Still a Long Way Away / La Chine est encore loin* (2008), refers to one of the Prophet Muhammad's sayings: "Seek knowledge, even if that means going as far as China." This study of contemporary Algerian schoolchildren is also, Bensmaïl tells us, shaped by the first film images that influenced him as a child, those of the father and son in Vittorio De Sica's neorealist masterpiece, *Bicycle Thieves*.[37] The film is set in Ghassira, a Berber village where, on October 31, 1954, a local Muslim governor (*caïd*) close to the French authorities and two newly arrived young French schoolteachers were shot in an attack considered to constitute the beginning of the Algerian War of Independence. Bensmaïl's particular concern with language is apparent as early as the opening titles, where Berber credits are constantly wiped away by incoming Arab ones, themselves supplemented by French versions.

As usual, Bensmaïl is concerned to get firsthand evidence and explore a whole range of issues around his stated central concern; these are the strengths of his work. But the director again dispenses with any kind of explanatory commentary, with the result that some of his concerns are masked. We see a group of schoolchildren uninterested in learning and unable to articulate their ideas, despite the patient efforts of their teachers. Bensmaïl makes clear in his interviews that he sees linguistic issues as a key to this failure. But the film itself does not make explicit that, since the Arabization of school teaching, pupils are taught in classical Arabic, not the Berber language or Algerian dialect they use in their life outside school. Nor is it emphasized that French is crucial to any possible higher education for the pupils, since this continues to be the language in which scientific university courses are taught in Algeria. Bensaïdi talks of "trilingual illiteracy"—an inability on the part of young people to communicate properly in French, classical Arabic, or Berber.[38]

As usual in Bensmaïl's work, the various sequences are interspersed with carefully composed shots showing the beauties of the Algerian landscape (these stand out partly because they were shot in Super 16, while the main scenes were realized in HDV with frequent recourse to close-ups). In addition to the key concern with school education (shot over a whole academic year), a number of other issues are explored, some with witnesses reaching the ends of their lives. Locals who participated in the 1954 shooting debate the exact circumstances, and those who were pupils of the two French schoolteachers who were shot (the husband fatally) record their memories of them in the classroom. The school cleaner, Rachida (who refused to speak directly to camera, but whose words are relayed over shots of her at work), recalls women's very constrained upbringing when she was young. An entrepreneurial parent, Azouz, reveals his desire to marry a French woman and revive the area's tourist industry, while the poet and musician Messaoud, nicknamed "the Emigrant," rails against just about every aspect of current Algerian life. The film ends on a note of optimism, however, with all the children enjoying an outing to the seaside.

The director has since released *The FLN's Secret Wars in France / Guerres secrètes du FLN en France* (2010). Bensmaïl's work over fifteen years provides an indispensable survey of key aspects of contemporary Algerian life and invaluable records of the remembered past.

* * *

Another Paris-based Algerian newcomer is **Fatma-Zohra Zamoun**, who was born in 1967 in Bordj-Ménaïel and studied at the École Supérieure des Beaux Arts in Algiers from 1985 to 1988. Then she left for Paris to study filmmaking, completing her diploma at the Sorbonne in 1995. She has wide-ranging interests beyond cinema: painting, which she has taught and about which she has written several studies, and literature. She has published two French-language novels: *A tout ce qui partent* (To all those who are leaving) (1999) and *Comment j'ai fumé tous mes livres* (How I smoked all my books) (2003). She also made several short films before undertaking her first feature-length work, *(Un)Lucky / Z'har* (2009). The catalogue of the film at the Dubai Film Festival gives a clear account of its structure:

> Fatma-Zohra Zamoun plays herself in this highly original and intriguing debut, interweaving a documentary-style account of her return to Algeria to shoot her film, employing members of her family along the way, with three mysterious artfully shot, fictional narratives. Alia, a photographer, is attempting to journey from Tunis to Constantine to see her sick father; Cherif, an aging writer, is grappling with the discovery of his own death via an announcement in the newspaper; their paths cross through Farid, the taxi driver who guides them through a fraught Algerian landscape.[39]

As Beti Ellerson has explained, "the overlapping of stories is not by chance, but rather as Fatma-Zohra Zamoun makes clear 'by obligation.'" Because of her inability to raise the needed funds, she chose this option which she took on as a challenge. What was meant to be a classic road movie with a departure and an arrival became a 'distanciation,' a mixture between fiction and documentary."[40]

Zamoun has recently completed a more conventional fifty-two-minute documentary, *Le docker noir, Sembene Ousmane* (2009). This account of Sembene's career from Marseilles dockworker to world-renowned novelist and filmmaker is focused largely on his film output and is beautifully shot (with Zamoun behind the camera). Our principal guides are the United States–based academic Samba Gadjigo, author or editor of three books on Sembene, and Ismaïla Diagne, a Dakar teacher who relates Sembene's films to the Senegalese capital where so many of them are set. There are also brief interventions from a wide array of interviewees, ranging from Abdou Diouf (former president of Senegal), Filippe Savodogo (minister of culture in Burkina Faso), Boudjemaa Karèche (ex-director of the Cinémathèque Algérienne), Amamata Salembere (founder member—with Sembene—of the Fespaco film festival), and Denis Pryen (Sembene's publisher at L'Harmattan in Paris) to closer figures in Sembene's life, his assistant Clarence Delgado, the actor Ibrahima Sow (nicknamed Pathé), and Sembene's two sons, Amadou and Alain. We also get glimpses of the house Sembene built for himself in Dakar and his production base there. The film uses well-chosen extracts from Sembene's films to illustrate the principal themes of his work: contrasting images of women (*La noire de . . .* and *Faat Kiné*), bureaucracy and corruption (*Le mandat* and *Xala*), and the colonial past (*Camp de Thiaroye*). The final image is of the aptly named Calle Ceddo—The House of the Free Man.

* * *

In **MOROCCO** a key newcomer to documentary in the 2000s is **Dalila Ennadre**, who was born in 1966 in Casablanca but grew up in Paris. She received no formal film training, but traveled widely and worked as a production assistant in a number of countries. Her first two documentaries were made in Montreal in the 1990s. She has since made half a dozen documentaries from a production base in Paris, all with European funding The subject matter of Ennadre's films is effectively captured by Fadwa Miadi: "The women of her home country. Not the stylish and emancipated citizens. The other ones, the forgotten ones, the outcasts. Those who, abandoned by their husbands, feed their children on hard bread dipped in tea. Those who slave away from morning to night for a meagre pay. Those who can't read or write. Those who have nothing but their will to pull through."[41] The director herself defines a documentary as "a film with the subjective viewpoint of the author"; she tries, in her films, "to create a place where the public can meet a character and communicate directly with him/her."[42]

El Batalett—Women of the Medina / El Batalett, femmes de la médina (2000) is Ennadre's tribute to the women of the Casablanca medina—the title means "heroines" in Arabic. The comments of a little girl, Zeinab, open and close the film and indeed punctuate the whole narrative with fascinating queries, dreams, and aspirations. Zeinab's mother, Saadia, who is the film's central character, begins by talking of her aspirations for Zeinab, hoping she will have a life which goes far beyond the two certainties for a woman of her own generation: marriage and death. Saadia and her neighbors are subsequently seen and talk to the camera while engaged in the endless succession of dreary and routine domestic duties—shopping, cooking, washing clothes. They have known no other existence since childhood—one talks of being married at twelve to a man three times her age. For a woman whose husband divorced her, the only way of supporting her mother, brother, and children has been prostitution—for a time in Spain. For those with husbands, there is little beyond the domestic routine and a concern for their children.

These women survive thanks to their system of mutual support, their good humor, and their basic acceptance of the way things are. Although they are uneducated—indeed, illiterate—they have a shrewd insight into the world immediately around them. They understand both the lure of emigration and the human costs that it would entail. They are able to laugh a lot (particularly at their own problems), but they also weep at television reports about the death of Hassan II (in August 1999), fearing social instability. They hope for new possibilities in the new millennium but are realistic about the likelihood of real change. At the end of the film—no doubt owing to the influence of Ennadre, who spent months shooting this project—Saadia goes to Rabat in March 2000 to participate in the

March for Women's Rights. Initially the women all found the idea that women have rights almost incomprehensible, but Saadia finds it an uplifting experience and returns full of enthusiasm.

I Loved So Much / J'ai tant aimé (2008) is the story of 75-year-old Fadma, who enrolled at the age of twenty to work as a prostitute for the French army during its war in Indochina and feels her services to France should be rewarded. The film opens with an equally aged veteran soldier, also seeking a proper pension from the French, who laments the use of Moroccan prostitutes as degrading to Moroccan men. This opening is followed by a collage of orientalist images of Arab women. The film concludes with Fadma's own response to seeing the film, a year or two after it was shot. In between, Fadma talks openly and amusingly about her life and the importance in it of what she calls "love." She displays no sense of shame or degradation concerning her past role, merely a joyful recollection of the Frenchmen who made such good lovers. Now she lives in poverty, but has nonetheless adopted and cares for two boys whose parents could not bring them up, earning a meager living begging and amusing tourists. This is the affectionate portrait of an indomitable woman who, despite all the tribulations of her life, still regards herself as free.

Ennadre, who does her own camera work, shows respect for her subjects, and in return she gets unaffected and honest answers from them. These documentaries reveal with real clarity the burdens on the lives of women who otherwise have no voice, except among themselves, within the domestic spaces of their homes or at the *hamam*. The camera work is always unobtrusive, and there are no technical gimmicks to detract from the force of the unaffected statements made, mostly, direct to camera. Although one learns intimate details of these women's lives, the films show no trace of intrusion, just a sharing of experiences. This is insightful, totally sympathetic documentary filmmaking of the highest quality.

* * *

In **TUNISIA** there is also no strong tradition of documentary filmmaking; yet one Tunisian documentarist who has found an international outlet for his work is **Néjib Belkadhi**. He was born in 1972 in Tunis, initially studied economics, and has since worked widely as a producer, director, and actor in film, television, and theatre in France. After making a number of shorter documentaries and commercials, he directed his strikingly exuberant feature-length documentary debut, *VHS Kahloucha*, in 2006. The subject is Moncef Kahloucha, a forty-five-year-old housepainter, who is also a passionate amateur filmmaker. His tastes range from the films of Alain Delon and Jean-Paul Belmondo to Hollywood genre movies, and he is currently at work on a new production, *Tarzan of the Arabs*. His films employ his immediate neighbors and use locations around his home district of

Kazmet—an area of Sousse not seen by its numerous summer tourists (a collage of whom Belkadhi includes, saying how much they love Sousse—in several languages). Kazmet is a run-down area, peopled by the unemployed and petty criminals, who happily participate in Kahloucha's films in exchange for a beer or a bottle of wine. The only difficulty is casting women, even older ones, since acting is viewed as disreputable by their menfolk.

Kahloucha has a keen local audience, and his fame even extends to the Tunisian community around Altamura in Italy, mostly illegal immigrants, who welcome scenes of people and settings from back home. Kahloucha's energy is limitless—he is happy to cut his own arm to provide blood for a fight scene or haggle in the souk to buy furniture for the climactic scene of his film, which involves setting fire to his sister's house. He himself is always the hero in his fictions—beating up criminals and saving women in distress—and he sees himself as sole author of his work (disparaging the contributions of his key collaborators, his cameraman and his editor). At the end, he reveals himself as the perfect male representative of his community, organizing the first screening of *Tarzan of the Arabs* in the local café, from which all the women of the community are, by definition, excluded.

An afternote, two years after the initial filming, reveals that Kazmet is a place where nothing really new happens: Kahloucha has not shot another film (though he has plans, of course) and various neighbors, who acted in his films, have been arrested, are on trial, or have just been released from prison.

Belkadhi's first feature film, *Bastardo* (2013), is a surprising development in his career, in which he discards all his documentary roots, to shape a very distinctive world not at all constrained by the conventions of realism. The protagonist Mohsen, called Bastardo because he was found abandoned in a garbage can, is an amiable figure. He loses his job as night watchman when he allows the glamorous Morjana, once a production line worker and now owner of her own fashionable shoe shop, to steal a truckload of merchandise. Although they never have as much as a conversation, the image of her as a model advertising her store obsesses him to the very end.

The district in which Mohsen lives could not be more different from this dream world. It is a totally enclosed, deprived area, dominated by Larnouba who, with his four pit bulls, uses violence and extortion ruthlessly. His rule is absolute and there is no socially organized opposition and no police presence. Larnouba is an overweight caricature of male dominance, vicious to all around him, but treated as if he were still a child by his even more grotesque mother, Khadra. Equally freakish is the girl, Bent Essengra, who went to school with Mohsen and Larnouba—she mysteriously attracts ants and other insects, which she allows to crawl undisturbed all over her body, even on her face. The inhumanity of this world is underlined by the constant references to animals (ranging from sexually active baboons to cuddly little rabbits); indeed, the DVD cover shows not the main characters but a collage of animal imagery.

Everything changes when a mobile phone antenna is installed on Mohsen's roof. The rental is generous and everyone—however poor—clamors to own a mobile phone. There is a huge party to celebrate the opening, into which Larnouba intrudes to re-establish himself as the boss. But his killing of Mohsen's business partner, Khlifa, is a step too far. The power gradually shifts to Mohsen (no longer addressed as Bastardo) who becomes a (comparatively) rich man because of his control of the antenna. He buys himself new clothes, but still does not have the courage to approach Morjana. The conflict with Larnouba continues, until Bent Essengra stabs him because of her unrequited love for Mohsen, who rewards her by raping her, amid her ants. Khadra's attempt to bring in a rival gang boss fails, and Mohsen establishes himself as the leading force in the community. But instead of helping it, he becomes as authoritarian as Larnouba. At the end, he is an isolated, sickly figure, who does not even notice the death of his beloved cat.

Whereas the film initially concentrates on the grotesquery of its characters and the violence of its setting, the final sequences aim at a kind of "magical realism." Larnouba is killed by Bent Essengra but raised from the dead to weep over the lifeless Mohsen. Khlifa, the cat, and Mohsen himself successively become ghosts, communicating together on the roof, next to the antenna.

Iraq

Most Iraqi documentary, like much new Iraqi feature filmmaking, is focused on Kurdistan. There are four Iraqi documentary filmmakers—all of them men— who made their feature debuts in the 2000s. One of them is Abbas Fahdel, whose documentary work is discussed, along with his feature film, in the section on feature filmmaking. The others are Layth Abdulamir, Hayder Mousa Daffar, and Zahavi Sanjavi.

Layth Abdulamir, who was born in Iraq in 1957, studied filmmaking both at the Sorbonne in Paris (1977–1979) and at the Fine Arts Institute in Kiev (1981– 1986). He subsequently worked as a freelance director in Paris and then, from 1999 to 2004, as a documentary director in Dubai, where he made a number of fifty-two-minute documentaries.

On Abdulamir's return to Paris, his first French-produced project was a full feature-length documentary about his homeland, *Iraq: The Song of the Missing Men / Irak, le chant des absents* (2005), aptly described in the pressbook as "a road-movie from the South to the North of Iraq, through the emblematic cities and places of history and culture in a shattered country." The film grew out of Abdulamir's frustration, while based in Dubai, at the way in which the situation in Iraq after the fall of Saddam Hussein was being reported in the foreign media.

Although the film marks his return to Iraq after an absence of twenty-eight years, it has none of the familiar marks of the "returnee" genre (no reunions with long-lost family members or old friends). Instead, the film sets the images of the present chaos and ruins of Iraq against the commentary's account of its glorious past. The film is well organized (complete with maps of the journey) and elegantly shot, but with a certain reticence. Perhaps this was due to the conditions of shooting, as Abdulamir has explained: "Most of the time I had to 'steal' images of reality, I was never able to install myself in a shot, in an interview, and thereby benefit from the time necessary for this type of operation."[43]

Abdulamir set out with a clear sense of purpose: "To understand Iraq, you have to go everywhere, to meet in their daily and ritual lives representatives of the different ethnicities and religions. That alone allows you to reach the essential of what is happening in the country and why." The scope of his enquiry was wide from the beginning:

> This documentary takes the form of a journey seeking out the identity of my country, which is so hard to pin down, seeking the shared basic common cultural, social and historical elements, which make Kurds, Arabs or Turkamen, Shiites, Sunni or Christians, villagers and city-dwellers, Iraqis as well.

What he found, however, was a lack of unity, that "Iraqi identity was broken, that everyone retreated to hide behind his community, his religion, his religious allegiance." This he blames on the occupation, which "has unleashed something completely negative and, in my opinion, this problem of identity is a bomb which could go off at any moment." He does manage to end his film on a lighter note, with an old shepherd in a remote part of the North refusing to sell his favorite sheep for any price (even if a woman is thrown in as part of the deal!) and running off cackling into the distance. On a personal level, the journey was in some ways a disappointment for Abdulamir: "Among the surprises and regrets created by my discovery of Iraq as it is today, the strongest, emotionally speaking, was to find myself, from one end of the country to the other, regarded as an outsider by the inhabitants."

Abdulamir's second, 53-minute documentary, *Christians of Iraq / Chrétiens d'Irak* (2011), explores one of the "bombs" set off by the US occupation, the halving of the Christian population in Iraq, at one time measured at around a million, since the fall of Saddam. As one Iraqi Christian observes, "the Americans didn't come here to help their fellow Christians, they came just for their own political and economic reasons." Christians had settled in Iraq from the first century A.D., and the film opens with shots of some of the impressive monuments—churches and monasteries—which were constructed over the centuries and which now lie empty, in some cases pillaged and vandalized. Similarly, houses in the old Christian Al-Dorra quarters of Baghdad have now been taken over by poor Shiite families, themselves often refugees from other areas of conflict and unrest. The Christians who have suffered persecution from Islamist militants or criminal gangs, who seem to enjoy police acquiescence if not overt support, tell their stories. Many of those who have not emigrated have sought refuge in Kurdistan, where greater tolerance reigns. Again, the director proves himself a reticent commentator—he does not reveal his personal religious affiliation or cite personal examples of persecution. Instead, he gives scope for the expression of both personal experiences and political debate (about constitutional issues in the new Iraq). This is a regional problem—almost all Christians have already been driven from Turkey—and the film can offer no hope of a favorable resolution. Abdulamir sets out the situation clearly and soberly, showing his sensitivity in the use of music to structure his film.

Hayder Mousa Daffar's *The Dreams of Sparrows / Rêves de moineaux* (2005) was one of the first feature-length documentaries, shot with an Iraqi crew, to explore the realities of Iraq after the fall of Saddam. The film begins with what is clearly intended as a symbolic sequence—the birth of a child in difficult circumstances which cause the mother to die in the process—to stand for the birth of a new Iraq. The voice-over announces, "This is the story of that child." But *The Dreams of Sparrows* does not, in fact, follow any single character; instead, we hear a mass of conflicting voices and attitudes from a wide range of witnesses. In many ways, this is a disoriented film, since it sets out to capture the day-by-day developments in a chaotic situation: the progress (or lack of it) in Iraq from the capture of Saddam Hussein to the US army's assault on the city of Fallujah.

As he makes clear at the beginning of the film, Hayder Mousa Daffar has no more idea than anyone else about what will unfold, but he realizes that this is too big a story for a single filmmaker and so enrolls four "contributing directors"— one woman, Khariya Mansour, and three men, Hayder Jabbar Fehed, Murtuda Sa'ady, and Rassim Mansour. These are all young people, recently emerged from education or training, who had not worked in Saddam Hussein's propaganda cinema. There are only a few archival clips in the film (such as the destruction of Saddam's statue in Baghdad and shots of him after his capture); essentially, *The Dreams of Sparrows* comprises the immediate responses of five people to a constantly changing and sometimes violent situation. The directors have no special status. They appear in their own footage as interviewers, but at times they become witnesses themselves as well, talking directly to camera about their responses, just like their interviewees.

The range of views expressed could not be wider. For one witness, the arrest of Saddam Hussein is "a beautiful day"; for others (especially taxi drivers), it is an irrelevance compared with the shortage of gasoline, which causes seemingly endless waiting lines, unknown in a country which is one of the world's leading oil-producing states. Some welcome the US invasion, others demand the immediate withdrawal of the occupying forces. There are dramatic differences in the experience of various groups. The smartly uniformed girls at a private school are already recovering, now drawing bright, cheerful pictures instead of the earlier images of war. Meanwhile, just down the road, poor children get no education and face a sordid life on the streets. Many people are now homeless, including the groups of Palestinians whom Saddam had encouraged to settle in Baghdad. Conditions could hardly be worse (six to a room) in the mental hospital in Sadr City, which houses many of those destroyed by torture under Saddam's rule. The name of his son Uday is constantly mentioned.

Various artists and writers reveal their deeply felt need to express their experiences under Saddam's rule and their responses to the current situation. Soldiers and officers from the old regime are interviewed; they acknowledge the cruelty under Saddam but deny any personal responsibility. As the days pass, the hostility toward the occupiers grows. Earlier, some people had welcomed George W. Bush as a new strong man, who would sort out Iraq's problems. Now, there are complaints about weakness and assertions that at least Saddam would have solved the problems of water, electricity, and oil in three months. Already there is talk of the beginnings of armed resistance (initially ill directed) against the Americans. Then comes the assault on Fallujah and the Iraqi response: challenges by young men eager to resist the occupiers. There are also images of shelled mosques, shot-up ambulances, and mass graves of unknown victims.

The Dreams of Sparrows, which began at a time of uncertainty, breaks off at a point of rising tension. There is a final epilogue and dedication for the film. Saad Fakher, associate producer and one of the team, was killed driving home one night. Fired on by Iraqi militants, he turned in the opposite direction only to come face-to-face with a US patrol. Next morning, his colleagues found his body; the car he was driving had 120 bullet holes.

There is a question mark concerning the fourth Iraqi, **Zahavi Sanjavi**. He was born in 1967 in Arbil in Iraqi Kurdistan and in 1975 sought asylum with his family in Iran. He subsequently studied filmmaking in Sweden and at VGIK in Moscow, returning to Iraq after a thirty-year absence in 2005. He has since worked in film and television production as both writer and director. Some sources list Sanjavi as co-director of a feature-length Kurdish-language documentary shot in Iraq, *All My Mothers / Toutes mes mères / Hamey-e madaran-e man* (2009). Others attribute this role to Abbas Ghazali, who produced the film. The universally agreed-upon second director is the Iranian Kurd Ebrahim Saeedi, who, in addition to co-directing *All My Mothers,* was also responsible for the photography and the editing of image and sound. Saeedi, who was born in 1965 in Mahabad in Kurdish Iran, studied filmmaking at the Arts University in Tehran and pursued a career as editor and/or cinematographer on numerous films, including five features. What is also certain is that *All My Mothers* was produced by the Tehran-based Iranian production company Sheherazad Media International.

The synopsis prepared for the International Documentary Film Festival Amsterdam in 2011 gives a vivid account of the film:

> The Kurdish women in *All My Mothers* are not introduced by their age or position in life, but rather by the number of people they have lost. Beautifully filmed with side lighting, a wrinkled old woman tells us how she has been waiting 23 years and six months for the return of her loved ones. During an Iraqi attack in the 1980s, she lost a total of 30 who were dear to her, and now she is just one of hundreds of women who are waiting. Women who remember, as if it were yesterday, how their husbands were called to a "meeting" in Kirkuk—never to be seen again.

The rain that hammers down incessantly in the background in many scenes reinforces the atmosphere of sorrow, absence, and loneliness. The women help one another get by from day to day by talking, crying, praying, and giving each other massages. And it is not only the older generation that mourns the dead—younger women miss their fathers and brothers, and realize that their chances of marrying are slight, as there are hardly any young men left in the village. A military funeral leads up to the grand finale, in which images of weeping, fainting women and archival footage of executions speak for themselves.[44] I regret that I have not been able to view the film or resolve the problem of its authorship.

Syria

The path to feature-length output in documentary has been pioneered by the Paris-based **Hala al-Abdallah Yakoub**, who was born in 1956 in Hama. Her experimental video autobiography, *I Am the One Who Brings Flowers to Her Grave / Je suis celle qui porte les fleurs vers sa tombe* (2006), was co-directed with Ammar al-Beik and has been followed more recently by two solo-directed films, *Hey! Don't Forget the Cumin / Hé! n'oublie pas le cumin* (2008) and *As If We Were Catching a Cobra / Comme si nous attrapions un cobra* (2012).

Al-Abdallah's *I Am the One Who Brings Flowers to Her Grave* is the archetypal exile film, clearly targeted not at a Syrian popular audience but at the international festival circuit. It is personal, self-reflective, self-indulgent, seldom overtly political, but crammed with themes of loneliness, regret, nostalgia, loss, memory, and pain. It opens and closes with images of migrating birds, and the personal allusions are enigmatic. The film as a whole is a collage of stories, many of which peter out inconclusively, and of images which are imprecisely located (in France or Syria?). *I Am the One* is held together by al-Abdallah's personality and her delight, as a professional producer, at being for once her own writer-director.

Al-Abdallah has since made another, more complex documentary feature, *Hey! Don't Forget the Cumin* (2008), which, despite its apparently upbeat title, is a study of sickness, madness, suicide, and death. Somewhat awkwardly structured for those in the audience unfamiliar with her subjects, the film tells the stories of three unconnected writers with tormented lives. Two of the tales are al-Abdallah's own interrogations of the lives and deaths of writers.

The first is that of the Arab short-story writer, journalist, and political activist Jamil Hatmal (1945–1995), whom the director knew personally. He suffered from a heart complaint and spent the last two years of his life in exile, confined to various hospitals in France. There, al-Abdallah tells us, his bed served both "as an office to write in and as a garden in which to encounter a past or future lover."[45] This scene becomes a ritual in the film, lyrically restaged by the filmmaker and enacted by a succession of beautiful women, who are shown endlessly circling in the seemingly limitless space at the end of Hatmal's bed.

The second tale is a more anguished questioning of the death of the young English playwright, Sarah Kane (1971–1999), who suffered from depression throughout her short life and who committed suicide at the age of twenty-eight. Her life is told largely through her own words, recorded in English. She wrote five plays, all marked by violent action and language, focused on extreme physical situations and mental states. Of her career as a dramatist, she wrote that she was attracted to the stage because "theatre has no memory, which makes it the most existential of the arts. . . . I keep coming back in the hope that someone in the darkened room somewhere will show me an image that burns itself into my mind."[46]

The third episode, which upsets the balance of the work somewhat through its directness, intensity, and dramatic power, is a filmic adaptation of a theatrical monologue acted out by its author, the Lebanese actress Darina al-Joundi (who had appeared in a number of Arab films by major directors, including Ghassan Salhab's *Beyrouth fantôme*, Yousry Nasrallah's *Gate of the Sun*, and Danielle Arbid's *A Lost Man*). This monologue, first performed onstage at the Avignon festival in 2007, was itself based on al-Joundi's autobiographical memoir, co-authored with Mohamed Kacini, *The Day Nina Simone Stopped Singing*. Al-Joundi's life has been a remarkable one. She was brought up by a very liberal father (and acquiescent mother) to despise religion and always to express herself fully (she first appeared as an actress on television at the age of eight). As a child, she was actively encouraged by her father to indulge in alcohol, cigarettes, and drugs—all against the background of the worsening civil war in Beirut, which began when she was seven. At fifteen, she was raped, made pregnant, and underwent an abortion. As a result, she lived a wildly abandoned life:

> My philosophy of life was very simple. I was convinced that I was going to
> die at any moment, so, hungry for everything, for sex, drugs and alcohol, I

doubled my efforts. I always had a bottle of whisky in my bag, a packet of cigarettes, and a candle that I would light on the sidewalk on the corner of Makhoul Street where I would spend hours by myself. I wanted to take sexual revenge. I made love like a madwoman, with anyone anywhere.

In her twenties she enrolled in the Red Cross and saw the atrocities perpetrated in the civil war at first hand, including the massacre at the Sabra and Shatila refugee camps. At the same time, she experienced three failed marriages, one to a man who physically abused her. Perhaps it is not surprising that, one day, she woke up to find herself chained to a bed in a mental hospital. This is the story which Darina al-Joundi recounts and acts out in harrowing detail, direct to camera, in the film.

The production of *As If We Were Catching a Cobra* (2012) was interrupted by the events of the Arab Spring in Egypt and the outbreak of civil war in Syria. The film began as a study of the art of caricature in the Arab world. Initial interviews were set up and filmed, with the novelist Samar Yazbek providing a narrative guide to the role this graphic form plays in the Arab world (it is from her description of the art that the film takes its title). Al-Abdallah shot conversations with, among others, the veteran Egyptian caricaturist Mohieddine Ellabbad and Syrian caricaturists Ali Farzat and Hazem Alhamwi. But then the filming was interrupted by the totally unexpected events of 2011, which rock the lives of all those involved: Yazbek is arrested and driven into exile in France, Ellabbad dies, and Farzak is beaten up and has his hands broken. *As If We Were Catching a Cobra* becomes an immediate and passionate reflection of the impact of this turmoil on the whole Arab world. In its completed form, the film has little visual analysis of the graphic art of caricature and its relationship to the Arab political scene. But, unsurprisingly, it contains examples of al-Abdallah's special talent: extracting raw and direct testimony from the participants in events over which they have no control. The film emerges as a vivid and intimate testimony to the courage and tenacity of its chosen Arab artists.

In the last decade, thanks to the growth of Syrian television and the advent of digital technology, new possibilities of production outside the General Organization for Cinema have arisen. A number of Syrian newcomers, most still in their twenties and thirties and many based abroad, are active, making short fictional and documentary works; but as yet few documentary feature-length works seem to have been made. The year 2009 did, however, see the breakthrough of several new young Syrian feature filmmakers. One Syrian documentarist who did manage to get her work shown internationally is **Soudade Kaadan**, who was born in France in 1979 but now resides in Damascus. *Damascus Roof and Tales of Paradise* (2010), produced by Al Jazeera Documentary, is an affectionate and nostalgic look at the big houses in the old district of Damascus, now deserted by the extended families who once lived there and threatened with destruction. It recalls through direct testimony and charming, childlike animation some of the traditional stories and legends attached to these buildings, which now risk being lost forever. The film is particularly poignant in being made before there was any hint of the political upheavals which would tear Syria apart beginning in 2011.

4 Feature Filmmaking

Arab filmmaking in the 2000s consists of many strands, one of which is the work of those filmmakers who are based in Paris. These might seem to constitute a typical exile group of the kind so ably chronicled by Hamid Naficy.[1] Certainly many of their films carry the marks of exile and diaspora, and some chronicle a return—real or imagined—to the filmmaker's roots. But the filmmakers' concern to make films set in their countries of origin meshes perfectly with the French government's policy of creating a network of worldwide cultural filmmaking with Paris at its center. Indeed, French policies toward cinema mean that the major problem of these filmmakers, like that of their predecessors, is less exile than potential integration and loss of Arab identity. The *beur* filmmakers who began in the mid-1980s with striking films focused on the immigrant community in France have now largely been absorbed into mainstream French cinema.

The previously useful distinction between the *beurs* working within the structures of French film production and the Algerians employed by the state film organization in Algiers is no longer valid, since many of those who previously worked in Algeria are now long-term residents in France. In the 1980s, those who had grown up within the immigrant community tended to be treated as belonging to a specific *beur* cinema, but in a 2002 survey of young French filmmakers by René Prédal, Mehdi Charef merits just a footnote, while Rachid Bouchareb, Karim Dridi, Malek Chibane, Abdellatif Kechiche, and Yamina Benguigui are fused effortlessly into a narrative dominated by their purely French contemporaries who choose to deal with similar subject matter. As Prédal points out, "The *beur* current is now twenty years old and no longer constitutes a separate entity apart from the rest of cinema."[2]

A further complexity is due to the definition of nationality for those born in Paris. A number of the new filmmakers—among them Nadia El Fani and Karin Albou—are of mixed descent, having French mothers and Maghrebian fathers. Many French-based Arab filmmakers now come from outside the Algerian community and have complex personal histories. Mourad Boucif, who is of Moroccan descent, was born in Algeria and reached Belgium, after a stay in France, at the age of four. Both Souad El Bouhati and Nadir Moknèche were transported across the Mediterranean by their families while they were still newborn babies—the former from Rabat to France and the latter from Paris to Algeria. The consequences have proved paradoxical. While El Bouhati has dealt exclusively with issues of Moroccan emigration and identity and Moknèche set his first three films in the Algiers where he grew up, both have made French-language features, with largely French production financing. For other filmmakers as well there is no immediate correspondence between birthplace and narrative stance. The early features of Abdellatif Kechiche (born in Tunis) and Rabah Ameur-Zaïmèche (born in Beni Zid in Algeria) dealt with subjects treated almost exclusively from an immigrant perspective, while the French-born Karin Albou (of part Algerian descent) set her second feature in Tunis during World War II.

In all, there are about a dozen feature filmmakers of Maghrebian descent who were born in France. As all of them identify themselves strongly with their perceived country of origin, they are considered here alongside those who have been brought up in the Maghreb (and whose own films may also owe much to French financing). There is a strong representation of women from across the Maghreb in this group—from Morocco and Tunisia, as well as from Algeria.

Algeria

A real renewal of Algerian cinema—in terms of a new generation—seemed imminent in 1992, with the appearance of **Malek Lakhdar-Hamina** who was born in 1962. The son of the great Algerian pioneer filmmaker Mohamed Lakhdar-Hamina, he was the first of those born after independence in Algeria to release a feature film and was, at that time, by far the youngest filmmaker active in the Maghreb. The director had appeared as a child actor in some of his father's films and, as an adult, in Mahmoud Zemmouri's comedy *The Crazy Years of the Twist* (1983) and his father's *The Last Image* (1986). Subsequently he acquired film training in the United States. He worked on his first feature, *Autumn—October in Algiers / Automne—octobre à Alger* (1992), which was made as a French-Algerian co-production, with an experienced team of collaborators, many of whom had already worked with his father.

In the film, Lakhdar-Hamina himself plays the leading role of Momo, a popular musician who has to support his wife and whole extended family, including his fundamentalist brother. Although the film is set at a time of huge popular unrest in Algiers (just prior to the army's clamp-down on the fundamentalists), much of the drama is domestic, and the comedic elements revolve around the problem of private domestic space (where can he make love to his wife?). These are characters very much on the periphery of the great events unfolding around them, and the film offers no real insight into the nature of the political conflict.

The focus is more on a general feeling of corruption and on the sense of hopelessness for Momo's generation.

Even at the beginning of the film, Momo is frustrated, proclaiming that he would give *both* his kidneys to get abroad. In the course of the action, he finds his music branded as decadent and is beaten up by both the police and the *barbus* (Islamists). When he does get involved in wider events, he is promptly shot dead by the police, Molotov cocktail in hand—the very image of a wasted life. *Autumn—October in Algiers* is an impressive debut, with moments of real dramatic power. But even though it was generally well received, Lakhdar-Hamina has not continued his career, either as an actor or as director.

* * *

Questions of national identity are continually raised by the films of second-generation immigrants born and living in France. Key examples of the ambiguities involved are offered by the film careers of three mid-1960s French-born filmmakers: Malek Chibane, Bourlem Guerdjou, and Zaïda Ghorab-Volta.

Malek Chibane, who has French nationality and lives in France, was born in 1964 in Saint-Vallier of Kabyle parents, who moved to Goussainville when he was three. He was one of the first of the 1960s generation to make a breakthrough into feature filmmaking, directing two initial, modestly funded French-language independent features in the mid-1990s, *Hexagon* (1993) and *Sweet France* (1995). But despite work in French television, Chibane had to wait thirteen years to make the third installment of what has been marketed on DVD as his "Urban Trilogy," *Neighbors* (2008). Each film is set in a different area of the Parisian suburbs (the *banlieue*): Goussainville, Saint-Denis, and Sarcelles, respectively, and gives an insider view of the lives of those residing and growing up there. In one sense, Chibane is a worthy successor of those who pioneered the *beur* film from the mid-1980s, the trio of Rachid Bouchareb, Mehdi Charef, and Abdelkrim Bahloul, in particular. From another point of view, he is a part of the mainstream low-budget French output dealing with the socially deprived in the suburbs surrounding Paris. René Prédal, for example, first considers *Hexagon* alongside the films of Mathieu Kassovitz and Jean-François Richet, Olivier Dahan and Thomas Gilou,[3] and then, in a later reference, links Chibane's work to that of Philippe Faucon.[4]

Hexagon / Hexagone (1993) is a realistic social study, which focuses on the lives of five young people—Ali, Staf, Samy, Slimane, and a young "beurette," Nacéra—as they try to achieve something in their lives. All except Nacéra have left school, but they struggle to get either training or real jobs. Their efforts are serious, sad, and at times pathetically comic: shoplifting but picking up only left-foot shoes (Samy), for example, or faking a diploma in English while being unable to speak the language (Staf). Still living at home, they struggle to find an identity, but in fact spend much of their time just talking on street corners. The film is set in the period leading up to the festival of Aïd El Kebir, but this is essentially a concern of their parents, not something for them. They find Goussainville suffocating but have no way to escape. Lovemaking is a furtive affair in someone else's borrowed apartment. A locally held dance is uninspiring and a financial failure for its organizers, while a trip into Paris merely reinforces their sense of failure to become a real part of the French society in which they live. *Hexagon* is largely a series of conversation pieces, convincingly acted but static. Action enters the narrative only at the end, when Samy is shot by the police and dies after a chase sequence. The film ends on a thoughtful note, but no real possibility of change has emerged for any of the remaining members of the group.

Whereas the characters in *Hexagon* are trapped by circumstances in Goussainville—not least by the lack of money—Moussa and his French friend Jean-Luc in *Sweet France / Douce France* (1995) find a totally unexpected way of escaping from the pressures of Saint-Denis. Both in their twenties, they are the chance witnesses of a jewel thief fleeing from the scene of his crime and are able to recover the loot he has dropped into a trash can before the police and the owner search the scene. Hence, they are able to set themselves up successfully in business, Moussa buying and running a café and Jean-Luc, a trainee lawyer, setting up a legal advice center in the back room. Their problems are emotional rather than financial, as they are attracted to two very different young women, who turn out to be sisters. Jean-Luc is attracted to Souad, a liberated, mini-skirted young woman who wants to live her own life, while Moussa is drawn to her younger sister Farida, who is lively and intelligent, wanting to become a teacher, but devout and still insisting on wearing a chador to cover her hair. For all of them there are problems with French authority figures, such as the police, education authorities, and concierges, and the three *beurs* have additional problems with their parents.

The actions of the four young people are neatly intercut in the early parts of the film, and the atmosphere of Saint-Denis is very well captured in the scenes set in Moussa's café. But the resolution of the film is less satisfactory, being scattered with incidents which are illogical or irrelevant: Farida having a (false) religious vision; Moussa somehow ending up in his concierge's bed, while his intended bride improbably manages to construct instantly a mannequin wearing her wedding dress, as she flees back to Algeria. The outcome for the guests at an Arab wedding when the bride has gone missing is not shown. Moreover, the film's supposedly happy ending involves the characters acting totally out of character: Farida renouncing her chador and Jean-Luc saying glibly that converting to Islam would be no problem if it will allow him to marry Souad.

Although *Neighbors / Voisins voisines* (2008) was made after a gap of ten years, there is a strong sense of continuity with the first two films. The setting is again the *banlieue* and the film is again composed largely of conversation pieces, with very little physical action. The two male leads from *Sweet France*, Hakim

Sahraoui and Frédéric Diefenthal, reappear, with the latter playing the key role of the Spanish-born concierge, Paco. The characters have a wider age range than in the two earlier films and come from very disparate national backgrounds— immigrants from various parts of Europe, as well as Arabs of Algerian descent. But they all inhabit the same apartment block, the Résidence Mozart, and their interactions, individually face-to-face or at tenants' meetings, form the bulk of the film.

The key difference here is the presence of Moussa Diop, a rapper living in a second-floor apartment and working on his new album, who provides the film with its musical accompaniment and voice-over commentary. While the latter is precise, the rap itself is very hard to follow because of the particular balance of the voice and the bass (Jackie Berroyer, who wrote the lyrics, proposed subtitles, but Chibane thought that this would damage the rap's authenticity).[5] Initially Moussa gets plenty of inspiration from the actions of his fellow tenants. When he finds a lack of fresh incident, he deliberately intervenes to provoke new actions and reactions, by jimmying open the door of Alice, an attractive young woman who is living alone but having an affair with one of her neighbors. Throughout, it is Moussa who gives the film both its flavor and its rhythm, as he successfully completes his album. The film ends with the collapse of the Arab owner of the building, Malouf (played by Fellag), whose body Alice and Paco take to his favorite spot, the Arab area in a nearby cemetery.

Throughout these three films Chibane's style is marked by long conversation scenes broken up by quirky and unexpected incidents, such as Paco's encounter in the hallway with a group of younger rappers. Arriving complete with a pit bull terrier, they look threatening but in fact serenade him, using no instruments but just their voices to provide both the rap and the rhythmic accompaniment. Chibane's strength as a filmmaker lies, as always, in his handling of his ensemble of players and his ability to mix comic and serious material effortlessly.

Chibane's fourth feature, *Poor Richard / Pauvre Richard* (2012), has a similar suburban setting but is framed as a light comedy. Here the stress is initially on the peace and tolerance of a multi-cultural urban community, until it is revealed that one of their number has won 124 million euros in the lottery. The winner, Omar, insists on keeping his identity anonymous, with the result that over the next seven days the community is torn apart by envy and suspicion. Because of a mistaken furniture delivery, Richard is thought to be the true winner, and his life falls apart in the face of hostility from just about everybody around him. Omar, meanwhile, briefly enjoys the privileges of wealth, but, drawn back to the community, is deeply hurt when his father refuses the luxury home he has bought for them both. There is a succession of misunderstandings and farcical events (such as a couple of failed kidnappings), but eventually Richard and Omar are reunited with the women they love. As the film draws to a close, Richard has the pleasure of tearing up a check for half of Omar's winnings, leaving the latter alone to face an endless waiting line of supplicants. The film, whose action begins in a bank and in which money dominates throughout, ends with Omar's father finding his vacuum cleaner blocked with (presumably high-value) euro notes. *Poor Richard* adopts a lighter tone than Chibane's earlier work but shows his continued gift for showing the dynamics of mixed-race urban communities and the complexity of young people's interactions.

Bourlem Guerdjou is a particularly good example of national confusions. While the director's parents are of Algerian origin, he himself was born in Asnières in France in 1965, has French nationality, and works as a writer-director in French television. His debut feature, *Living in Paradise / Vivre au paradis* (1998), is a French-Belgian-Norwegian co-production, adapted from a French-language novel published in Paris and co-scripted—with French dialogue—by two French writers. It also has Europeans in all the key production roles. Yet it was awarded the top prize (the *Tanit d'or*) at the 1998 Journées Cinématographiques de Carthage in Tunis as an Algerian film.

Whatever the uncertainty about the national identity of *Living in Paradise / Vivre au paradis* (1998), there can be no question about the quality of the film, which fits perfectly into the vein of immigrant (*beur*) filmmaking established in the mid-1980s in France. The film looks back at the surge of immigrants arriving from Algeria during the early 1960s to work in the French construction industry. The setting is the slums of Nanterre (three kilometers from Paris), where so many of the immigrants are housed, crowded into leaky shacks without basic facilities such as running water and electricity, or even the most fundamental forms of privacy. This is also a world of exploitation, domestic violence, and sickness, subject to both "taxation" by the FLN and random intrusions and violence by the French police.

Yet this is a world into which the film's protagonist, Lakhdar, who is convinced he will be granted a municipal apartment, invites his wife Nora and two small children over from Algeria. His obsession with the idea of a modern apartment turns him from being a helpful and respected member of the community into one of those who prey on more vulnerable or newly arrived immigrants. Meanwhile, Nora, initially shy and dominated by her husband, gradually finds strength through her association with other women, particularly the FLN militant, Aïcha. While she becomes more in tune with the mood of the community, supporting the collective struggle for Algerian independence, Lakhdar becomes increasingly alienated. His schemes fail; he throws out his wife and children and proceeds to gamble away his last resources.

The film is stronger at depicting the specific details of interactions within the family and in the community than in conveying the wider political movements which form the background to their lives: the routine harassment; the horrific police brutality on October 17, 1961, when over two hundred unarmed Algerian protesters were murdered in Paris; and the celebrations which mark the final achievement of Algerian independence on July 5, 1962. Lakhdar's last decision is to return with Algeria with his family (with whom he is reconciled on Independence Day). But a final title reveals that returning immigrants were not welcomed by the new government in Algeria and that it took seven years for the immigrants living in the Nanterre slums to be rehoused.

   Zaina, Horsewoman from the Atlas / Zaïna, cavalière de l'Atlas (2000), Guerdjou's second feature, is a very different, French-language project, set in a traditional world of family feuds and rivalries and located against the glories of the Atlas Mountains. The film opens with the burial of Selma, witnessed by her tearful young daughter, Zaina. Selma's life had been torn between two men, Mustapha, her first husband, who repudiated her without knowing she was pregnant with his child, and the powerful Omar, who subsequently married her and was unintentionally responsible for her death. The two men remain hostile rivals, and the film makes full use of the melodramatic possibilities offered by Zaina's need to choose between the two of them. She is always hostile to Omar, but on a twenty-day trek through the mountains, she forges a real bond with Mustapha. There is no evidence that Zaina had ever ridden a horse before this trek, but she establishes a close relationship with Mustapha's prize thoroughbred stallion, Zingal. During the trek, she seals her growing maturity in dramatic fashion, by riding to Mustapha's rescue, proclaiming herself to be the legendary queen Fatyn and putting marauding horse thieves to rout. In Marrakesh, the end of their journey, she emulates her mother's feat by winning the Agdal, a race which draws champion riders from across the Arab world and in which she is matched specifically against Omar. The mass of women, as well as Mustapha, hail her as champion. Whereas *Living in Paradise* is a sober study of failure, set in a precisely located time and space, *Zaina* is a fantasy of improbable success, set against the backdrop of a timeless Morocco.

   Zaïda Ghorab-Volta was born in Clichy in 1966 and is based in France. She began her career in the social sector and worked as a scriptwriter with the French director Romain Goupil. Her own first film is a fifty-nine-minute fiction in which she plays a leading role, *Remember Me / Souviens-toi de moi* (1996). This is a film in the traditional immigrant mold, the study of a family living in the Parisian *banlieue* and split in terms of generations. The father works in construction, while the mother stays at home in traditional style, to look after the family. But the members of the new generation have different sets of values. One daughter has already left home and disappeared, and the son Hamid cannot accept his father's attitudes toward women. But the focus is mostly on the two remaining daughters, Mimouna and Salima, who dream of living like young Frenchwomen, having boyfriends of their own choosing and not accounting for time spent away from the house. The annual family holiday with their relatives in Algeria allows them to experience with their cousins the traditional Arab life of female seclusion, but this will not change their attitudes.

Ghorab-Volta's two full-length features continue the filmmaker's concern with women's lives and relationships, but now without the immigrant dimension. *Leave a Little Love / Laisse un peu d'amour* (1998) deals with the changing lives of a woman in her fifties who has taken early retirement and her two daughters, one of whom is studying music at the conservatory, while the other is recovering from a breakdown which had confined her to hospital. *Gilded Youth / Jeunesse dorée* (2002) deals with two teenage French girls, Gwenaëlle and Angéla, who have grown up in the *banlieue* and are bored with family life, domestic pressures, and the life around them. They decide on a photo safari across France, but the actual nature of their project, photographing housing blocks that have grown up in the middle of nowhere, means that they merely encounter again the kind of images and people they are familiar with at home. When they eventually reach farming territory in the Pyrenees, they are introduced to new landscapes and a couple of pleasing young men. But these encounters do not lead to any emotional discoveries or sexual involvements, and they return home without having undergone any apparent change during their journey.

* * *

Nadir Moknèche is a filmmaker of quite different stature, whose career illustrates even more vividly the complexity of distinguishing between *beurs* and Algerians and of defining the complex trajectories of the Paris-based exiles. Born in 1965 in Paris to working-class parents, he was brought up, from the age of one month, in Algeria, which he did not leave until he was eighteen, to take his *bac* (*baccalauréat*) in Paris and to begin two years of law studies. After abandoning law, he joined the drama school at the Théâtre National de Chaillot, where he spent three years acting and directing. He also discovered the power of cinema in Paris and names Pier Paolo Pasolini's *Medea* as a key influence. Subsequently, he spent some time in London and received his training in filmmaking at the New School for Social Research in New York, where one of his shorts was titled *Medea*.

Moknèche has described himself as a product of the Algeria of Boumediene and Chadli, of Arabization (he learned French only at the age of nine), and of Islamization.[6] Despite this, he is generally considered a *beur,* largely because he draws his financing from conventional French production sources, uses French crews, and makes his films with French dialogue, even when shooting in Algiers (where his first three films are set and two were shot). All of his features— *Madame Osmane's Harem / Le harem de Madame Osmane* (2000), *Viva Laldjérie* (2004), *Paloma Delight / Délice Paloma* (2008), and *Goodbye Morocco* (2011)—are dominated by strong female characters.

Madame Osmane's Harem is a paradoxical work. Widely distributed and often regarded as a key film, re-establishing Algerian cinema after the virtual cessation of production in the late 1990s, it is a work from which Algeria itself is largely absent. It was shot by a French-based filmmaker, using a French crew and shooting on location in Morocco. The film's dialogue is in French, and the leading role is played by the Spanish actress Carmen Maura, best known for her appearances in the films of Pedro Almodóvar. The film's disjointed narrative is also dominated by absence—that of the men who would be expected to live in the apartment block occupied solely by women and dominated by Madame Osmane. They are abroad, called up for army service or perhaps fighting in the resistance to the government.

Madame Osmane is the film's central figure, whose stated aim is to keep the house in better order than any man would. A former resistance fighter (Madame Osmane was her *nom de guerre*), she married for love. But her husband left her for a Frenchwoman and now lives in France. She is preoccupied by appearances, dresses immaculately, and pays much attention to her bleached hair. Always confrontational, she spends most of her time controlling the life of her daughter, Sekkina, when not cajoling and spying on her female tenants. Perhaps even more flamboyant is her maid, Myriem (forcefully played by the Algerian actress Biyouna), who, with her own daughter, is really part of the family. The film focuses almost exclusively on the boisterous, often hysterical and violent interactions of the women, and the initial tone is broadly farcical, with a succession of theatrical quarrels and confrontations within the apartment block. The women's only outing is a joint expedition by car to the sea and to the female celebrations of a marriage. After this, the tone changes abruptly, as Sekkina is killed when out after dark following a quarrel with her mother. The delivery of her coffin to the apartment block brings the film to its end.

Throughout the film, the role of men is almost non-existent; they are all shadowy figures: the gigolo who seduces one of the tenants; Sekkina's timid, mother-dominated suitor; a workman who strips naked on the rooftop to impress Madame Osmane (who treats his offering with total disdain). Otherwise, men are largely anonymous figures: the soldiers manning roadblocks and the policemen delivering the coffin. The impact of the returning husband, back to witness his daughter's engagement but thrown out of the taxi by Madame Osmane on the way back from the airport, is minimal. His only role is to sign the papers for the return of his daughter's body. Although the film is set in 1993, the events of the civil war are barely touched upon, and Sekkina's death occurs off-camera. Moknèche's sole concern is his gallery of female portraits within their enclosed spaces.[7]

Moknèche's second feature, *Viva Laldjérie* (2004), takes its title from a slang mixing of the French "Algérie" and the Arabic "El Djzaïr." The film follows the same narrative pattern as its predecessor, focusing on two main characters: a middle-aged woman (in this case, Papicha, played by Biyouna, who was the servant in the earlier film), proud of her past; and her twenty-something daughter, Goucem, who leads a liberated life style but is totally obsessed with marriage. Again the film ends with the killing of a young girl, but this time it is Goucem's prostitute friend, Fifi, who is killed cold-bloodedly by her "protector when he suspects her of stealing his revolver (which was in fact taken by Goucem). Unlike the off-screen killing of Sekkina, this is developed into an emotionally powerful chase scene. The ebullient Papicha, now reduced to sharing a hotel room (and a bed) with the daughter who supports her, finds consolation only in the past. She laments the loss of her youth, her money, her house, and most of all, her popularity as a star dancer at the Copacabana nightclub. The one strand of the plot that ends optimistically is the possibility that the nightclub will in fact be reopened and not turned, as is currently planned, into a mosque.

Goucem's story, by contrast, shows the difficulties faced by a young woman in today's world, in a society torn between Muslim tradition and Western-style modernity. Her greatest desire is to marry her lover after his divorce, but when he does split from his wife, it is to marry someone richer and of higher social status. He sees Goucem as no more than a mistress. In a sense, Goucem mirrors his attitude in her disdain for the unemployed Samir, who loves her but has nothing more to offer than a ride on his scooter. Although the film opens and closes with documentary-style shots of anonymous crowds on the streets of Algiers, and Moknèche has spoken of "the failure of the authoritarian attempt to create a national identity which is visible today,"[8] the film offers no real analysis of the social, political, and economic issues arising from Algeria's emergence from civil war. But what Moknèche does offer, like his contemporaries Raja Amari and Laïla Marrakchi, are striking and—for Algerian audiences—potentially shocking images of modern sexuality, such as adultery, open promiscuity, prostitution, homosexuality, and nudity, issues which Arab cinema has traditionally ignored.

Moknèche's third film, *Paloma Delight,* retains the almost exclusive concern with women's lives, as well as key cast members from the earlier films (Biyouna as Madame Algéria, Nadia Kaci as Shéhérazade, and Fadila Ouabdesselam as Mina). But the film's structure is more complex, and its focus on Algeria's social problems, especially corruption, is much sharper. *Paloma Delight* begins with Madame Algéria's release from prison, and as her day unfolds, we are given flashbacks to the events which landed her in prison, commented upon by Madame Algéria herself in voice-over. At the start of the action, she is on top of the world, with her collaborator, Shéhérazade, running a business which solves everybody's problems—ruining a business rival, getting rid of an unwanted husband, and so forth—through bribery, deceit, the use of a crooked lawyer (played by future director Lyes Salem), and her list of call girls. She sees herself as head of a family which includes Shéhérazade, her own deaf-and-dumb sister Mina, and her spoiled son Riyad, to whom she adds a new recruit, the waitress Rachida, whom she renames Paloma (after a dessert she has just eaten).

In fact, almost all the women have assumed names. In truth, Madame Algéria is Zineb Agha, and Shéhérazade's real name is Zouina. Everyone also has a dream: Italy (where he imagines his father lives) for Riyad, a husband and children for Shéhérazade, becoming a dancer for Paloma, and most ambitious of all, ownership of the Caracalla thermal baths, dating from Roman times and about to be privatized, for Madame Algéria. This latter proves to be the step too far that brings about her downfall: she is confronted by the unimaginable demand that she prostitute her own son and is unmasked as the criminal she is. Emerging from three years in prison, she finds her world destroyed. Shéhérazade is now married to an Islamist and has two children (with Mina as "grandmother"); Riyad and Paloma have vanished; and her own treasured apartment has been trashed by the police. She observes in her commentary that anyone who drinks alone drinks with the Devil. But at the end of the film, drinking beer from a bottle on the street, she is in just that position, preoccupied with a new and even more impossible dream of herself as the well-loved grandmother of Riyad and Paloma's children.

Goodbye Morocco is Moknèche's first film not to be set in Algeria, but the sense of continuity in his work is stronger than the shift in locale. Once more, an archeological site plays a key part, but it is not a specifically Moroccan one. Again the focus is on a powerful woman, Dounia (played by Lubna Azabal, Gloucem in *Viva Laldjérie*), who is amoral in her drive for success. She may suffer troubles and setbacks, but she is dogged and unbreakable, ultimately indifferent to the men around her, who seem either ineffective or uncontrolled by comparison. She has already scandalized her family and lost the custody of her son thanks to her decision to live with her handsome Serbian lover, Dimitri. Together they run a development site in Tangier. The site, which is heavily protected by dogs and staffed exclusively by African workers from Ghana and Nigeria, is clearly profitable, but a collapse of the soil covering an underground tunnel reveals real potential riches: a fourth-century Coptic cemetery, presided over by a beautiful fresco depicting a woman at prayer. Dounia's plans to sell the fresco privately at a huge profit are thwarted by Gabriel, one of the workers. He has stolen a skull, thinking it would be valuable; but learning it will bring him bad luck, he tries to return it and is mauled to death by the dogs. Disposing of his body brings Dounia closer to her devoted chauffeur, Ali (played by director Faouzi Bensaïdi). They grew up together (his mother is Dounia's mother's maid), and now Ali falls totally in love with her. Failing to get the response from her he had hoped for, he beats Dimitri to death. Two people have been killed, Ali is taken to prison, Dimitri's coffin is shipped back to Europe, and the fresco has been claimed by the state, but

Dounia is seemingly unmoved. Our last sight of her is her playing contentedly with her son.

Nadir Moknèche's films offer a striking series of portraits of forceful middle-aged women, usually surrounded by female acolytes, who are driven by memories of the past and struggle to survive with dignity in the present. The world of women is depicted as neither tender nor moral, but the bonds between the women are intense, even if the expression of their mutual feelings involves angry shouting as well as exuberant laughter. Moknèche's heroines operate in a world of male power; but this is always kept in the background, and the individual men never match the women's drive or amorality. In *Paloma Delight,* we get a most striking image of the male world of money and corruption—at the Miami nightclub, where male patrons pay millions of dirhams in a competitive auction to dedicate songs to their girlfriends (a scene based on the director's personal experience). In *Goodbye Morocco,* we see a woman's basic indifference to the deaths she has inadvertently triggered. Moknèche has never been concerned about the nationality of his actresses—Carmen Maura (Madame Osmane) is Spanish, Lubna Azabal (Goucem and Dounia) is Belgian, and Aylin Prandi (Paloma) is Argentinian—but he has been able to draw consistently powerful performances from all his key players. Another strength is his use of physical contrasts between his characters (Dimitri versus Ali in *Goodbye Morocco*). While the thematic material is consistent, and it is always a death which triggers the action or brings it to its conclusion, Moknèche's taste for ever more complex narrative construction in his thriller plots has grown from film to film, leading to occasional incoherencies in the later works.

* * *

Two French-born women directors making their feature debuts after 2000—Yamina Benguigui and Karin Albou—have made a real impact. Their backgrounds and formative experiences are very different. Benguigui, who trained within the industry, was already an experienced documentary filmmaker when she made her feature debut. By contrast, Karin Albou, who had studied filmmaking formally in Paris, preceded her feature debut with two striking, independently made short films.

Yamina Benguigui, who was born in 1957 in Lille, is a self-taught filmmaker who has been making documentaries for French television since the mid-1990s. She entered politics in 2008, becoming deputy mayor of Paris, with responsibilities for human rights and the fight against discrimination. As a documentarist, Yamina Benguigui is best known for two 1990s television series, each comprising three 52-minute videos: *Women of Islam* (1994) and *Immigrants' Memories: The Maghrebian Inheritance* (1997).

Women of Islam / Femmes d'Islam (1994), made for the France 2 channel, looks at the role and status of women in Islam worldwide. Part 1, *The Veil and the Republic,* begins in Marseilles and deals largely with life in France for mi-grants from the Maghreb. The issues raised are those which will recur: the veil and women's position in society, female circumcision, and men's interpretation of Islam for their own advantage. A particular emphasis is on young Maghreb-ian women joining husbands in France in arranged marriages. Part 2, *The Veil and Fear,* begins with Algeria and considers the disillusionment of women who fought for a freedom now denied them. There is more space and opportunity for women in Egypt, and especially in Morocco, but difficulties remain. Part 3, *The Veil and Silence,* takes the filmmaker to Mali, where the discussion is about polygamy; to Indonesia, where the issue of girls' education is raised; and to Yemen, where the focus is on the burka and women's own disparate attitudes to it. In all, we are given a sweeping and thought-provoking survey of women's life worldwide under Islam.

Immigrants' Memories: The Maghrebian Inheritance / Mémoires d'immigrés, l'héritage maghrébin (1997), made for Canal+, has a similar three-part structure, this time looking successively at the three constituents of the family. It looks first of all at the fathers, the men who came initially from Algeria to work in factories, in the building trades, or on the land, sustaining a dream of return and with no thought of settling in France. Then the focus shifts to the mothers, the women who were eventually allowed to join their husbands. They expected paradise and in fact got slums and huge housing developments. They were faced with living a traditional life of arranged marriages and large numbers of children in an un-known, alien environment. Last, there are the children—the second-generation *beurs.* They speak French and accept the French way of life in a manner impos-sible for their parents. They have no memories of Algeria and so no thoughts of a return; they are French Muslims. Where their parents were cowed, they are assertive, even aggressive, in their new identity. The film employs a succession of powerful interviews from a wide range of personal experiences of immigration. The presentation of historical information and use of archive footage are excel-lent, but the real strength of this documentary, like its predecessor, is the direct personal statements by the immigrants themselves, telling their personal stories.

In the 2000s, Benguigui made a number of individual fifty-two-minute documentaries for French television, such as *The Perfumed Garden / Le jardin parfumé* (2000), *The Glass Ceiling / Le plafond de verre* (2005), and its companion piece, *The Pioneers / Les défricheurs* (2005), as well as a fictional telefilm, *Aïcha* (2009). Her full feature-length work includes a final documentary, *9.3 Memory of a Territory* (2008).

9.3 Memory of a Territory / 9-3 mémoire d'un territoire (2008) begins with footage of the Paris riots of November 2005 and includes scenes from the funeral of the two young men whose deaths triggered the violence. But the film is less an examination of the causes of this than a historical reflection—taking in a century and a half—focused on the area of Seine–Saint-Denis, which in the municipal re-organization of French departments in 1964 was given the number 93, which had previously been that of the department of Constantine in French Algeria. In the mid-nineteenth century, while Paris flourished as an elegant world capital, heavy industry began to be established to the northeast. Although the factories offered appalling working conditions and polluted the whole area, the chance of employment drew in successive waves of immigrants, first from Spain, then from those countries where the French had established their overseas rule: the West Indies, Algeria, and sub-Saharan Africa. Benguigui's film offers fascinating interviews with descendants of these very diverse groups and also traces the authorities' mostly failed attempts to deal with their housing and social needs. The last wave, as it were, comprises the thousands of young men, largely with prospects of education or work, who participated in the 2005 riots. The filmmaker's approach is distanced and detached—there is no social critique here—and the tone is resolutely upbeat: the film ends with a roll call of those who originate from this area but have gone on to have distinguished careers, including the actor Roschdy Zem and the film director Rachid Bouchareb.

Yamina Benguigui made her first and so far only feature for cinema release in 2001. *Inch'Allah Sunday / Inch'Allah dimanche* is a fictional account of many of the issues raised in her documentary *Immigrants' Memories*. The protagonist, Zouina, arrives in France, accompanied by her mother-in-law, to join her husband, who had left Algeria for France ten years before. The new life is difficult for her: the landscape is alien, the neighbors are hostile, her mother-in-law constantly tries to humiliate her, and her husband is largely hostile, beating her on the slightest pretext (for going out alone or wearing lipstick, for example). Her greatest consolation and source of knowledge is the radio, which introduces her to novel French ideas on love and sexuality. Her Sunday outings are devoted to seeking out another immigrant family with which to celebrate the festival of Aïd El Kebir. She fails in this, but by the end of the film she has managed to overcome some of her isolation and to discover a new self-assurance. It is she who will take the children to school next day. There are a few weaknesses in the acting and dramatic structure of the film, but it is a revealing and touching portrayal of the realities of immigrant life.

Karin Albou, who was born in 1968 in Paris of part Algerian descent, followed her film school training with work in television before beginning her filmmaking career. She has always been attracted to controversial subject matter. Her first seven-minute short, *Chut . . .* (1992), is a chilling study of child abuse, while her first fiction, the thirty-five-minute *Aïd El Kebir* (1998), opens with an infanticide and ends with the protagonist, Hanifa, joyfully giving birth to the child that is the result of an adulterous affair with her brother-in-law.

Albou's first feature, *Little Jerusalem / La petite Jérusalem* (2005), is set in the Parisian district of Sarcelles, given its nickname because of the predominantly Jewish population. The community, as we see, is subject to occasional racial violence but remains cohesive. The eighteen-year-old Laura lives in a strict Sephardic orthodox family, alongside her mother, her sister Mathilde, the latter's four children, and her devout brother-in-law, Ariel, who is very much the head of the family. Albou captures perfectly the domestic rituals of table manners and successive religious festivals, which shape the family's life, observing closely and capturing the minutest details but never being judgmental.

Laura's own sense of being an outsider to her background is beautifully captured early on in the film, when Albou intercuts between Ariel, putting on his full religious garb for his—inevitably solitary—morning prayers, and Laura, taking off her clothes for bed after a night of study. Her sister, Mathilde, is weighed down with domestic duties and troubled by her belief that the Torah forbids women from experiencing pleasure in sexual relationships. But after receiving counseling, she is reassured, and our last sight of her in the film is of her actively caressing her husband in bed. Laura's life follows a similar, if more dramatic, trajectory toward freedom and desire, after she falls in love with a trainee Arab journalist. Though passionate (and deeply opposed by both sets of parents), the affair does not last. But Laura has acquired a new freedom of mind through her intellectual studies. This had allowed her to contemplate a Jewish-Muslim relationship, and it now enables her to free herself and to face life alone with tranquility.

In this, Laura is following the filmmaker's own stated beliefs. Explaining her approach to filmmaking, Albou has said, "I prefer creating from my doubts than from my certainties, and perhaps freedom signifies just that for me: to be content with questioning rather than seeking answers at any price."[9] Albou has also fulfilled another of her stated aims for *Little Jerusalem,* "to leave the meaning as open as possible, so that the spectators are given space to create their own interpretations, and so that the screen becomes a mirror."[10]

Albou's second film, *The Wedding Song / Le chant des mariées* (2008), is an even more explicit film about female sexuality, full of scenes of nudity and sexual intimacy, this time set in Tunis in 1942, under the German occupation. It begins with a child's song about a bride who lacks just one thing. The song recurs throughout the film, and at the end the lack is revealed: a husband. The film is focused on two 16-year-old girls, Nour and Myriam, one Arab and the other Jewish, who have grown up as neighbors and close friends and who are now both on the point of getting married. The two girls face very different prospects in marriage.

Nour is in love with her cousin Khaled, but the wedding can only take place when he gets a job. But the only work he can obtain is for the Germans; he gradually absorbs their ideology and tries to prevent Nour from seeing Myriam.

Myriam's prospects are equally troubling, but very different. Her mother, Tita (played by Albou herself), is faced with a real problem when the Germans impose a huge fine on all Jewish residents. She solves this by, in effect, "selling" Myriam to a rich Jewish doctor in his forties, Raoul. When he decides on an "oriental" marriage, Myriam is violated according to traditional custom (and by other women) by having her pubic hair painfully removed by a hot wax treatment, which Albou shows in graphic, unrelenting close-up detail. The marriage takes place but is not consummated, as Raoul, who had thought he could remain safe by collaborating with the Germans, is nonetheless sent off for forced labor at the front, in an ominously closed railway carriage.

The focus is resolutely on Myriam and Nour, who despite all the pressures upon them remain close. The wider social and political issues are not analyzed and are important only in so far as they affect the characters. As in her earlier film, Albou concentrates with remarkable sureness on the intimate moments of her characters' lives, with the gentle closeness of the two girls being united in total opposition to male patterns of dominance, but never crossing the line into actual sexuality. For Albou, what are important are the details: "I think this is the way I see life, these little situations are very intimate. And above all, I think that art in general is all about details."[11]

For Albou and other French-born women filmmakers, the depiction of female nudity and sexuality and intimate relationships between women is totally natural. What sets Albou apart is the fact that she is part Jewish, and both her features deal with Jewish-Muslim interactions. Also distinctive is Albou's concern with adolescent girls on the verge of major changes in their lives.

* * *

Among the newcomers to feature filmmaking in the 2000s who were born in the 1950s in Algeria, three women born in Algiers but with very different backgrounds have made the greatest impact: Yamina Bachir-Chouikh, Djamila Sahraoui, and Nadia Cherabi-Labidi. All three had to work extensively for years in the media before being given the resources to direct a feature film.

Yamina Bachir-Chouikh was born in Algiers in 1954 and stayed there throughout the killings and chaos of the 1990s, working as a film editor, especially on the films of her husband, Mohamed Chouikh. *Rachida* (2002), Bachir-Chouikh's sole feature to date, is her reflection on the experience of living through Algeria's civil war. It is also, significantly, the first 35mm feature directed by an Algerian woman in Algeria, though all the production financing came from French and European sources. The film is an extremely moving study of the plight of a defenseless woman in a dysfunctional society, set during the period of Islamist unrest. The narrative is disjointed, full of little incidents—some joyous, some brutal. At one moment, for example, the classroom is magically full of bubbles blown by the children; later, toward the end of the film, it has been ransacked. Often two totally contrasting moods and incidents are cut together abruptly, thereby capturing perfectly the uncertainty of the times and the troubled spirit of the heroine.

At the beginning of the film, Rachida is a lively modern young woman, who wears lipstick, goes unveiled, and is committed to her job as a teacher. But when she is shot and wounded for refusing to plant a bomb in the school where she works, she is traumatized. Her mother takes her to a nearby village, where the headmistress has loaned them a house, hoping this will help her daughter's recovery. But reminders of the all-pervasive violence are to be found here as well. Traditional attitudes still hold sway in the village, whose inhabitants—in the absence of any visible police or military presence—have no way of protecting themselves or their property. Zohra, a girl from the village who has been kidnapped, escapes and returns through the forest. But because she has been raped and made pregnant, she is deemed to have brought shame on her whole family and is publicly rejected by her irate father. The film's climax is the long-prepared and eagerly anticipated wedding of another of the village girls. It begins joyously for all but is brutally interrupted by the band of terrorists, who kill men, women, and children indiscriminately and kidnap the bride and some of the other younger women. Rachida, who has hidden in the forest caring for an abandoned child, hears herself mentioned as a possible victim. Next day, her mother is ready to abandon the village, but Rachida recovers her courage and leads at least some of the children back into the classroom. In the film's last shot, as she begins the day's lesson, she turns and looks directly at us, the viewers.

Rachida, despite all the horrors it contains, is a quiet and restrained film. Almost all the violence occurs off camera, except for the shooting of Rachida, which provides the film with its best-known image. The wider political issues of Algeria's situation are largely ignored; the film keeps close to the immediate narrative and to its characters, observing the women respectfully and offering no overt critique of traditional values and customs. Many of the most telling moments are quiet scenes of women alone together: the women of the village welcoming Zohra by baring their heads and symbolically covering her shame with their scarves, or Rachida's mother, seated beneath a fig tree, telling her about the shame of her own divorce when her husband took another wife: "A divorcee is always a divorcee, even if she's a saint." Though often understated, the film offers a powerful and moving image of the savage times in which it is set and of the essential powerlessness of those caught up innocently in the violence. Bachir-Chouikh has succeeded in her stated aim of capturing "the confusion of ordinary citizens hitherto considered as mere statistics in the lists of statistics. A people taken hostage between so-called legitimate violence and barbaric violence, and young people without guidelines, humiliated and ready to adopt any extremes."[12]

Djamila Sahraoui, who was born in 1950 in Algiers, studied at IDHEC in Paris. She settled in France in 1975 and began her documentary career in the 1990s. After an initial fictional short, *Houria* (made in 1980, presumably as part of her studies at IDHEC), she worked as an editor and assistant director before beginning to direct her own documentaries. She first achieved prominence in the mid-1990s with a series of feature-length documentaries.

Half of Allah's Heaven / La moitié du ciel d'Allah (1995) was shot in France and Algeria and looks at the status of women in the latter country during the forty years since independence. Early images of women's role in the liberation struggle and their memories as participants are followed by accounts of how they were "put back in their place" by the post-independence FLN government, which talked of their duties as women, not their rights. The 1984 family law (*code de la famille*) is denounced as the infamy law (*code de l'infamie*) by its women opponents, who participate in the founding of a supportive organization, SOS: Femmes en Détresse. The film also deals with the growing threat to women posed by Islamic fundamentalism on its rise in the 1950s, whose ideology leads the fundamentalists to consider women as mere "breeding machines." But the determination of younger women now entering the struggle and a 1994 demonstration ("No Iran! No Sudan! An Algerian Algeria!") together allow Sahraoui to end her film on a note of hope. The film skillfully combines contemporary interview footage (much of it shot in close-up) with black-and-white archival footage and a scattering of songs. But its strength lies in the testaments of the women interviewed, all well handled, many moving, some inspiring.

Sahraoui tells us in the voice-over commentary at the beginning of *Algeria: Life in Spite of It All / Algérie, la vie quand même* (1998) that this film marked her return to her birthplace, Tazmalt, a backwater in the Kabyle mountains, after an absence of twenty years. The opening captures something of the tone of Merzak Allouache's *Omar Gatlato* twenty-two years earlier, with direct-to-camera comments by both of the protagonists—"Why is she filming us?"; "I think she must fancy us." It ends in the same vein: "Stop the camera, Bachir, that's enough." Between these two points, the film draws an affectionate portrait of two young men, of a kind known in Algeria as "hittistes" because they spend their lives propping up walls. Abdenour, Sadek, and their friends constantly complain of the tiredness caused by doing nothing all day, every day. For these two 25-year-olds, who still live with their parents, there is absolutely no prospect of a proper life or family. They are indifferent to politics and religion, and girls are an alien race, about whom they know nothing ("God created all that, and it's not for us"). To keep themselves going, they have nothing but their friendships and their sense of humor. They speculate about going abroad, to Rwanda or Ethiopia (arriving at Orly would just cause a heart attack!), but they know they are going nowhere, seemingly mocked by the trains which speed through the village without stopping. They are indifferent to the rise of fundamentalism: it would mean that they would have to pray five times a day, but as one of them observes, the government keeps them on their knees all the time now. The film is beautifully shot, excellently shaped, broken up by occasional snatches of melancholy song, and full of precise insights.

For *Algeria, Life Goes On / Algérie, la vie toujours* (2001), Sahraoui loaned a camera in October 2000 to her nephew Mourad in Tazlat, and his monthly letters to his aunt give the film its sparse voice-over commentary. Apparently, when they saw themselves on Arte television, the young people who had been filmed in *Algeria: Life in Spite of It All* realized that their district, the Cité des Martyrs, looked like a slum. As a result, they agreed to take part, unpaid or for a very minimum wage, in various projects to improve its appearance: raising money, planting trees, painting walls, and so on. As a villager himself, Mourad was able to get close to the other young men: "They know I am not a professional and that they are not taking any risks." The old people cooperated as well, expressing their views, singing, and reciting poems for the camera. *Algeria: Life in Spite of It All* unfolds entirely on a social level, with no domestic interior scenes. It captures excellently the rapport between the young men and the old women of their parents' or grandparents' generation, affectionately referred to as "aunties," whom they encounter on the streets (curiously, there are no young women to be seen in the film—presumably they are in domestic seclusion). Day-to-day life continues: Aïd El Kebir is celebrated; the old lament the lack of health care; Noureddine continues his struggle to get his car working.

Then, seemingly out of nowhere, come the first political protests. A sit-down demonstration leads to confrontation with the security forces, the killing of two protesters, and a mass turnout for the funeral of one of them, followed by calls for freedom in Algeria. Now, for the first time, the film expands its horizons to take in the wider picture of political life in Algeria, as many of the young people, along with Aunt Ouardia, take part in the mass demonstration in Algiers against President Bouteflika. Back in Tazlat, the older people sympathize with the difficulties faced by the young: no prospect of a job, constant hunger and humiliation, and at the same time, awareness of general corruption within the country. But at the end, *Algeria, Life in Spite of It All* reverts to the tone of the previous film. Two young men, with nothing to do except go out into the countryside and try to catch goldfinches to sell, indulge in the fantasy of the film turning them into film stars, hired to act alongside Jean-Claude Van Damme and Jackie Chan. It is this sense of intimacy, of young people feeling free to talk even of their most absurd fantasies, which gives the film its power to engage.

And Trees Grow in Kabylia / Et les arbres poussent en Kabylie (2003), Sahraoui's third film in the series, is essentially an eighty-six-minute extended and re-edited version of the previous fifty-two-minute film which was made for

Arte television. Most of the material to be found in *Algeria, Life Goes On* is present in the new work (though often edited into a new order), and additional material seemingly shot at the same time (2000–2001) is also included, particularly scenes set in the Cité des Martyrs during the aftermath of the initial outbreak of violence. Aspects of the previous film which are omitted include the voice-over of Mourad's letters to his aunt, which shapes and informs the previous film; the material shot in Algiers during the anti-Bouteflika riots; and the striking scene of the two young men dreaming of a career as international film stars. The only new material shot in 2003 is a single shot of the main street in the Cité des Martyrs, now with its trees flourishing, which precedes the end title: "In 2001 the riots in Kabylia led to 120 dead. In 2003 the riots in Kabylia continue. . . . And trees grow in the Cité des Martyrs."

Sahraoui made her first fictional feature, *Enough! / Barakat!* in 2005. The film is ostensibly a road movie and displays many of the narrative incoherences typical of the genre, which in general relies on a succession of often totally unexpected incidents rather than a logical, tightly plotted sequence of events. The plot, to which the filmmaker deliberately gives a vague location—"somewhere in Algeria in the 1990s"—involves the search by a young doctor, Amel (Rachida Brakni), together with an older companion, the nurse Khadidja, for her journalist husband Mourad, who has mysteriously disappeared. But we never see Mourad or learn precisely what has happened to him. Slimane, the radical Islamist leader of a group based in the mountains, whom they meet, provides no help. Indeed, although he knows Khadidja from their shared time in the resistance to the French colonizers, he still allows the two women to be treated as captured French colonizers were treated back then—being made to walk barefoot through the mountains. Slimane is a cameo role played by Mohamed Bouamari, one of the key directors of 1970s Algerian cinema, whose wife, Fettouma, plays Khadidja.

The core of the film is the growing closeness of Amel and Khadidja, which develops on their long trek back from the mountains. They represent different generations—those who fought in the resistance to the French and those born since Algeria's independence—and though initially they are far apart in their attitudes, they become virtually mother and daughter during their travels. The most striking aspect of the film is not the story line but the successive scenes showing the divisions within 1990s Algerian society. At the end it is Khadidja who passes judgment on this society, tossing the women's handgun into the sea, with a single word, "Barakat!"

Whereas *Barakat!* was largely French funded, with just a little money from Algerian television and none at all from the Ministry of Culture, Sahraoui's second fictional feature film, *Yema* (2013), was essentially an Algerian-funded film, though with some help from the Fonds Sud and scripting assistance from a couple of European festivals as well as from the Gulf. *Yema* means "mother" in Algerian Arabic, and the central focus throughout the film is on the mother, Ouardia. On one level, this is a highly personal film. Sahraoui grew up in Kabylia, and as she says, "The gestures Ouardia makes, my parents made them, and me too at a certain age. Sowing, watering while economizing with water. . . . I know all that." As for Ouardia's clothes, "I was inspired by the peasant women I knew, my mother, my aunts. What strikes me, is that they are always impeccable, as if they weren't working in the fields. They have a sort of elegance and grace. As they don't have the constraints of women in the towns, with the veil for example, they have a sort of liberty and dignity too."[13]

Yema is also a fresh look at the themes which have obsessed Sahraoui throughout her career: "There's the violence of Algeria, of its history, violence against young people, against women, the state of total despair and the question of knowing how to revive, to live, even."[14] Another very personal aspect of the film is that in addition to writing and directing the film, Sahraoui plays the leading character, Ouardia, though she had never acted before.

Though personal in so many ways, *Yema* is in no way self-indulgent. It is a sparse, pared-down film, shot at a slow pace and often from a distance, so that we observe the characters rather than being directly drawn into their actions. The narrative, too, is leisurely. The background is only gradually filled in, deaths occur off-screen, and many crucial incidents are left unexplained. The plot, however, has the simplicity of an ancient Greek tragedy. Ouardia has two sons, who grow up to hate each other, particularly as they both fall in love with the same woman, Malia. When she dies in childbirth, the identity of the child's father is uncertain, and the brothers go their separate ways.

The film opens with a long sequence of Ouardia burying her dead son Tarik, who had joined the army, in a bleak winter landscape. The crucial drama is played out between Ouardia and Ali, who has become a militant leader and whom Ouardia holds responsible for Tarik's death. Mostly they are hostile and aggressive toward each other. Ouardia, for example, withholds morphine from Ali when he is wounded, presumably to bring home to him how his brother died, without medical help, in her arms. Later Ali dies in an unexplained shooting incident, seemingly shot by a fellow militant who had to guard (or perhaps imprison?) his mother This is a bleak tale, from which Ouardia emerges indomitable. After forty days, she puts away her funeral clothes and begins to dress in the colorful clothing customarily worn by peasants in the mountains. The garden she tends so lovingly grows, and the fruit ripens. This is a tale of survival, with the newborn baby, whom she names Tarik, offering hope for the future.

Nadia Cherabi-Labidi was born in 1954 in Algiers. She studied sociology at the University of Algiers before obtaining her doctorate in cinema at the Sorbonne in Paris in 1987. While continuing her studies, she worked from 1978 as a director of production in the Algerian Film Center (CAAIC), and then from

1991 as assistant director to Ahmed Lallem at the Algerian newsreel organization (ANAF). In 1994, at a time of the liberalization of the state monopoly, she set up her own production company, Procom International. At first the company specialized in documentary and television productions, but toward the end of the 2000s it turned to 35mm feature production. The first film produced was Cherabi-Labidi's feature debut, *The Other Side of the Mirror* (2007), followed by two features made by established directors, Saïd Ould Khelifa's *Women Alive! / Vivantes! / A'ichate* (2008) and Abdellatif Ben Ammar's *Wounded Palms / Les palmiers blessés* (2010).

Before undertaking her first feature, Cherabi-Labidi made three short documentaries, of which the best known is *Fatima Amaria* (1993), which reveals some of the paradoxes of Islam. Fatima was born and lives in a tiny isolated village, Aïn Mahdi, in the Sahara, where the women are completely veiled, leaving their homes only for prayers or a visit to the *hamam*. The men are largely absent, working in the South and returning only once or twice a month. Fatima, who learned singing from her mother, performs at the local religious ceremonies of her tijany sect. But she is also allowed by the leaders of the community to have another life, outside the village. She travels to big cities—Dakar, Oran, Algiers—to perform with a (largely male) group, singing traditional songs but also *raï* and even Bob Marley songs. Here she dresses in a headscarf and jeans, makes recordings, and dreams of stardom. But always, as custom demands, she returns to her village to take up her traditional role there. Amaria states at the end of the film: "Sometimes I want to leave this place because I am suffocating, I want to be free. . . . But I will always return to the place where I was born." For Cherabi-Labidi, the lesson of the film is that "we cannot imagine modernity without referring to our cultural environment. By no means should it serve to alienate us. . . . It is good to strive for the modern—but based on one's own roots. It is possible to reconcile the two."[15]

The Other Side of the Mirror / L'envers du miroir / Wara al-mir'at (2007) began with a script written by the veteran director Sid Ali Mazif, whose feature film directing career began in 1972 and who is best known for *Leila and the Others* (1978). When Mazif became too ill to direct the film, Cherabi-Labidi took over the project and adapted the script. Initially the story is simple. Thrown out of her lodgings by an unsympathetic landlady, Selma is desperate to find a home for her newborn baby, eventually leaving it in the back of a cab driven by a car mechanic and part-time taxi driver, Kamel. Her choice could not have been more fortunate: Kamel was himself a foundling. When Kamel discovers the baby, he leaves it with his mother and sets out to find the woman who left it in his cab, but without success. Eventually he decides to adopt the child. At this point, we are told nothing about Selma's past, but we see her reduced to a life on the streets, only narrowly avoiding being forced into prostitution. Eventually, she is saved by a rich and sympathetic man, who offers her his home and the opportunity of a new life. The exact relationship between the two is never spelled out. After a chance confrontation between Kamel and Selma, Selma rediscovers her child and the truth is revealed: Selma was raped by her stepfather. There is a melodramatic confrontation between the two, in which Kamel intervenes. Despite the difficulties caused by Selma's past misfortunes, the film ends with the implication that she and Kamel will form a couple and jointly care for the child.

When discussing her film, Cherabi-Labidi has argued that the problem with Algerian cinema is not a hostile board of censors but self-censorship on the part of filmmakers. She was aware that she was tackling a sensitive subject. For her the key issue was the abandoning of the baby: "One of the major things I wanted to convey was that every child has the right to live and be respected as a human being, whatever the conditions of its birth or conception."[16] It was for this reason that she held back details of the child's origins until the end of the film. She remembers, like every Arab, watching Egyptian movies as a child, but deliberately rejected all traces of that popular style. Although she uses emotive music throughout, she tells us that she "wanted to tell a simple story, from the inside, using social not cinematic codes, putting emphasis on what is not said, delving into human reactions. For other cinemas that may appear banal, but directed at an Algerian audience, it was bold."[17] Cherabi-Labidi's boldness is emphasized in Christiane Passevant's account of the film:

> The film indeed deals with several taboo issues: rape, incest, and being an unmarried mother in a society which does not recognize single mothers. It's a film by a woman about women, their rights, their social role, their status in the family, their choices. Can women be individuals in a society ruled by a family code that, since 1984, makes them minors for life?[18]

* * *

Three French-born male filmmakers of Algerian descent, all born in the first part of the 1960s—Chad Chenouga, Lyèce Boukhitine, and Azize Kabouche—followed a similar trajectory: they studied drama in Paris, went on to work as actors, and subsequently directed two or three short films before completing, in the early 2000s, a single feature film set in France.

Chad Chenouga, who was born in 1962 in Paris, began by studying economics, then turned to drama. He studied at the Cours Florent in Paris, where he later became a teacher. He has acted in a number of French films and television dramas and made four shorts (including a first version of the subject of his feature film).

17 rue Bleue (2001) is an autobiographical study of growing up in the immigrant community, being of Algerian descent but born in Paris and never being taught Arabic (on a visit from Algeria, Granny is a linguistic as well as cultural alien). The opening scenes show the happy times of his mother, Adda, generously looked after by her rich French industrialist lover, M. Merlin, who treats both her children as if they were his own, though he is the biological father of only the second, Samir. Adda has a rich family life, with her two sisters as well as her sons. All this changes when M. Merlin dies unexpectedly of a heart attack, before he has made the will which he had promised would secure Adda's life. Adda forges the will he intended to make and goes to court against his widow, in a case which drags on for years but which Adda eventually loses. The family unit disintegrates, with Adda's elder sister, Yasmine, moving out to lead her own life and her younger sister, Leila, having an abortion and being packed off to Algeria. The two boys, now adolescents, have little life outside the home. They quarrel jealously—and at times quite violently—until Samir is taken into care as a result of his mother's illness.

The core of the film is the close (at times almost incestuous) relationship between the older son Chad and his mother, as her physical and mental health steadily decline. The film is, it seems, largely autobiographical, and its sense of authenticity is enhanced by the fact that Chenouga has not shaped his personal story into a conventional dramatic narrative. Instead, he offers a succession of individual, intimate, and often difficult scenes, separated at times by disconcerting gaps—akin to those in an album of family photographs. Although there are still moments of touching closeness between mother and son, Chad is less and less able to cope as his mother declines, and the film's ending—when he discovers her body and has to contact the police—becomes inevitable. The film is dedicated to Chenouga's brother, who was (understandably) deeply upset when the film was first shown. But he shows himself more accommodating in the discussion between the brothers which accompanies the DVD of the film, released ten years later, though maintaining that his own family memories are very different.

Lyèce Boukhitine, who was born in 1965 in Digoin, studied in Lyon as well as Paris and made a number of film appearances as an actor. His first—and to date only—feature film is *The School Mistress in a Swimming Costume / La maîtresse en maillot de bain,* made in 2001, which reunites the three-man cast of Boukhitine's first co-directed short, *A Bad Start / Faux départ* (1995). The title, more graphically described in the subtitled DVD as *Teacher in a Bikini,* refers to a small graffiti drawing on a wall done years ago by three small boys, Eric, Jean, and Karim, overwhelmed by the appearance of their teacher at a swimming lesson. The three, still friends but now all unemployed in their early thirties, are inordinately fond of the drawing (the film's action shows they have not really grown up where sex is concerned). A running joke in the film is constituted by their efforts to protect it from a council employee with orders to remove it.

The film is a light comedy of small town life, capturing the frustrations of not being able to afford a cup of coffee or buy gas for the car one of them owns. The theft by Jean of a television camera, which they hope, unsuccessfully, to sell, threatens to change their lives when it results in their obtaining footage of a burst of gang warfare. But the comic tone is maintained, as the gang of supposedly vicious thugs turn out to be surprisingly accommodating and not at all vicious toward them. For a while, they actually believe the gang will pay them a fortune for the tape, but of course this is not to be. A postscript shows their later lives. Jean, who fancied himself as a gangster, is a hotel doorman; Eric is married with a child he dotes on; and Karim is doing social work and learning Arabic (from a very attractive teacher, as the little boy sitting next to him in class comments). This is an untroubling and amiable comedy, offering a clear portrait of French provincial life but providing no particular insights in the specific lives of Muslims who form part of this community.

Azize Kabouche, who is of Kabyle descent, was born in 1960 in Lyon. He studied acting at the ENATT in the rue Blanche and at the National Conservatory. He has extensive experience as an actor in the theatre, film, and television and as a stage director. He wrote and directed two short films in the 1990s before making his feature debut with *Letters from Algeria / Lettres d'Algérie* (2002), which deals with a theatre group which bases a play on the "Letters from Algeria" column in the newspaper *Le Monde*.

* * *

Four male directors born before the 1960s also made their feature debuts in the 2000s: Mostéfa Djadjam, Kamal Dehane, Liazid Khodja, and Mohamed Lebcir. Their backgrounds are equally varied as those just discussed, though their success has been less striking.

Mostéfa Djadjam was born in 1952 in Oran and began his career as an actor, playing the lead in Merzak Allouache's *The Adventures of a Hero* (1978), which won the top prize at the Journées Cinématographiques de Carthage (JCC) in Tunis in 1978. In addition to his appearances as an actor on screen and stage, he worked as assistant director (for Werner Schroeter and Mahmoud Zemmouri) and as a scriptwriter before beginning to make his own short films and documentaries in 1982. Djadjam's sole feature to date, *Borders / Frontières* (2002), traces the progress of a very mixed group of six young Africans from Senegal to the Mediterranean coast and, as they hope, on to Europe.

They are an extremely varied group in terms of their origins and ambitions and their interactions are complex, particularly after they are joined in mid-journey by Amma, a would-be female migrant. Under the physical pressures of the journey, they develop friendships and rivalries, even the beginnings of a love affair (between Sipipi and Amma). They develop a sense of solidarity, but jealousy is not far below the surface. Their personalities emerge as they help but also betray each other. Above all, what unites them is that they become commodities, to be passed from hand to hand by their successive traffickers, always in exchange for money, unpaid work, or (in the case of Amma) sexual favors. The film begins with them already underway—on the water in a small boat at night—and the tone is set when they land, to find that the agreed-upon cost of their journey has already doubled.

Their modes of travel are varied—boat, car, refrigerated truck, cattle truck, bus, train—and they travel through a variety of landscapes—deserts and major towns—to reach the coast and the Straits of Gibraltar. But as they get separated and meet up again, it becomes clear that this is a single route used over and over by the people smugglers. Inevitably, when they make their final night crossing from Tangier, the Spanish police are lying in wait for them in armed speedboats equipped with searchlights. Three of the would-be migrants end up in Spanish custody, but Joe (who really does have a European woman in love with him and there on shore in Spain to meet him) has been drowned in the chaos of attempting to evade the Spanish police boats. *Borders* has a well-structured narrative and a nicely varied cast. If its final outcome is inevitable, the film holds one's attention through its detailed exploration of human character under pressure and the skillful handling of its varied settings. In 2009, Merzak Allouache, who had introduced Djadjam to cinema in the late 1970s, tackled an almost identical subject in *Harragas*.

Kamal Dehane, who was born in 1954 in Algiers and grew up near the Algerian Film Institute (Cinémathèque d'Alger), is a graduate of INSAS in Brussels, where he now teaches. In Belgium he found "a slightly strange cinema which didn't set up barriers between documentary and fiction," and the experience was very positive: "At INSAS I found myself and was able to express my political ideas."[19] Dehane made a series of fifty-minute documentaries during the late 1980s and 1990s. Several of these were portraits, notably *Kateb Yacine: Love and Revolution / Kateb Yacine, l'amour et la révolution* (1989) and *Assia Djebar: Between Shade and Sunshine / Assia Djebar, entre ombre et soleil* (1999). His best-known documentaries are those concerned with wider issues in Algeria after independence, such as the situation of women and the lives of children in the new Algeria.

Women of Algiers / Femmes d'Alger (1992), deals with a subject Dehane knows at first hand—it is dedicated to, among others, his seven sisters. The impulse behind the film, made when he was preparing his study of Assia Djebar, was the winning of the legislative elections by the Islamist movement:

> If they took power, the first people to be crushed would be women, as was the case in Afghanistan. I told myself I had to give a voice to other women, not

just Assia Djebar. It was a reality you couldn't ignore, even if it was risky for us. The women I filmed were full of hope, modernity, and progress, confronting a fascism which was there and which risked plunging the country into obscurantism.[20]

The documentary begins, as it will end, by intercutting between shots of Delacroix's celebrated painting, *The Women of Algiers,* and a traditional women's dance group. But after a pan across contemporary Algiers, most of the film comprises verbal testimony by a range of women (including a former militant and a radio journalist), with, occasionally, equally eloquent looks from those unable or unwilling to speak on camera. The novelist Assia Djebar talks of the tradition which makes a woman feel naked if she talks of herself and of her own ambition to give a voice to those condemned to silence. The women's comments, ranging from reminiscences of their freedom during the liberation struggle to the aggression of the contemporary male look, and including thoughts on the context of the family and the need for women's education, are interspersed with songs and scenes at a demonstration demanding greater freedom and full citizenship for women, at a historical moment when the views of Algerian Islamists were increasingly influential.

In *Algeria: Children Speak / Algérie, des enfants parlent* (1998), which was shot on video, Dehane compares his own childhood in Algeria, growing up during the war of liberation, with that of children in the 1990s as they experience firsthand the violence involved in the Islamist struggle against the Algerian government. Dehane uses the children's words to construct his plea for tolerance.

Dehane's first feature is *The Suspects / Les suspects* (2004), adapted from the novel *Les vigiles* (The watchmen), written by the Kabyle writer and journalist Tahar Djaout, who was murdered by Islamic terrorists in 1993. For Dehane, it was a return to his obsessions but with a new way of working; he gives as his example the treatment of an incident of rape: "The only problem with a documentary is that when you respect people, you cannot ask them, out of modesty, to go beyond a certain moment. It's a question of respect. But in fiction, what struck me was that I could ask the actors to perform it, because they are not revealing their own lives."[21] The official synopsis of the film reads:

> In the Algerian hospital, Samia (Nadia Kaci), a young psychologist who has studied abroad, treats and gathers testimony from former fighters in the war of independence. She hopes to write a book about the traumas left by the war. This modern young woman, who rejects the religious fundamentalism ravaging her country, and her partner are placed under surveillance and prosecuted for their nonconformism. Their opposing visions of life and of Algerian society and culture provoke differing reactions in response to the oppression.[22]

The character of Samia and the whole psychological dimension are additions by Dehane and his co-scriptwriter, Mahmoud Ben Mahmoud, to Djaout's original narrative. Olivier Barlet has noted the contemporary relevance of "this reflection on the continued integration of violence and intolerance in and after the struggle for independence"—a situation which Algerians find difficult to put behind them. He also notes that "it is not easy to convey just how far compromise has been able to eat up the country's soul."[23]

* * *

Two more directors of this generation made features that attracted comparatively little attention. **Liazid Khodja** studied film in Paris and worked in film production in Algeria before making his first feature, *The Rebel* / *L'insoumis* / *Si Mohand U M'hand* (2004), in collaboration with the editor-turned-director Rachid Benallal (whose own solo feature, *Ya ouled,* was made in 1993). **Mohamed Lebcir** worked for many years in television before completing his sole feature, *My Friend, My Sister* / *Mon amie ma soeur* (2003).

* * *

Among the Paris-based filmmakers born after 1960, one in particular stands out. **Rabah Ameur-Zaïmèche** is a self-taught filmmaker who studied sociology at university. Though born in 1966 in Algeria, his closest links are with the immigrant community in France, where he arrived at the age of two. He used his immediate family as the cast of his first feature and shot his second in his home village of Beni Zid, using a dozen or so of his relatives there to play key roles. He also played the lead role of an immigrant in each of his first three features.

Wesh Wesh—What's Happening? / *Wesh Wesh, qu'est-ce qui se passe?* (2002) is very much a family affair, with Ameur-Zaïmèche playing the leading role and another of the major parts played by his co-scriptwriter, Madjid "Madj" Benaroudj. Most of the rest of the cast are members of the director's extended family, who were given a month to rehearse, confined to an apartment at the top of one of the tower blocks. Although the film was fully scripted in advance, the script was put aside when the shooting, which was spread out over a whole year, began: "We worked by instinct, spontaneously."[24] *Wesh Wesh* is also a self-financed film, funded initially by the director and his brothers, though it later received some CNC funding under the *avance sur recettes* scheme. Shot with a Sony digital camera and subsequently transferred to 35mm, *Wesh Wesh* is set in the Cité des Bosquets, Seine–Saint-Denis, which houses a largely immigrant population, and offers clear insight into contemporary life in the Parisian *banlieue*.

The narrative traces the failure of an immigrant, Kamel, returning illegally from his expulsion to Algeria, to reintegrate himself into the *beur* community in

France. The ending is deliberately ambiguous. Kamel is chased by a policeman, who opens fire on him, but we are not told whether he is hit or whether he escapes. Almost all the action involves Kamel's family and their neighbors. While the daughter has received an education, works, and is integrated into French life, the sons, their male cousins, and their friends have no positive role. Their main occupation is avoiding police harassment. The father is a broken figure, whose dreams of returning to Algeria—very common among the first generation of Maghrebian immigrants—have come to nothing. The mother's attitudes are more complex. Still speaking only Arabic, she is very supportive of her own daughter's independence but utterly hostile to Kamel's French schoolteacher girlfriend, Irène, even though she intervenes with the police to support Kamel's younger brother when he gets into trouble. The mother dotes on her sons, doing everything for them. As Ameur-Zaïmèche points out, this typical Maghrebian treatment of sons as "little princes" goes some way toward explaining their later problems: "Once they have left the family circle, they lose this privileged status, which creates a rather strange kind of disorientation."[25]

Wesh Wesh, based on Ameur-Zaïmèche's own research into the problems of the Cité des Bosquets area, offers a convincing, up-to-the-minute account of both the parallel economy based on drugs and the multiple dissatisfactions among the young people there. On its release, the film won the Prix Louis-Delluc for best debut feature of the year.

The director's second film, *Bled Number One* (2006), which received production support from the CNC, was produced along similar lines as the first. Ameur-Zaïmèche again plays the lead and there are just two professional actors: Abel Jafri, who plays Bouzid, and Meriem Serbah, who takes the role of Louisa. The script was later modified to make use of her talent as a jazz singer. All the rest of the cast are villagers or members of the Ameur-Zaïmèche family. *Bled Number One* deals with Kamel's earlier experiences in Algeria, following his expulsion from France. Although he is warmly welcomed and invited to the local feast (the *zerda*), which involves the ritual slaughter of a bull, he finds himself unable to fit into a society where the segregation of women is unquestioned and violence constantly threatens.

A vicious attack on his beer-drinking cousin Bouzid by young Islamists rallies the community and provokes the setting up of roadblocks. But Bouzid proves himself equally violent toward his own sister, Louisa, who has left her husband and is subsequently repudiated by him. Kamel and Louisa, both increasingly ostracized, are drawn together. Louisa, after submitting to traditional "cures" and attempting suicide, finally achieves her ambition to perform as a jazz singer, but only within the confines of the psychiatric hospital in the city of Constantine. Kamel is driven back to France, where, as we know from the earlier film, he will be unable to re-integrate.

While preparing the script of the film, Ameur-Zaïmèche did not revisit his ancestral village, but instead relied on his memories of holidays there. When on location, he was not interested in current social problems concerning "the youth of today." Instead, he felt it necessary "to bring to the fore ancestral cultural practices"; for him, "getting to know our roots, knowing the practices of our country of origin" was fundamental. But he deliberately avoided political issues having to do with present-day Algeria and the legacy of the civil war (the integrationists are referred to as "desperados" in the film). Similarly, he does not see the problems encountered by Louisa as being specifically Algerian: her situation "is found everywhere in the world and has been since the dawn of time." His focus in making this film was on re-creating "an ambience, the atmosphere of the Algerian land," and in this he succeeds admirably.[26]

Last Resistance / Dernier maquis (2007) marks a return to the immigrant community in France and employs a manmade setting, the towering piles of vivid red pallets stored on the premises of a transport company, to which the formalized tracking and panning shots of the opening and closing sequences of the film are devoted. Within this stylized framework, a minimal narrative is sketched out, open to the viewer: "Everyone who views the film has every opportunity to construct the narrative line. The film's ending, for example, can be interpreted in a multitude of ways. . . . Our idea is to open up as many possible points of view as possible." A detailed dialogued script had to be written to get support from the various funding bodies which support independent filmmaking, but for Ameur-Zaïmèche this was just the beginning: "When you begin shooting, you begin by filming from a distance, and then you hurry down the hill and put yourself at the height of the people, at the height of their hearts and you discover the characters."[27] Just as the script of *Bled Number One* was reshaped to incorporate Meriem Serbah's singing talents, so too the script of this third film was reworked to make the most of the setting they discovered during preparations for the shooting.

As far as the plot is concerned, the boss, Mao, sets up a mosque for his Muslim workers, but chooses the imam himself instead of leaving the choice—as Muslim tradition demands—to the community of worshippers. This leads to divisions in the workforce but also new kinds of solidarity. Mao's motives are ambiguous—he seems both religious and manipulative—but like Ameur-Zaïmèche's earlier protagonists, he ends in failure, beaten up and face down in the mud.

Ameur-Zaïmèche has a real sense of his own independence. Although he admits to having liked filmmakers such as Renoir, Ford, and Murnau as a child, the only one of his contemporaries for whom he has real admiration is Jim Jarmusch. His own films have slow and disjointed linear narratives, with key moments (such as Kamel's shooting in *Wesh Wesh* and Louisa's beating in *Bled Number One*) taking place off-screen. For the director, his films are an extension of his university studies in sociology: "You continue to explore, to unravel social facts, structures of domination and exploitation."[28] One of his complementary strengths is his handling of domestic and intimate scenes: those involving the mother in the first film, for example, the moment when Louisa sings—in English—to Kamel in the second, or Mao musing alone in his mosque. There is great poignancy, too, in the breakaway shots from the ugly *banlieue* and the factory to beautifully framed landscape shots: the lake which is a refuge for Kamel (and the scene of his possible death) in *Wesh Wesh* and the canal with its crane viewed briefly in *Last Resistance.* The beauty of the Algerian countryside, in which Kamel cannot find his place, in *Bled Number One,* plays a similar role. The use of jazz also plays a key role in distancing and shaping the spaces within the action and in emphasizing the persistent gap between the banality of the events and the formal organization of the films' visual imagery.

For Ameur-Zaïmèche, his fourth feature, *Songs of Mandrin / Les chants de Mandrin* (2012), marks a fresh departure. Although he again plays the lead, the film looks back into French history, shedding all the director's former concerns with the contemporary immigrant community. In this sense, the director completes his assimilation into French film culture. Louis Mandrin was a celebrated outlaw and popular hero in France, executed in 1755 in Valence.

The film is a surprisingly slow-paced and lyrical account of the band of his followers, who are ostensibly smugglers but are shown mostly distributing their loot free to local villagers. They lead an idyllic life, with no tensions within the group or with the locals they encounter. They have that essential freedom which Ameur-Zaïmèche's earlier characters could hardly have dreamed of. The sense of a shared friendship uniting the group reflects, it would seem, the way in which the film was shot collectively. Ameur-Zaïmèche has revealed that the actors and crew formed a unity, so that all those behind the camera (except the director of photography, Irina Lubtchansky) also appeared as performers, with the editor playing one of the smugglers and the two soundmen featuring as soldiers.[29] The fighting depicted in the film is minimal, and without any loss on their own side, the Mandrins come out on top in their various skirmishes and confrontations with the small numbers of royal hussars sent to pursue them. Their major preoccupation is to ensure the printing of a collection of Mandrin's poems, which will perpetuate his memory. Early on, they incorporate a peddler and a wounded deserter into their group and encounter the marquis de Lévezin, who is seeking material for the book he is planning to write about Mandrin, whom he visited in prison before his execution. The film ends in the marquis's château with a recital of his poem in homage to Mandrin, accompanied by violin and electronic hurdy-gurdy and leading into a lively and uninhibited dance involving the Mandrins and local women.

*   *   *

Of the other newcomers born after 1960, two contrasting figures stand out: Lyes Salem, an actor-turned-director specializing in comedy, and Tariq Teguia, an avant-garde filmmaker whose work explores very distinctive narrative structures.

Both have close links to Paris, with Salem having studied drama there and Teguia working there as a photographer before beginning his film career. Two less innovative French-born newcomers are Mohamed Hamidi, who was born in 1972 and whose background is in theatre, and Rachid Djaïdani, born in 1974, who published three novels, before turning to filmmaking.

Lyes Salem was born in 1973 in Algiers but has lived in Paris since the age of fifteen. He followed studies of modern languages at the Sorbonne with drama training at the École du Théâtre National de Chaillot and the Conservatoire National d'Art Dramatique. He has appeared widely in theatre, television, and film, playing, among other roles, that of the shady lawyer in Moknèche's *Viva Laldjérie*.

Prior to making his first feature, Salem had made several very well received comic shorts. These include the seventeen-minute French-language monologue, *Jean-Farès* (2001), in which Salem plays a young *beur*, Driss, who is over the moon at the birth of his first child, a son. But Driss finds that problems arrive as soon as he has to phone the two sets of grandparents, his own Algerian mother and father and his French in-laws, to announce the news and try to agree on the child's name. The film is a little tour-de force, wonderfully acted and offering a small but significant insight into the problems of mixed relationships.

With *Cousins / Cousines* (2003), a thirty-minute piece shot in 35mm, he turned his attention to contemporary Algeria, tracing the return of Driss for a holiday with his family in Algiers. This intimate film (Salem used his own family to portray Driss's relatives) explores the cultural differences which separate men who have grown up in Algeria and experienced its increasing Islamization from those, like Driss, who have been shaped by life in the freer atmosphere of France. Initially Driss is warmly welcomed by his distant male relatives, as well as by his immediate family. He is astonished that men and women still dine separately. His greatest impact is on his female cousins, who find the idea of couples living together without being married inconceivable. They welcome his openness to their concerns—helping them to participate in a demonstration to protest the shooting of a woman who refuses to wear the *hijab* and taking them for an evening visit to the beach, an outing their brothers and male cousins would never consider. His greatest impact is on a distant cousin, Nedjma, whom he has not met before. His influence provokes her to a timid revolt against her sequestered existence. *Cousins* is a lively, nicely acted film which looks acutely but never judgmentally at Algerian society. It won the 2005 César Award for best short French film of the year.

Lyes Salem's first feature film, *Masquerades / Maskerades* (2008), is a gentle and lighthearted satire on life in a backward Algerian village where nothing seems to happen except the regular passing of a cavalcade of large black cars, which never stop but throw a pall of dust over the village. They belong to a clearly important local figure, "the colonel," for whom the film's protagonist, Mounir, works as a gardener (or, as he prefers to term his role, "horticultural engineer"). But we never see this representative of (presumably official) power, and indeed the film, which received backing from the Algerian Ministry of Culture, contains nothing to offend the government or to blame it for the condition of the village. A later scene, where Mounir acts as a con man—a role to which he is well suited—and acquires an ill-deserved 10,000 dinars by claiming political influence, involves only a couple of local rogues, with no hint that government officials or politicians could actually be involved. In *Masquerades,* farce blocks out any social comment.

Mounir is an amiable character, whose minor pretensions bring only the scorn of his neighbors. He is happily married, with a small son, but burdened with responsibility for his daughter, Rym, who is beautiful and bright but unfortunately falls asleep all the time (she suffers from narcolepsy). Returning drunk from town one night at midnight, Mounir awakens the village by shouting that he has arranged to marry his daughter to an improbably named Swedish-American multi-millionaire, William Vancooten. The villagers are taken in and, within days, presents and offers of services for the wedding pour in, as the rumors—in the hairdressing salon, in the café, and on the bus—take on increasingly exaggerated forms. Although Mounir assures his wife, Habiba, that he has everything under control, he is under mounting pressure to provide the groom. His problem is solved when his best friend, Khliffa, who has been in love with Rym for years (regularly sleeping outside her window so that they can talk through the shutters), awakens the villagers for a second time with the proclamation of his forthcoming marriage to Rym. A friendly but not too bright passing imam, attracted by rumors of a wedding, fulfills Khliffa's wishes by taking him and Rym through the words and gestures of the wedding ceremony, in effect marrying them. All can now end happily, with Mounir and Habiba drawn closer together and Khliffa driving off with Rym, shouting excitedly that he has cured Rym's narcolepsy, while she sleeps soundly at his side.

Masquerades is that rare event in contemporary Arab cinema: a highly enjoyable comedy, which is lightly scripted and well acted by all members of the varied cast. Whether it can bear the symbolic weight which Lyes Salem attributes to it, is, however, more doubtful. Asked about the choice of narcolepsy, Salem has said that he wanted Rym to symbolize Algeria, "the heroine of the movie . . . torn between her brother and lover: the former still clings to the past and seeks to impose his will, even if through lies. As to her lover, he is open and looks to the future with an open mind, but he is hesitant."[30]

Tariq Teguia, who was born in 1966 in Algiers, studied both philosophy and art and design before beginning work as a photographer, first in Algiers for the daily *Alger-Républicain* and then, from 1993 to 1995, in Paris. Although he studied film theory in Paris, he is self-taught as a filmmaker. His first four short works, two 16mm films and two videos, were made between 1996 and 2002. Since 2003 he has also taught the history of contemporary art at the École Supérieure des Beaux-Arts in Algiers. In his two Fonds Sud–funded features, he displays a taste for complex (if minimal) narrative structures, which is unique in Algerian filmmaking.

Rome Rather than You / Rome plutôt que vous / Roma wa la n'touma (2007) presents a vision of Algiers and its suburb La Madrague of a kind never seen before in Algerian cinema. Teguia trained and practiced as a photographer, and this is a film in which the image plays an essential role, with every shot calculated and held for its maximum duration and impact. But this is not a form of camera work which concentrates on intimate gestures or the relation of figure to landscape, but rather one which denies intimacy and shows its landscape as an empty, silent, often dark and threatening void. The film also shows numerous interiors, but often these are places on which the camera focuses not because of the significance of the action occurring there but simply because nothing is happening. The wider context is never specified precisely, but casual remarks indicate that the film looks back to the period of Algeria's civil strife, with its curfews, bombings, and mindless killings, in which the young (Kamel and Zina) are of necessity disoriented, along with everyone else.

The film's plot is minimal—a search for a person, Bosco, or more precisely for the documentation he can perhaps provide. Kamel, who has no passport, hopes this documentation will help him to establish himself abroad. But first he will have to devise a way of leaving Algeria clandestinely. Our introduction to Kamel—in a studio, having what is presumably a passport photograph taken— mocks his aspirations in the following wider shot, which frames him against some ideal dream holiday location. Kamel is sure he wants to leave but has no clear view of his destination. We first see Zina reading a Chester Himes novel, the first of a number of references to American culture, which include talk of Eldridge Cleaver and the soundtrack music of Archie Shepp and Ornette Coleman. During their first conversation, Kamel invites Zina to accompany him to Rome, but she seems unsure, only half-committed to the project. But she accompanies him on the search for Bosco.

The couple's joint trajectory is hesitant, often disrupted by seemingly random events. Some of these they spontaneously organize (a soccer match with small boys on a beach, which has no relevance to the narrative which is unfolding), while others intrude upon them unexpectedly (their arrest by the police, in a scene which parodies Algerian justice at this time). Most remarkably, their journey takes them through a labyrinthine landscape of streets, which are empty by day, most often threatening and in total darkness at night (when there is the pressure of the police curfew). The drive around La Madrague is perhaps the most striking exemplification of the void in which the action occurs, since this is less a suburb than a seemingly abandoned building site, where few of the houses are fully built and virtually none inhabited.

The couple's stifled relationship matches the void through which they travel. We often see them in shots taken from behind or showing them turned away from each other. If they are in love, they indulge in no gestures which would indicate intimacy. The final two scenes seem to indicate the death of a relationship which has never, for whatever reason, been able to assert itself. Presented with a woman's passport and a male green card for residence in the United States, which Zina has found in the kitchen of the dead Bosco, Kamel does not offer the passport to Zina. Instead he rejects it with the words "What good is that to me?" Even more enigmatic are the last images of the film. Driving away, to return to Algiers, they encounter for the first time in the film people on the street. But these are gunmen, who fire on them, fatally wounding Kamel. His last words are about listening to music, to which she replies (in a full close-up which is freeze-framed): "Cretin."

Inland / Gabbla (2008) is very much a companion piece, shot on video with a small crew and transferred to 35mm film. Again we have two disparate characters who meet up and travel together and an attempted emigration that does not finally take place. Malek is a surveyor in his forties commissioned to delineate the landscape of a remote desert region. One day, returning to his base camp, he finds a young black girl hiding there. They do not share a language and she refuses to tell him her name, but he assumes that she is trying to emigrate and begins to take her toward the Moroccan border, the natural destination for emigrants. But if she had earlier set off to try to reach Europe, she is now tired and has changed her mind. She traces quite another direction on his map, a trajectory which will take them to the heart of the uninhabited desert.

As in *Rome Rather than You* the pace is slow and very little happens: Malek is watched by a young shepherd; a group of villagers, some of them armed, come to find out who he is; the police who make a routine investigation; from a distance Malek sees a body hanging from a tree. Again, the background is as important as the figures in the foreground. It is a desert landscape, with its own inner variations and its own history, once the site of fundamentalist violence. Now only traces remain, but these the film explores with a gaze unlike that to be found elsewhere in Algerian cinema.

Mohamed Hamidi initially studied and then taught economics for ten years before becoming involved in theatre, working in particular with the actor Jamel Debbouze, who appears in his debut film alongside a newcomer, Tewfik Jallab. Hamidi had planned this first feature, *Homeland / Né quelque part,* for many years, and though it was released in 2013, it reflects none of the excitement and hope for change which followed the Arab Spring. It is, in fact, a variant on the familiar tale of the returnee. Farid, a young man of immigrant descent who was born in France, is a trainee lawyer and sees himself as essentially French; he is forced by circumstances to visit an Algeria which he does not know at all. In working to save the family house, which his father had struggled many years to build, he gets to know his extended Algerian family and the community in which they live. This much of the story reflects the director's own personal experience.

The dramatic twist in the film is that the cousin whom Farid gets to know best (who bears the same name and whose father was originally intended to be the one sent to France to help support the family) steals his passport and papers. The French-born Farid now finds himself at the mercy of an Algerian bureaucracy, which refuses to acknowledge his status as a French citizen. Driven to despair, he joins the mass of young men from the village who are planning illegal immigration to France. Almost inevitably, the group is discovered by the police in Marseilles, and only Farid is allowed to stay. *Homeland* is an agreeable dramatic comedy, which touches on two key issues: the guilt which the children of immigrants feel when they encounter their disadvantaged Algerian cousins and the desperate need of a whole generation of Algerian young men to emigrate to Europe.

Rachid Djaïdani, born into a working-class family in France, is a self-taught filmmaker, who before making his feature debut worked successively as a laborer on building sites, as a security agent on the film locations of Mathieu Kassovitz's *La haine,* and as a boxer. He played small parts in television before spending five years on tour with Peter Brook's drama company. The first of his three novels appeared in 1999. After a number of documentary films, he released his first, well-received feature, *Rengaine,* in 2012.

Rengaine—the title means literally "the same old story"—reflects Paris-born Djaïdani's own mixed parentage (an Algerian father and a Sudanese mother); it begins with a simple declaration of love between a young Algerian woman, Sabrina, and her black African (and Christian) lover, Dorcy. They have been together for a year, and now both wish to get married. The film is described on the DVD as a fairy tale (*un conte*), and this perhaps explains how it is that Sabrina has no fewer than forty brothers. When the eldest of these, Slimane, hears of the proposed marriage, he sets out to organize his brothers to oppose it. The film is not about the personal problems of the two racially disparate lovers—they have none—but about how their union is viewed by the male world. The African and Algerian men we see clearly live quite amiably in a shared community (from which white males are noticeably absent). They drink, converse, and insult each other, but basically they respect each other as well. For virtually all of them, however, the idea of a racially mixed marriage is inconceivable. Although they are living in twenty-first-century Paris, the weight of traditional beliefs and assumptions about women—their sisters in particular—still shape their thoughts and opinions.

Slimane sets out to rally his brothers, who have a whole range of different jobs—taxi driver, boxer, rap singer, mechanic, and so on—and his encounters provide the film with a series of encounters which are mostly funny, albeit almost always couched in offensive language. Meanwhile Dorcy, oblivious to all this, pursues his career as a debutant actor, failing to land a role in a production of the classical play *Cinna* but accepted for a major role in a short film shot by a young Frenchwoman. This provides the film with its most dramatic reversal. We are led to believe that Slimane has hired thugs to beat up Dorcy, and the result is a gruesome torture scene. Acted with great intensity, this is, we later discover, a scene in the short film in which Dorcy is acting—his first great screen moment—except that there is no cassette in the camera . . .

Djaïdani did not go to film school, but the credits list him as the person principally in charge of image, sound, and editing, as well as script and direction. His chosen style is to be as close as possible to his characters, using a handheld camera, even if this means disconcertingly shaky images some of the time. The editing follows the same pattern: raw and jagged, with plenty of "errors' in terms of classical continuity-style editing. The sound, too, is often difficult to understand, with passages shot silent for no apparent reason. But the personalities shine through, and the vigor of Djaïdani's approach is sustained throughout. Slimane has his own secret: a blonde Jewish girlfriend whose existence is unknown to the family. When he is confronted about this by another of his brothers, excluded from the family because of his homosexuality, Slimane realizes the error of his treatment of Sabrina, and the film ends with his apology to Dorcy.

Morocco

Throughout the 2000s, in Rabat, the Centre Cinématographique Marocain (CCM) has maintained an open and eclectic funding policy. As a result, there has been a stream of first works by older filmmakers shown at Moroccan National Film Festivals during the 2000s. Most of the ten or so to make a breakthrough had been active for many years in some sort of commercial production activity, mostly in relation to foreign films and television productions shot on location in Morocco. Among the newcomers is the largely self-taught filmmaker **Ahmed Boulane**, who was born in 1956 in Salé. He studied drama in Rabat, then began (and promptly abandoned) film studies in Italy. After returning to Morocco, he worked as an actor and as assistant on Moroccan and foreign productions. His first feature was *Ali, Rabia and the Others / Ali, Rabia et les autres* (2000). He followed this with *Satan's Angels / Les anges de Satan,* which was the top Moroccan box office success in 2007. Other former assistant directors and production managers include **Mohamed Hassani** (born in 1952), who made *Two Lakes of Tears* (2008); **Aziz Salmy** (born in 1955), who directed *Veiled Love / Amour voilé* (2008); and **Hamid Zoughi** (born in 1942), who made *Kherboucha* (2008).

The great comic actor **Bachir Skiredj** (born in 1939), a major star in both Moroccan theatre and cinema and best known internationally for his leading role in Mohamed Abderrahman Tazi's *Looking for My Wife's Husband* (1993), made his directing debut at the age of sixty-eight with *Once upon a Time, Twice upon a Time / Il était une fois, il était deux fois* (2007). Others turned to film directing after successful careers in other media. **Mohamed Zineddaine** (born in 1957) had worked as a photographer before turning to filmmaking in the 1990s and directing two features after 2000: *Awakening / Le réveil* (2003) and *Do You Remember Adil? / Tu te souviens d'Adil?* (2008). **Lahcen Zinoun** (born in 1944) had already established himself as a choreographer in theatre and cinema and collaborated with Martin Scorsese (on *The Last Temptation of Christ*) and Bernardo Bertolucci (on *The Sheltering Sky*) when he directed his first feature, *Scattered Beauty / La beauté éparpillée* (2006).

* * *

Key contributions from this group of older filmmakers were made by two Moroccan filmmakers, both of whom studied and trained abroad: Mohamed Asli, whose links are with Italy, and Abdelhaï Laraki, who studied in Paris. Their subsequent work as feature filmmakers in Morocco shows clearly those formative influences.

Mohamed Asli, who was born in 1957 in Casablanca, trained in Italy, where he worked on numerous documentaries and telefilms. On his return to Morocco, he founded the Kanzaman studios in Ouazzarte and a film training center in collaboration with Cinecittà and the Luce Institute. There are genuine echoes of neorealism in Asli's first feature, *In Casablanca Angels No Longer Fly / À Casablanca les anges ne volent pas* (2004), since he had worked for some years in Italian documentary production and used an Italian production crew to shoot his first feature. At times, it explicitly recalls the theories developed by Cesare Zavattini after his period of collaboration with Vittorio De Sica. The film is focused on adult poverty, describing the lives of three Berber waiters who are trying to make a living in Casablanca. The central story, with which the film opens and closes, is that of Saïd, who has been forced to leave the Atlas Mountains to find a way to support his family. The move has been made against the wishes of his wife, who sees Casablanca as a devourer of people which is holding him prisoner. The working conditions are appalling; the café owner regards them as riffraff and refuses Saïd permission to leave, even when his wife is about to give birth. His fellow waiters have equally strong but very different obsessions. Ottman, remembering the proudest moment of his childhood—riding with the men of the village in a fantasia—longs for his magnificent stallion, for which he sends home sacks of stale bread. Ismail, in contrast, falls in love with a pair of boots he sees in a shop window. They cost three months' salary, but he imagines that if he wears them they will totally transform his life.

All three realize their dreams, which turn out to be nightmares. Ismail buys the boots, but a succession of tiny comic misfortunes (worthy of Zavattini) show him that they are completely impractical in Casablanca, and he ends up wearing them wrapped up in black trash bags. Ottman saves his horse and rides it proudly into Casablanca. But the noise and chaos of the city cause it to throw him and bolt, vanishing into the traffic and leaving him devastated. Saïd's fate is tragic. When he does get to the village, he finds his wife gravely ill after giving birth. He tries to get her to the hospital, but she dies on the way, whereupon he is thrown out of the taxi and left by the roadside, where passing motorists, fearful of the consequences, refuse to help him. Only an old man with a mule is willing to give assistance. This instance of freely given aid is virtually the only such act in the whole film. It is not angels which fly over Casablanca but vultures, which circle the city and its highways. Throughout the film, while emphasizing the harshness of their existence, Asli shows great sympathy for his protagonists' lives, dreams, and defeats and weaves their tales together beautifully. The film deservedly won the top prize (the *Tanit d'or*) at the Journées Cinématographiques de Carthage in Tunis in 2004.

Abdelhaï Laraki, who was born in 1949 in Fez, studied filmmaking at the École Louis Lumière and film history at the Sorbonne in Paris. Although he only made his feature filmmaking debut in 2001, Laraki belongs, in terms of age, to the generation which dominated Moroccan cinema in the 1990s. He shares the concern of such contemporaries as Jilali Ferhati and Abdelkader Lagtaâ to bring to light the darker aspects of Morocco's past under Hassan II (a preoccupation shared by few of the other, mostly younger filmmakers making their debuts in the 2000s).

Laraki produced *Mona Saber,* a French-language film, as his debut work in 2001. It traces the search of a young Frenchwoman, Mona, for the Moroccan father she never knew she had. Armed only with an old photograph and a letter, she sets off to an unknown Morocco, to be confronted with an official denial of her father's existence, as well as a mystical encounter with the forces of ancient traditional Morocco. Finally she finds peace with the families of others who, like her father, were tortured and murdered in the infamous prison of Derb Moulay Cherif under the rule of Hassan II.

Laraki has since completed a second feature, *The Scent of the Sea / Parfum de mer / Rih al-bahr* (2007), based on an actual incident in 2003. In his statement of intent, Laraki states:

> [The film] is a black social drama, set, on the one hand, in the traditional, artisanal world of the ordinary fishermen from the medina, the old city, and,

on the other, in the urban world of petty drug smugglers installed in the "new city." Two cultures, two communities, which live alongside each other and ignore each other, according to an order and its principles: the results of a social and economic equilibrium. The film tells how this equilibrium is broken in a chance, violent, and irremediable collision between these two worlds and shows how an opening to modernity can be made without alienation and archaism can be renounced without, at the same time, renouncing true values.[31]

* * *

Nabil Ayouch is both one of the first of the Maghrebian directors born after 1960 to be able to make a feature debut in the late 1990s and also the Moroccan filmmaker with the widest range of output: two thrillers, two realistic studies of street children, an English-language musical, and a very personal feature-length documentary. Undoubtedly, the diversity of his filmmaking stems, in part, from his complex background. He was born in Paris in 1969, and, as his documentary *My Land* reveals, he is of mixed Muslim and Jewish descent. He was brought up in France and has French nationality. Though self-taught as a filmmaker, he studied drama in Paris but later took up residence in Morocco, where he set up his production base, Ali'n Productions. He began his career making commercials and, for his entry into fictional filmmaking, used the structures of support and funding provided by the CCM (the Centre Cinématographique Marocain). He first came to international attention with three short fictional films in the early 1990s, the best known of which is the first, *The Blue Stones of the Desert / Les pierres bleus du désert* (1992). He has since used his position as one of Morocco's leading filmmakers to act as producer for some of his contemporaries and also to foster filmmaking by younger Moroccan filmmakers.

Ayouch began his feature film career with a fairly conventional thriller, *Mektoub* (1997), which, perhaps because it confronted the issue of corruption, proved remarkably successful with Moroccan audiences. When an eye surgeon, Taoufik, falls ill on a visit to Tangier, his wife, Sophia, is seized and subjected to a form of ritualized rape by some of the rich and powerful of the city. Taoufik's response leads only to further violence and killings, including that of his policeman brother-in-law. But despite all that they have endured, Taoufik and Sophia are able to rediscover themselves and their relationship through a flight to find redemption in the South.

Ayouch's second feature, *Ali Zaoua / Ali Zaoua, prince de la rue* (1999), a dark study of three Casablancan street children, is a far more substantial work that recalls both Italian neorealism and the Luis Buñuel of *Los olvidados*. In more local terms, it also marks a further stage in the development of a specifically Moroccan style of realist filmmaking, which grew to prominence from the 1970s to the early 1990s. The film opens with a disconcerting sequence reflecting Ayouch's own first experience during the months in which he researched the film with a video camera and thereby discovered the dreams, as well as the actual lives, of urban street children. In what turns out to be a television news item, we hear the fifteen-year-old Ali talking about his dream of an island with two suns, his ambition to become a sailor, and his fantasy about being "Ali Steel Teeth," who can pull cars with his teeth and who has left home because his mother is planning to sell his eyes. The children in the film are all played by genuine orphans and abandoned children, and Ayouch worked closely throughout with the professionals concerned with Casablanca's actual street children. Although the children contributed enormously to the film through their performances and though certain scenes were improvised, the film is fictional. The overall structure was pre-scripted by Ayouch and Nathalie Saugeon, with the assistance of another French writer, Philippe Lamblin, with Arab adaptation and dialogue by the Moroccan dramatist Youssef Fadel (who had worked in the same capacity on *Mektoub*).

An interplay between dream and reality is fundamental to the film's overall structure, in which animated sequences of children's drawings, illustrating Ali's dream island with two suns, constantly recur. Ali himself is killed in a confrontation with a gang led by the evil, if slow-witted, Dib (played by one of the film's few professional actors, Saïd Taghmaouï, star of Mathieu Kassovitz's celebrated study of the Parisian *banlieue, La haine*). But his three younger companions, Kwita, Omar, and Boubker, determine to keep Ali's memory alive. The trio's efforts to give a worthy burial to their "prince"—hindered by the disorder in their lives caused by constant glue sniffing—form the core of the film, and the performances Ayouch extracts from the three young non-professionals are never less than compelling. We come to learn their strengths (sticking to their task), their weaknesses (bullying those weaker than themselves), and their own dreams of love and affection (constantly inventing non-existent families).

The children are treated kindly within the narrative, but no attempt is made to disguise either the total waste these lives represent or the moments of real nastiness to which they are driven by the world as they encounter it. There is no way that they can carry out their self-imposed task, and ultimately adults need to intervene to enlighten and assist them. This ending undoubtedly softens the film's impact, since, unlike the children, these adults are sentimentalized figures. Ali's mother reveals the source of Ali's story of the island with two suns: it was a fairy tale on the tape she used to help get him to sleep. But the mother herself (played by the director's sister, the actress Amal Ayouch) is a very beautiful and romanticized whore, seemingly untouched by the reality of her life. The fisherman Hamid, for whom Ali had longed to work and who arranges his burial at sea, resulting in the discomfiture of Dib's gang, is a deus ex machina, whose actions have no narrative motivation.

Nonetheless, *Ali Zaoua* offers a very powerful and lucid personal view of the poverty and deprivation—but also the dreams—to be found on the streets of Casablanca. Ayouch's combination of thorough research and sensitive use of young non-professionals with careful script writing and a very conscious shaping of the plot gives *Ali Zaoua* its particular power. This is no detached documentary about poverty as seen from afar, but a fictional *auteur* film, which succeeds in achieving authenticity through its closeness to its subject. The characters are not simply helpless victims; they have their histories, failings, and dreams, and they can therefore engage us emotionally as spectators, despite the fact that they have—in Nouri Bouzid's memorable phrase—defeat as destiny. *Ali Zaoua* became the second most popular Moroccan film ever at the box office and won the top prize (the Étalon de Yennenga) at the Pan-African film festival FESPACO at Ougadougou in 2001.[32]

Ayouch returned to the thriller genre with *One Minute of Sunshine Less / Une minute de soleil en moins* (2002), the plot of which is triggered by the killing of a dissolute young drug dealer in Tangier. This is a gang killing, organized by the man's uncle, but suspicion falls on Touria, the victim's servant and mistress. The crime is investigated by a young police inspector, Kamal Raoui, who leads a solitary life and whose closest friend is a transvestite dancer. Kamal takes care of Touria and her seriously ill younger brother Pipo (played by Hicham Moussoune, one of the young boys in *Ali Zaoua*). The pair embark on an affair, which is depicted very frankly, with a great deal of very French-style explicit nudity. For a time, Kamal's life is transformed, but the relationship is always precarious, and it comes to an end when Touria and her brother are both shot down by the original killer. Kamal is very much a conventional screen detective, taciturn and morose, and hence not generating much emotional involvement. But as a whole, *One Minute of Sunshine Less* is well paced, skillfully directed, driven by a throbbing soundtrack, and full of striking, if sometimes flashy, editing devices (there is even a moment of fantasy to recall *Ali Zaoua,* when Kamal's car is shown flying in a pinkish-orange sky).

On one level, Ayouch's move toward Hollywood-style, commercially oriented moviemaking is concluded with his English-language musical, *Whatever Lola Wants* (2007), a simple Cinderella story, shot in English but with a French crew and an international cast. On another level, as he admits in the film's pressbook, the film is motivated by deeply personal questions about his own identity. He admits to having always "run after his roots" during his childhood and to experiencing a sense of "floating" owing to his lack of roots. He had a profound sense of being simultaneously both Eastern and Western. These personal questions, hidden at the beginning of Ayouch's career, no doubt explain the way in which he could identify so profoundly with the disturbed children of *Ali Zaoua.* They are explored openly in his subsequent feature-length documentary, *My Land.*

The issue of moving from one culture to another is reinforced in *Whatever Lola Wants* by the decision to cast an actress, Laura Ramsey, who could neither sing nor dance and who had in fact never taken dancing lessons. As a result, she had to undergo four months of intensive daily training in both modern jazz dance and oriental dance. Curiously, Carmen Lebbos, who was cast as Lola's teacher, Isfahan, is also a non-dancer. The tango she dances with Lola in the garden, which marks Isfahan's emergence from solitude, had a particular poignancy for her, because her own late father was a teacher of tango who had always wanted to teach her, requests she had always refused. The problem of rendering the film's title song was solved by the choice of a singer whose own origins mirror those of the director. Natacha Atlas was born in Belgium to an Egyptian father and English mother and brought up in Brussels, Egypt, Greece, and England. It is her recording of *I Put a Spell on You, Because You're Mine* which Elia Suleiman uses in his eye-to-eye confrontation with an Israeli settler in *Divine Intervention*.

Lola is a twenty-five-year-old postal worker (like her father and brothers) who vainly aspires to succeed as a dancer in New York. Her life is transformed by two key moments. She is introduced by her gay Arab friend Youssef to oriental dance through a tape of the legendary star Isfahan; and a disastrous attempt at dancing in the restaurant where Youssef works introduces her to a handsome Egyptian, Zack, with whom she has a passionate (but discreetly shot) three-week affair. The combination of these two events impels her to set off for Cairo, where she seeks out Zack (who has reverted from free-living US MBA student to dutiful Egyptian middle-class son) and the dancer Isfahan. The latter now lives in seclusion after a scandal which brought her career to an end.

The aim throughout *Whatever Lola Wants* is to please the audience, with tales of failed love interspersed with dance and song routines. Despite Ayouch's own preoccupations, there is no attempt in the film to explore in any meaningful way the cultural gulf between American and Egyptian cultural attitudes. Instead, differences are simply turned into jokes: "When a Westerner falls in love, he marries the woman. When an Arab falls in love, he marries someone else" (in this case, his second cousin). The totally unprepared Lola is never shown to be seriously in danger when she explores, alone, the streets and nightclubs of Cairo. The rifts and jealousies between her and her fellow (Egyptian) dancers are rapidly turned into smiling friendships. Lola herself rises with incredible speed to Egyptian stardom. The message is clear: if you are blond, strive hard enough, and keep believing in yourself, everything is possible. At the end, all is neatly resolved. Lola can return to New York as a star, after confronting her ex-lover and publicly acknowledging her debt to her teacher. Isfahan is (for one night at least) rehabilitated by an applauding audience and reunited the next day with the lover who had previously failed her. *Whatever Lola Wants* is a thoroughly professional product, slickly directed and making good use, in its set-piece numbers, of the considerable production resources provided by the producers, Pathé. The performance of Laura Ramsey is spirited; she captures convincingly the combination of drive and naiveté which both brings Isfahan out of seclusion and establishes a real bond with Isfahan's five-year-old daughter, Reem. This role is played by Ayouch's own daughter, and what we see on screen reflects a real personal relationship, as Ramsey helped the young girl relax into a role she sometimes found daunting.[33] There are also some nice filmic allusions: a clip from *The Red Shoes* and a manservant to recall Erich von Stroheim's role in *Sunset Boulevard.*

Ayouch's most unexpected film, *My Land* (2010), is a feature-length documentary which stems from his hitherto little-known personal situation, which he explains in the opening words of the film: "Born in France of a Moroccan Muslim father and a Tunisian Jewish mother, I always suffered from the conflict which resonated within my two families." His way of confronting this problem in *My Land* is to film the testimony of those Arabs, now mostly in their seventies and eighties and living in Lebanese refugee camps, who still remember vividly the Nakba, their 1948 expulsion from their homes in what is now northern Israel. This material Ayouch then presents to a range of Jewish Israeli citizens, mostly young people in their twenties, who were born and now live in settlements established on the site of former Arab villages.

The testimonies of the Arab men and women are consistent with those of all the other Arabs of their generation interviewed in dozens of documentaries. They tell of the totally unexpected intrusion of armed Israelis into their villages, which, as unarmed farmers, they had no way of combating. They talk of atrocities, terror, and flight, of leaving behind everything they owned. But the memory of what they left is vivid, even after fifty or more years: precise locations, homes, space, trees, plants, fields, olive groves—contrasting so poignantly with the squalid present-day reality of an overcrowded refugee camp. None of the young Israeli Jews included in the film refuse to look at the testimonies of the Arabs who preceded them in the occupancy of northern Israel. But their initial comments show the extent to which they have absorbed, during their schooling, the dominant Zionist message: "They lost, so why are they complaining?" or "They left, why do they expect to come back?" With the passing of the years, these young people, born and brought up within the boundaries of Israel, have developed their own personal, undeniable links with the land which once belonged to Palestinian Arabs. Some are indifferent to the Arab testimony, some are moved by it, but none can offer even the beginnings of a way forward.

With *Horses of God / Les chevaux de dieu* (2012), Ayouch returned to fiction and to the bleak urban world of slum children which he had explored in his most successful feature, *Ali Zaoua*. The film's title refers to the term used by Islamists to designate those they regard as martyrs, and the film is inspired by the five suicide bombings which took place almost simultaneously in Casablanca on May 16,

2003. Of the forty-five dead, twelve were bombers brought up in the slums of Sidi Moumen. Ayouch carried out months of research there, drawing on the experiences of local social workers (as in *Ali Zaoua*) and choosing his non-professional cast from among Sidi Moumen residents.

In narrative terms, *Horses of God* is very straightforward, unfolding chronologically, with four sections set in 1994, 1999 (the year of Hassan II's death), 2001 (when the Twin Towers were attacked), and finally in 2003. What is striking stylistically is the counterpoint between the repeated overhead image of Sidi Moumen as "an open-air prison" and the close-in images of the four main protagonists themselves. The startling overhead shot was taken using a Belgian technical innovation, a camera strapped to a two-meter-wide helicopter "drone" able to fly just above rooftop level.[34] Equally striking (though easier to obtain) are the intimate images of the central characters as they make their progress from slum kids to suicide bombers. Typical of the detail which Ayouch obtains are the shots of the group just prior to the attack: the shared joy and amazement at seeing the big city for the very first time and then their reversion to childhood, as they splash in a stream and play an improvised game of soccer during their wait in the mountains.

In 1994, Hamid is already a streetwise kid of thirteen, fearless and violent, who participates fully in the vulgar abuse and vicious sexual bullying which characterize life in Sidi Moumen. Even the game of soccer, with which the film opens and which serves as a symbol of some sort of a different life, degenerates into a brawl. Hamid is constantly concerned with his more timid ten-year-old brother, Tarek, who calls himself Yashine because his idol is the Russian goalkeeper Lev Yashin. Home life is difficult, money has to be made scouring garbage dumps, education is non-existent, and the police are corrupt. When the narrative resumes in 1999, the boys are now adolescents, still part of a gang culture where the younger and weaker members are regularly taunted and beaten. Hamid, wanting as ever to stand out, shows off by throwing a stone at a police car. Inevitably, he is arrested and sentenced to two years in jail, leaving behind Yashine, who fares badly in his absence.

When Hamid returns, he is a changed man, having been converted to radical Islam in prison. The Islamists now form a separate force in the community, unafraid of police violence and with their own strict codes of behavior. Hamid enrolls Yashine and two of their friends in the Islamist group, and the film traces how they are steadily drawn away from their families and former concerns (a typical moment being when Yashine is separated from his treasured photograph of the Russian goalkeeper as they prepare for the attack). Their appearance, as well as their behavior, changes, as the Islamist group of "friends" begin to constitute their new family, with the men eating, sleeping, and praying together. After Hamid, Yashine, and their two friends have been told that they have been chosen to become martyrs, the training is intensified and so are the tensions within the group, with Hamid showing his first signs of hesitation. At the moment of the assault on a Spanish tourist hotel, after their two friends have dropped out, it is Yashine who now emerges, for the first time, as his brother's leader.

Horses of God is a powerful study of an endlessly perplexing issue: what makes a young man become a suicide bomber? As Ayouch has made clear, "the film doesn't judge, it simply shows."[35] In the case of Hamid, who is violent as a child and always wants to stand out from his contemporaries, there is a logic in his development. His prison conversion gives him a new focus for his energies, but interestingly, he is the one who, at the end, begins to hesitate. The case of Yashine is more fascinating. Always timid and fearful as a child and growing up under his brother's domination, conversion allows him to realize himself in a new way and find a confidence he has always lacked.

Although Ayouch usually works with a script collaborator, he always originates his own work. Yet it is impossible to define a typical Ayouch protagonist or find a consistent set of thematic concerns. The key to his approach is constant innovation, exploring the possibilities of differing genres and facing fresh technical challenges. His comments on the overhead helicopter shots of Sidi Moumen spell this out most clearly:

> It took us eight hours to complete this shot. It was the most complicated in all the film. I'm really pleased to talk about it, as it is for shots like this that you struggle to make films, for this magic you can seize at the moment of shooting.[36]

* * *

Two French-born Moroccan filmmakers, Zakia Tahiri and Nabil Ben Yadir, both started out as actors, but their debut features could hardly be more different.

Zakia Tahiri, who was born in 1963 in Lille of Moroccan descent, was taken by her parents at the age of three months to Casablanca, where she spent her childhood. She returned to France at the age of seventeen, first to study drama and then filmmaking in Paris. In France she worked in a variety of production roles and back in Morocco appeared in films by directors as significant as Farida Benlyazid and Mohamed Abderrahman Tazi. Subsequently, in Paris, she collaborated (under her married name) with her husband, Ahmed Bouchaâla, on two features, *Krim* and *Control of Origin*. For the first she is credited as co-scriptwriter, while for the second she was co-director. The couple also together co-scripted Abdelhaï Laraki's debut feature, *Mona Saber* (2001). It was in Morocco that Tahiri was able to make her first solo feature as writer-director, *Number One* with her husband as co-producer. The film, a light comedy on relationships between the sexes, was second in the box office listings for Moroccan features in 2008.

The starting point of *Number One* is ostensibly the Moudawana, the Moroccan family code, revised in 2004 to give new rights to women (including that of being able to sue for divorce). But this code, the film's opening title tells us, is little known and seldom used. Here in the film it is, in fact, mentioned only in passing, since the film's plot actually turns on a magic spell cast by a wife, Soraya, on her domineering husband, Aziz, who is a petty tyrant both at home and at work. Aziz's problems begin when he and his wife are invited out to dinner by a female French clothing distributor, Mlle. Morel, who has come with an order for eighty thousand pairs of jeans. He has never taken his wife out to a restaurant before, frets about how she should dress, and tells her to watch other diners and behave as they do. She takes her cue from an amorous French couple at the next table, hence drinking wine and smoking, while making up a totally fictitious account of her life. The inevitable row back home forces Soraya to act and cast her spell.

Overnight, Aziz finds himself transformed into a caring, feminized person, cooing over babies, sympathetic to his workers' child care needs, and eager for his wife to take on a Westernized existence (a fresh hairdo, new clothes, and even a personal bank account). He finds himself helping old ladies up the stairs, hanging out the washing, and even trying his hand at cooking. His new attitude upsets the lives of his friends, whose chauvinistic attitudes are exposed and who find their wives now demanding that they behave like Aziz. The peak of this new identity crisis comes when Aziz is chosen as "man of the year" by a women's magazine. But all ends well. The spell is lifted, and Aziz can resume his former life, but with a new personality. He is now a caring husband and manager, and in the film's final, jolly ending, the workers welcome him back.

Arab audiences are starved for domestically produced comedy, and one can understand the popularity of this well-acted, if loosely structured, film. Situations of women transgressing (if only in the eyes of their dominant males) and, especially, of men taking on traditional female roles and duties cannot fail to be amusing for audiences whose own lives are still so strongly shaped by tradition. For Tahiri, Aziz's story represents that of a country undergoing change, but the fact that the film's plot turns on magic rather than on the emerging self-awareness of a new generation of women limits its relevance as a social document. Much more significant is the fact that here in *Number One* we have a woman film director capturing the mood of a popular audience in her debut feature.

The Belgian-born actor, **Nabil Ben Yadir**, who was one of the leading players in Mourad Boucif's *Beyond Gibraltar,* made his own first feature, *Barons / Les barons,* in 2010. The self-styled "barons" of the title are anything but that—a trio of layabouts of Maghrebian descent who live on benefits and by faking car accidents in Brussels. They acquire a big car to reflect their assumed status. The focus is on one of their number, Hassan, who has aspirations to leave this milieu and create a real life for himself as a stand-up comedian. He has a role model in Malika, the sister of his friend Mounir, who has become a television newscaster. But instead, Hassan gets a job as a bus driver and allows himself to be pushed into an arranged marriage (which his friends gleefully sabotage). During the early scenes, the film is structured as a light comedy, and there are plenty of indications of Ben Yadir's actorly concern with performance: asides to camera; a fluidity in moving from the real to the imaginary (as when Hassan revisits his childhood). The film has a clear autobiographical tone, since it so evidently reflects the director's own formative experiences. Throughout, the tensions are not between immigrants and the host nation but between first- and second-generation immigrants, with the latter showing no ability to live up to the traditional values of their elders nor to create real lives for themselves in the wider community.

As the film progresses, the mood darkens. Hassan is savagely beaten up by Mounir (for breaking the gang's rules and getting involved with Malika without permission), only for Mounir himself to be killed in an accident. The film's ending is open. There is no indication that Hassan himself will succeed in leaving the immigrant ghetto which still mentally imprisons him, but the remaining "barons" get a new recruit in the form of their perpetual hanger-on, the Belgian Franck, who designates himself Baron Number One.

Ben Yadir followed this debut film with a more ambitious piece, *The March / La marche* (2013), for which he assembled a very strong cast, including many of the leading young actors of Maghrebian origin working in France. Although the scriptwriter, Nadia Lakhdar, apparently began work on the script in the mid-2000s, it captures excellently the post-2011 mood in its tale of a largely forgotten peaceful march against racism and police violence in 1983 (when the director was just four). The march involved thirty or so young second-generation immigrants, most of them from the Lyon suburb of Minguette, who set out on foot from Marseilles to make their way to Paris, where they were greeted by a welcoming crowd of around 100,000 people. Although many of the participants are still alive, this is not a documentary but a fictional rendering of the events, with the participants renamed. The actual initiator of the march, the twenty-year-old Toumi Djaidja, was hailed as a Gandhi figure by the press at the time, and Ben Yadir maintains that the march was inspired by Richard Attenborough's film *Gandhi:* "I thought it just and indispensable to bring it back to the cinema, since it began there."[37] This is a version of events, however, that is denied, by Djaidja, who has stated that "it was not the film on Gandhi which created the idea of the march. It was a bullet I received when I tried to help a young man who was being attacked by a police dog."[38]

* * *

Every two years in the early 2000s, the Moroccan National Film Festival screened ten or a dozen new feature films, and much of this output was by young filmmakers born in the 1960s and 1970s. In place of the commercial filmmaking experience of their elders, they often brought formal film qualifications obtained in Paris. There is undoubtedly work of real quality here, but since it receives virtually no international distribution, there is no way of assessing it from outside Morocco. Newcomers in 2002 include **Kamal Kamal** (born in 1961), who studied at CLCF in Paris and worked in television and on video commercials before making *Tayf Nizar* (2002) and *Moroccan Symphony / Symphonie marocaine* (2004). The veteran Hakim Noury's commercial success with his comedy *She Is Diabetic and Hypertensive and She Refuses to Die* (2000) was equaled by the two features of another 2000s newcomer, **Saïd Naciri** (born in 1960), with his own hit comedies *The Bandits / Les bandits* (2004) and *Abdou with the Almohades / Abdou chez les Almohades* (2006), both of which topped the Moroccan box office chart. The year 2006 brought two additional newcomers. **Hamid Faridi** (born in 1968), who had studied journalism in Rabat, worked in advertising and published a first novel. His first feature film, *The Bike / Le vélo* appeared in 2006. A recruit from television, **Mohamed Ali El Mejoub** (born in 1968), who had studied film at ESEC in Paris, presented *The White Wave / La vague blanche* (2006).

New filmmakers also emerged at the 2008 festival. **Mohamed Chrif Tribeck** (born in 1971) developed his interest in film through the Moroccan film club movement and went on to study at FEMIS in Paris. He initially worked in television and made short films before receiving funding from the Fonds Sud for *The Time of Comrades / Le temps des camarades* (2008). **Yassine Fenane** (born in 1978 in Rabat), who had studied drama in Paris and worked extensively in Moroccan television, showed *Skeleton / Squelette* (2008). Two new women filmmakers appeared in 2008.

Aicham Losri studied film and made the first of her four short films in 2002. She also made numerous commercials before directing two feature films, *The Iron Bone / L'os de fer* (2007) and *People of the Clock / Le peuple de l'horloge* (2007). **Stéphanie Duvivier** (born in 1974 and possessing Moroccan citizenship despite her name) studied filmmaking at Université de Paris VIII and at ESRA and worked as assistant director on a number of productions before completing a first feature film, *A Thriller / Un roman policier* (2008). **Hassan Rhanja** made *Argana* (2007), and **Ziad Ahmed** made *Real Premonition* (2007).

Yet another new wave of young directors emerged at the 2010 National Film Festival. **Hicham Alhayat**, who was born in 1974 in Marrakesh, studied at ESAD in Geneva and now has Swiss nationality. His first feature was *Punishment / Châtiment* (2010). **Mohamed Ahed Bensouda** (born in 1969 in Tétouan) studied filmmaking at the Sorbonne and in Canada. He worked widely in film production and television before making his first feature, *The Story of a Mchaouchi Wrestler / Histoire d'un luteur Mchaouchi* (2010). **Mohamed Lyounsi** (born in 1966 in Fez) worked in film, radio, televison, and the theatre before completing his first feature, *Hello 15 / Allo 15* (2010). **Ismaël Saidi** was born in 1974 in Belgium, where he studied at the Free University of Brussels and the Catholic University of Louvain. He worked for ten years as a police inspector. His first feature film is *Ahmed Gassiaux* (2010). **Mohamed Mouftakir** made his feature debut with *Pégase* (2010).

* * *

In general, the key innovations in Moroccan cinema of the 2000s tend to be less stylistic and more in terms of the widening of access and opportunity for filmmakers, as the range of newcomers shows. There are three major areas from which new voices have emerged: filmmakers from the Berber community express their concerns in their own language; Moroccan-born filmmakers, born to emigrant families abroad or residing there for decades, make films describing their particular experiences; and a new and forceful generation of women filmmakers achieve a new prominence.

As far as Berber filmmakers are concerned, a significant contribution to the development in Moroccan cinema was made by **Mohamed Mernich** (born in 1951), one of the founders of Berber (Amazigh-language) cinema in Morocco, who followed twenty or so short films, mostly shot on video from 1992 onward, with two feature films, *Tilila* (2006) and *Tamazighte Ouflla* (2008). He was backed up by one of the younger generation, **Badr Abdelilah** (born in 1963), whose *Bouksasse Boutfounaste* (2006) continued the breakthrough.

As is the case with other Arab countries, many of Morocco's filmmakers were trained, live, and often work abroad. The films by the younger filmmakers of the 2000s often reflect their director's foreign training and residence. **Hakim Belabbes**'s two features, *Fibers of the Soul / Les fibres de l'âme* (2003) and *Why the Sea / Pourquoi la mer* (2006), as well as **Jérôme Cohen Olivar**'s *Kandisha* (2008), are shaped by their director's years spent in the United States. **Mahmoud Frites** (born in 1961), director of *Nancy and the Monster / Nancy et le monstre* (2007) and *Ex Chamkar* (2008), describes himself as dividing his time between Norway, Belgium, and Morocco.

In Morocco, more than any other Arab country, filmmaking has become a family business in the 2000s. **Imane Mesbahi** (born in 1964), who began her sole feature in 1994 and finally released it in 2002, is the daughter of the pioneer Moroccan filmmaker Ahmed Mesbahi. **Hichem Ayouch** (born in 1976), director of *Edges of the Heart / Les arrêtes du coeur* (2006) and *Cracks / Fissures* (2010), is the younger brother of the internationally acclaimed Nabil Ayouch. **Omar Chraïbi** (born in 1961), one of the most prolific of the younger generation, with three features in the decade—*The Man Who Embroidered Secrets / L'homme qui brodait des secrets* (2000), *Rahma* (2003), and *Woven by Hands from Cloth / Tissée de mains et d'étoffe* (2007)—is the younger brother of Saâd Chraïbi, best known for *Women . . . Women / Femmes . . . et femmes* (1998). The most recent additions to the ranks are Swel and Imad Noury, who are the sons of Hakim Noury, director of a number of acclaimed realist films in the 1980s and 1990s, as well as two hit comedies at the beginning of the 2000s.

Swel Noury and his brother **Imad** were both born in Casablanca (in 1978 and 1983, respectively). They started in very different careers, Swel studying in Paris and becoming a financial analyst, while Imad was a rock guitarist. But both worked on some of their father's features, and together they made a number of short films beginning in the late 1990s. In 2001 they both moved to Madrid to enroll in the film school there. They have since co-directed two feature films from the production base they set up in Spain: *Heaven's Doors* and *The Man Who Sold the World* (2010).

Heaven's Doors / Les portes du ciel (2005) is a striking first feature full of uninhibited shooting and jagged editing, enigmatically held long shots and unexpected transitions, bursts of every kind of music from hip-hop to grand opera. It offers sympathetic images of young people struggling to make a living in contemporary Morocco, alongside such classic symbolic figures from traditional Arab literature and culture as the mad old woman who proffers words of wisdom and the old drunk who offers profound insight into the protagonist's future. The film comprises three acts (as they are described in the end credits), each featuring different lead characters and preceded by a long written caption reflecting philosophically on the action to come.

Act one begins with a young man, Ney, bursting into an apartment and initiating a shooting in which a man dies, his wife is gravely wounded, and Ney himself is killed. The rest of the act traces the events which lead to this situation and reveal Ney's background. Needing money because he has to care for his little sister and blind mother (with whom he has a difficult relationship), Ney turned to crime. The man he killed was the local gangster Mansour, who had double-crossed him. The act ends with a replay of the opening shooting and its aftermath, as discovered by a ten-year-old child, Salim.

Act two continues the story, not by showing what happens to Ney's family but by following the subsequent life of Salim. He and his comatose mother Souad are taken in by his dead uncle's American widow, Lisa. After a difficult start, the pair achieve a real rapport. For Lisa, Salim comes to represent what she has never had, while Salim appreciates the fact that, though she drinks bourbon, she does not beat him as his father did. The budding relationship comes to an end when Salim's other uncle (whom we never see) emerges to exercise his legal claim to take control of his sister and nephew. Lisa is left planning a return to San Francisco, to rebuild her relations with her own family.

Act three has only tenuous links with the earlier stories, though it contains tantalizing tiny flashbacks to the narratives of acts one and two and the occasional linking sequence, as when the new protagonist, Smail (played by the directors' father Hakim Noury), is almost run over by two of Ney's friends when he is crossing the street. This, like the story of Ney, is a tale of betrayal and desire for vengeance. Emerging from fifteen years in prison, Smail has two things in mind: to look after his dying mother and to seek revenge. His mother dies after a few weeks, so then he concentrates on vengeance. Eventually, however, perhaps influenced by the encounters he has had since leaving prison, he merely shoots his betrayer in the leg.

Heaven's Doors is a structurally flawed work. Having established our sympathy and involvement with one set of characters, it frustrates us by ignoring them to move on to others. Nothing is definitively resolved. The basic theme of the difficulty of human interrelationships is clearly stated in all three acts, but it is difficult to see how these constitute a single narrative, and wider conclusions are hard to draw.

*   *   *

The influence of growing up in Europe or of living there for decades has shaped the work of two talented members of the 2000s generation. Mourad Boucif was brought up from the age of four in Belgium, where he still lives, whereas Nour-Eddine Lakhmari has chosen to live for the past twenty-four years in Norway, where he received part of his education and training. Boucif and Lakhmari are highly individual filmmakers with very little in common: Boucif's work looks at the immigrant community in which he grew up, while Lakhmari uses his situation to bring a detached but lucid gaze to aspects of Morocco's past and present.

Mourad Boucif was born in 1967 in Algeria but is of Moroccan descent. He spent part of his childhood in France and reached Belgium, where he still lives, at the age of four. He began his career by making amateur videos and co-directed his first (and so far only) feature, *Beyond Gibraltar / Au-delà de Gibraltar* (2001), with his close friend and fellow immigrant, the Turkish-born Taylan Barman. In it they explore life in the Moroccan immigrant community in Brussels. The film is focused on Karim, whose graduation as an accountant coincides with the sacking of his father. His inability to find work generates tensions with his father, who expects him to take over as head of the family. Further problems are generated when Karim falls in love with a Belgian girl, Sophie. As well as the emotional problems owing to their differing backgrounds, Karim's trajectory brings out a whole set of issues facing the immigrant community in Belgium: constant police harassment, unease with outsiders (such as Sophie), poverty, and unemployment. But it also offers images of the more vibrant life of the community: a popular hip-hop display and dance, as well as a traditional Moroccan wedding celebration (that of Karim's sister). Ironically, it is Sophie who helps Karim understand his community's roots by taking him to see Yamina Benguigui's *Immigrants' Memories*.

At first the couple's relationship goes smoothly, but a return to Tangier for the funeral of his younger brother, who has been killed in a drunk-driving accident, reminds Karim forcefully of his Maghrebian roots. It gives him a fresh insight into his father, but also reminds him that he has an intended bride within the wider family community. Karim and Sophie break up temporarily but meet up again when Karim's father and Sophie's brother are both being treated at the same hospital. Their eventual reconciliation takes place against the background of an immigrant confrontation with the police. It is with images of this riot that the film ends.

The narrative pattern of *Beyond Gibraltar* is straightforward, though perhaps too reliant on coincidence. At the beginning, Karim receives his diploma on the very day his father is loses his job, and at the end, the couple both have relatives treated in the same hospital on the very same day, enabling the eventual reconciliation. The dialogue—improvised by the largely amateur cast—rings true and the direction is assured. The film is a passage of discovery for Karim, who obtains a greater insight into his own culture—especially via the funeral visit to Tangier—and a fresh awareness of Belgian attitudes via Sophie. But his social experiences are never profound. The family is poor but can afford the daughter's traditional wedding and the funeral trip to Tangier to bury their son. There is police harassment on the streets, but Karim is always an onlooker. Insofar as there is a background of racial hostility, Karim is himself unaffected by it personally. Nor is he caught up in any political activity or in the events which trigger the concluding riot. Despite these reservations, the film does give a vivid and sympathetically drawn picture of its immigrant Brussels community.

Nour-Eddine Lakhmari, who was born in 1964 in Safi, has been resident in Norway since 1986. He originally planned a very different career, studying pharmacy at Nancy in France and then modern languages and chemistry in Oslo. When he turned to filmmaking, his early videos allowed him to gain access to the Oslo Film and TV Akademie. He subsequently undertook further study in Paris and New York, and from the mid-1990s made a succession of short films, many of which were well received at international festivals. He has subsequently also worked in television.

Lakhmari's first feature, *The Gaze / Le regard / Blikket* (2004), typifies the heterogeneous elements that so often form part of exilic filmmaking: it is a Norwegian-Moroccan co-production, shot largely in French with a French protagonist but using a Norwegian production team. Although it deals with a key moment in Morocco's past, there is little space in the film for a Moroccan viewpoint. The action is preceded by a title which adds a further element of diversity by citing Khalil Gibran: "And how shall you punish those whose remorse is already greater than their crime?"

This is a tale of memory and guilt which concerns a seventy-year-old French photographer, Albert Tueis, who is preparing an exhibition of his life's work in Paris when he realizes that one episode of his life is missing—the time he spent as a nineteen-year-old army photographer in Morocco toward the end of the French colonial occupation. Impulsively, he decides to return to Morocco to recover a couple of reels of film he had hidden there because he could not face up to the images which they contain, which document his cowardice at the time. He witnessed atrocities but did not intervene to prevent them. In particular, Albert feels that he is responsible for the death of one militant, Issa Daoudi, with whom he could communicate because he had fought with the French army in Indochina.

The reels of film he hid away have vanished after fifty years, but Albert is continually haunted by memories of himself fifty years earlier. Searching the market and using local contacts, he manages to find two of the photographs he shot back then: one of him posing alongside the French soldiers and their prisoners and the other a battered close-up of Issa's face. Eventually, he even finds Issa, who survived the French but subsequently spent ten years in a Moroccan prison for political activities. To Issa, now a broken man, rendered mute and imprisoned in a psychiatric hospital, Albert is able to express his plea for forgiveness, and new photographs of Issa's still-impressive face allow Albert to complete his exhibition.

The Gaze is technically well realized—the shots are excellently composed and the frequent transitions between past and present are well handled. But Albert's journey into his own past creates little dramatic tension, and a subplot concerning the unspoken love of Réda, the local photographer who helps him, for Aïda, a beautiful girl who dances in the neighborhood café, adds little. The scenes of French atrocities are plausible enough, but not filmed with enough intensity to motivate a fifty-year obsession. *The Gaze* is a competent first feature, but does not match up to Lakhmari's earlier short film work.

CasaNegra (2008), the director's second feature, generates the power missing from *The Gaze* and became one of the most commercially successful Moroccan films in the year of its release. As its title implies, it offers a bleak vision of Casablanca, which is often filmed at night and in its most run-down districts. The film's opening sequence shows the two protagonists, Adil and Karim, both unemployed men in their early twenties, squabbling as they run away from the police. The narrative then moves back in time three days to explain their predicament. Though friends since childhood, they have very different current situations. Karim is concerned to help his family, in particular his sick father and his sister, who needs support to pay her school fees. Adil's concern is to cope with the domestic nightmare of a brutal stepfather who regularly beats his mother. His dream is to escape to Europe (illustrated by a postcard of the Swedish city of Malmö, sent to him by one of his uncles who has emigrated there).

Karim and Adil both try, not very successfully, to hustle a living on the streets, organizing child cigarette sellers and stealing a pizza deliveryman's motorbike and pizzas, until they meet up with a real mobster, Zrirek. He is truly a fascinating figure, who combines psychopathic violence (running a protection racket) with a passion for his tiny beribboned dog and for singing sentimental songs in his mistress's drinking club, the ironically named Où Tout Va Bien (where he compels the other clients to sing along and to cheer his musically inept efforts). The first job Zrirek gives them introduces the pair to an inconceivable world of luxury and depravity (collecting money from a rich French-speaking transvestite). While awaiting their second, bigger assignment, both go on with their lives. Karim embarks on an affair with Nabila, the beautiful owner of a shop selling luxury goods, only to discover the social gap which separates them. Adil finally confronts his stepfather but only indirectly, by setting fire to his car and selling his beloved television set. The pair's second assignment, doping a horse, which Zrirek has backed to lose, inevitably goes wrong and leads to the situation with which the film opens. A little epilogue shows Karim and Adil back where they started: Karim's family is no more secure, and though Adil has persuaded his mother to return to her own family, she knows that as a woman who has left her second husband, she will not be welcomed.

CasaNegra has the well-handled action sequences and driving musical rhythm missing from the plot of *The Gaze*. This time the violence is dramatically effective, and the basic film noir plot has a real coherence and force. The film offers a searing portrait of its setting, Casablanca, a city which combines daytime wealth and beauty with a dark and violent night-time underside, peopled by those with no real hope of a better life. *CasaNegra* is a film that runs over two hours, and Lakhmari's second concern—beyond the narrative as such—was to talk about Morocco's young people. As he told an interviewer, 70 percent of the population comprises young people, but these are totally neglected. Returning from Norway and going out at night, he met "an enormous number of aggressive people." But as soon as he got to know them, he found them "gentle with lots of love to give and receive . . . victims of a very brutal society."[39]

Karim and Adil illustrate perfectly Lakhmari's view of Moroccan society. Although they like to see themselves as tough and can indeed be brutal on occasion, they are no match for real crooks like Zrirek and the people Adil encounters in the medina (one fears the vengeance Zrirek will wreak on them for having both failed and opposed him). Just as Adil cannot cope with his mother's acceptance of domestic violence, so too Karim is unable to tolerate the harsh working conditions which allowed his father to bring up a family. They are lost on the streets, and their dreams—Karim's for Nabila and Adil's for emigration to Europe—are doomed to failure. They are concerned with their immediate family problems, but there seems to be no way they can possibly establish families of their own. Poverty inhibits their every move, and Adil is clearly ashamed when he performs a good act (rescuing a child's beloved tortoise). Casablanca is shown to be beautiful at night and at dawn, but it offers no hope to the young.

Zero / Zéro (2012) is a further exploration of the filmic world to which Lakhmari is most attracted, the Hollywood film noir, again transposed to Morocco at night. The film opens with a totally enigmatic scene of a man scrubbing every inch of every wall of a room, which is totally empty except for a wheelchair, in which he is initially shown seated. The man, we discover, is the film's protagonist, a policeman known to all as Zero.

Zero is a contradictory character. Much of his time is spent in this room, caring for his elderly wheelchair-ridden father, an ex-army veteran and total soccer fanatic (a magnificently exuberant performance by the veteran actor Mohamed Majd in a role that matches in its ferocity that of the gangster of *CasaNegra* and almost unbalances the film). Zero does not have a home of his own, and although he shows infinite patience, the relationship with his father is far from pleasant. Zero nurses and bathes his father, providing him with drugs (kif) and, on occasion, the services of a prostitute, but the only reward for Zero is constant abuse, invective, and insults about his mother (we never learn whether she has died or simply left home because of her husband's treatment).

In his work life, Zero is similarly downtrodden. He has none of the attributes of police authority, no real physical presence, no gun, not even a uniform. His day job is listening to the endless pleas and complaints of those seeking help. Only one of these catches his attention: a mother seeking her missing seventeen-year-old daughter, who has come to Casablanca with no money and despite having no friends or relatives there. In his free time—the evenings—Zero wanders the streets, drinking incessantly from the bottle he always has in his pocket and operating a scam with a young prostitute to put middle-aged men in a situation where he can threaten an arrest and take in a large payment in lieu. But his superiors know all about his supposedly secret life and treat him with the same contempt his father shows, beating him and taking his supposed "earnings."

The film's opening image reappears, now fully understandable. Zero's father has died. This could be the end of a narrative about frustration and failure, but instead it proves to be the necessary catalyst in the protagonist's life. Zero is transformed from being a victim of those with authority (his father within the Moroccan patriarchal society and his superiors in a corrupt police force) to a man with a mission. With demonic energy, Zero sets out to find the missing seventeen-year-old. He assaults and viciously humiliates a tattoo artist whom he rightly assumes is involved with Casablanca's prostitution rackets (decorating the bodies of young prostitutes). He then goes on to kill his immediate superior (leaving his body hanging from a meat hook in a restaurant refrigerator). Then, pursuing his quest, Zero shoots the owner of the brothel above the upscale restaurant and, though wounded, stabs his police chief, who has been enjoying the fruits of his corruption in the brothel. Driven on, he finds the seventeen-year-old, but he cannot rescue her and restore her to her mother. As most of the audience will have assumed, she is already working as a teenage prostitute, catering to the sexual whims of an extremely rich client, whom Zero, surprisingly, does not kill.

The film's epilogue has further twists. Zero is a film noir hero, but nonetheless it is astonishing that, despite the murders he has committed, Zero is not placed under arrest. Instead, he emerges, wounded but undaunted from the hospital, seemingly about to begin a new life. But the tattoo artist whom he had humiliated (one of the film's quirkiest characters) emerges to stab him dead. The film's final shot is an overhead image of Zero lying dead on the street.

As in *CasaNegra,* Lakhmari reveals a totally bleak vision of life in Morocco's largest city. Neither tradition (Zero's father) nor modernity (the modern police force) offers any hope for progress. Zero, by any measure, is a failed hero. The few moments of luminosity in a very black film are provided by the appearances of the woman doctor (marvelously named Kenza Amor) whom Zero meets up with. But their passionate lovemaking is filmed in such a way that it could equally plausibly be Zero's imaginings. Certainly there is no possible future for the relationship.

Like *CasaNegra, Zero* proved immensely popular with both Moroccan critics and audiences. It won best film and four other awards at the 2012 Tangiers National Film Festival, and Lakhmari again topped the year's box office listings, with over 200,000 admissions. But on its release in France it received a very mixed reception. While for *Le Monde* "the film brings fresh proof that in the Morocco of today, cinema can provide an outlet for a society perverted by venality," for *Première* it "shows a total incomprehension of its model" (*Taxi Driver*), while the reviewer in Critikat sourly observed that "not everyone who wants to be Brian De Palma, can be."[40]

* * *

Two Moroccan-born but Paris-based filmmakers—Hassan Legzouli and Ismaïl Ferroukhi—have close artistic connections, even to the extent of choosing parallel forms and subject matter. Their debut features, both released in 2004, are highly personal road movies, each of which offers a young man's reflections on growing up in France and discovering only later in life his father's values.

Hassan Legzouli was born in 1963 in Adrej in Morocco and studied film in France, where he has lived since 1980, and at INSAS in Belgium. His *Testament / Tenja* is a warm, if somewhat conventional, road movie. It has a personal dimension, since the village at the end of the trajectory is Adrej, where the director was born. The film also develops some of the themes treated in the director's earlier thirty-eight-minute fiction, *When the Sun Makes the Sparrows Fall / Quand le soleil fait tomber les moineaux* (1999), a look at everyday life and death in this same village deep in the Atlas Mountains. *Testament* has the same measured pace, patterned narrative, and very composed—but never self-indulgent—imagery. The story of *Testament* is a simple one. Nordine (played by the best known of all actors of Maghrebian origins in France, Roschdy Zem) is asked by his mother to fulfill his father's dying wish—to be buried in his native village in the remote Atlas Mountains. Nordine has never visited Morocco. When he was fourteen, his father attempted to take the family back there, but Nordine's papers were not in order and so the family had to turn back. His father never attempted to make the trip again. When Nordine sets out this time, in a van with his father's coffin in the back, he again finds his papers are not in order, but because of the circumstances he is allowed through and reaches Tangier without serious problems.

Legzouli is concerned with the human details of the relationship. We learn of Nordine's father's pride at being selected for work in the mines of northern France—he showed everyone in the village the green stamp on his hand that marked his acceptance by the French recruiting agent. Nordine finds his Moroccan identity constantly questioned—he is taken for an Algerian, because the immigrant Arabic he speaks has been so strongly shaped by the *beur* immigrant majority of Algerian origin. The crucial aspect of *Testament* is not the rigor of the journey but the nature of Nordine's two main encounters. The first, at the Tangier morgue, is with Mimoun, a slightly crazy young man, barred from the nearby café because of his past behavior (to which he responds by peeing in the teapot). Although he wears a Moroccan soccer team T-shirt, his dream is to emigrate to Australia, where a girl he once met lives. Despite their differences, Nordine and Mimoun are drawn together, and at the end, Nordine helps him by funding his clandestine passage to Europe.

The second and more significant encounter is with Nora, an attractive young girl who accompanies him to the village of Aderj. She is one of the numerous Maghrebian graduates who has been unable to find a proper job. Instead she has become the mistress of a man wealthy enough to set her up in an apartment in Casablanca. At the moment she meets Nordine, she is weeping by the roadside, having been thrown out of his car after a quarrel. Initially, she wants to visit her parents, but when the moment arrives, she cannot face them: they think the monthly check she sends them comes from her work as a civil servant. Instead she uses the journey to rethink her life.

Nordine arrives in Morocco as an outsider, and he has a tourist's expectations of the souk to which Nora takes him: he is surprised not to find pottery and carpets. Instead he discovers Berber music of the kind his father played constantly and shocks Nora by playing it in the car. For him this is celebrating his father's life, while for her it is like dancing on his grave. Unfortunately, like many a tourist, he insists on sampling the local food, only for it to make him sick and delirious. The couple are drawn closer together, as she nurses him and takes over the driving. The possibility of a more permanent relation is hinted at as they kiss goodbye, but they go their separate ways, she to reflect on her life, he to meet up with Mimoun in Tangier and to make his way home. *Testament* is a reticent and understated film, but the couple's growing relationship is subtly indicated, as they move from the banter of their first real conversation—"Are you married?" "Are you looking for business?" "You couldn't afford me!"—to their final embrace. Nordine has discovered his need for his cultural roots at his father's grave, and the experience will shape his later life.

Ismaïl Ferroukhi was born in 1962 in Kenitra in Morocco and studied film in France at the Établissement Cinématographique et Photographique des Armes at Ivry. Ferroukhi subsequently settled in France, where he worked in television and as scriptwriter on three films by the French filmmaker Cédric Kahn. After three fictional shorts, he began his feature film directing career with *The Long Journey / Le grand voyage* (2004), which is the most austere of road movies, with Fowzi Guerdjou's lyrical score one of its few concessions to overt emotion. Nevertheless, the film has very personal origins, being based on the car journey made by the director's own father when he himself was just a child.

The film is focused on its two protagonists, Réda, a teenager obliged to drive his father from France to Mecca for the hadj, and his father, who disapproves of just about every aspect of his son's life: his Westernized lifestyle, his French girlfriend, his indifference to Islam. Nicolas Cazalé and Mohamed Majd convey their mutual incomprehension admirably as the five-thousand-kilometer journey progresses. The father is implacable, as he gradually strips his son of everything that links him to his life at home. He refuses to address him in French (though he speaks this with total fluency), throws away his mobile phone, and confiscates his only photograph of his girlfriend. He slaps Réda's face furiously when Réda questions giving alms to a destitute woman. When the boy demands to have meat to eat, his father swaps Réda's camera for a live sheep, which escapes in one of the film's few comic touches.

By the time they reach Mecca, Réda is totally lost. Since he does not speak or understand the Arabic of the Koran, he is unable to communicate, as his father can, with neighbors among the millions from around the Arab world who are driven by a faith of which he has no comprehension. His father's sudden death plunges him into despair. But there had been one point on the journey when the two did make real contact and when his father gave him his blessing. As he enters the airport to return to France, Réda pauses to give money to a beggar woman—a first lesson, perhaps, has been learned.

The austerity of *The Long Journey* is deliberately intended by Ferroukhi. Unlike Legzouli, Ferroukhi offers a pared-down, abstract relationship between father and son. He gave his characters few personal traits, because he wanted "them to be considered above all like two human beings confronting the father/son relationship, and facing a spiritual conflict. I did not want their Moroccan or Muslim origins to take over the rest."[41] The difference between Legzouli's film and Ferroukhi's is sharply revealed by the dream sequences each contains. Nordine's vision, in *Testament*, though provoked by his fever, is of a warm and friendly conversation with his father, dressed in his best Sunday suit, where they enjoy a closeness they rarely achieved in real life. By contrast, Réda's dream is a nightmare, symbolically representing his growing isolation by depicting him being sucked down by quicksand. Interestingly, both families had the same linguistic gap at home—the parents conversed in Arabic and the children replied in French. But in *Testament* the gap is bridged in the dream sequence, as father and son both converse in Arabic.

The people encountered on *The Long Journey*—the mysterious old woman who hitches a lift, the friendly Turk who helps and then robs them, their fellow pilgrims—remain symbolic figures rather than developed individual characters. Similarly, there is a blurring of the varied national landscapes through which father and son travel, because, as the director has said, "their inner evolution was much more interesting for me than their geographic one."[42] *The Long Journey* won the prize for most promising newcomer at the Venice Film festival in 2004.

Ferroukhi's second feature, *Free Men / Les hommes libres* (2011), presents itself as fiction, though two of its key characters, the head of the Paris mosque, Si Kaddour Ben Ghabrit, and the mosque's Algerian-born chief singer, Salim Halali, are both historical figures. The film is set at a time which is now hardly imaginable: 1942, when Arabs and Jews living in or deriving from the Maghreb saw themselves as part of the same community. It is also the moment when the Allied invasion of North Africa was about to begin, and when the Vichy government and the German occupiers in Paris tightened their grip on Jews, communists, and members of the French resistance. As Benjamin Stora, who served as historical advisor on the film, points out, at the outbreak of war there were perhaps 100,000 Maghrebian citizens working in France; "these are 'invisible men' with no legal or cultural existence, relegated to the bottom of the social ladder."[43] These were largely illiterate men from Kabylia, recruited for factory work and forced to live apart from their families left back in the Maghreb. Perhaps half of them left at the outbreak of war; some went along with the policies of Vichy France; others, especially those who learned to read, were influenced by French trade union activity, in some cases fighting for the resistance and/or for independence back home. The role of the Paris mosque—and that of its head— was ambiguous. Though forced into collaboration with the Vichy government and the German occupiers, it did certainly save some Jews, and Si Kaddour Ben Ghabrit was awarded the resistance medal at the end of the war. The film's fictional hero, Younes, is a petty black marketeer, forced by the police to spy on the Paris mosque. As he carries out his imposed duties, his awareness of the situation steadily grows. He is impressed by Ben Ghabrit (who realizes his situation); is drawn into friendship with Salim Halali, who is actually, he discovers, a Jew; and sees Leila, a woman to whom he is drawn, arrested and destined for deportation. He himself is humiliated on the street by the Nazis. Under the influence as well of his cousin Ali, he begins to see things differently, personally saving a little Jewish girl, refusing escape to North Africa, and eventually becoming part of the armed resistance. *Free Men* is the well-told story of an episode in Franco-Maghrebian relationships (and Arab-Jewish closeness) which will be unknown to most of its audience. It is well paced and beautifully acted, and the Rabat mosque, in which parts of the film were actually shot (Ferroukhi was refused permission to shoot in the Paris mosque), makes a visually intriguing and totally convincing location. The use of music (particularly the singing of Pinhas Cohen—in "Arabic of course, but with Judaic inflexions"[44]—is powerful throughout. This is a serious and important piece of filmmaking, only slightly marred by the manner in which Younes evolves (at the end he is less an individual character than a symbolic figure of Maghrebian resistance) and by the addition of a slightly awkward postscript, set in 1944.

* * *

The most stylistically innovative of the new young directors screened internationally is **Faouzi Bensaïdi**, who was born in 1967 in Meknès. He studied at ISADAC in Rabat, before moving to Paris in 1995 to study at the Conservatoire National Supérieur d'Art Dramatique. He gained wide-ranging experience before undertaking his first feature film: he worked as a theatre director on several productions and began a career as a film actor, appearing in several important Moroccan films—Nabil Ayouch's *Mektoub* (1997), Jilali Ferhati's *Braids* (1999), and Daoud Aoulad Syad's *The Wind Horse / Cheval de vent* (2000). In 1999, he co-scripted the French director André Téchiné's *Loin,* in which he also appeared. He made three internationally acclaimed short films—*The Cliff / La falaise* (1997), *Journeys / Trajets* (1999), and *The Wall / Le mur* (2000).

The director's visual style in his first feature, *A Thousand Months / Mille mois / Alf shahr* (2003), which was refined in his trio of shorts, is characterized by lengthy fixed takes and highly complex patterns of narration. This makes the film both difficult and rewarding for the viewer. Set in 1981, at the start of the month of Ramadan, it confronts the realities of Hassan II's rule, though the underlying violence always occurs off-screen. Bensaïdi is interested in an "intimate" form of history, "its traces and after-effects on the lives of people who do not see it occurring."[45] Equally, although religion plays an important role in the film, Bensaïdi is not interested in expressing his own beliefs about Islam.

Within *A Thousand Months* there is a mass of fascinating individual detail and lots of tiny moments of comedy to draw in the spectator, although the overall narrative is bleak and unrelenting. The choice of a strictly chronological unfolding of the plot and the wide array of characters included means that the spectator has to hold a myriad of stories simultaneously in mind, constantly switching from one to the other, with no clear immediate indication of what is important and what is not. Key moments are underplayed, either because they are omitted from the on-screen narrative or because they are shot in such extreme long shot that their impact is defused.

The film's opening sets the pattern for the unfolding two-hour narrative, posing two questions to the spectator. The first is, why are all the villagers standing on the hillside watching the sky? This is swiftly resolved when a title tells us that this is Ramadan, the beginning of which is marked by the first sight of the waxing moon. For an answer to the second question—why is seven-year-old Mehdi carrying a chair around all the time?—we have to wait about ten minutes, when we learn that it is Mehdi's honor and privilege to be in charge of his schoolteacher's chair. Even then there is no way of knowing the important role that the chair is to play as a leitmotif running through the entire narrative. In fact, the differing roles played by the chair as the story progresses are paralleled by the shifting perceptions we have of the various characters, as new layers of information are given to us. Indeed, the film could easily have been called *The Chair,* on the lines of *The Cliff* and *The Wall.* The key to the understanding of the film is Mehdi. Although the story is not shown through his eyes, it is his level of perception (or failure to perceive) which shapes the whole of *A Thousand Months.* He does exactly what little boys do: tells stories when he's lost his satchel; beats up a smaller boy who annoys him; wants to pee when out walking with his mother. As the teacher's pet he is given his "first lesson in being a teacher" when he is made to cane other boys. Inevitably, the boys in class beat him in turn, although the effect of this is defused by being shown in extreme long shot.

The second key character, Amina, Mehdi's mother, has the typical Maghrebian role of female victim, with her husband in prison for almost a year without trial and with little money to live on despite working as a servant for the *caïd.* At home she is put upon by her in-laws; at the prison, she raises her voice in protest at being refused permission to see her husband, only to be accused of insulting the state and being beaten by the police. Later, raising money to live on by selling her wedding ring, Amina is promptly robbed of it all by rapacious beggars in a scene worthy of Buñuel. Her scenes with her husband Samir (played by Bensaïdi), in which the possibility of a new life seems to offer itself, are abortive, but beautifully played by the couple. For Bensaïdi, "it's a film about looking, about what you see and what you don't."[46] He leaves to his audience the task of fitting together the pieces of the mosaic and of giving each piece its appropriate weight. *A Thousand Months* is a remarkable work, and its austerity and authority provoked justified comparisons with the films of Robert Bresson.[47]

A Thousand Months, which is firmly situated in relation to a whole forty-year tradition of socially committed Moroccan filmmaking, won for Bensaïdi the prize for the most promising newcomer at Cannes. But he has spoken of wanting to break with these conventions rather than rebuilding and renewing them. For his second feature, the director decided to do something very different: "I wanted to try something different, mix genres and tones, and to begin a dialogue with a part of cinema of which I am not 'a natural, cultural descendant,' but which is nevertheless mine."[48] As if deliberately to mock his more serious-minded critics, Bensaïdi made, as his second feature, *WWW—What a Wonderful World* (2007), a totally frivolous comedy thriller about a professional hitman and the policewoman he loves. Unfortunately it lacks the narrative logic and drive of the best examples of the genre. The rules of the thriller are parodied rather than adhered to, and the actions are always openly depicted as a kind of game with the spectator, played by a very detached director. Perhaps *WWW* is best seen as an elaborate and virtuoso audiovisual exercise, and as such it offers numerous moments of pure enjoyment. There are a number of visual gags, many shaped by memories of silent cinema, and a succession of references to Bensaïdi's favorite films (none of them Arab). While *WWW* does not engage one emotionally, it displays constant wit, invention, and imagination. Faouzi Bensaïdi is a complex filmmaker, just beginning to find expression for the range of his talents.

Death for Sale / Mort à vendre (2011) is again a fresh departure, this time an intended homage to the classic Hollywood film noir: "American film was influential to me. I would go to the movies three times a week when I was young. . . . When you take the instances of these classic genre films and set them in different locations and socio-political realities, something happens. This was an homage to a part of cinema without directly copying film noir."[49] It was also a very conscious decision to turn away from the style adopted in *WWW*:

> I wanted to move to a classic construction, not to woo the public, but because I didn't want to repeat my previous film, which was built precisely on deconstruction. I wanted to set out in the opposite direction, taking on the codes of the film noir, while adding my personal touch. . . . I was much inspired by the film noir of the 1940s and 1950s, but also the work of Martin Scorsese and Brian De Palma in the 1970s, two directors, among others, who have known how to play with the constraints of the genre film, while adding their own touch.[50]

Although *Death for Sale* was planned as a genre movie, it has many personal aspects. Bensaïdi had originally intended to shoot the film in Tangier and spent eight months living there with his family to explore locations, But a visit to Té-touan, where he had lived for a year as a child, made him change his mind and shoot *Death for Sale* there instead. The three central characters, he tells us, are based on "young men I knew when I was a teenager. I was a good student, and overall a good kid, so my parents gave me social liberties. I was allowed to go out into the neighbourhood at night and I met these guys—they weren't model citizens. . . . I think, at 17 or 18, I wrote notes about this story that had to do with three friends and a robbery."[51] Another personal aspect of the film is that Ben-saïdi himself plays the role of the "corrupt and perverted" Inspector Dabbaz. As he has observed, this was not intended when he wrote the script: "That came as a challenge. I'd never played a character like Dabbaz before."[52]

The film opens with Allal, the oldest of the group, emerging from prison to be welcomed by his two closest friends, Malik and the much younger Soufiane. They are a group of layabouts, with little prospect of making a living except by petty crime. Early on, Soufiane shows his proficiency at bag snatching. More sig-nificantly, Malik meets Dunia, who is working as a prostitute in a local nightclub, the Passerella, and falls in love, quite literally at first sight. Particularly after the three are called "chicken thieves" when they are thrown out of the nightclub, Al-lal rages against their lack of status. But before he can do anything about it, he has to flee to his grandfather's house in the mountains, as the bosses of the drug gang he works on the fringes of are rounded up by the police.

While Allal is away, the lives of the other two fall apart. Soufiane fails in one of his bag-snatching raids on a rich schoolgirl and is caught by her class-mates. They beat him up, make him apologize, and then hood him and tie him up in a tree, while they picnic and drink alcohol underneath him. His rescuers are a group of club-bearing Islamists who cut him down, tend to his wounds, and convert him swiftly to their own violent ideology (he was, he says, "an empty dustbin"). Malik, meanwhile, frames his stepfather/uncle, whom he blames for causing the death of his sister, for selling drugs to children. When Dunia herself is arrested by the police, he gets even closer to Inspector Dabbaz, agreeing to become a police informer in order to secure her release.

When Allal returns with plans for a big jewel robbery, the trio is no longer united, and Allal makes things worse by raping Dunia in order to break up her love affair with Malik. It is therefore a totally disorganized gang which under-takes the robbery. Soufiane is uninterested in the money, but wants "to please God" by killing the Christian shopkeeper. Malik has already informed Dabbaz of the raid, on the understanding that Allal will be shot by the police; while Allal seems blissfully unaware of the consequences of his assault on Dunia. The result is mayhem: Allal is indeed shot dead; Malik is also shot at by the treacherous

Inspector Dabbaz; and a blood-stained Soufiane emerges from the shop to confront the police, convinced he has done God's will. In a final twist, Malik does escape to keep his rendezvous with Dunia at the railway station, but she promptly steals the proceeds of the robbery and walks away unseen.

While this ending is perfect for a classic film noir (the femme fatale strikes again), the rest of the plot is not. In a classic 1940s or 1950s thriller, the robbery would, of course, come at the beginning, and the disintegration of the group would follow, when they have the proceeds ready to divide up. If confirmation were needed that Bensaïdi is merely toying playfully with genre conventions, one need only consider the final shot of the film, which would have been inconceivable in any of the hundreds of thrillers I saw in my youth. It begins conventionally as a high-angle long shot of Malik leaving the station and pans down to follow him under the camera point. But Bensaïdi does not cut there as any classic Hollywood director would have done. He continues the downward panning shot, so that Malik appears to be moving upside down. It is on the image of Malik when he stops, seemingly hanging upside down like a bat, but illogically, from the pavement, that Bensaïdi freeze-frames for the superimposed credit titles.

But if *Death for Sale* is hardly a classic film noir, it is a wonderfully realized image of a world on the brink of the Arab Spring. There is no prospect of meaningful work for the young men who lounge about on the streets; crime seems the only option. Women's work consists of drudgery in vast warehouse-like factories, where the women are hired daily at the owner's whim and searched as they leave at the end of the day. Domestic violence is rife and traditional constraints on women's freedom still apply, in a society where crushing poverty and police corruption go hand in hand. All of this Bensaïdi captures in *Death for Sale,* which proceeds at a pace which allows every detail to be appreciated and with imagery which is always impeccable both in its framing and in the relationship it posits between the characters and their environment.

* * *

Women also achieved a new prominence in Moroccan cinema during the 2000s, constituting a sixth of the thirty or so new directors. The oldest of the women to begin her career after 2000 is Souad El Bouhati, who was born in 1962 in Rabat but brought to France at the age of two weeks. Unsurprisingly, she has been fascinated since the beginning of her career by issues of emigration and identity. Three other Moroccan-born but foreign-trained women directors also made their mark in the early 2000s: Narjiss Nejjar, Yasmine Kassari, and Laïla Marrakchi. All were born in the 1970s and began their careers with internationally shown short films and subsequently provoked a mixture of acclaim and controversy with the striking feature films they made on their return to Morocco from film school study abroad. All three deal with ignored aspects of the lives of women, rich or poor, in contemporary Morocco. The most recent key woman filmmaker born in the 1970s to make a real impact is the French-educated former journalist Leila Kilani. She won the top prize at the 2011 National Film Festival with her first feature, *On the Edge,* having initially established her reputation with the feature-length documentary *Our Forbidden Places,* which was awarded the fiftieth national anniversary prize at the 2008 festival.

Souad El Bouhati was born in 1962 in Rabat but brought to France at the age of two weeks. She studied film at the Sorbonne and has made two intense, loosely structured films about the ambiguities of emigration and national identity. The more reticent of the two, the thirty-minute short, *Salam* (1999), begins with an unaccompanied coffin being shipped off to Morocco. Ali, who watches it go, has now retired after many years of working in France and has to leave the hostel he shares with dozens of others. This very mixed community— sub-Saharan Africans and Maghrebians, Christians and Muslims—has been the focus of his life, and the film now follows the events stemming from his decision to return to Morocco. The most significant of these is saying goodbye to his closest friend, whose school-age daughter has kept all the shoes he gave her on successive birthdays and offers him a pair as a keepsake. The film is a sympathetic, almost documentary-style portrayal of a saddened man, going off to a future we (and perhaps he too) have no way of imagining.

El Bouhati's more forceful debut feature, *French Girl / Française* (2008), is an interesting variation on the theme of emigration, since its heroine Sonia was born in a French provincial town. She grows up there quite happily, working hard at her studies and considering herself totally French. She is startled when a teacher refers to her as an African, and her life is shattered when her father, unemployed and unhappy with his life in France, makes a sudden decision to return to Morocco. Ten years later, she is a determined young woman, still concerned with her studies but obsessed with the idea of returning to France, which she sees as her true home.

While the rest of her family have settled comfortably into life in a farming community in rural Morocco, Sonia does not fit in. Study is her chosen means of escape, and initially she enjoys her studies at the girls' college. But she desperately wants her father to give her her passport when she completes her studies, confident she can get work in France. She ignores all warnings that, as a Moroccan, she will not fit in there: she sees herself as French. The traditions of Moroccan life do not suit her at all, although her father gives her every freedom (except possession of her passport). She prefers working in overalls alongside her father on the farm to living the conventional sheltered domestic life of a Moroccan woman. Although she has a boyfriend, she vehemently rejects the prevalent idea that a girl should get married as soon as she completes her studies. More and more desperate, she proclaims that if she has to stay, she will die, and quarreling violently with the headmistress, runs away from college. Alone in the dark streets, with nowhere to go, she drifts toward the harbor, where she is eventually picked up by the police and returned to her family. Even now, she is prepared to make no concessions, stridently rejecting all thought of compromise. She retreats more and more into herself; none of her family can make real contact with her anymore. Her hitherto unsympathetic mother, who hears her reading Baudelaire's "L'invitation au voyage" to herself at night, finally relents and gives her her passport. The outcome is unexpected. Instead of a triumphant arrival in France, what we are offered at the film's conclusion are images of a now more relaxed Sonia, an elegant, modern young woman working as a translator in the city.

In these two assured, well-focused fictions, El Bouhati gives fresh expression to the conflicting demands of national identity. While never explaining quite how an obsession with one's birthplace can take over one's life, she chronicles the often-troubling consequences, which, in Ali's case, lead him to plunge into the unknown, and which, for Sonia, drive her close to suicide.

Narjiss Nejjar, who was born in 1971 and studied at ESRA in Paris, caused controversy with her debut feature, *Cry No More / Yeux secs* (2002). This began as an idea for a documentary about rural prostitution, but when this proved difficult to achieve, Nejjar transformed the project into a poetic feature film (the basis upon which it received CCM support). The film is prefaced by a declaration by the filmmaker: "A people is great when it knows how to talk of love without shame." It is set in a remote village in the mountains, inhabited only by women, whose sole source of income is prostitution. The film begins and ends in realist style. At the start, we see Mina released from a twenty-five-year prison sentence and returning to her native village, driven by Fahd, a former prison warder who is now a bus driver. She is recognized by some of the older women but not by her daughter Hala, now the village leader, who rejects the initial advances of Fahd.

The transformation of the film from documentary-style realism to a dreamlike symbolic melodrama comes with the revelation of the villagers' "cemetery of virginities," where each of the mass of red flags marks the transition of a young village girl from virgin to whore. The middle portions of the film are focused less on Mina than on Fahd, a man very different from the shepherds who are the villagers' normal clients. Accustomed to entertaining children on the streets of Casablanca on Sundays, he suddenly appears dressed as Charlie Chaplin to dance and delight the children. But when he witnesses the degradation of a mere child, Zinda, as she is forced into prostitution, he breaks down totally. Dressed in drag, complete with eye makeup and badly applied lipstick, he tries symbolically to take on the pain of the young prostitutes. He ends up screaming—mad and naked—on a snowy, picturesque mountaintop. Then, in an abrupt return to realism, we see Mina in the final images struggling on with her efforts to teach the young village girls weaving, so that they will have an alternative source of income, while Fahd (now abruptly restored to sanity), Hala, and Zinda drive off to seek a new life.

Members of the cast and inhabitants of the village where it was shot felt they had been exploited and tried unsuccessfully to sue the filmmaker. This has not prevented her from making two more features, the first titled—appropriately perhaps—*Wake Up, Morocco* (2006) and the other *Angels' Terminus / Terminus des anges* (2010).

Yasmine Kassari (born in 1972) abandoned her studies of medicine to enroll at INSAS in Brussels. She made her initial reputation with two internationally shown short films. *Stray Dogs / Chiens errants* (1995) is a purely visual seven-minute exercise, with an opening explanatory title but no dialogue or narration. When the municipal dog killers are around, those with dogs keep them at home; but the homeless have no such luck. By contrast, her major documentary, *When Men Weep / Quand les hommes pleurent* (2002), is a fifty-seven-minute documentary based largely on interviews carried out by the (unseen) filmmaker, interspersed with three poems by Mahmoud Darwish. Direct to camera, Moroccan workers in Spain talk of their problems: the difficulty of obtaining proper papers, the low wages they are paid, the difficulties they had in reaching Spain, the racism and exploitation they have encountered there, and their appalling living conditions in settlements of three to four hundred men. They are unable to circulate in towns or villages, barred from cafés, and have no prospects whatever of a better life. Unable to support themselves on the wages they earn, let alone send money back to their families, the thought of ever returning to the people and places they left fills them with shame. Utterly unpretentious, *When Men Weep* is a powerful document on the lives of illegal immigrants in Europe.

Kassari's first feature film, *The Sleeping Child / L'enfant endormi* (2004), shows the other side of the coin: the lives of women left behind in Moroccan villages. The title derives from a pre-Islamic tradition that the fetus of an absent father could be "put to sleep," so as to be born on the latter's return. Originally there was no time limit, but amazingly, in the 1950s, a maximum of twelve months of pregnancy was established in Moroccan law. Kassari is in no way making a case for the validity of an ancient tradition (although it is real for her illiterate peasant characters). For her, it symbolizes the sexual frustration of women whose husbands have been forced by economic circumstances to depart for work in the city or abroad.

The old ways hold sway in the (unnamed) remote village in the Atlas Mountains where the action takes place, and the wedding ceremony with which the film opens will only be valid if all the traditional rules are followed. One of these is the seclusion of the bride, Zeinab, who is first seen symbolically caged behind a muslin veil. Next morning, her husband Hassan joins the local group of men leaving to seek their fortune abroad, together with her cousin Halima's husband, Ahmed. Tellingly, it is their mothers the men embrace as they leave; no public demonstration of emotion between husband and wife is allowed, even on the day after the wedding. The pan across the landscape, which marks their departure, conveys the stark isolation of the hamlet rather than any sense of natural beauty.

Left behind are two families without men: Zeinab, her mother, and grandmother; and nearby, Halima and her little daughter, Siam. There is no news from the men for months, and learning she is pregnant, Zeinab decides on the traditional "magic," which will keep the baby asleep and unborn until her husband returns. There are strict rules on keeping the talisman secure and rituals to undergo when the child is to be awakened. Eventually the women gather around the only television set in the village to see and hear a videocassette recorded by the men, but there is no good news: none of them has found a job. For the women, the daily routine of washing, milking the goats, preparing food, and gathering firewood goes on as before, interrupted only by the death of Zeinab's mother. A brief respite, when the two women, Zeinab and Halima, bathe in the river, is interrupted by the arrival of a man, Amziane. Halima lingers to talk to him, an innocent act for which she will later be savagely beaten by her in-laws. Afterwards, while she is secluded, Amziane visits her secretly. They talk not of love but of the conditions Amziane experienced during his own sojourn abroad.

The second communication from the men indicates that their situation has not improved and that Ahmed has disappeared. In despair, Halima screams out her anguish on the mountaintop, then leaves to sue for divorce, abandoning her daughter, Siam. Although the hamlet is barely an hour's ride from the city, there are few intrusions from the outside world: the local television set and a video camera with which the women make a cassette to send to their husbands. There is a modern-style school which even a little girl like Siam can attend but which interferes, as far as the grandmother is concerned, with the traditional rhythms of village life (and where the teacher discovers, not altogether surprisingly, that no one knows the meaning of the word "democracy"). In the little town of Taourit there is a photographer's shop, where Zeinab, her grandmother, and her niece get themselves photographed for Hassan. When he returns the photograph with no other message than the instruction never to visit Taourit again without his permission, Zeinab discards her talisman, breaking the spell and symbolizing that she, like Halima, has lost all hope.

The Sleeping Child is a reticent, slow-paced film which makes great use of long-held, static long shots and never patronizes its illiterate, superstitious women characters. Except for Rachida Brakni, who plays Halima, all the cast are amateurs who had never acted before, though Zeinab is played by Mounia Osfour, granddaughter of the pioneer Moroccan director Mohamed Osfour. Any sense of the picturesque is avoided, despite the opportunities which the Atlas

Mountains provide; the setting is bleak in its beauty. The film does not have a strong dramatic line; scenes like the mother's death are filmed from a discreet distance, but the gradual loss of hope by the two women is powerfully conveyed. As Denise Brahimi aptly notes, we are close here to the "violent silence" of Moroccan cinema's artistic beginnings with Moumen Smihi's *El chergui*.[53] The film, a Belgian-Moroccan co-production, received a number of awards at international film festivals and eventually won the top prize at the 2005 National Moroccan Film Festival.

Laïla Marrakchi, who was born in 1975 and studied film in Paris, provoked a scandal in Morocco when her first feature film, *Marock* (2005), was released, and perhaps as a result, the film topped the Moroccan box office list that year. Whereas the films of Najjar and Kassari deal with women's sexual frustration in rural communities in the absence of their menfolk, *Marock* deals with the all-too-present opportunities for sex in a major Moroccan city. The film is a study of rich upper-class Casablancan youth in the 1990s.

In the pressbook that accompanied the release of the film, Marrakchi says, "I wanted to show and share my memories by making this film. For me, and my generation, it's like a tender and nostalgic photo album."[54] But in fact, although the film has little explicit nudity, its frank depiction of youthful sexuality and indifference to religion provoked outrage in the Moroccan media. The director has denied that the film, the main plot thread of which concerns a romance between the Arab heroine, Rita, and a Jewish youth, Youri, is autobiographical. But she admits that the film comes directly from her own and her contemporaries' experiences: "When I started writing, I brought all my friends together. Together we remembered our adventures, the funniest and the saddest. This is the way I started constructing the framework of *Marock*."[55] In addition, Marrakchi grew up in Anfa (the prosperous Casablancan suburb where the film takes place) and has chosen to set the film in 1997, when she herself was in her early twenties. Brian T. Edwards has noted that "from press photos and in film festival appearances, it is striking how much Marrakchi herself looks like and dresses like her own characters."[56] On a deeper level, Marrakchi is married to the Paris-based Jewish director Alexandre Aja (born Alexandre Jouan-Arcady), who is the son of the *pied noir* filmmaker Alexandre Arcady and who worked as artistic advisor on the film.

The film's title, *Marock,* is a deliberate pun on the French word for the country, *Maroc,* and Marrakchi presents the film as a testament to "her" generation. The overall narrative structure is straightforward: about twenty successive scenes, chronologically arranged and each ending with a fade to black. Brian T. Edwards sees it as a variant on the conventional Hollywood "teen pic," and certainly the film has the typical vibrant colors and slow pans through luxurious (upper) middle class villas and lush gardens, accompanied by a soundtrack of popular teenage music—with David Bowie's "Rock 'n' Roll Suicide" used as a constantly returning motif. The tone is set in an early sequence in which the camera pans from an old man knelt in prayer in the middle of a car park to a car in which a couple are kissing. When a policeman breaks in upon the couple— "Where do you think you are, Sweden?"—the seventeen-year-old Rita, the girl in the car, shows her total contempt for police authority, indeed warning the cop that he will be in trouble if he tries to stop her from walking away.

No real tension or suspense is created in the film—Rita and Youri fall in love at first sight, and their relationship proceeds with all the expected passionate incidents and temporary misunderstandings which invariably accompany first love (in the cinema at least). He dies in a car crash before the full ramifications of the relationship have to be faced. He is a Jew, and in Morocco, as Marrakchi has noted, "Only religious marriage is recognized. Not civil weddings. Converting to another religion than Islam is also forbidden. So 'mixed' marriage is impossible, like living together, which still remains illegal in 2005."[57]

The group of which Rita forms part, along with her closest friends Sofia and Asmaa, consists of students preparing for their graduation exam, the *bac*. They enjoy every luxury, with the girls chauffeured to and from college, the Lycée Lyautey. But with their parents absent or indifferent, they spend their time drinking and taking drugs, dancing and partying. While the girls gossip and flirt, the boys race in their sports cars through the empty morning streets. The group is defined by shared class and money and comprises Jews from wealthy families as well as the children of the Arab rich and powerful. They all converse in French; Arabic is reserved for talking to the servants (depicted as happy, smiling people, devoted to their masters) and the occasional dirty song at a party. Religion plays no part in the group's life, and Rita is typical in her attitude toward Ramadan. For her, it is not a time for fasting, but for romance—she bets her girlfriends that she will "get" Youri before the month is over.

This is the group to which Rita's brother, Mao, returns from Europe. We assume he was once like all the others (we later learn that he killed a child in a driving accident, which the family are hushing up by paying compensation). But now Mao is a changed man, with cropped hair and bearded face. He does observe the demands of the Muslim faith and calls Rita a whore when he sees her made up to go out partying. When he is taunted about his sister going out with a Jew, he causes a violent family row at home (virtually the only time any members of the older generation are seen). But Rita refuses to be disciplined and makes love to Youri in the scene which most shocked Moroccans, in that he hangs his Star of David around her neck so she doesn't have to be troubled by it. They do discuss their problem—briefly—each proposing that the other change faith; but Youri, always a reckless driver, is killed in a car crash before the issue needs to be confronted publicly. Rita is devastated, but in the happy ending so necessary in this genre she is reconciled with Mao. When she daydreams on the plane taking her to Paris two months later, however, it is her two girlfriends, not Youri, that she remembers.

If the film's most shocking scenes (for a Moroccan audience) are those depicting the love affair between an Arab girl and a Muslim boy, its iconic image is that of the seventeen-year-old heroine, clad in pink hotpants and skimpy top, looking uncomprehendingly down at her elder brother, Mao, as he kneels in traditional prayer. Rita's words show just why the film caused offense: "Mao! Where are my jeans? But . . . are you ill, or what? Mao, what have you done? You've fallen on your head? You're crazy? You thought you were in Algeria, or what? That's it, you're going to become one of the Bearded Ones. Is that it? Daddy, Mummy, here's your son, who's gone completely mad!" As Edwards has noted,

> In the public debate that ensued upon the film's general release *Marock* and Marrakchi herself quickly came to stand for multiple positions—freedom of speech, the young "rock" generation, intellectual and artistic honesty, and humanism, on the one hand, and disrespect for Moroccan tradition, diasporic elitism cut off from the homeland, neo-colonial pandering to Europe's Islamophobic preoccupations, and savvy self-publicity/provocation, on the other.[58]

As Edwards adds, these positions are, of course, "not mutually exclusive." The debate provoked by the film was enormous. Not only did the film top the cinema box office in 2006 and receive a vast amount of newspaper coverage, it was pirated on the streets, and discussions of the film also raged on the Internet, in blogs and chatrooms, from 'bladi.net' to Islamist sites.[59] *Marock*'s reception went far beyond that of a conventional feature film.

Marrakchi's second feature, *Rock the Casbah,* made eight years later and set in Tangier in the wealthy upper-class Moroccan society which the director knows so well, is in many ways a surprising work. The death of Moulay Hassan brings together his wife and three daughters for three days of mourning. The sisters have chosen very different lives for themselves. Miriam, frustrated in her marriage, has turned to extensive plastic surgery, while Kenza, a schoolteacher, accepts the limitations of her life without question. The outsider is Sofia, who emigrated to the United States and made a career for herself starring in movies, in which she habitually plays the role of an Arab terrorist. There are inevitably tensions and conflicts between the three young women and with their mother. During the three days of mourning, the reality of their seemingly unassailable bourgeois existence is exposed: deceit, adultery, even incest. The young women learn that the family servant's illegitimate son, Zackaria, is in fact their half-brother, and that their elder sister Leila, who committed suicide, had not gone to London to study drama but to have an abortion, because, in all innocence, she had begun a relationship with Zackaria.

Given Marrakchi's previous film and the new film's title, *Rock the Casbah,* one might have expected a searing comment on the hypocrisy of Moroccan upper-class society to stem from such a narrative. In fact, the tone is set, not by rock 'n' roll, but by the music actually used to introduce the film's setting: Bing Crosby and Bob Hope singing "The Road to Morocco." Each of the acts is introduced and commented on by the dead father (Omar Sharif, charismatic in ill-fitting white pajamas). He accepts no responsibility for his own actions and trivializes the very real turmoil he has created. The fig tree he once planted provides the film with its first and last images, and he has the final word: "Never make a woman cry. Allah counts her tears." Unbelievably, in a film ostensibly concerned with women's utterly real problems in the Arab world, patriarchy reigns supreme.

Leila Kilani was born in 1970 in Casablanca, but she was brought up in Tangier and studied economics, history and social science in Paris. She began but did not complete a PhD at the École des Hautes Études en Sciences Sociales. From 1997, she worked as a journalist, and although she had received no formal training, turned to film two years later. Her first documentary, *Tangier: The Dream of the "Burners" / Tanger, le rêve des brûleurs* (2002), was supported in the scripting phase and subsequently co-produced by the French film funding system, including, at the final stage, the Fonds Sud. The film received a wide international festival distribution. The "burners" of the title (a term invented in Morocco in the 1990s) are the would-be migrants who flock to Tangier, from which Gibraltar (and another world, that of Europe) can be viewed whenever the weather is fine. This is a world which can be seen but is inaccessible, though barely half an hour away by speedboat.

Choosing as her principal characters a Ghanaian man, a Moroccan man, and a woman, Kilani offers an intimate study of individuals who burn driven by an unquenchable desire to reach Europe and who, if they manage the perilous illegal crossing, will literally burn their passports and other documents so as to try to forestall any official moves to repatriate them. For them, there will be no going back. In addition to offering these personal studies of frustrated striving, Kilani is also concerned to give a distinct sense of the unique identity of the city of Tangier itself, which is quite literally—and crucially for these would-be migrants—the border between Africa and Europe. A child growing up and spending her weekends in Tangier, Kilani found that this border was crucial to her own youthful dreams: "This physical presence of the border was impossible to ignore. It magnetized us all."[60] Unsurprisingly, her identification with the characters in her film is intense. As she said in another of her interviews, in Tangier "you are not bogged down, even if you are obsessed: it's a dream, which brings a sort of quasi-metaphysical transcendence. It's this dream that I want to narrate: these are cowboys, not desperados. When you are desperate, you don't 'burn'; you don't have the energy. You "burn" when you have the strength to dream and to confront death. A burner dreams, imagines, waits. The waiting is physical, but the dream is abstract. These are heroes."[61] The actual outcomes for these dreamers in Portugal, where so many ended up, are graphically and tragically documented, as we have seen, in another of the key films of this new generation of women filmmakers, Yasmine Kassari's *When Men Weep,* which was made the same year.

The following year Kilani completed a less widely distributed fifty-minute documentary about a Middle Eastern musician, *Zad Moulataka* (2003), whose work, like that of so many contemporary filmmakers, embraces influences from both sides of the Mediterranean. She also made an even less widely known documentary, *From Here and Elsewhere / D'ici et d'ailleurs* (2003), which is about, it seems, industrial memory in France.

In 2004, the new king, Mohamed VI, set up an Equity and Reconciliation Commission to look into the abuses of state power under the rule of his father, Hassan II. This led to a greater freedom for Moroccan filmmakers to deal with the period commonly known as the "Years of Lead" (*les années de plomb*), when individuals perceived as hostile to the regime were systematically killed, tortured, imprisoned, or simply disappeared. A number of older filmmakers have made fictional features dealing with these issues, but the subject has largely been ignored by the younger filmmakers born since 1960. An exception is Kilani's well-received feature-length documentary *Our Forbidden Places / Nos lieux interdits* (2008). Work on the script of this film began, it would seem, at the same time as *Tangier: The Time of the "Burners"* and was originally intended to be a similar study of inner feelings, this time of family members who had lost loved ones and did not know whether they were alive or dead. The emergence of the debate in the public domain meant the film had to take on a wider focus, exploring both intimate and public spaces, but it remains "a film of whispers, rarely of cries," filmed in chiaroscuro.[62] At the heart of the film is a record of the questions, doubts, and silences of three generations of a family. For Kilani, in the lives of the anonymous families with whom she deals, the key is "being totally off track, of completely losing the father's role in the historical conflict," as the questioning occurs only within the family circle. Kilani's focus is on the difficulty of handling these grave issues in the present rather than on exploring what actually happened in the past. The film is not an indictment of the past regime, but rather, as Olivier Barlet observes, a way of feeling and hearing the resultant mix of "solitude, austerity, despair, uncertainty," a world where one victim does not want to talk about the torture he has endured because it would be "boring."[63] As a result, there is no discussion of what motivated the regime to act in this way against its own citizens, only a touching portrayal of the enduring results of this tyranny. The film, which was largely French financed, encountered no censorship problems in Morocco and was in fact awarded a specially instituted prize at the festival celebrating fifty years of Moroccan cinema, as well as the prize for best documentary at FESPACO in 2009. The 350 hours of footage shot have been archived to help future scholars examine the issues involved.

Kilani has since turned to feature filmmaking, with *On the Edge / Sur la planche* (2011), again made with French scripting assistance and co-production funding, but focused entirely on Morocco. It is set in Tangier, but offers a very up-to-date and, in many ways, surprising image of the city. This is not the popular Western view of Tangier as a tourist center and magnet for expatriate writers (Paul Bowles et al.). Instead we find a capitalist-driven production center, drawing in cheap labor from the city and its surroundings. The film opens with a striking pre-credit sequence in which the main protagonist, Badia, dances to and fro in front of the camera, often going out of focus. As she does so, we hear her voice-over, blurting out her view of life: "It's better to be held up by your own lies, than to be stretched out, crushed by other people's truths." She spells out the details, which will be illustrated in the drama as it unfolds:

> I don't steal, I get my money back. I don't burgle, I get back what's mine. I don't deal illegally, I trade. I don't prostitute myself, I invite myself to act. I don't lie, I am already what I want to be. I'm just ahead of the truth, my truth.

The outcome of this approach to life becomes clear at the very beginning of the main narrative, which is told as an extended flashback: Badia is shown alone and under arrest.

In the preceding weeks, the lives of Badia and her friend Imane are split between day and night, and this division is reflected in the film's visual organization. By day, the two work in a modern, brilliantly lit, white-walled factory, and their clothing—white overalls, white caps, and white facemasks—matches this completely. Here the shooting is formally composed, mixing well-framed close-ups with telling long shots of the factory setting. What the imagery cannot convey, but what obsesses Badia, is the stench generated by the factory activity—shelling shrimp—which permeates the workers' hands, faces, and clothing. Badia is constantly washing her clothes and scrubbing her face and hands, in order to clean herself of the pervasive fishy smell.

In reaction to this regimented daytime worklife, the two girls prowl the nighttime streets of Tangier, with Badia in tight jeans and a black leather jacket. Now they make their own rules, seeking enjoyment and indulging in petty crime, cheating all the men who come their way. Badia's voice constantly comments on what drives her. At one point she notes (explaining the film's title): "I'm on a springboard, the edge of a diving board." These nighttime sequences are shot in a way that matches their frenetic activity—handheld shots, made as close as possible to their bodies, mostly in semi-darkness, and abruptly cut together.

On the course of their journeys around Tangier by night, they encounter two other twenty-somethings, Nawal and Asma. They have better jobs, working for Western-owned companies in the newly established Tangier Free Zone, to which access is denied to ordinary Moroccans lacking the proper work passes (although Badia bluffs her way in). Nawal and Asma have the same intention of enjoying themselves after the end of the working day, and much of the film is devoted to the interactions of the four. Badia is very much the driving force, as they move from initial acquaintance to friendship and collective enjoyment, then on to doubts, mutual suspicion, and potential hostility. In the end, as the opening of the film indicated, the tensions between the four come to a head and Badia is betrayed—characteristically, when she stays behind at the scene of their biggest burglary to wash herself and her clothes.

On the Edge is a remarkably assured first feature, distinctively shot and with a firm grip on the narrative. It is narrated at the level of the characters, without explicit comment on the economic situation in which the four principals find themselves or moral verdict on the choices they make. But this does not lessen the film's revelation of little-seen aspects of contemporary Moroccan life. Like the would-be migrants in Kilani's first documentary, these are characters who "burn"—driven by inner forces to commit acts about which they do not reflect. They want a different kind of life and pursue relentlessly the limited opportunities they are given.

Despite her background in sociology and her work as a journalist, Kilani has never attempted to offer detached, distanced analyses: "On becoming a film-maker, I left the neutrality of a researcher to draw on my own subjectivity, to say 'I.'"[64] As a result, although all her films deal with important political issues—emigration, state brutality, the situation of the young in contemporary Morocco—she is not a political filmmaker. What she said about her first film holds true for all her subsequent work. She did not want to make a film about a category but "about individuals, characters. Not an essay or a journalistic treatment, but finding the proper subjective vocabulary to tell a story which is an epic and which will not stop tomorrow." She is convinced that it is her refusal of "a journalistic treatment, an exhaustive history, an informative narration" which convinced the funding bodies to give her the backing she needed.[65] Certainly the intensity of her identification with the obsessive, albeit circumscribed, views of her characters, real or imagined, is the key characteristic of her work. While keeping totally to the level of personal experiences of those involved, Kilani's films offer real, moving insights into the wider political issues.

Tunisia

There are a number of directors with very different backgrounds, born in the 1950s, who made a first feature film in the 2000s, among them Khalid Ghorbal, Nawfel Saheb-Ettaba, Nidhal Chatta, Khaled W. Barsaoui, and Ibrahim Letaief. Ghorbal came from the theatre, Saheb-Ettaba and Chatta are marked by lengthy

periods spent abroad, and Barsaoui and Letaief are products of the Tunisian enthusiasm for ciné clubs and amateur filmmaking.

Khalid Ghorbal, who was born in 1950 in Tunisia, is based in France; his
earlier work, except for the short, *The Chosen One / L'élu* (1996), was in theatre,
which he had studied first in Tunis (at the Centre d'Art Dramatique) and then
in Paris (the Université Internationale du Théâtre de Paris and the École Jacques
Lecoq). He directed the most widely distributed film by any of this group of older
directors, *Fatma,* in Tunisia in 2001. The film sets out to confront the practice
of repairing a woman's vagina—just three stitches required—after she has been
raped. It is Ghorbal says, "a strange compromise which seems to sort out things
for everyone: the future husband, whose honor will be safe and his virility intact,
as well as the young woman, who will have a husband and in that way become a
wife and mother." But underlying this is a basic hypocrisy, "which weighs only
on the woman."[66]

The film recounts, with almost excessive modesty, the sexual misfortunes of
its young heroine, who grows up in Sfax and is raped by her cousin at the age of
seventeen. Later she has an affair, which she cannot sustain, during her studies in
Tunis. Eventually she falls in love with a doctor while working as a schoolteacher
in the remote South. But now she needs to have her vagina repaired before the
marriage takes place. Unfortunately, the surgeon who performs the operation is
an acquaintance of her husband, and although he gives no sign of recognition,
her meetings with him trouble her deeply. Finally she feels compelled to tell her
husband the truth, which he has no way of handling.

Ferid Boughedir has remarked on the absence of fathers in Tunisian film
narratives,[67] but here it is the mother who is dead, so Fatma has no one to turn
to when she is assaulted. Her sense of guilt shapes the whole of the rest of her
life, but when she decides to have the operation, our concern for her as a rape
victim is lessened by the fact that she has had an extra-marital affair in Tunis.
The director shows great confidence that a simple chronicle of events, without
real surprise or suspense, can sustain the film's two-hour structure. The film is
slow paced, with many long-held scenes observing his rather inexpressive protagonist from a discreet distance. Fatma displays one moment of forceful anger,
when she orders her assailant out of the house; otherwise the film is essentially
a tale of the stereotypical passive female victim, forever denied happiness. The
negativity of the approach is enhanced by the fact that both of Fatma's lighthearted companions at the University of Tunis are also denied the happiness and
security of married life, Radhia because of an affair with a married colleague and
Samira because her marriage has quickly ended in divorce. Ghorbal tells these
stories with great sympathy and shows great respect for his heroine, but *Fatma*
generates only limited passion or involvement because of the protagonist's innate
submissiveness.

Ghorbal has since made a second feature, *Such a Beautiful Journey / Un si beau voyage* (2008), yet another tale of a man who returns to his homeland. This time the protagonist is a retired worker, Momo, who exchanges a lonely life in Paris for the attractions of the Tunisian South. Again the narrative is minimal and the pace slow and pensive.

Nawfel Saheb-Ettaba, who was born in 1959 in Tunis, studied and worked in Canada before making his feature debut, *The Bookshop / La librairie / El-kotbia*, in 2002. The film is in the realist tradition and deals with two couples. Jamil returns crushed from years of exile and finds work in a Tunis bookshop owned by his contemporary, Tarek. Tarek's widowed mother, Aïcha, is drawn to Jamil, although he is fifteen years younger. He is attracted to her as well, despite the age gap, finding in particular that she is the one person to whom he can talk openly about himself. But both are hesitant about anything more than friendship, and eventually a more self-confident Jamil leaves to reunite with his family in rural Tunisia. Tarek, meanwhile, suffers marital problems with his wife, who has ambitions to become a singer. Against his wishes, she begins singing professionally at wedding ceremonies and eventually leaves him. But finding herself five months pregnant with Tarek's child, she seeks a reconciliation, aided by Aïcha and Jamil. Saheb-Ettaba has said that in *The Bookshop* he wanted "to talk about the difficulty of being, by introducing fragile and attaching characters faced with the ambivalence of feelings."[68] In this he has succeeded, as the film is a muted and understated study of difficult personal relationships and largely suppressed emotions, fully justifying its DVD release title, *The Dark Side of Love / Le côté obscur de l'amour*.

Like Saheb-Ettaba, **Nidhal Chatta** received Fonds Sud support for his debut feature, *No Man's Love* (2001). Chatta, who was also born in 1959 in Tunis, studied in England and worked for the BBC before returning to Tunisia. *No Man's Love* reflects the director's studies of marine biology and ecology and his experience of shooting marine documentaries for the BBC. It offers a unique combination of (very professionally shot) deep-sea diving and the traditional Maghrebian therapeutic journey to the South. It is also full of unexpected plot twists and revelations. The protagonist, Akim, is a diver, who lives with his lighthouse-keeper brother, Issa, a very orderly, responsible man. Akim, by contrast, is a tormented figure, involved with the sea but ambiguous about it, haunted by the death of his handicapped sister, who committed suicide by rolling her wheelchair off a jetty. He instantly falls in love with Aicha when he meets her and immediately breaks up with his current girlfriend, only to have his car smashed and himself beaten up by her brothers.

When he has recovered, he decides to change his life and goes to see Monsieur Ferid, the local gang boss, who—for reasons the film does not explain—wears a metal head brace. Akim is given a mission: to go south and recover three boxes from the bottom of a well. En route, he meets up again with Aicha, who is also going south, in search of healing which modern medicine seems unable to provide. The couple make love and then separate at a railway station. Akim tackles the well, which proves very dangerous; at one moment he has a vision of his sister beckoning him to join her in death. He finds nothing and returns north. Another film might end here, but *No Man's Love* has fresh plot twists for us. Aicha is in fact Monsieur Ferid's daughter. She was at the station to meet Issa, who takes her to a mountain shrine where she is offered fresh hope. When confronted by Akim, Monsieur Ferid admits that the trip was all just a test, which Akim has passed. He is now, as it were, a "made man." *No Man's Love* won the prize for best first film at the JCC in Tunis in 2000.

    Khaled W. Barsaoui, who was born in 1955 in Souk al-Arba, studied sociology at the University of Algiers. He began making 8mm films as a child and is the latest in the series of Tunisian filmmakers to emerge from the amateur film movement (FTCA). His best-known short film is *The Child Who Wanted to See the Sea / L'enfant qui voulait voir la mer* (1998), a complex, convoluted twenty-two-minute fiction which mixes images of meeting and separation with spectacular, if touristic, landscapes and curious dream dance elements. The whole is overlaid with a diverse musical accompaniment (traditional Arabic and Western religious and operatic) and a succession of Arabic narrating voices. Barsaoui made his first feature, *Beyond the Rivers / Par-delà des rivières / Bin el-widyene*, in 2006. The plot is simple. At the very moment that she is about to be married to the husband chosen by her parents, her cousin Ikbal, Aicha elopes with the man she really loves, Mahdi, who has just returned from abroad. The pair are pursued by Ikbal, a former helicopter pilot. Picking out the filmic allusions (Truffaut, Tarkovsky, Hitchcock), Olivier Barlet notes that the film plays with genre conventions "to escape them through a spiraling construction of flashbacks, which allow a depiction of the disappointed hopes of the generation that witnessed independence and of the desire to get back to one's roots."[69]

    Ibrahim Letaief, who was born in 1959 in Kairouan, discovered film at the local ciné club, and after studying communication sciences in Paris involved himself in filmmaking. He began work as a producer in 1994, founding his own company, Long et Court, in 1997. Among the features he has produced is Saheb-Ettaba's *The Bookshop*, and he has also supported young filmmakers by producing a series called *Ten Short Films, Ten Looks / Dix courts, dix regards*. Letaief turned to directing at the beginning of the 2000s, making a number of short films and then a feature-length comedy thriller. *Cinecittà* (2008) is set in the film production milieu the director knows so well. The story concerns a filmmaker who, frustrated by his inability to raise financing for his new film, decides to rob a bank with two friends. Things do not turn out as he expects, however, when he finds himself involved with real villains. But all ends well and the film is indeed made. *Cinecittà* (as its title suggests) is an homage to Italian cinema: "It's an homage to cinema in general and to one period in particular, the neorealism of Fellini and De Sica. There are parodies where I echo scenes from cult films such as *La dolce vita* and *Bicycle Thieves*."[70]

*   *   *

Two Tunisian-born but Paris-based filmmakers have achieved contrasting forms of success. Abdellatif Kechiche has achieved by far the greatest popular acclaim of any member of this generation, winning a clutch of national and international awards. The lesser-known Karim Dridi, in contrast, has made as many features as any other Arab-born filmmaker of his generation outside Egypt, but only one of these deals with specifically Arab issues.

Abdellatif Kechiche was born in 1960 in Tunis but has worked exclusively in France, where he began as an actor, in the theatre and on-screen, taking leading roles, for example, in Abdelkrim Bahloul's *Mint Tea* (1984) and André Téchiné's *The Innocents*. Kechiche's five features have won a host of awards, including the prize for the best first film at the Venice Film Festival, the Palme d'Or at Cannes (in 2013), and two successive sets of Césars (the French domestic equivalent of the Oscars) for best film.

Kechiche began his feature filmmaking career with *Blame It on Voltaire / La faute à Voltaire* (2000), which opens with a young Tunisian illegal immigrant, Jallel, being coached in how to behave toward the French authorities (talk about liberty, equality and fraternity, praise Voltaire . . .). Pretending to be an Algerian political refugee, Jallel finds the process of getting a temporary permit (a trifle unconvincingly) easy, and he ends up in an all-male hostel, where he soon makes close friends. *Blame It on Voltaire* has no great narrative drive, as it moves slowly from one inconclusive situation to another; Kechiche's real talent seems to be the depiction of group scenes of heavy verbal interaction that get out of hand (a spontaneous dance in a café, a wedding ceremony that doesn't quite happen, a game of *pétanque* which goes disastrously wrong), and all these have the air of being very convincingly improvised.

Jallel is a very passive hero. Although he talks about supporting his family back home, his work aspirations do not rise above selling cut-price vegetables in the metro during the daytime and over-priced single roses in cafés in the evening. Jallel's sexual adventures are portrayed with the (European-style) openness of his expatriate female Arab contemporaries, but with little actual joy. Both of the relationships depicted in the film are characterized by frustration and inhibition. The French waitress and single mother Nassera is attracted to him, but she puts formal limits on their relationship. She agrees to the marriage which would give him resident status, appears in a wedding dress at the ceremony, but at the last moment refuses to go through with it. While Jallel suffers a breakdown which means he must be hospitalized, Nassera vanishes without any explanation from his life and from the narrative. While in the hospital, he embarks on an inconclusive relationship with a second woman, Lucie, who is suffering, it seems, from nymphomania. She rejoins him, pregnant (but not by him), after her release, but their tentative relationship, during which he tries to "cure" her, is cut off abruptly when he is unexpectedly arrested and deported by the police. The world which Kechiche depicts in *Blame It on Voltaire* is one where nothing is forcefully sought and nothing is resolved. Characters come and go with no sort of control over their lives, and none of the eventual outcomes are apparent: Why did Nassera leave? What will happen to the pregnant Lucie? How will Jallel fare back in Tunisia?

Games of Love and Chance / L'esquive (2004), which was shot digitally and uses largely unknown or non-professional actors, offers a very close-up view of life in the Paris *banlieue,* where so many members of France's immigrant community live. The film is focused on a group of adolescents with different ethnic origins preparing an end-of-school-year production of the 1730 Marivaux play, *Games of Love and Chance.* The film's opening revolves around the choice by the film's heroine, Lydia, of an elegant gown for her part in the play and the effect that her appearance wearing it has on one of her classmates, Abdelkrim, known as Krimo. He is another passive Kechiche protagonist, in the mode of Jallel in *Blame It on Voltaire,* unable ever to articulate his feelings. Much of the film consists of verbal confrontations—games, rivalries, arguments, involvements—between the young people, and Kechiche makes great play of the contrast between the formal, classical diction of Marivaux's play and the jumbled, semi-coherent language of the young people among themselves, a mixture of Arabic turns of phrase and mispronounced or misapplied French words which even a French critic has admitted would require subtitles to be fully understood.[71] Nothing much happens during the film's two-hour timespan, as the group, under the energetic direction of their French-language teacher, moves toward the eventual on-stage production; but as always, Kechiche is entirely sympathetic toward his characters despite their evident inadequacies. The play is used to prompt them to discover new sides to themselves, never to underline a gap between them and mainstream French society. There is the perhaps inevitable clash between members of the group and a vanload of heavy-handed French police, but this time there are no repercussions. The film ends with the actual end-of-year production—an event of totally multicultural harmony, enjoyed by all—and with Krimo's final failure to express his feelings.

The Secret of the Grain, also known as *Cous Cous / La graine et le mulet* (2007), Kechiche's major work, was in fact the first feature-length film project he devised in the mid-1990s, originally envisaged as a Super 16 film to be shot in Nice, where he grew up, and to feature members of his own family. By the time *The Secret of the Grain* was shot, however, Kechiche's father was dead. The film, though now purely fictional and with a refashioned script, retains a personal, autobiographical tone, not least through the casting of one of his father's friends, not a professional actor, in the central role of Slimane. The film's location is shifted to Sète, on the Mediterranean coast, where a mixed community—French, but also with Arab and even Russian immigrants—struggles in difficult economic circumstances.

We are introduced to Sète through a tourist boat ride, interrupted by a sexual encounter between the guide, Majid, and a blonde Frenchwoman, which seems gratuitous but eventually plays a key role in the film's dénouement. The sixty-one-year-old Slimane, later revealed as Majid's father, who has worked as a fisherman and on the docks for thirty-five years, loses his job but initially reacts passively (a typical Kechiche male protagonist). The complexities of his life are revealed as he delivers the fish given him by his friends on the dock: to his ex-wife Souad, to his married daughter, and to the woman he currently lives with, Latifa, the owner of a hotel overlooking the harbor. The opening is slow-paced, with no hint of what is to come. Kechiche concentrates on personal interactions revealed in intensely dialogued scenes, initially at Slimane's daughter's house (about the price of nappies) and then at his ex-wife's home, where there is a huge family party—to eat Souad's fish couscous—which Slimane does not attend. A plate of the couscous is, however, delivered to him by his two sons, Majid and Riadh, revealing both the tensions between Slimane's two families and the extent to which Rym, Latifa's daughter, feels him to be her real father.

It is Rym who is his closest helper as his retirement plan gradually emerges. Although he has no experience in running a restaurant, he decides to use his severance pay to buy a dilapidated boat and borrow from the bank to convert the boat into a restaurant, which will serve his ex-wife's fish couscous. The audacity and absurdity of his plan are discussed in great detail by a group of musicians, who meet to drink tea and talk outside Latifa's hotel—they agree that they will help, if they can. Despite Rym's efforts, Slimane faces reluctance and delay from the bureaucrats whom he needs to give him the necessary permissions. So he decides to invite them all to a special party meal on the boat, with food put together by his ex-wife and children. All goes well, and after an intense confrontation, Rym even convinces her mother Latifa to attend.

But Majid has caught sight of his French mistress and her husband among the guests. He drives off, inadvertently taking with him the container of his mother's couscous grain—the meal cannot be served. Slimane's efforts to find his son fail, and his moped is stolen by teenagers who mockingly urge him to run after them. He tries but collapses, helpless, in the street. Back on the boat, however, the disastrous wait is made good. Latifa comes up with the necessary couscous, and Rym displays an unanticipated talent by performing an energetic and totally involving belly dance to keep the guests amused.

Kechiche's first three features delineated a very distinctive world, which created a very positive response from both French audiences and critics. The director's prime concern was with his actors, and his great strength is his handling of group scenes, which are evidently tightly scripted but appear as spontaneous interactions: the conversations between Jallel and his colleagues in the hostel in *Blame It on Voltaire,* the rivalries between the adolescents in *Games of Love and Chance,* and the family gatherings, meals, and confrontations (Souad and her daughters, as well as Latifa and Rym) in *The Secret of the Grain.* The typical Kechiche male protagonist is a laid-back, withdrawn individual who never fully articulates the project which drives him forward. The end result is a kind of failure: Jallel unexpectedly picked up by the police and deported, Krimo still inarticulate, Slimane collapsing as his project is about to come to fruition. There is no sense of a tightly structured narrative line: things just happen, developments cannot be foreseen. But within this framework there is space for actresses to give dazzling performances: Aure Atika as Lucie, Sarah Forestier as Lydia, and Hafsia Herzi as Rym.

Black Venus / Vénus noire (2009) is a departure from Kechiche's customary style, leaving behind both the modern-day setting and the immigrant context in which his previous work operated. For the first time, too, the protagonist is a woman, Saartjie Baartman, the so-called Hottentot Venus, who, in the early nineteenth century, was exploited as an object of curiosity in the proletarian sideshows of London and then the bourgeois drawing rooms of Paris. It is not surprising that she shares much of the awkward inarticulateness of Kechiche's earlier male protagonists, as the director has admitted that all his films "are self-portraits, even if they are not only that."[72]

The notion of performance is also a common feature of all Kechiche's work—Jallel reciting poetry while begging in the metro, the Marivaux play, Rym's belly dance—but here the nature of the activity and hence the audience's involvement in it is new and altogether different. The opening sequence, in which Saartjie is an object, not a participant, sets the tone. Charles Cuvier enters the lecture hall of the medical academy to applause from his audience of scholars and students. A bronze bust of Saartjie is theatrically unveiled and a jar containing her excised sexual organs is circulated among the audience, as Cuvier begins his racist lecture purporting to demonstrate that African blacks are closer to monkeys than to white "human beings."

From the date of her arrival in London in 1810, Saartjie was exploited, first as an exotic "savage" curiosity, then, more troublingly, as a sexual oddity in Paris. What is most disturbing for the audience is her acceptance of her fate. Although she objects to some of the things she is required to do, basically she is submissive. When an opportunity to assert herself is offered, at criminal proceedings brought by three members of the African Institution in London seeking to free her from "slavery," she protests, defining herself as a paid performer. But never, in the 247-minute narrative, is she shown to enjoy any aspect of her successive performances or to have any sense of rejoicing in being flamboyantly displayed. We follow her decline to working in a brothel and then alone as a prostitute on the streets, and attempt unsuccessfully to probe the enigma which she represents. But this is a very uneasy situation for any viewer, since we align ourselves, however unwillingly, with those who pay to witness (or participate in) her constant humiliation. The film completes its cycle by returning to the moment when the lecture hall is about to be opened, but the unease remains. Kechiche has said that his interest in the subject was aroused when the South African government petitioned in 2002 for the return and proper burial of Saartjie's remains. But the inclusion of celebratory newsreel footage of this event in the end credits does nothing to assuage the feelings of disarray that the film provokes.

Kechiche reinvented himself again for his next feature, *Blue Is the Warmest Color / La vie d'Adèle chapitres 1 et 2* (2013), which won acclaim at the Cannes Film Festival, where Kechiche became the first African-born filmmaker since the Algerian Mohamed Lakhdar-Hamina in 1975 to win the Palme d'Or. But the film is in no way a reflection of Kechiche's birth in Tunis or his Arab upbringing within the immigrant community. Its origins lie in a comic strip by Julie March, *Le bleu est une couleur chaude* (hence the title used for the film's English-language distribution), and it is a mainstream French commercial production, which provoked its intended controversy through its very explicit depiction of lesbian sexuality and, arguably, Kechiche's exploitation of his two young stars. In the interview contained in the pressbook prepared for Cannes, Kechiche talks of Léa Seydoux, the older of the two actresses, possessing "an Arab quality (*arabité*), something of the Arab soul" and expresses his real pleasure in the fact that the Christian name of the other actress, Adèle Exarchopoulos, used to replace the comic book's original name Clémentine, "means justice in Arabic."[73] But *Blue Is the Warmest Color* is in no way a contribution to Arab cinema.

Karim Dridi, who was born in 1961 in Tunis, with a French mother and Tunisian father, has, like Kechiche, worked consistently from a production base in France. Dridi is an illuminating example of a foreign-born filmmaker who has ceased to be an outsider and has been assimilated into the host country's production structures. Whereas most of his Maghrebian-born contemporaries had to wait until after 2000 to begin their careers, Dridi was also one of the very few Arab filmmakers born after 1960 to make a debut as early as the mid-1990s. He began his career with two short fictional films in the early 1990s and quickly moved on to feature filmmaking. His striking debut feature, *Pigalle* (1994), is a mainstream French film, set in the seediest quarter of the French capital. It offers a close-in view of its four interconnected main characters—a stripper, a petty criminal, a pickpocket, and a transvestite—and includes explicit scenes of sex, homosexuality, and violence.

Dridi followed this with an equally forceful study of the French immigrant community, *Bye Bye* (1995). Set in Marseilles, it deals with two brothers, the adult Ismaël and his twelve-year-old brother Mouloud, who arrive from Paris to spend two weeks with their aunt and uncle prior to Mouloud's return back to the *bled*. From the opening sequence, the film paints a vivid picture of immigrant life in the slums around the port. The overcrowding at home is paralleled by close intermingling on the streets, where sex, violence, and racism are turned inward by the community, so that anyone, friend or neighbor, is a potential victim. Ismaël cheats on his white friend with the latter's Arab girlfriend Yasmine, while Mouloud is drawn by his cousin Rhida into a world of drugs and vandalism. Both brothers are sympathetically portrayed and hold our attention throughout, but they are no innocents. Nothing indicates that, back in Paris, Ismaël will show greater maturity, or that Mouloud will, in future, keep away from the lure of drugs and violence. Dridi's view of immigrant urban life is harsh and uncompromising. He keeps his (often handheld) camera close to the action, as in the scene of sexual passion between Ismaël and Yasmine on the stairs. As in *Pigalle,* the director is not afraid to shock, as when the source of the flames which haunt Ismaël's mind are explained in a frighteningly convincing scene in which his other, crippled brother is set alight in an accident for which he is responsible. Although Dridi is of Tunisian, not Algerian, origin, *Bye Bye* fits well within the tradition of *beur* filmmaking established from the mid-1980s onward by older filmmakers such as Mehdi Charef, Abdelkrim Bahloul, and Rachid Bouchareb.

A dozen years later, Dridi's second, equally forceful study of juvenile delinquency, *Khamsa* (2007), was presented at the JCC in Tunis as a Tunisian film. But this tale of a young gypsy who runs away from care and tries unsuccessfully to reintegrate himself with his family, is a wholly French production, set in the South of France. Dridi's other films are equally remote from any concern with Tunisian or Arab immigrant life. *Out of Play / Hors jeu* (1998) deals with two hard-up young actors who find themselves by chance at a film-star party and decide to profit from this by taking their hosts hostage. *Cuba feliz* (2000) is a break from Dridi's usual fictional concerns, a personally narrated "musical trip" though Cuba. *Fury / Fureur* (2003) is a return to fiction and to the central concern of Dridi's early fictional short films, boxing. Set in the 13th arrondissement of Paris, it traces the difficult relationship between a young Chinese girl (who is engaged to a rich and nasty Thai businessman she does not love) and a Frenchman involved in the boxing world, managing his brother's career.

The Last Flight / Le dernier vol (2009), in sharp contrast, is set in the Sahara (and shot in Morocco). It takes full advantage of the filmic possibilities of the limitless desert landscape, which, in truth, overwhelms the fairly minimal narrative, set in the French colonial world of the early 1930s. The indigenous Tua-regs play the role accorded to Indians in a John Ford western, while the whole focus is on the Europeans, specifically on the growing relationship between an insubordinate French lieutenant and an upper-class female aviator seeking her English lover, who has crashed his plane in the desert. The film, though sumptu-ously shot, does not manage to avoid the clichés that seem inherent to the co-lonial film genre (the chauvinistic captain who combines a belief in the French nation's civilizing mission with a total contempt for the Arabs, the sensitive sub-ordinate officer who speaks the language and respects the locals, the travails of a lone woman in a male world, etc.). It contributes nothing to Arab cinema.

* * *

In addition to Kechiche and Dridi, there are half a dozen or so other male new-comers, most of whom have been trained in Paris but are largely based in Tunisia. These include Moez Kamoun, Moktar Ladjimi, Jilani Saadi, Mehdi Ben Attia, and Elyes Baccar.

Moez Kamoun, who was born in 1962 in Tunis, followed film training at ESEC in Paris with extensive work (as many as fifty films) as an assistant director on Tunisian and foreign productions. He made four short films and a documen-tary before completing his two fictional features.

Word of Honor / Parole d'hommes (2004) begins in the idyllic seaside village of Nefta and traces the lives of three boys, Sassi, Abbes, and Saad, and their girl companion, Khadidja. The four play, quarrel, make promises to each other, and above all, are entranced by the Mercedes car, driven by town dwellers from Tunis, which for them represents total success in life.

Thirty years later, the narrative resumes in Tunis, where their lives and in-teractions are very different. Saad is the one who has made it: the wealthy owner of a shop, winner of the lottery, husband of Khadidja, and owner of their child-hood dream car, which he keeps in his garage and is reluctant to drive in public. For him, secrecy is the key component of his life. Sassi, by contrast, has failed in his life; we first see him as he is about to be fired from his university post, hav-ing foolishly opposed an intelligent student from a wealthy family, Olfa, who flirts with him and submits a thesis which is in fact plagiarized. She proves to be much more powerful than he, lures him on and then gets the family servants to beat him up. Failure drives Sassi to turn his anger toward Saad, whom he resents because he has stolen Khadidja from him. As before, Abbes is the go-between, who, of course, never succeeds in winning the lottery. Failing as well in his efforts to find funding for the children's books he wishes to publish, he tries to make money dealing with Saad about the book Sassi has written, which will reveal everything about his life. The book finally comes to nothing, and instead Sassi sets fire to Saad's shop.

Word of Honor offers a very disillusioned view of contemporary life in Tunis, a society where everyone is concerned only with his or her own interests. One of the few Arab films of the 2000s to be adapted (if very freely) from a novel— Hassan Ben Othman's *Promosport*—the film is awkwardly shaped as a dramatic narrative. It fails to focus on the core conflict between Sassi and Saad—they meet only at the very end, when the shop is on fire—and Sassi never gets to speak to the secluded Khadidja, who is no more than a shadowy figure in the film. Instead, the narrative puts its emphasis on the three male characters' largely failed personal relationships with other women: Sassi's confrontation with Olfa; Abbes's affair with his secretary, Selma; and Saad's involvement with a widow, Faiza, whom he takes as a secret "second wife." *Word of Honor* is confidently shot and directed and presents a trio of interesting, well differentiated characters, but its lack of narrative coherence limits its dramatic impact.

Late December / Fin décembre (2010) offers a much more interestingly structured story line. After the breakup of his current relationship, Adam, a doctor working in a Tunis hospital, finds himself drinking heavily and feels the need for a complete change. He arranges a transfer, so as to become the GP in a remote village, and almost immediately experiences the shock of being in another world when he is made to wear dark glasses when attending a woman having problems in childbirth. But he finds that the place suits him, and soon he is accepted there and becomes a lure for women with his nighttime guitar playing. Aicha has a very different experience, having left a life of drudgery and unwanted male advances in a nearby factory with no clear plans for the future. Her life changes utterly when her boyfriend suddenly and unexpectedly emigrates and she finds herself pregnant. Adam is totally supportive, and she is momentarily torn between him and Solifene, a neighbor who returns to the village from France in search of a bride. But when she learns that Solifene's intent is to capture a virgin he can keep isolated in his tenth-floor apartment (not in Paris but in the *banlieue*), there is no real choice to be made, and the film ends with the possibility of Aicha and Adam beginning a relationship.

Late December is structured as a tragicomedy, with multiple plot strands. Ibrahim, a taxi driver who fancies himself a poet, plays a key comic role. There is a lively view of village life, seen through the eyes of Ibrahim's daughter Emna, who realizes that Dalila, her stepmother, is cheating on her father. There are also a number of well-realized comedy scenes, such as the silent formal meeting of Solifene and Aicha, as prospective marriage partners, and her mother's subsequent prayer, when she hopes she is not wasting God's time. The couple's eventual breakup also has lively comic elements, while at the same time revealing reactionary male impulses to keep women "in their place." Above all, while offering an engaging dramatic narrative, *Late December* does not shy away from depicting real social issues, such as abortion, with Adam's matter-of-fact acceptance of this pointing the audience to a new social perspective on the place of women in a new Tunisia.

Moktar Ladjimi, who was born in 1975 in Monastir and studied at IDHEC in Paris, where he now lives. After making four short films between 1994 and 1997, he completed his first feature-length documentary, *Colonial Cinema / Le ciné colonial* (1997). With the sole exception of the early 1920s work of Albert Samama Chikly—the short, *Zohra* (1922) and the feature-length *La fille de Carthage / Aïn el-ghezal* (1924)—all the films made in Tunisia were shot by French directors and aimed at audiences back in France. The settlers were generally uninterested, and the Arab population were more interested in imported Egyptian or Indian movies, although local audiences were eventually sought for works of propaganda through the use of a wide-ranging cinébus distribution system. Chikly's daughter, Haydée Tamzali, who scripted and starred in both of her father's films, is present to comment on his work. In addition, a number of film critics and several post-independence Tunisian directors—Ferid Boughedir, Omar Khlifi, and Farida Benlyazid, along with the producer Ahmed Attia—give their views on aspects of the French colonial productions. There are also clips from twenty or so films of the period to illustrate the argument, some of these by major French filmmakers such as Jean Epstein, Jacques Feyder, and Julien Duvivier.

Film reached the Maghreb in the 1890s, when Louis Lumière (three of whose shorts are included) shot and screened films there. Subsequently the deserts and casbahs of the Maghreb became favored locations. Much of this filming was shaped by Western fantasies of the East, but at the same time, these are the only filmic records of the Maghreb at this period. Of course, the true history of colonization is never told. The films inhabit a fantasy world of stereotypical characters, where the gallant French legionnaire pursues a course of "pacification" solely for the benefit of the local inhabitants, and Arab women, mostly dancers or prostitutes, exist only for the sexual gratification of the warriors. The soldiers are seldom actually seen on their missions of pacification; more often they are depicted as lured and seduced by an incomprehensible Orient, or isolated and trapped by hostile forces. For some of those interviewed, this conscious colonial propaganda is to be taken seriously; for others, such as Ferid Boughedir, it is no more than an equivalent of the Hollywood western, with the legionnaires and Berber tribesmen standing in for the cavalry and the Indians. Only in the years immediately preceding independence does a countercurrent emerge, most notably in the work of René Vautier, who was to go on to play a key role in the development of an independent Algerian cinema. The story told in *Colonial Cinema* is a complex one, full of paradoxes, but Ladjimi handles his narrative well, fusing a complex mass of material into a satisfying and informative whole.

A Thousand and One Oriental Dances / Mille et une danses orientales (1999), also French produced, opens with clips from Egyptian musical films and the observation that everywhere in the world people dance. The film uses paintings, photographs, and graphic images, as well as extracts from almost twenty Hollywood, French, and Egyptian films. These range from Loie Fuller, as shot by Pathé in 1905, to Ladjimi's own 1999 documentary *La nuit du henné*. The film's range is wide, taking the audience from the worlds of ancient Egypt and India through to contemporary avant-garde theatrical performances. The recurring image—constantly reinterpreted and found irresistibly enticing by actresses and dancers alike—is that of Salome. Throughout, Ladjimi stresses the interaction between East and West in the development and interpretation of oriental dance, which not only influenced the flamenco in Spain but also fired the erotic imagination of orientalist painters across Europe. The crude colonialist image found in certain 1930s French films is transformed into the total glamour of Hollywood's imaginary East, which in turn influences Egyptian cinema as it develops its own mature style in its own golden age in the 1930s and 1940s, with dancers such as Tahiya Carioca and Samia Gamal.

In Ladjimi's view, oriental dance as a spectacle is now degraded to postprandial nightclub entertainment in the East, but other forms of dance continue to play an important part in women's lives there, especially in situations where women are together without men. The two contrasting examples given are the celebrations at all-female gatherings at wedding ceremonies and the exorcism rituals practiced by certain Tunisian religious cults. Meanwhile, in the West, oriental dance is flourishing, with the opening of hundreds of studios teaching it. In addition, a reinterpretation of oriental myths fascinates certain dancers and choreographers, the two examples offered being avant-garde productions of "Salome" and "The Dance of the Seven Veils," both staged in Paris. A similar mix of archival material, interviews, and contemporary footage characterizes Ladjimi's next documentary compilation, *L'orient des cafés* (2001), an equally wide-ranging study, which traces the development of the Orient through the changing patterns of the café lifestyle which forms a key part of Eastern culture and society.

Viva the Cinema: The Cinema of the South Facing Globalization / E viva le cinéma, le cinéma du sud face à la mondialisation (2010), which runs a full ninety minutes, is an equally broad survey. The core of the film consists of an interwoven set of short passages from interviews with directors from a variety of countries: Congo (Bassek Ba Kobhio), Venezuela (Atahualpa Lichy), Algeria (Malek Bensmaïl and Mohamed Lakhdar-Hamina), Zaire (Mweze Ngangura), Iran (Mohsen Makhmalbaf), Morocco (Daoud Aoulad Syad), Tunisia (Abdellatif Ben Ammar), Brazil (Carlos Diegues), and Taiwan (Hung Hung). Each talks directly to camera, with no questions or interventions from the interviewer (Ladjimi) included. These director interviews are backed up by interviews with a range of film critics and festival organizers. The intervening images consist of shots of audiences at various film festivals (where the interviews were presumably recorded), together with images of film posters and film extracts (mostly unidentified and unrelated to the director whose words overlap with them). The result is a rich and stimulating collage.

The definition offered of "Cinema of the South" is that it is a term invented by the North, with reference to a North-South dialogue, highlighting the geocultural, economic, and aesthetic specificity of a certain form of filmmaking. Obviously Africa, Asia, and Latin America have a huge variety of national cinemas, some—like Egypt—totally self-sufficient, others (those included in the definition of "Cinema of the South") poor, marginal, and in need of assistance. Confronting these cinemas are the forces of globalization—exemplified in terms of cinema by the continuing power of Hollywood—which regard film as a product to be marketed and exploited like any other. Fortunately, there are opposing views, in particular those held by the French, who, thanks to their notion of the "cultural exception," take on the task of offering support to the impoverished cinema of the South.

The type of cinema which emerges from this kind of assistance is inevitably an art cinema focused on the filmmaker as *auteur*. But for such a filmmaker, aiming to offer a personal vision linked to a locally rooted culture, such aid comes with obvious dangers. The script that is necessary to receive such funding will need to be read and approved by Europeans with their own view of the South. Compromise may be demanded and be difficult to resist. Even if the filmmaker maintains his own vision, he will be forced to take on the role of producer, even make his own attempts to distribute the film. At home, this will be difficult, as satellite television is increasingly reducing cinema audiences everywhere and pirated DVDs are ubiquitous. New technology, such as digital cameras, offers new, potentially fruitful options, but in the end it is up to the individual filmmaker to provide a rich new insight into the hidden aspects of the South: "a suburb of Tunis, a district of Mexico City, Ougadougou, an arterial road in Rio or an isolated village in Senegal."

Moktar Ladjimi's documentaries are complex works, packed with information and opinion. They are well organized and edited, offering genuinely fresh insights into their chosen subjects. He made his first and so far only feature film, *Summer Wedding/ Noce d'été / Bab el arch*, in 2004. The central theme of *Summer Wedding* is set out in the pre-credit sequence. In time-honored fashion, an old grandmother has gathered a ring of children around her on the roof terrace to tell stories. But now the terrace also contains satellite dishes, and when an equally small child emerges from behind one of them, dressed in a Spiderman costume, the children rush off screaming: the worlds of tradition and modernity are in collision.

The central figure is Hamid, an aspiring journalist, frustrated by the censorship that prevents the publication of his investigative journalism, undertaken with his ebullient photographer friend, Elyes. Currently he is not being properly paid and has to repeatedly cadge money from his mother. At home, his attitudes contrast strongly with those of his two brothers, Alaya, who struggles to maintain traditional values, and Sami, who is seeking to make a career in computing without the necessary backing from his family. Now age thirty, Hamid allows himself to be pressured by his father into a traditional marriage, arranged by the two families, with a neighbor's daughter, Rym. Although they are formally engaged, he refuses all contact with her, and she only comes alive when Elyes photographs her. Hamid glumly submits to the wedding ceremony, but walks out on the wedding night to take refuge with Elyes. A tearful Rym is left alone to remove her clothes and cut herself to provide the requisite bloodied sheet. In the absence of his editor, the glamorous divorcée Sara, Hamid manages to get his article on stealing satellite dishes into print. Sara forgives him, even though it will mean a fine, and even seduces him when they go back to her apartment. Next morning, when they are drinking and dancing in celebration with Elyes, the vice squad arrives.

The ending is open but marked by the havoc Hamid has wrought on those close to him. His father-in-law, Ansalem, who engineered his release from prison, has since been physically abused and threatened by Hamid. But he is last seen trying vainly to make fresh contact with Hamid. Our final image of Rym is of her weeping in her room, refusing to open the door to her mother. Sara and Elyes are left in custody with the vice squad. Hamid himself is seen from behind, walking off—somewhat uncertainly—into the distance along the railway line. Although Nouri Bouzid, Tunisian cinema's most gifted portrayer of tormented young men, contributed to the script, the major problem with the film is the figure of Hamid. The aim is clearly to show the situation of an individual caught between the pressures of tradition (which remains strong) and the frustrations of life under a dictator. But Hamid fails to gain our sympathy, as he is from the very start totally self-centered, weak, ineffectual, and self-pitying. He gets a visa for Paris but makes no serious attempt to leave. He declares he hates marriage but has allowed himself to become engaged and even goes through with the ceremony, even though he has no intention of consummating the marriage. He pronounces himself a journalist but objects to writing pieces about singers or soccer players, and shows little of the intensity and risk taking which one would expect of the great journalist he is convinced he could become. As one example, he leaves the stadium where a soccer match which he has been assigned to cover is taking place. In the local café, where he has taken refuge, he learns of a riot, which would have provided good copy for any reporter. He constantly complains: that he gets no recognition as a journalist, that nobody loves him, that he never had a sister. Why the attractive, self-assured, and successful Sara seduces him at the end of the film is a mystery: he never looks her (or anyone else, for that matter) straight in the eye. At the end of the film, he leaves behind a set of blighted lives, and his own future is obscure.

Summer Wedding is well shot and beautifully acted, with the portrayal of Rym outstanding (the scenes of her mild flirtation with Elyes and her stark self-mutilation are among the most powerful in the film). As one would expect from Ladjimi's documentary work, the organization of the editing is excellent. This is a very promising—if flawed—feature debut.

Jilani Saadi was born in 1962 in the small town of Bizerte and studied film-making in Paris. He made two short films in the mid-1990s before his feature debut, *Khorma: Stupidity / Khorma, la bêtise* (2002), set in his birthplace In the film he creates a sense of strangeness in the narrative, provoking a shifting emotional response in the spectator that is due to the choice of a very unconventional protagonist. Khorma (the name means stupidity in Arabic), with his red hair and pale complexion and habit of singing and dancing on the beach, is stereotypical outsider. His only real friends are children—adults treat him as a sort of village idiot. He is taken on as assistant (out of pity?) by an old man, Bou Khaleb, who tends the cemetery and carries out public announcements.

When Bou Khaleb dies, the villagers appoint Khorma his successor, but the results are not what they expect. Success goes to his head: he dresses up as Haj Khorma and calls himself Billal, a companion to the Prophet. Having laughed at him earlier along with the villagers, the spectator now finds himself laughing with Khorma at their discomfiture. But Khorma goes further and begins to exploit those weaker than himself, in particular an orphan girl. The community turns on him with real anger and shows no mercy: he is beaten, stripped, tied up, and smeared with honey (to attract insects). We have our third image of Khorma, a sacrificial victim (Christlike in Western terms). Only next morning does a child rescue him. Khorma does his little dance, as in the film's opening, but then goes off alone, a silent, defeated figure.

Khorma is a complex work, a kind of moral tale, but what is the moral? Should we rejoice that Khorma had his brief spell of power? Or pity his total defeat at the end, when he has nowhere to go? Perhaps both. Saadi's second film, *Tender Is the Wolf / Tendresse de loup* (2006), which uses the same lead actor (Mohamed Graya), takes place in a single dark night in Tunis medina. It tells of the gang rape of a pretty young prostitute, Saloua, and the savage punishment meted out by her brothers on the least violent of the perpetrators, Stoufa, who is beaten, stripped naked, and humiliated. Saadi clearly feels concerned with those on the margins of society (the village idiot, the prostitute), but the violence and personal humiliations in his films are extreme and his vision is bleak. There is the possibility of redemption here, along with the violence, but the films' endings are ambiguous as to what will happen to the characters after the most brutal of assaults.

Mehdi Ben Attia, who was born in 1968 in Tunis, studied sociology and politics in Paris and initially worked as a journalist. He began his film career as scriptwriter, writing sitcom episodes for Canal+ as well as working on several feature films in France. His first feature, *The String / Le fil* (2007), is one of the few openly gay films to be made in the Maghreb. Although there were problems at first with the authorization to film in Tunisia, the shooting, according to Ben Attia, went without a hitch,[74] although it seems unlikely that the film will receive much, if any, commercial distribution in the Arab world.

The thirty-year-old Malik, who has trained as an architect in France, returns home to live with his mother after the death of his father from cancer. She is a demanding, domineering woman (played by Claudia Cardinale), but he is relaxed, even in the face of her expectation that he will settle down, marry, and have children, and he resumes what was presumably his normal promiscuous homosexual life in Paris. Tensions threaten when he falls in love with his mother's twenty-five-year-old handyman, Bilal. Despite the gulf which separates them in terms of wealth and education, their affair proceeds smoothly, every step depicted in graphic detail, with some scenes of an explicit sexual nature. Even the awkward (potentially disastrous) moment when his mother catches the two of them naked in bed is smoothed over. His cousin Sirene's parallel lesbian relationship with Leila, which they hope to take further with Sirene bearing a child, is fully accepted by her parents. Even the fake wedding of Malik and Sirene (to give the child a name and a position in society) takes place without dissent or protest within the extended bourgeois community in which the two families live.

The "string" of the film's title refers to Malik's deep sense of being constrained, which he claims shaped his life as a child and adolescent; but there is no sign of this in his present demeanor. Everything in his life proceeds smoothly and without real tension; even when his mother is taken to the emergency room at the hospital, the problem turns out to be a mere allergy, from which she recovers in a day or so. *The String* is smoothly directed and makes the best possible use of its Tunisian setting and its upper middle class interiors. Ben Attia has said that "in France, the film would have had no interest; we've seen hundreds of stories about love between boys."[75] But despite the fact that he has set and shot his film in Tunisia, he has erased any hint that homosexuality might be problematic in a country with Arab culture and strong Islamic religious traditions. This is a world of wishful thinking, where class, culture, and religion do not intrude on personal sexual relations, not a clear examination of the tensions inevitable even within a French-speaking urban elite living in the Arab world.

I Am Not Dead / Je ne suis pas mort (2013) was from the outset conceived as a fantasy film.[76] It is a disorienting work which makes great demands on its audience's sense of reality and grasp of narrative logic. Although both Yacine, an ambitious young Arab-born philosophy student, and his French philosophy professor, Richard Artaud, a successful author about to be awarded the legion of honor, have difficult relationships with their fathers, they could otherwise hardly be further apart. There is, however, an ambiguous scene between them, when Yacine, who supports himself by working as a courier, delivers the proofs of Richard's latest book and is offered unexpected help with his career. But nothing prepares the spectator for the moment of Richard's death, when Yacine bursts in to reassure Richard's wife Eléonore and his friend Eugène that Richard is not dead and that he, Yacine, is in fact Richard.

The subsequent confusions about Yacine's identity—he appears to have forgotten his own identity and even his relationship with his brother Jamil—no doubt reflect Ben Attia's own cultural confusions when, arriving in Paris from Tunisia at the age of eighteen, he spent four years studying and, at the same time, turning himself mentally into a Frenchman, "a model Parisian."[77] In a sense these confusions of identity are resolved when Yacine makes love to Eléonore (attracted to him just as her husband had been). They talk lightly about whether Richard might be watching them and find this causes them no problem. Yacine moves in with Eléonore, in Richard's house, and all seems resolved. But Ben Attia maintains the ambiguity to the very end. Yacine's final "memory," with which the film concludes, is of himself as a five-year-old Richard, saying farewell to his mother stretched out in her open coffin.

Elyes Baccar, who was born in 1971 in Tunis, combined study at CLCF and FEMIS in Paris with work as assistant director with Ferid Boughedir and Ridha Behi. He has made short films and directed in the theatre. His first and to date only fictional feature is *Him and Her / Lui et elle / Hiya wa houwa* (2004). The official synopsis of the film reads as follows:

> On a winter's night, a young man who has been living as a recluse in his apartment for months, receives a visit from a young woman who comes in against his will. He rejects her, pretends to ignore her, but she ends by changing his perception of reality. Maybe she was not as real as all that . . .

The film, made on a tiny budget, with a single set and just two actors, was apparently the first digitally shot Tunisian film, although it was distributed as a 35mm film. After a press showing, one journalist wrote: "with its intellectual appearance, provocative style, and freedom of tone, this film which appears elitist could find its place in the commercial circuit."[78]

The film seems, however, to have achieved little popular success. In contrast, Baccar provoked great interest with his documentary about the Arab Spring, *Red Word / Parole rouge* (2011). Between these two very different films, Baccar produced *Wailing Wall* (2010), a two-hour documentary on the Palestinian situation and the Wall, produced by Al Jazeera. The approach adopted by Baccar is apparent from the synopsis he provides:

Hear the testimony of the people of Palestine as they voice their stories of suffering centered around a wailing wall. Their cry for help, for peace and freedom. They demonstrate against the separation wall that destroyed lives and demolished homes. Listen to the people as they grieve for the spilt blood of innocent children and loved ones.[79]

* * *

Three Tunisian women directors were active in the 2000s: Raja Amari and Nadia El Fani, both appearing at the beginning of the decade, and Ayda Ben Aleya, appearing at the very end. Their trajectories are very different. Amari was born in Tunis and studied filmmaking in Paris, while El Fani (born in Paris) and Ben Aleya (born in Tunis) both worked extensively in the film business before getting the opportunity to direct.

Raja Amari is the Tunisian woman director who has made the greatest international impact. Born in 1971 in Tunis, she studied at FEMIS in Paris and began with a widely shown thirty-minute fiction, *April / Avril* (1998), before making her feature debut in 2002. That film, *Red Satin / Satin rouge* (2002), established her as the most important Tunisian woman director since Moufida Tlatli and provoked scandal.[80]

Red Satin is the tale of Lilia, a respectable middle-aged widow who seeks release by dancing professionally in a nightclub. The film's inspiration comes not from personal experience but from the old Egyptian movies Amari watched with her mother as a child. *Red Satin* was not intended as a general study of women's place in Tunisian society: "I started out with a specific character. I wanted to study her evolution and how she's going to journey through the film. I didn't want to set the character against society."[81] The essential aspects of Lilia's situation are beautifully captured in the film's opening three-minute tracking and panning shot, showing her cleaning the room, pausing at a photograph of her dead husband, and then dancing demurely to the sound of the radio.

Her life changes when she goes at night to a neighboring cabaret searching for her absent daughter. Here she crosses a line from "the world of the day, strict, dominant, prudish" to "the world of the night, relaxed, marginal, lascivious."[82] She is gradually drawn more deeply into this unknown world, starting as a dressmaker, then trying on a dress and dancing for herself, and finally appearing on stage, in public. Life gets complicated as we discover that her daughter, Salma, also has a secret life, as well as a secret lover, Chokri, the nightclub's drummer. Unaware of this complication, Chokri and Lilia have a brief fling. If this was not shocking enough for Tunisian audiences, the ending actually celebrates Lilia's liberation. An almost regal Lilia, full of the confidence her secret life has given her, greets Salma and her shocked future son-in-law Chokri, and then dances, in red satin, at their wedding.

The narrative of *Red Satin* is beautifully shaped, moving easily between its two world and two generations, with the constant leitmotif of dance in all its social forms—as private self-contemplation, adolescent amusement, cabaret turn, and a key to the celebration of marriage. The parallels, contrasts, and dramatic ironies are well worked out, and the pace maintained through the intercutting of the various segments is admirable. What caused the scandal surrounding the film is, of course, the character of Lilia, who does not fit the social stereotypes of the older woman as victim or as upholder of tradition. Lilia transgresses, but instead of being punished—as women who act outside of male authority guidance always are in Arab cinema—she is instead shown flaunting herself before her respectable guests, almost as brazenly as in the cabaret.

Raja Amari followed her highly acclaimed first feature with a documentary on the traveler Isabelle Eberhardt, *Seekers of Oblivion / Sur les traces de l'oubli / Ala khoutta al nessyan* (2004). Eberhardt led an amazing life. Her aristocratic Russian mother left her husband (the St. Petersburg chief of police) to live with her children's anarchist tutor in Geneva, where Isabelle was born. Isabelle never knew who her father was and seems to have sought father figures in the various Algerian sheikhs she encountered in her later life. She grew up in Geneva at a time when it was full of Russian revolutionaries, including Lenin, and for a while she was tempted by political action. But instead she opted for an uncompromisingly individual life. In 1900, at the age of twenty-three, she left Geneva for Algiers, and for the six remaining years of her life Africa was her spiritual home. There she initially lived a disreputable life, among criminals and prostitutes. Very much the outsider in Geneva, she had habitually dressed as a sailor, a workman, or an Arab, and she spent much of her time in Algeria disguised as a man, Mahmoud. Indeed, it was while disguised as a man that she first met Slimène, the Arab soldier who would become her husband, and it was also as a man that she converted to a strict Muslim sect. She worked as a journalist but kept her real writings private, to be published only after her death, which came unexpectedly in a rare flash flood in the little town of Aïn Sefra.

A woman of violent contractions, Isabelle Eberhardt was passionate about the Arabs but also acted as a spy for General (later Marshal) Lyautey in his "civilizing mission" in North Africa. She would have made a fascinating protagonist for an Amari fictional film. But this documentary does not wholly capture "her real journey," described by her biographer Annette Kobak as being "from the new world to the old, from clutter, mental and material, to space, from inherited guilt to redemption, from seething complications to some measure of peace; and from mystery back to mystery."[83] The problem is largely the lack of relevant visual material: the life that Isabelle led did not leave physical traces— the sites where she lived and died are now all deserted or ruined. The film is likewise constrained by the fact that Amari's interviewees are fans rather than real scholars and hence able to offer only limited insights into the life of a very remarkable woman.

Raja Amari's second fictional feature, *Buried Secrets / Dowaha* (2009), is both a return to the claustrophobic world of her first short, *April,* and a venture into the world of mainstream gothic horror. In *April* she draws a fascinating portrait of two frustrated, slightly weird middle-aged sisters, who bring in a ten-year-old girl as a servant to work for them but gradually shift their attitude toward her, so that the child becomes a sort of fragile doll, to be cherished and stroked—a fate she seems to welcome. The film ends troublingly with a close-up of the child's knowing smile. *Buried Secrets* has the same social gulf, between servants and masters, set this time in a vast and largely dilapidated mansion. The former owner's servant family—the mother and two daughters, Radia and Aicha—are secretly living in poverty in the cramped basement quarters. Their living routine is disturbed when Ali, the grandson of the former owner, moves in upstairs with his very young girlfriend, Selma. They begin to make secret visits upstairs, with the younger daughter particularly fascinated by the girl's high heels and makeup, which she disturbs when the couple are out shopping. Her mother and elder sister, both more sexually aware, become obsessed with the half-naked body of the sleeping grandson, making successive ghostlike silent intrusions into his bedroom. All three begin to make use of the bathroom for private preening.

Aicha is tied up by her mother, after behaving in ways likely to betray them. Her cries are heard by Selma, who breaks into the basement to try to rescue her but is instead captured by the family. She is distressed when Ali, instead of searching for her, moves another girl in upstairs. Gradually she comes to terms with her captivity, befriends Aicha, and in effect becomes the fourth member of the family group. The turning point comes when Aicha takes her to her own secret place, the supposed grave of a dead baby. To her astonishment, she finds a dead dog buried there instead. Everything she has ever been told is now called into question, and this triggers a moment of total madness. The long-hidden secrets of the family unravel with devastating speed and horrendous results. Discovering that her "sister" Raida is in fact her mother, she responds by suffocating the grandmother who deceived and dominated her. Fearing discovery, Raida then kills Selma as she tries to escape, only to be cut down herself with a razor by Aicha, now wearing Selma's long white gown. After participating in this welter of violence, Aicha seems to find a curious sense of liberation. Our last view of her is walking in her white, blood-stained dress down the main street of Tunis—with the air of an innocent passer-by.

The atmosphere, built up through a set of powerful performances from four very different women and aided by Amari's meticulous set design and precise camera work, is greatly aided by a score marked by the haunting repetition of a cradle song. Like Faouzi Bensaïdi's choice of a comedy thriller to follow the universally praised *A Thousand Nights,* this move to the horror movie is a bold one for Amari. Her immense talents as a director are obvious, but the end result points to the difficulty of re-creating mainstream commercial genres (inspired by Egyptian melodrama) in an art-film production context.

Nadia El Fani, who was born in 1960 in Paris of Tunisian descent, worked as assistant director for numerous major directors, including Roman Polanski, Franco Zeffirelli, and Nouri Bouzid. She made her sole fictional feature, *Bedwin Hacker,* in 2002. Like her Maghrebian-born contemporaries, Raja Amari and Laïla Marrakchi, she offers a distinctive view of women, one far removed from that presented by the male filmmakers of the previous generation. On the one hand, *Bedwin Hacker* is a high-tech thriller, in which the characters make so-phisticated use of computers and converse by video link. On the other hand, it is almost a domestic drama, in that the two powerful, bisexual protagonists, the hacker Kalt and her pursuer, the special agent Julia, are intimately connected, having known each other since university. The film's casual images of nudity and indications of a lesbian affair give it an atmosphere rare in Tunisian cinema.

The tone of the film is set in the opening in the pre-credit sequence, where President Truman's television statement about the discovery of nuclear energy is overlaid with images of a cartoon camel, the Bedwin Hacker of the title. The action gets underway at Midès, an oasis in the desert, where the hacker Kalt and her friends see footage of a police raid on an immigrant group in Paris on televi-sion. Recognizing one of her friends, Frida, in the mêlée, Kalt resolves to go to Paris to rescue her. This she does, using her computer skills to convince the police that Frida is the king of Morocco's niece. She returns to Midès, pausing only to sleep with Frida's roommate, Chams. Then, with her niece, she undertakes her first piece of satellite hacking, breaking into an international soccer transmission with images of Bedwin Hacker and a message in Arabic. The French authorities put out a statement that Bedwin is a "technical error"—a statement the camel refutes in a series of further appearances.

The agent assigned to investigate both incidents is Julia, who takes the be-trayal by Chams, the journalist who is her lover, remarkably calmly. She suspects that Kalt, with whom she once had an affair, may be responsible and pursues her ruthlessly. She even uses Chams to spy on her, although she realizes this means that they will resume their relationship. Though knowing the noose is tightening around her, Kalt continues her activities, putting a free Arab voice on the Euro-pean airways. Ironically, it is not all the state's high-tech equipment but a child's postcard that eventually leads Julia to the oasis for a final confrontation. The narrative patterning of the film, which constantly switches between Paris, Midès, and Tunis, is disjointed and occasionally confusing, and the ending does not suc-cessfully resolve either the personal or ethical issues. But the film is lively and original, shot through with humor. Kalt emerges from betrayal and discovery unbowed and, with her friends, offers a vivid and unexpected set of images of liberated young Tunisian women who go off without men to drink and party with remarkable freedom. Chams meanwhile has the role usually assigned to women in Arab cinema, being the unwitting pawn used in their conflict by two more powerful women.[84]

Nadia El Fani has since completed two feature-length documentaries. *Ouled Lenine* is a personal tribute to her political activist father, who played the role of the writer whom Chams is ostensibly in Tunisia to interview in *Bedwin Hacker*. By contrast, *Secularity, God Willing / Laïcité Inch'Allah* is a study of events preceding the Arab Spring in Tunisia.

Ouled Lenine (2007)—the title means "children of Lenin"—begins as an affectionate tribute to Nadia's father, Bechir, the former director of the National Library and a lifelong communist supporter. Born in Paris but growing up in Tunis from the age of ten, Nadia El Fani enjoyed the best years of her life, she tells us at the film's outset, because she had a secret: she was the daughter of communists (the party was at that time banned in Tunisia). Her father talks of the importation of ideas such as revolution and communism from France in the 1950s and of his own conviction that nationalism alone was not enough. The pre-independence era was a period of hope, when everything seemed to be possible for the internationally minded communists, whose ranks were open to both men and women and recruits from any race or nationality. But the rise to power of the nationalist leader Habib Bourguiba crushed all their hopes. A foiled military coup gave Bourguiba the opportunity to ban the Communist Party (although it was not in any way implicated), and any chance of influencing the development of Tunisia vanished. There seems not to have been much actual violence toward party members (although some were imprisoned), and from this account Bechir seems to have lived a quiet, uneventful life.

From these early accounts of her father's hopes and dreams, often recorded as the two stroll in the sunlight through Sidi Bou Saïd, the streets of Tunis, or the medina in Sousse, El Fani widens the scope of her film to take in a more general picture of the history of the Tunisian Communist Party, through interviews with veterans (both men and women) and people of her own generation. The Tunisian Communist Party was never a major force in the country—it does not merit even a single index entry in Kenneth Perkins's 250-page *History of Modern Tunisia*. Yet as El Fani's interviews show, its supporters were intelligent, eloquent, and liberal minded. The director's respect for them and for their views is very clear. The party's early problems were those of defining an alternative to Bourguiba's nationalist vision, but later, like other Arab communist parties, it subsequently had to sort out its relationship with Islam. Opposing Islamic fundamentalism is self-evident, but Bechir El Fani is well aware that many of those giving their lives for Arab liberation are practicing Muslims. Despite his own confident atheism, he cannot reject such freedom fighters, and interestingly, Nadia El Fani herself admits that, faced with the question of whether she is a Muslim, she has no answer. The director's last question to Bechir is whether he is still a communist. He hesitates a little, then admits that he is. He is certainly opposed to injustice wherever it is to be found, even if he is a little unsure of what exactly the party can do in the contemporary world. The film ends with El Fani's dedication of her work to her daughter, her nieces and nephews (who will know nothing of this story), and with the old comrades individually singing passages of the "Internationale." *Ouled Lenine* is a perfect example of a contemporary Arab documentary genre, the affectionate family portrait.

Secularity, God Willing (2011) begins and ends with footage shot in August 2010, six months before the fall of President Ben Ali, while the protests (and government responses) were still peaceful. The army is obstructive, but the protest is allowed to go ahead without interference. The demonstrators are predominantly young and chant slogans demanding freedom, democracy, and dignity. They are unafraid and sing that they are willing to die for their country. The only jarring note is the appearance of an equally peaceful group of demonstrators who are demanding an Islamist state.

There is a public debate, in which Nadia El Fani plays a leading role, about the relationship between religion and the state, with demands for a revision to the Tunisian constitution, which defines Tunisia as a Muslim state. El Fani, whose mother is a Catholic and whose father is a Muslim (while she herself is "by the grace of God" an atheist), is well qualified to participate in this debate. The participants are largely middle class and well educated, and it is noticeable that the discussion is largely in French. El Fani's stated aim is to film the paradoxes of her society, which are very apparent at the meeting, with some (particularly older speakers) clear in their demand for a separation between state and religion, while others, mostly young people, admit to confusion.

The central portion of the film—presumably the documentary El Fani initially set out to make—examines a subject very relevant to the secularity debate: the way in which Tunisians behave during Ramadan. The sequence opens with an outward view of Tunis during Ramadan—tracking shots of empty streets and deserted street cafés. Later, there is a televised address from the Grand Mufti, giving precise instructions as to how the festival is to be observed.

But El Fani is keen to probe beneath the surface, to uncover the kind of contradictions apparent in the debate on secularity. She meets wine merchants who are more than happy to have a month off and sees the curtain in the supermarket designed to hide alcohol even from foreigners (who are not expected to observe the fasting and abstention from alcohol). But on the eve of the festival there are plenty of people (El Fani included) who are busy filling the trunks of their cars with beer and wine. She meets workmen who openly resist fasting (although one admits that his wife is very unhappy about this) and waiters who will only serve foreigners with alcohol (and, perceptively, are a little doubtful about her status in this regard). She stages a picnic on a summer beach, but this provokes no hostile reaction—people hardly bother to look. On another occasion, in Sousse, she enjoys the ritual end of a day's fasting at a meal which brings family and friends together and where each of the women has contributed a dish or two. Tunisians are split: the mosques are full, with the call to prayer accompanied by a reminder that papal Constantinople was captured by an army of fasting Muslims; but at the same time, behind closed doors and opaque windows, the cafés too are crowded, although the customers are anxious not to be filmed. El Fani repeatedly makes the point that there is no law to make people fast during this month, but one of her interviewees points out that this is not the point: Ramadan is sacred. *Secularity, God Willing* contains unique footage of the mood of the people in Tunis in 2010, when the overthrow of Ben Ali, which the young demonstrators call for, was still inconceivable. It is also a lively, informal account of individual opinions which are both informative and entertaining.

No Harm Done / Même pas mal (2013; co-directed with Alina Isabel Pérez) is an intensely emotional look at two patterns of events occurring between 2010 and 2011, both explicitly referred to in terms of "cells" in the film's introduction. The first concerns the cancer cells which, during the shooting of *Secularity, God Willing*, El Fani discovers have quite unexpectedly invaded her body. The successive stages of treatment—countless pills and then chemotherapy—recur regularly throughout the film, until El Fani is finally pronounced cured. The passages from the shooting of the earlier film show that the people's revolution involved men and women of all ages and had two aims: freedom and democracy. But the attempt to screen El Fani's film at the AfrIcArt cinema in Tunis, under its original title, *Neither God nor Master / Ni Allah ni maître,* is prevented by a violent (all male) Islamist protest (the "Salafi cells," in El Fani's words). Worse is to follow. Her admission in one of her interviews that she is an atheist (both her parents were communists) provokes vile abuse on the Internet, which takes a vicious delight in the baldness caused by her chemotherapy that she has made no attempt to disguise. *Secularity, God Willing* not only shows the strikingly brave manner in which El Fani publicly confronts her cancer but also provides immediate testimony on the manner in which the advances achieved by popular demonstrations in the "Arab Spring" were rapidly subverted by Islamist extremists. El Fani has made her own position clear:

> My rebellious spirit certainly developed because of my family history—it's not insignificant to be the daughter of communists—but also because of my profound need and hence desire for freedom. I have always considered that my films spoke of just one thing: freedom.[85]

Despite the filmmakers' very different initial trajectories, there are fascinating parallels and contrasts between the feature work of El Fani and that of Karin Albou, who is also Paris based. Both were born in Paris, with a French mother and Maghrebian father, and both have spoken of their closeness to their grandmothers. El Fani's grandmother lived with her when she made *Bedwin Hacker;* the film is dedicated "to my grandmother Bibi, who has always inspired in me the courage to resist." For both filmmakers the depiction of female nudity and sexuality and intimate relationships between women is totally natural. There is, however, a major difference (beyond the fact that Albou is half Jewish): while El Fani deals with mature women, securely located in their chosen worlds, Albou is primarily concerned with adolescents.

Ayda Ben Aleya, who was born in 1966 in Tunis, has followed her own personal trajectory. She worked extensively in Tunisian film production, as production manager, executive producer, and screenwriter, before presenting two fictional features at the JCC in 2010. The shorter of the two, *Dar Joued,* aka *Sinners / Pécheresses,* is set in 1903 in the Dar Joued women's prison, located in the Tunisian medina. It deals with four women who have transgressed the patriarchal order of the time: Nefissa, who wants to be rid of her aged husband; Mahbouba, who is seeking a divorce; Zina, who has refused the husband chosen for her by her father; and Hasna, who has protested after finding her husband with another woman. The narrative is built from their varied reactions—from submission to revolt—as they face up to the realities of their lives in prison.

Chronicle of an Agony / Chronique d'une agonie (2010), by contrast, is the story of a contemporary female victim, the twenty-five-year-old Donia. She has been abandoned by her parents and has the task of looking after her grandfather. Though totally dependent, he is foul-mouthed and abusive, both directly to Donia and about her mother for bringing disgrace on the family by leaving home. From the outset, Donia's situation is bleak. Her father abandoned her as a child and her grandfather despises her (complaining and calling her a whore every time she returns home to care for him). At work she has no close friends, just a boss who expects her to have sex with him. Her lover, Jamel, to whom she is ostensibly engaged, recoils from the mere mention of marriage, and when she lies to him that she is pregnant, responds only by proposing an abortion. Her life is monotonously repetitive and offers her nothing in the way of positive emotional return for the efforts she makes. The only exception is Adam, who becomes obsessed with her, following her everywhere. But he is a bearded and disheveled homeless tramp, unable to speak and with nothing to offer her apart from mute devotion. Together, however, they do share three dreamlike moments, as she dances for and with him in a deserted theatre. When this outlet too is closed, after the caretaker discovers them, she abandons everything to live rough, in the open, with Adam for a week or so. When she attempts to return to her old life, all gates are closed. Her lover has a new mistress, her grandfather has died, and her mother has returned only to sell the house and render her permanently homeless. Donia begins to doubt even Adam, thinking his silence may be faked and rebuffing his first tentative physical advances. When they are separated, Adam becomes totally distraught and Donia is driven, seemingly inevitably, to suicide. The only sign to commemorate Donia's life is Adam, sitting silent and motionless, looking at the river in which she drowned herself.

With its unrelenting tale of defeat, *Chronicle of an Agony* is a difficult film. There is not a single positive moment in Donia's life: her lover is never convincing in his affection, her grandfather never makes a single positive statement, her father is absent, and her mother is seemingly unconcerned about her, while Adam is, of necessity, mute. This is evidently a low-budget film, returning constantly to the same low-key locations, offering no sense of a wider social world (location in a specifically identified city, for example). The settings are always drab and the narrative pattern is set from the beginning, so that Donia's downward trajectory is unremitting—a world resolutely without hope.

Egypt

The three thousand or so feature films made within the constraints and possibilities of the Egyptian film industry fall outside the scope of this volume.[86] But since the late 1980s, a small number of Egyptian filmmakers have turned away from the conventional funding and production structures of the Egyptian film industry and sought French co-production funding and/or Fonds Sud aid. The model here is Youssef Chahine (1926–2008), a filmmaker whose work has on occasion proved very controversial in Egypt, but who is widely admired by subsequent generations of filmmakers across the Arab world. Ferid Boughedir, for example, describes him as "the true founder of most of the trends that have characterized or now characterize our Arab filmmaking, from the 1950s up to the present." Chahine is a director "continually forging new alliances in order to guarantee the possibility of experimenting with new paths, far from the commercial obligations of Egyptian cinema."[87] Since *Farewell Bonaparte* in 1985, Chahine's way of maintaining his independence had been to make all his films as co-productions between his own Misr International Company and French producers, especially Humbert Balsan. Two of the subsequent eight features—*Alexandria Again and Forever* (1990) and *Destiny* (1997)—received Fonds Sud support. As a result, Chahine acquired a huge reputation in France, where all his later films were been given a cinema release as well as being reproduced and sold as videos and/or DVDs. Among the numerous prizes and awards Chahine won in a career that spanned thirty-four feature films and fifty-seven years of directing was the Special 50th Anniversary Prize at the Cannes Film Festival.

A number of Chahine's former assistants, spanning the period from the late 1980s to the present, have followed his example. Their work comprises mostly fictional features, but in the 2000s one ex-assistant, Nadia Kamel, made one of the feature-length documentaries dealing with her own family of a type much in vogue throughout the Arab world in the past decade (her work is discussed in the previous section on documentaries). Key examples of Franco-Egyptian cooperation in the 1980s and 1990s are the co-productions of Yousry Nasrallah (born in 1952) and Asma El Bakry (born in 1947), which fall outside the scope of this volume. But in the 2000s, their example of seeking French support for at least some of their feature film work has been followed by two younger filmmakers: Khaled El Hagar and Atef Hetata, both of whom were born in the 1960s. Although they have very different backgrounds and training experience, both served at one time as an assistant to Youssef Chahine and both made their first features in co-production with Chahine's company, Misr International Films (MIF).

Khaled El Hagar, who was born in 1963 in Suez, began by studying law in Cairo before turning to filmmaking, at the age of twenty-one, to work as assistant to Youssef Chahine. El Hagar also has strong foreign links: he studied in the 1990s at the National Film and Television School (NFTS) at Beaconsfield in the United Kingdom. He subsequently made one of his features as an English-language film in London and currently lives between Birmingham and Cairo. He has also received co-production financing from Germany, beginning with his first feature, co-financed by ZDF.

After a number of short films, El Hagar made *Little Dreams / Petits rêves / Ahlâm saghîra* in 1993. This offers a bleak view of Egyptian history and society, set in Suez, the city where El Hagar grew up, and opening with a funeral procession. It is not apparent until the end of the film that what we have witnessed is the burial of the protagonist, the thirteen-year-old Ghareeb, since it is his narrative voice-over which introduces us to his family and to his own origins. The same curious, dreamlike effect is reprised at the end of the film, when it is the dead Ghareeb who speculates, again in voice-over, about the kind of life his young half brother will lead when he grows up, as we watch images of a defeated people.

Ghareeb's actual life is portrayed in graphic, realistic detail. He grows up in poverty after his father Sayed is killed in action during the Suez crisis, when Ghareeb is just two. His mother Hoda has to work as a seamstress; he leaves school at the age of eight to work in a printing company run by Saleh, who repeatedly urges Hoda to marry him, while treating Ghareeb with regular brutality. Saleh is everything Ghareeb's father was not: violent, reactionary, and a coward. But he does manage to seduce Hoda, make her pregnant, and marry her. There is no space for Ghareeb to dream, either at home or at work, but he does find an alternative father figure in Mahmoud, a crippled activist who was his father's friend and comrade in the army.

Ghareeb throws himself with whole-hearted enthusiasm into the activist cause, even secretly printing some of their leaflets as he comes to see Gamal Abdel Nasser as a godlike figure. His disappointment is therefore very real when Nasser's anti-Israeli actions lead to the utter Egyptian humiliation of the Six-Day War. Suez is devastated by Israeli planes, and dozens of his neighbors are killed. He hears at firsthand Nasser's broadcast admitting defeat and offering his resignation, and Ghareeb feels totally betrayed. Still unable to comprehend fully what is happening, he is caught up with the crowds who pour out onto the streets shouting "Do not leave us!" and "We will fight!" In the turmoil and confusion, he is hit and killed by a van covered in Nasser portraits.

This meaningless death caused El Hagar real problems in Egypt. The film was initially denied any television screening and upset his Egyptian producer. El Hagar reports that, when he saw the film, Chahine was very angry, "because, he said, 'you killed our generation by killing the little boy at the end,' but I said that this was my feeling about this time." Chahine "even threatened not to show the film in cinemas if I didn't change the end, but he eventually agreed that it was the right decision for the film."[88] Certainly nothing could be further from the ending of *Little Dreams* than Chahine's own filmic treatment of Nasser's televised resignation speech on July 9, 1967. In *The Sparrow* (1973), Chahine, who had had his own difficulties and differences with the Nasser regime, has his protagonist, the ordinary woman of the people Baheya, take to the streets to lead what becomes a flood of humanity shouting "No!" to the resignation and to the very idea of national defeat. Twenty years on, we are used to unusual and unexpected dramatic endings; yet here, after we have developed such sympathy for Ghareeb, El Hagar's decision to have him killed in a pointless traffic accident is still jarring.

In many ways, the English-language feature, *Room to Rent / Chambre à louer* (2000), which followed, could hardly be more different, but it contains a similar mix of realist and dreamlike elements, culminating in a totally unexpected ending. If *Little Dreams* was based on El Hagar's experience of growing up in Suez, the new film is even more openly autobiographical—the protagonist Ali is an aspiring Egyptian screenwriter trying to survive and make a living in London while his student visa is running out. It reflects, as El Hagar has stated, his own personal experience and the puncturing of his given assumptions about East-West relations: "I learned a lot renting rooms in different parts of London. Mixing with the English and adopting their way of life, I lost the clichés I'd had for years."[89]

Ali discovers the complexities of English heterosexual relations (with his married dance pupil Vivienne), the explicitly sexual nature of London's show business (thanks to his friendship with Linda, who works as a Marilyn Monroe look-alike), and the hitherto unknown world of homosexuality (through Mark, from whom he rents a room). All this is far removed from the traditional world of

Ali's family, brought back to him in phone calls to his mother. None of these fresh discoveries is explored in any depth, however, as El Hagar adopts a style which attempts to blend English whimsical humor (Ali is accompanied on his travels by his pet goldfish) with the characteristic bizarreries of Pedro Aldomóvar, whose style the director has sought to emulate.[90] Realistic probing of cultural, sexual, or age differences is never part of El Hagar's agenda. In the early parts of the film, Ali's scripted fantasies become mixed up with the real lives of those on whom they are too closely based. At the end, the film moves into a totally surreal mode, as Ali accepts wholeheartedly the delusion of the blind, seventy-two-year-old Sarah Stevenson (played by Anna Massey) that he is her reincarnated childhood lover. They even get married (solving his visa problem), but the inherent difficulties of such a relationship for the twenty-something Ali are avoided, when she promptly dies idyllically. He is left with his English residency, her property, and to complete it all, Sarah's reincarnation as a beautiful twenty-year-old would-be lodger.

It is reported that El Hagar's fifty-minute NFTS graduation film, *A Gulf between Us* (1994), the story of a love affair between an Arab student and a young Jewish girl, "caused an outrage and great anger in the Egyptian press when it was shown in Cairo in 1995," such that the El Hagar "who not only made [it] but also played the main role, was accused of promoting normalization with Israel and could not go back to Egypt until 2003."[91] Whatever the precise circumstances, El Hagar made a triumphal return to the Egyptian film scene with his new feature, *Women's Love / L'amour des femmes / Hob al-banat* (2004), which won seven awards at the 2004 Egyptian National Film Festival.

The film's opening premise is that a womanizing multi-millionaire Egyptian businessman (nicely named Abu Hagar) has left his fortune to be divided equally among the three daughters—Nada, Roaya, and Ghada—whom he had with successive wives and who barely know of each other's existence. The one condition is that they live together for a whole year in his luxurious apartment in Cairo. This is unproblematic for the home-loving cook Nada, who looked after their father during the last five years of his life, but less so for her half sisters. Ghada, the youngest, has been brought up in Alexandria, in an environment that has made her aggressively independent, very competitive, and utterly hostile to men. Roaya, by contrast, has grown up in a very Westernized context in London and feels herself an outsider both in England and in Cairo. The fourth key figure is their new neighbor, Moheib, a psychiatrist who spies on them from his apartment, becomes involved emotionally with all three in succession, and continually offers trite counseling on "how to live."

Inevitably, there are lively arguments and wrong decisions, questionable involvements and moments of self-revelation. But love conquers all. Nada resolves her tortured relationship with her now-divorced ex–college sweetheart

Omar and becomes a celebrated television chef under his guidance. Ghada melts enough to admit an involvement with one of her mature students, and Roaya, after a flirtation with a handsome but self-absorbed film star, settles for the ever-understanding Moheib. All can end with a party to the strains of "That's Amore" (sung in English).

After the musical *None but That / Rien que ça / Mafesh gher kada* (2006), which was loosely based on Bertolt Brecht's ballet *The Seven Deadly Sins* and "exposes the current desire for instant fame and wealth in not just contemporary Egypt but Africa, whatever the cost,"[92] El Hagar resumed his examination of contemporary Arab society with *Stolen Kisses / Baisers volés / Qubulaat masruka* (2008). Like so much of El Hagar's work, this is a film which changes tone and direction as it proceeds. It begins, as its title implies, as a romantic comedy, tracing the difficulties of a number of young student couples who have family problems at home and few opportunities in the world of work outside. The central character, Ihab, is an engineering graduate who cannot get a decent job in Cairo or obtain the visa necessary to emigrate. He is forced to work pumping gas in a garage, a job which means he cannot afford to set up house and is certainly not going to recommend him to the wealthy businessman father of Marwa, the girl he loves. Ihab's sister, Hanan, is in love with a serious, slightly older student, Ezzat, but neglects her studies and embarks on an affair with her middle-aged professor. Their friends, Hola and Mohsen, are saving for marriage, but Hola's father steals their savings (to support the family) and tries to marry Hola off to a wealthy, much older man. On the fringe of the group is a fellow student, Layla, who, unknown to them all, is working in the evenings as a prostitute to support her own impoverished family.

It is Layla's desperate act of committing suicide by setting fire to herself which marks the film's transition to full-blooded melodrama. Thanks to his treacherous friend Selim, the naive Ihab is caught up in a vice racket making pornographic videos and then implicated in the murder of the woman who had seduced him. The latter part of the film is full of ugly threats and violent confrontations, with the couples separated and Ihab eventually sentenced to a year in jail. But in one final, unexpected (and unmotivated) change of mood, the three couples are shown reunited and embracing—as if nothing had happened—on Ihab's release from prison. Despite this contrived happy ending and the numerous Egyptian prizes it won, *Stolen Kisses* proved highly controversial in Egypt. There was much concern expressed about the sex scenes (quite mild by contemporary Western standards), and El Hagar even received death threats on the Internet for "debasing the image of Egyptian girls."[93]

Lust / L'envie / El shooq (2011) was made as a French co-production and with considerable French government assistance, as well as post-production funding from the Doha Film Institute, but it is essentially a mainstream Egyptian feature.

One indication of the gap between El Hagar and his contemporary Arab colleagues outside Egypt is that he does not act as his own scriptwriter (and does not even claim a co-writing credit). *Lust* was scripted by Sayed Ragab, just as *Stolen Kisses* was written by Ahmed Saleh, yet both films connect thematically with El Hagar's earlier films. The director has provided a very clear view of his ambitions in making *Lust,* which, he says, "brings us into the lives of the inhabitants of a marginalized street in Alexandria, the second largest city in Egypt. Familiar, moving, and funny, each character is isolated in their fierce, yet fragile dreams."[94]

The film opens and closes with images of the sea, and many of the songs interspersed throughout the narrative refer to the power of the sea. Against the openness and freedom of the seascapes are set the constraints and oppressions of the poor Alexandria backstreet that is the setting for most of the action. Here people live in close proximity, with the young frustrated in their emotional ambitions and their elders too scared to be bold enough even to try to change their situation. In this context, it is not surprising that when Saad, the young son in the Shooq family, falls ill, the family has no ready way to pay for his hospital treatment. In these early scenes, the action is convincingly shaped as a realistic, fragmented study of urban deprivation. But even at this point, one character stands out from the rest, Saad's mother Oum Shooq, who tells her neighbors' fortunes and experiences moments of communication with (she is convinced) the spirit world, during which she rocks to and fro, banging her head and risking injury.

It is with Oum Shooq that we enter the familiar world of Egyptian melodrama. We gradually learn that she was disowned by her family twenty years earlier for marrying—out of love—her husband, who is now a habitual drunkard who takes little interest in or responsibility for their family (they also have two teenage daughters). Faced with the need for money, Oum Shooq resolves to attempt reconciliation with her family, sets off to Tanta, and then recoils at the last moment. On impulse she boards a train to Cairo, where, finding she cannot get a job, she decides to beg on the streets. By the time she gets back to Alexandria with money to pay for his treatment, her son is dead, but she continues her double life, leaving regularly, ostensibly to collect more of her inheritance in Tanta but actually to continue to work as a Cairo beggar.

But working as a beggar is socially degrading; Oum Shooq determines that she has to dominate the street in order not to be humiliated. This she does by using her insight into human behavior and her newly acquired wealth. She continues her trips to Cairo, but one day, inevitably, she is recognized by someone from the street in Alexandria. Her aim, after the death of her son, was to ensure the future of her daughters; but in fact the opposite happens. In her absence, and without any sort of parental oversight, both of her daughters have allowed themselves to be seduced by strangers on a first date. *Lust* is not altogether convincing, even as a melodrama. Can a woman, even in deepest despair, really kill herself by banging her head on a wall? Do Cairo beggars earn, quite literally, sackfuls of money? But the film is skillfully made and proved very popular with Egyptian audiences and critics. Certainly, after the death threats he received for *Stolen Kisses,* one can only admire El Hagar for daring to include explicit scenes of the girls' seductions and allowing the pair to walk off unpunished at the end, looking forward to a new life, away from the street, to be funded by their mother's sackfuls of money.

Khaled El Hagar is a talented, prolific, and versatile filmmaker who has made short films, features, and television programs in both Europe and Egypt and provoked much controversy. His career offers a fascinating variant on the pattern, typical of so many of his generation, according to which a filmmaker of Arab birth or descent, after being trained and working in exile, is subsequently absorbed into the host nation's mainstream production. Obvious examples of this are the Tunisian-born Abdellatif Kechiche in France or the Syrian Ruba Nadda in Canada. El Hagar's progress is the reverse of this. After years of living abroad, he has accomplished a return to his origins in the Egyptian film industry. Losing his youthful enthusiasm for European alternative cinema (most notably Pedro Aldomóvar), he has been able to re-establish himself in the heart of Egyptian national cinema, gaining large local audiences, winning national film festival awards, and even obtaining the top prize at the Cairo International Film Festival in 2010. His later films offer fascinating insights into Egyptian society on the brink of the Arab Spring, with *Lust* heading the box office listings two weeks before the revolution began.

Atef Hetata was born in 1965 in New York City but was brought up as a child in Egypt. His father is a doctor, novelist, and activist, and his mother is Nawal El Saadawi, the celebrated feminist activist and author of such books as *The Hidden Face of Eve: Women in the Arab World* (1980), *The Fall of the Imam* (1989), and *A Daughter of Isis: The Autobiography* (1999). He studied at Cairo University, where he won a literary prize for his first collection of stories, before graduating from the Faculty of Engineering (Department of Communications) in 1988. He subsequently spent some time in Paris, where he had a brief attachment to FEMIS and made his first short film, *Salut Barbès* (1989), about the Parisian district of that name. On his return to Cairo in 1989, he worked as assistant to a number of directors, including Youssef Chahine, and made two more short films, *The Violin / Al-kamanja* (1990) and *The Bride of the Nile* (a denunciation of arranged marriages; 1993). The best known of these short films is *The Violin,* produced by the Arab Women's Solidarity Movement, which was founded by his mother. This twenty-two-minute film has no dialogue but an almost continuous music track, comprising a mixture of Saint-Saens and Massenet. It opens and closes with a woman violinist in a park, and the intervening collage of often-enigmatic little scenes presumably represents her thoughts, memories, dreams, and fears.

Hetata's only feature to date is *The Closed Doors* / *Les portes fermées* / *Al-abwab al-moghlaka* (1999). He has said that his intention in making the film was "to make a film about adolescence, and to set it in Cairo because that is a city that I know. . . . I also wanted to tackle the political and economic influence of the Gulf War, another subject that the Egyptian cinema has rarely taken on." A third subject which forced itself upon him was Islamic fundamentalism: "I could not avoid this subject while speaking of adolescence. It's not I who has chosen this subject; it's the subject that has imposed itself on me." Fortunately, this is an issue on which he has a clear opinion: "I definitely believe that the best way to avoid fundamentalism is to be as open as possible and to resolve the fundamental problems of society. Freedom of speech is not the least of these. Corruption and economic issues too."[95]

The film is indeed set during the Gulf War, and there are constant short clips from television and radio broadcasts, but the tensions and confusions of adolescence remain the main focus of the film throughout. It opens with a close-up of Hamada's eye looking through a hole in the wall, as he neglects his studies to look at the innocuous behavior of the girls in the neighboring school. After having been suspended temporarily from school, he gradually begins to skip classes, as he replaces his ambition of becoming an airline pilot with the reality of working and earning money by selling flowers to passers-by on the streets. This transition is beautifully captured by Hetata. As a school presentation makes clear, Hamada admires his only real possession, a set of homing pigeons, for their sense of freedom. It is these birds he sells to finance his first set of roses when he turns to street-selling.

The role of school in shaping Hamada's upbringing is taken over by the mosque (one of the few doors always open to him), where he is confronted with the fundamentalist Islamic teachings of the local imam, Sheikh Khaled. His tales of heaven and hell and the need to purge the world of sin do not help Hamada come to terms with the contradictions of this particular moment of his life. Despite the growing hold of fundamentalism on his thought processes, he cannot prevent himself from committing acts of "sin," eyeing the thighs of a mini-skirted tourist or pulling off the veil of a young servant at the mosque. The mosque's eventual solution to his family's financial problems—that he marry Sheikh Khaled's daughter and his mother become the second wife of another imam—fills Hamada with visible apprehension and is totally unacceptable to his mother, Fatouma.

It is in Hamada's home that the tensions grow toward their climax. Fatouma's husband left her for a much younger woman years ago, and she has had sole responsibility for supporting and bringing up Hamada. His older brother Salah, who was sent to work in Iraq by their father, was conscripted into the Iraqi army at the time of the Iran-Iraq War and has not been heard of since. Fatouma is as uncertain as her son about his identity at this age. On the one hand, she invites him to sleep with her, "as he did when he was younger," when she suffers from flu. On the other hand, he is her "little man," and there is a moment when she gets them both to pose in front of the mirror (troublingly, like a married couple) in new clothes they have both just acquired. These tensions and ambiguities are exacerbated by Fatouma's friend and neighbor, his "aunt" Zeinab, who is a sexualized version of his mother. Ostensibly a nurse, she is in fact working as a prostitute to support her family. Learning this, Hamada on one occasion leaps on her like one of her clients, only to run away humiliated by what he has done. Yet later, at a moment of crisis, he needs her to hold him in her arms like a child.

In this increasingly complex set of relationships, Fatouma becomes one of the women Hamada spies upon. He is suspicious when his teacher Mounir offers him home tuition free of charge and views the growing relationship between Mounir and Fatouma with horror. Hamada rejects the idea of a second "father' possessing his mother. When he tracks them down to Mounir's apartment, where they have been making love, he bursts in and stabs them both to death. As he sits between the two bodies, hardly comprehending what he has done, there is a loud banging on the closed doors of the apartment—he has presumably been discovered. The film dissolves to black, so that "the ending leaves us with nothing to hold on to."[96]

The Closed Doors is a complex film, dealing sensitively with a delicate subject. It sets the action convincingly in a society characterized by the huge gulf between the very rich (the "Monsieur" and Madame" for whom Fatouma works) and the kids struggling to make a living on the streets. Unlike most Egyptian melodrama, the film allows its characters and their interactions to develop slowly toward its genuinely shocking climax. It is full of subtle visual touches. On Hamada's last day at school, the pupils revolt and tear up their exam papers, which demand knowledge they have not been taught. Hamada remains at his desk, making and throwing a paper airplane—the film's last allusion to his lost career ambitions. With regard to *The Closed Doors,* one can only echo Chale Nafus:

> What is surprising and disheartening is that, for unknown reasons, Atef Hetata has not made any more films since 1999. His views of the Egyptian Uprising of 2011 could be truly fascinating, and hopefully there will be such a film.[97]

* * *

By definition, much low-budget independent Egyptian cinema, which does not follow the Chahine pattern of seeking funding from European sources, will not receive foreign attention, international distribution, or release in subtitled DVD format. For that reason, this section on new Egyptian cinema cannot be more than partial, dealing only with the few who have been able to gain wider international acclaim for their work. Four Egyptian independents, who began their feature filmmaking in the latter part of the 2000s, stand out. Ibrahim El Batout, Ahmad Abdalla, Ahmed Rashwan, and Maggie Morgan all have considerable documentary experience and are resolutely opposed to the structures and modes of production of the Egyptian commercial entertainment industry, even though this means that they have to work with very limited resources. All four produced work immediately related to the Egyptian Arab Spring.

Ibrahim El Batout was born in Port Said in 1963 and graduated from the American University of Cairo in 1985. From 1987 to 2004 he worked as a war correspondent, making reports and documentaries, largely for international television companies, filming twelve wars in over thirty countries. The experience left him exhausted: "I had lost my faith in documentary; I was making all these films in war zones, I was taking all these risks because I thought the films could change something. But after eighteen years, I realized that the documentaries changed nothing." After a spell of working as a carpenter, El Batout returned to filmmaking with a fictional film, *Ithaki* (2005), which taught him that, acting as his own cameraman and using his own camera, he could work "without a budget, or with a very small budget." El Batout is very much a product of the digital age. He used the same method for his second, better-known feature, *The Eye of the Sun / Ein Shams* (2008): "As we lived under an extremely repressive regime, I told myself that this was the only way we could make films that could really escape the control of the regime. Because of that I didn't ever write a script, didn't present scripts to the censorship authorities and never sought permission to shoot."[98]

Ein Shams combines documentary and fictional elements. El Batout has described the origins of the film in these terms:

> *Shams* was inspired by an encounter in September 2005. At the time I had just finished my first fictional film *Ithaki* and was involved in a project teaching children living in Upper Egypt how to use the art of theatre and filmmaking. Mohamed Adel Fatah, a teacher and a director who was also participating in the project, put forward the idea of positioning my next film in his neighborhood, Ein Shams. . . . Being a place that has long haunted and fascinated me, I took up his evocation and I wrote a story that was appropriate for Ein Shams. In this film I use footage from my last visit in Iraq, thus bringing full circle my documentary work that was marked by my first project in the Ein Shams neighborhood almost 20 years ago.[99]

His own synopsis of the film reads as follows:

> From once being the capital of Egypt during the Pharaonic era and a sacred location marked by the visit of Jesus and the Virgin Mary, Ein Shams has become one of Cairo's poorest and most neglected neighborhoods. Through the eyes of Shams, an eleven-year-old girl inhabitant of this neighborhood, the

film captures the sadness and magic that envelops everyday life in Egypt. In a series of heart-rending events, the diverse characters of the film showcase the intricacies of Egypt's political system and social structure, and give a glimpse into the grievances of the Middle East region and the complex relationships of its nations.[100]

El Batout's third feature, *Hawi* (2010), was made using a team of students from a film school in Alexandria, where he was acting as an advisor. The cost of the shooting was just $6,000, and El Batout managed to raise a further $100,000 to complete the film and show it at the Tribeca Film Festival in Doha. There it won a major award and was granted a further $100,000, which allowed the cast and crew to finally be paid. The plot is structured to reflect the generational gap between two 40-year-olds returning to Alexandria—Brahim from exile in France and Youssef from years in prison—and the daughters they are eager to see again after so many years. But it also contains "a number of seemingly unconnected subplots, concerning a group of aspiring songwriters, a satellite TV executive searching for a show host, an elderly juggler leading his sickly horse through the city streets, and so on."[101] The film ends with a song by Maser Egbari:

> I became a juggler
> I am addicted now to holding back my tears, when grieving the most . . .
> It is because I got used to seeing my dreams pass me by
> That I gave up and left the dust on my face untouched.

El Batout's subsequent feature, *Winter of Discontent / El sheita elli fat* (2012), is a vivid, if oblique, account of the Arab Spring (the events in Tahrir Square can be heard but not seen from the protagonist's apartment), culminating in Hosni Mubarak's resignation. The key characters are Amr, a political activist whose 2009 torture is shown in graphic detail, his girlfriend Farah, a television presenter who resigns in disgust at the lies she is expected to tell, and behind all these events, the imperturbable, inscrutable state security officer Adel, who combines brutal sadism and ritual humiliation during his working hours with a tranquil and untroubled domestic life with his wife and small children. The film is full of penetrating insights into a disconcerting situation, masked and distorted by the authorities, which bewildered Egyptian citizens can only begin to understand by watching BBC television broadcasts.

The much younger **Ahmad Abdalla** was born in Cairo in 1978 and initially studied music. Although he never undertook formal film training, he worked from 1999 as an editor, both on documentaries and, from 2003, on feature films, including El Batout's *Ein Shams*. But most of the films on which he worked were mainstream Egyptian musicals, which taught him a great deal about how the commercial system works:

> In the commercial cinema, the star says, "I don't like my face in that shot, let's cut it," and in the end we discovered that the project didn't in any way resemble the initial ambitious project, not because they had begun by saying "I want to make a stupid commercial film," no, they'd said, "I want to make a serious film, a good film for once, we want to change everything and make a good film." But they accepted all these changes.[102]

Although there are differences in style and working practices between the two directors, the outcomes for both El Batout and Abdalla are similar: "We end up with the same idea as the one we set out with."[103]

Abdalla's first feature, *Heliopolis* (2009), is an independently made fictional feature about a number of young people on a single winter's day in the Cairo suburb of Heliopolis: "Their paths cross and their stories overlap, but they are caught up in their struggle and are oblivious to one another against the background of what used to be one of Cairo's most glamorous neighbourhoods."[104] Perhaps only someone who, like Abdalla, had spent years working in the Egyptian commercial cinema could have come up with a narrative so resolutely remote from that industry's fictional patterns and structures. Heliopolis was built by and for Egypt's expatriate community, who left en masse in 1956 with the advent of Gamal Nasser. Now it is crowded but run-down, a shadow of its former self, with only a handful of inhabitants from the old days.

A key figure in the film is Ibrahim, whose MA researches into the past of Heliopolis are hindered by the reticence of his interviewee and by the refusal of the police to allow him to video in the area. Some of the characters are trapped in the suburb, such as Engy, a hotel receptionist who deals drugs on the side to raise money and help convince her parents that she is actually in Paris. There is also an anonymous, often sleepy soldier, whose role, it seems, is merely to watch those passing by and whose only friend is a stray dog. Hany, a doctor, is trying to emigrate but finds his papers are not in order and fails to sell his apartment, as the would-be buyers do not turn up in time. Hany is also uncertain about what to do with his dog, or how to cope with leaving his girlfriend behind, as against his will he is drawn back into the Christian community. Ali and Maha, who want to move to Heliopolis and buy the apartment, are worn out and frustrated by the pressures of supermarket shopping and Cairo traffic. They seem to be on the brink of breaking up.

No one has a positive outcome to the day: nothing has been achieved. Hany and Ibrahim find that their relationships have terminated, and only Maha, after being dropped off by Ali, offers a positive note, when she returns to the car to tell Ali she loves him. One of the characters remarks that this has been a wasted day, only to receive the response that tomorrow will be no different—a sentiment the film wholeheartedly endorses.

Abdalla's second feature, *Microphone* (2010), which won the top prize, the *Tanit d'or,* at the Journées Cinématographiques de Carthage in 2010, had a larger budget, being produced "by a guy of the type who makes two or three commercial films a year and then one non-commercial film."[105] As in the earlier film, Abdalla worked without a formal script or fixed dialogue, just twenty or so written pages. Despite Abdalla's claims to the contrary, *Microphone* is essentially a two-hour documentary interspersed with short fictional episodes, rather than a fully fledged fictional narrative. The film's structure follows the pattern of Abdalla's own discovery of Alexandria: "It all started when I was wandering the streets of Alexandria like a tourist. The city had been as unfamiliar to me as it is to many Cairenes who are used to spending a week or two there in the Summer."[106] His discovery of Alexandria's alternative cultural scene—dozens of pop musicians, graffiti artists, amateur filmmakers, and even skateboarders—furnished him with the subject for his film, and the stories told by the individual artists he met gave him much of his material.

Although the film opens with a spirited rendering of "Welcome to Alexandria," the situation of Abdalla's alter ego, Khaled, who similarly wanders through the city streets, is initially bleak. In the seven years of his absence, his father has been plunged into silent depression and his former girlfriend Hadeer is planning to leave to study for a PhD in London. But Khaled is reinvigorated by his encounters with the uninhibited (often verbally offensive) heavy metal bands, hip-hop groups, and rap singers (the girls needing to mask their faces so that their parents will not find out), and he plans a concert for them. Just as Khaled represents Abdalla the author exploring his subject, so a couple of students making their graduation film about the bands mirror the filmmaker's own production methods. Magdy and Selma's use of a tiny video camera, often concealed in a box to capture a direct image of their subject, parallels Abdalla's own approach:

> I chose to make an independent low-budget film, with a crew of no more than eight people. I decided to use a camera that was never used before for such a film, which is a Canon D7, a photo camera that shoots video. . . . We used the natural lighting of our locations to achieve some visual credibility, along with photographic lenses that gave an image close enough to the eye's vision.[107]

The result is a real closeness to the action and some striking imagery of the city of Alexandria, shown in a way tourists never see it.

As in *Heliopolis,* there is no sense of narrative progression in *Microphone.* The concert to which the film seems to be building up never happens, thwarted finally by conservative elements such as the police and the worshippers at a neighboring mosque. The greatest barrier to innovation and creativity is the caricatured bureaucrat Saleh at the National Cultural Center. He constantly tells everyone that he is really an artist himself and has so many projects to undertake, hindered only by his administrative duties. He gets his come-uppance at the end of the film, when the graffiti artists paint "Fuck You" in large letters on the wall opposite his office window. Saleh is an interesting fictional caricature, but the most fascinating example of Abdalla's concern with improvised performance is the depiction of Khaled's only meeting, in a café by the sea, with Hineer. The film returns to this scene six or seven times, but what we see are not fragments of a long encounter but a set of clearly improvised variations on how the meeting may have gone. Most of the other personal stories in the film are no more than sketched-in episodes, which do not reach any dramatic resolution (although the fish found live at the market early on is returned to the sea at the film's muted ending).

Abdalla offered a fascinating (pre-2011) comparison between his first two films:

> *Heliopolis* is a very nostalgic film, and *Microphone* isn't. In my opinion, if you compare the two, *Heliopolis* is a film which tries to analyse what happens in our lives, in relation what has happened in the last 60 or 70 years and how we got here from there. By contrast, *Microphone* seeks to analyse what's happening in the present in relation to what will happen in the future and what we hope to see. That's the big difference.[108]

This seems a very apt description, which is borne out by comments in Mohammad Mirbashiri's review of the film:

> Though the film was completed in 2010, it is all the more relevant now, given the recent uprising in Egypt. It is easy to imagine that those who poured into Tahrir Square in the Spring of 2011 were none other than the same disillusioned youth portrayed in *Microphone,* desperate for a platform to express themselves under a regime which, among other things, sought to stunt creativity.[109]

Rags and Tatters / Farsh wa ghata (2013)—the title refers apparently to one of the styles of Sufi poetic recitation—opens with authentic video footage of Tahrir Square (material not shot by Abdalla himself but used as a leitmotif throughout what is otherwise a fictional narrative). The tape, depicting actual fighting and killing, is accompanied by a voice-over, "I made this video to show what really happened." Eventually it is delivered to the organization concerned with preserving and putting together this firsthand—often amateur—footage, the organization for which Abdalla worked at the time. The video's statement, "I made this video to show what really happened," sums up Abdalla's ambition in *Rags and Tatters.*

The unnamed protagonist is one of those prisoners unexpectedly released in the immediate aftermath of the Tahrir Square uprisings, when police and prison guards simply relinquished their posts and opened the prison gates. The prisoners who emerge from prison do not encounter immediate freedom but instead enter a world of darkness, sporadic violence, and total confusion. The protagonist, himself lightly wounded, befriends a more seriously wounded ex-prisoner, who entrusts him with the video he has shot in Tahrir Square (no doubt the reason for his imprisonment). Making his colleague as comfortable as possible, and promising to return, the protagonist makes his way, as might be expected, to his family home. But, although warmly welcomed, he cannot reintegrate himself after his years away.

He becomes increasingly concerned with the man he has left behind and eventually reaches the place where they both sheltered. But there is no sign of his fellow ex-prisoner, who has presumably died and been buried in an unmarked grave. He continues his wanderings through a Cairo in turmoil after the uprisings. Everywhere community defense groups guard their local streets and brutally beat up any intruders from outside, however little threat they might offer. Orthodox mosques and Sufi houses of worship offer precarious places of refuge for those wounded in the upheavals. The recitations he hears there become a point of fascination for the protagonist, and they are given their full value (it may be recalled that the director's first studies were of music).

As in his earlier films, Abdalla is using the encounters of his constantly moving protagonist as a voyage of discovery, a means of widening his own experience—hence the immediacy of so many of these fleeting encounters. Once more he had set out with no more than twenty or so pages of script, and the film has barely any passages of sustained dialogue. The comments to camera are those of real people, encountered during the shooting, not pre-scripted sequences. The protagonist eventually comes upon the Coptic Christian community of Cairo, which ekes out a precarious living by recycling the city's waste. But this is the moment when the community is about to be attacked and burned out by Islamic extremists, and the protagonist meets his death when he tries vainly to offer help.

Rags and Tatters is not factually accurate in its historical detail—the (very real) assault on the Copts came later than the film implies. But the film's pessimistic vision may well prove a more authentic view of Cairo's Arab Spring than many other immediate accounts, which reflect the fleeting optimism of the moment. Abdalla shows the deep poverty and deprivation of people from different communities across Cairo, Muslim and Christian alike, which triggered the uprising. But these ordinary citizens, so long denied any semblance of liberty, show no ability to create a coherent political strategy, and their efforts to protect their immediate communities are, if anything, more mindlessly brutal than those of the police they have replaced. The film's deep pessimism—the protagonist's journey can lead only to his own death—gives it its narrative power.

Ahmed Rashwan was born in Alexandria in 1969 and developed a passion for cinema during his childhood. After studying law in Alexandria, he moved on to study filmmaking at the Higher Film Institute in Cairo, from which he graduated in 1994. Although the institute essentially offers training for the Egyptian commercial film industry, Rashwan turned resolutely to the independent sector, making a number of short films and numerous documentaries (some for Al Jazeera) from the mid-1990s onward. He also co-authored a book on Arab independent cinema with Hossam Elouan in 2002 and went on to direct his first feature, *Basra,* in 2008.

Basra has a very basic narrative structure: it begins with a divorce and ends with a burgeoning new love relationship for the narrator, Tarek. He introduces himself to us, in voice-over, as someone who does not keep a diary to preserve his memories. Instead, as a professional photographer and constant drinker, he stores memories through the photographs he takes and, quirkily, on dozens of wine corks, all bearing the names and dates of his various encounters. The film looks at the lives of Tarek and his friends, a group of thirty-somethings who indulge in smoking, drinking, and partying. Events succeed each other, sometimes predictably, sometimes surprisingly, but not shaped to create suspense or dramatic tension. Even the sudden death of Tarek's best friend, Hamada, is underplayed and left unexplained. There are clearly autobiographical elements here: the lament for the Alexandria of old, characters who have studied law or trained in film, people who make images out of compulsion or television commercials out of financial necessity. In the background, revealed through the ubiquitous television newscasts in homes, hotels, and cafés, is the 2003 US invasion of Iraq, which has an unsettling effect on all the characters, with the fall of Baghdad coming as a profound blow to their sense of Arab identity.

Inevitably, Rashwan found himself very much caught up in the Arab Spring, which had a profound effect on him:

> I realized that my relationship with reality was a truncated relationship, that I was living inside a safe shell. My decision to engage with reality has changed my character, as it changed also the characters of millions of Egyptians in a positive way. It made me believe more in the need to practice my political rights, and not to be withdrawn and just accept that someone can manipulate my life.[110]

Born on the 25th of January / Moloud fi khamsa wa aishreen yanair (2011) is a hugely immediate and intensely personal documentary which traces developments in Tahrir Square from the beginning of the protest through to the resignation of Hosni Mubarak. Rashwan, whose voice-over shapes the film, reveals his own initial doubts, his growing enthusiasm (which leads him to involve his own small children in the demonstrations), and his eventual hesitations about what will come next.

Maggie Morgan was born in Alexandria and studied at the American University of Cairo, where she now teaches. Despite the name, she describes herself as "100% Egyptian. Cairophone the way some people are francophone."[111] She worked as a producer with the independent production company MediaHouse in Cairo and directed a number of shorter films before completing her first feature, *Asham,* in 2012. Asham is an Arabic word with no precise equivalent in English or French, meaning "fragile hope." Here it is used as the name of the male linking figure, who appears regularly throughout the film to help weave together a narrative which involves half a dozen women and couples who have no immediate personal connections or even awareness of each other's identity. Asham appears successively in a number of guises: a gaudily clad street seller, offering toys and balloons to children; an elevator operator, proud of his smart uniform; and finally a casually dressed man, making conversation on a park bench.

Asham is not a film of social analysis cataloguing the external difficulties of life in twenty-first-century Cairo. Although it must have been shot and edited during the Arab Spring, the film has no specific political message—there is just one fleeting reference to one of the characters taking part in an unspecified demonstration. Instead, the film is about the everyday, dealing with the ordinary moments of anxiety, dream, and ambition which all of us experience from time to time.

For Dalia, who has ambitions to open an art gallery, the question is whether to give up her own life and go off with her boyfriend to Malaysia, where he has just been offered a prestigious job. She decides to stay. For Ahlam, a naive girl from the countryside, it is figuring out how to deal with city life and work her way up from her initial job as a bathroom attendant. She succeeds both in getting a far better job as a shop assistant and in acquiring a new boyfriend. An ambitious hospital assistant, Ibtesam, manages to get her recognition as a qualified nurse, but the doctor she is in love with is indifferent to her and goes off to pursue his own career, leaving her to look after his aging mother. A middle-aged woman develops doubts about her husband's health (although he constantly assures her he is fine). Rather than fretting, she decides to take steps to change both their lives. As a personal challenge, she decides to take driving lessons and her first solo outing after passing her test brings the film to its muted finale.

Morgan's debut film offers no dramatic highlights or riveting enigmas. But the combination of a script reflecting her own experiences and the use of improvisation to allow the players to make their own personal contributions sets the tone of the film, which is also helped by the evident authenticity of the film's settings. Above all, the director's positive attitude to life and her evident warm affection for her characters have gained the film a good audience reception wherever it has been shown.

Lebanon

Lebanon has become one of the dominant filmmaking forces, aside from Egypt, in the Middle East during the 2000s, but, as Lina Khatib observes, it is "still not an industry, though it has the seeds of one. . . . Lebanese cinema remains a collection of films made by disparate filmmakers."[112] As the testimonies collected by Khatib make clear, the civil war remains the central preoccupation of this generation, all of whom grew up while it was occurring, many of them living in Beirut as children at the time. Bahij Hojeij's stance is typical, when he says of his first feature:

> I had not grieved over the war until I made this film; I could not conceive of making my first film without it being about my experience during the war and what we had to endure during the war. . . . I wanted to exorcise the war from within me.[113]

For Philippe Aractingi, the experience was similar: "The war is an essential part of our identity today. . . . The first thing you talk about is the wound."[114] Others cannot conceive of the present without also remembering the past. Jean-Claude Codsi, for example: "The war should be remembered, so it won't be repeated. Representing the war would also help us get over it and move on."[115] Or Randa Chahal:

> I will go back to making films about the war, whether fiction or documentary. . . . We should talk about the past when talking about the present. If we don't talk about the war, what else are we going to talk about?[116]

Although they share a common experience, Lebanese filmmakers show a striking range of attitudes, preoccupations, and narrative styles in their treatment of it.

Fifteen years or more after the end of the civil war, at least two directors, Philippe Aractingi and Nadine Labaki, made conscious efforts to put all thoughts of war behind them in their debut features, *The Bus* and *Caramel,* respectively. But the fresh foreign aggressions of 2007, ironically occurring just as their films were in release, meant that in their second features both felt they had either to confront the actuality of war or to fantasize how war might be avoided.

* * *

Among the older directors breaking into feature filmmaking in these years are two established Lebanese filmmakers, both born in the 1940s, who made their early reputations with documentary work in the 1990s: Jean Chamoun and Bahij Hojeij. Both reflect on the war and its aftermath.

Jean Chamoun, born in 1944, studied drama at the University of Lebanon and filmmaking at the Université Paris VIII. He is best known for his documentary work with his wife, Maï Masri, beginning in the early 1980s. This comprises a masterly series of well over a dozen documentaries, dealing largely with developments in war-torn Palestine. But having made a single solo fictional film, *In the Shadows of the City / L'ombre de la ville / Taif al-madina* (2000), Chamoun is a new voice in Lebanese feature filmmaking.

In the Shadows of the City is a slow-paced, thoughtful film which traces the life of its protagonist in three successive episodes, separated by black-and-white newsreel footage. Initially, Rami is forced, as a twelve-year-old, to leave his home in Southern Lebanon in 1974 because of Israeli bombardments, but arrives in Beirut on the eve of the civil war. We see the events of 1975 unfold chronologically through his eyes: a seemingly idyllic childhood (complete with his little friend Yasmin) destroyed, first by tensions within the community, then by steadily increasing violence, which forces families apart and culminates in the shooting of Nabil, an old man who sings in the café where Rami works. The second episode, twelve years later, shows Rami transformed from ambulance driver to militant fighter when his father is kidnapped. The civil war is fought out in the very area where he lived as a child and features his former childhood friends now fighting on opposite sides. But Rami, though troubled, is never totally corrupted by the mindless killings. A short epilogue, after the war, shows a wounded Rami now teaching children to paint and discovering that Yasmin is a happily married woman with a child of her own. Those who have survived most prosperously into the postwar world are the former gang chiefs, who, as militia leaders, were once deadly rivals in the killing, but who can now salute each other politely in the street when they pass in their shiny new limousines. Chamoun's fictional debut is a solid piece of work, thoughtful and committed, but lacks the bite and immediacy of the documentaries he has made with Masri, covering largely the same time span.

Bahij Hojeij was born in 1948 in Zahle. He studied philosophy, drama, and filmmaking before establishing himself as a documentary filmmaker for both Lebanese and French television. But in his first feature he was keen to avoid the pitfalls of sectarianism and depict his protagonist's experience from a more detached, analytical perspective:

> I wanted to make a film set in Beirut—it doesn't matter if it's East or West; about a person's experiences—it doesn't matter if he is Muslim or Christian or Druze. I did not want the main character to have a defined identity like that. I wanted him to remain a bit abstract.[117]

Ring of Fire / La ceinture de feu / Zennar el-nar (2003), the first of Hojeij's two features, is set in 1985, when Hojeij would have been thirty-seven, about the same age as his protagonist, Chafic, who is also, like him, a university professor. Chafic is, as Hojeij states in an interview included with the DVD of the film, "the mirror image of himself." The film opens with Chafic returning for the new semester at his university in Beirut in good shape. But almost immediately the basic pillars of his life start to crumble. His students desert his classes, called out on a general strike, and Asbo, the new concierge in the apartment building which contains his apartment, works steadily to dispossess him. Chafic reacts passively as Asbo makes himself at home in his apartment, moves a pregnant woman and her child into his spare room, fills his apartment with contraband goods, and finally installs a new steel door to the building (to protect his smuggled goods rather than the tenants), for which a key will cost Chafic two thousand pounds.

The crucial event for Chafic, however, is an intense sexual encounter with one of his female students, when he and the students are in a cellar in total darkness, sheltering from the bombing outside. Chafic never gets a chance to see the girl's face, and from this moment on he is constantly trying to identify her among the students he teaches. The girl also obsessively haunts his dreams, which invariably turn into nightmares. Since dream and reality are shot in exactly the same way, it is often impossible to distinguish the two. The scene where he is wounded in the shoulder is clearly imaginary, since the wound has vanished in the light of day. But does he have a real or imaginary encounter with a woman who accuses him of murdering her son? Does the checkpoint where he is twice arrested in his dreams really exist? At the end, Chafic likewise has no way of separating nightmare and reality. Almost our last sight of him is a long shot taken from high above, as he screams that he will not move his car unless his papers are checked. But there is no checkpoint, and a neighbor has to play out the role before Chafic will move on.

Hojeij has said that the key thing in *Ring of Fire* was to emphasize "the environment that he (Chafic) lived in, which stifled human beings, oppressed the expression of love, oppressed freedom, prevented progress."[118] The film's meaning is underlined by two literary/verbal parallels which it contains. The text that Chafic has chosen for his translation class is Albert Camus's *The Plague*. The way in which the plague invades and engulfs the city of Oran has clear analogies with the way in which violence has infested Beirut: "This virus destroys societies. During war, people are prevented from communicating, one cannot realize one's identity, one cannot dream."[119] The two most intense dialogue scenes in the film involve Chafic and his colleague Dr. Amale, the second of which is shot as a love scene, so that one is waiting for them to touch each other. But Dr. Amale tells of how, just by shaking hands with a friend, she was infected with *zona* (or shingles, as it is known in English). The disease gave her great pain, threatened her eyesight, and has left her terrified of human contact. The disease is popularly known in Arabic as *zennar el-nar* (ring of fire).

Hojeij's second feature, *Here Comes the Rain / Que vienne la pluie / Chatti ya dini* (2010), has its origins in a documentary film he shot in 1998, *Kidnapped*. From the extracts which are included with the DVD, this seems to be a conventionally structured documentary about the reputed seventeen thousand Lebanese citizens who were kidnapped and lost during the civil war. The film is constructed out of the moving testimony of relatives (fathers. mothers, wives, and siblings) who still wait for the (increasingly unlikely) return of their loved ones. It is also an examination of the various laws enacted in Lebanon to allow those kidnapped to be declared legally dead, without any sort of investigation into the circumstances of their kidnapping. There are, it seems, too many powerful ex-militia leaders who have now become government ministers for the truth ever to be revealed and for those responsible to be punished. One of those mentioned in passing in the documentary is Nayfeh Najjar, a woman whose thirteen-year-old was one of those kidnapped. She published a series of letters to/about him in the local Assair newspaper, before committing suicide as the anniversary of her son's disappearance approached. Short, black-and-white reenactments of Najjar composing these letters occur half a dozen times in *Here Comes the Rain,* punctuating the main action and providing some of the film's most poignant moments.

The principal plot lines of the film are in part predictable, in part unexpected. Out of the blue, Ramez Haddad is released from prison twenty years after being kidnapped. But his well-dressed wife, Marie, who has remade her life during the years of separation, with a job and a lover, does not recognize the shabby, stooped, and broken man who is her husband. Three months later Ramez is still a stranger in his own home. His children, Elie and Nadia, are now adults with their own lives, to whom his reappearance is an irrelevance. When his wife cooks for him and tries to restore their intimacy, he is critical and withdrawn. Ramez is left alone to wander the streets, collecting decorative shopping bags, which he classifies by size and cleans as necessary—actions which offer no insight into his thinking and are singularly lacking in symbolic meaning.

Ramez finds the warmth lacking in his own family in a growing, if initially awkward, relationship with Zeinab, whom he meets by chance and who turns out to be waiting for the reappearance of her own husband after twenty years of absence. The pair grow closer, and he proposes an outing to the Corniche and a boat trip, during which he experiences his sole moment of joy since leaving prison. But he is taken ill on the boat and needs intensive care in the hospital. There he talks of Zeinab to his wife, who fetches her to his bedside, to join her and the children gathered there. Ramez now finally finds the courage to tell Zeinab that, despite earlier denials, he had in fact shared a cell with her husband, Khalid. Khalid had died after a year, but not before asking Ramez to tell Zeinab how much he loved her. The film ends with shots of a seascape caught up in a storm.

Here Comes the Rain is a difficult film to evaluate. Totally sincere in its approach to the terrible crime of kidnapping in Lebanon and winner of several prizes at international film festivals, it somehow lacks the harsh narrative logic the subject demands. The key to its failure to generate emotional power is Hojeij's decision to omit any reference to the crucial first three months after Ramez's return. As a result, there is no poring over old photographs, no exploration of mutual memories, no extended family reunion, no festive family outing—any of which could have led to at least the beginnings of a rapprochement between Ramez and his family. The growing relationship and smooth flow of empathy between Ramez and Zeinab merely emphasizes what is lacking in the primary narrative line, a real exploration of the immediate relationship between a returning prisoner and his family. Whereas, in *Ring of Fire,* the protagonist steadily loses control of his life as the story progresses, here Ramez has, from the start, no real link with the world into which he emerges. In Hojeij's universe, failure is the only outcome for his protagonists, but the responsibility they themselves bear for this outcome—through their essential passivity—is somehow glossed over.

* * *

Some very disparate filmmakers born in the 1960s had already begun their careers in the late 1990s before making some of their most notable work after 2000. The key figures are Ziad Doueiri, who had studied in the United States; Samir Habchi, whose film studies had taken him to the USSR; and the team of Joana Hadjithomas and Khalil Joreige, who studied together at ALBA in Beirut but received no formal film training.

Ziad Doueiri, who was born in 1963, lived in Lebanon for twenty years until 1983 and then went to the United States, studying first at the University of San Diego and then at UCLA. Trained as a cameraman, he worked as assistant cameraman on the early films of Quentin Tarantino, including *Reservoir Dogs, Pulp Fiction,* and *Jackie Brown.* His debut feature was *West Beyrouth / Beirut al-gharbiyah* (1998),[120] a semi-autobiographical tale of three young people growing up at the outbreak of the civil war, capturing brilliantly the uncertainties of the time. Perhaps because the film is told through the eyes of adolescents, lacking political or religious insights and largely uncomprehending of what is happening around them, the film has a distinctly positive and upbeat tone. No one close to the central trio is killed. Doueiri's camera work is exuberant (as befits someone who once worked as camera assistant to Quentin Tarantino), and his film focuses as much on the comic absurdities of war as on its horrors. Like so much recent Lebanese cinema, it offers entertainment as well as insight. Its impact on Lebanese audiences is clear from Lina Khatib's personal reaction:

Watching *West Beyrouth* for the first time, I felt proud. Here was a Lebanese film where the characters resembled me. They spoke in the Lebanese dialect but sounded natural. And the film was entertaining. The film marked a new era in Lebanese cinema.[121]

Doueiri subsequently made a French-language feature, *Lila Says / Lila dit ça* (2004), which, though set in the Arab district of Marseilles, has a very un-Arab and explicit approach to teenage sexuality. The pre-credit sequence introduces us to the protagonists, the nineteen-year-old Chimo, who is beginning a diary about his obsession with a sixteen-year-old blonde, Lila, who describes her own good (and bad) physical features direct to camera. We hear Chimo reading from his diary throughout the film, which begins with a vivid picture of the Arab quarter, in which Chimo and a trio of friends, Mouloud, Bakary, and Big Jo, hang out, stealing, mocking the police, and visiting the mosque only to pass the time. Chimo's talent as a budding writer is recognized by his French teacher, who tries to persuade him to develop it in Paris, but such a move is mocked contemptuously by his friends.

Chimo and Lila (who has just moved to the district to live with her aunt) are immediately attracted to each other when she passes for the first time in the street. From the start, Lila is totally provocative, sexually and verbally, in ways with which the shy Chimo cannot cope. Lila, who does not wear underwear, takes the lead role in their relationship throughout. At their first meeting, she invites him to look up her dress, as she swings back and forth, her legs open, on a child's swing. Later, when they are riding on her scooter, she stands up so that the wind will blow up her short skirt and she masturbates him as he drives. When she is sunbathing in her garden, she invites him apply suntan cream to her back and buttocks. But this is the last time they have any physical contact, although Lila talks openly in front of other people about their having sex. Chimo is totally unable to cope with either her open sexuality or her uninhibited frankness, and subsequently they do not even kiss or hold hands.

Inevitably, Lila increasingly attracts the attention of Mouloud and the rest of the gang. They begin to accost her in the street, and later, seeing her get out of an expensive Mercedes, they conclude she is a whore. On his birthday, Mouloud treats his friends to a trip to a brothel, but Chimo angers them all by refusing to take part. Lila continues to provoke him every time they meet, including revealing her own fantasies by showing him an explicit adult cartoon book, depicting the group rape of an all-too-willing blonde, but Chimo still holds back. Eventually, Lila provokes a public scandal by claiming to her aunt that she is possessed. A priest is summoned and the whole neighborhood becomes agitated. Now the narrative can achieve the ending toward which it has been moving with slow inevitability. Mouloud, and his two friends get drunk, tie up the aunt, and while the others watch, Mouloud rapes Lila, who despite her provocative behavior is still a virgin. Chimo, who bursts onto the scene, is arrested along with his former friends, and by the time he is released, Lila and her aunt have moved out. He is able to tell Lila he loves her on the phone but makes no attempt to meet her. For him, the experience is now over. He passes his diary to his teacher for editing and moves on to a new life in Paris (the film is based on an autobiographical novel by a writer called Chimo, who had just such an experience).

Lila Says, which curiously received some of its funding from the UK Film Fund, is provocative, smoothly constructed, and fluently directed. Though set in an Arab community, it is very much a French film in its style, content, and narrative shape. But it does offer a striking dual portrait: on the one hand, powerful, youthful, female sexual desire, and on the other, the inhibited, ultimately self-destructive sexual hesitations of the young Arab male.

The Attack / L'attentat was first shown in 2012, but its scripting, undertaken by Doueiri with his wife, Joëlle Touma, predates the Arab Spring, going back to 2006. Based on a novel by the (male) Algerian writer pseudonymously known as Yasmina Khadra, the film opens with a totally self-confident protagonist, Amin Jaafari, receiving a top award from the Jewish medical authorities. Although he is a Palestinian Israeli, he has risen to the top of his profession as a surgeon, working at one of Tel Aviv's major hospitals. At the ceremony, he cannot take a call on his cell phone from his wife, Siham, but is relaxed enough to tell his mainly Jewish audience that "every Jew is a bit of an Arab, and every Arab is a little bit Jewish." Then his life is turned upside down. Called to the hospital to operate in the wake of a suicide bombing (seventeen dead, including eleven children attending a little girl's birthday party), he is stunned to learn that his wife—to whom he has been married for fifteen years—is the police's chief suspect.

The mere fact that these opening sequences of a French-backed movie were shot on location in Israel was enough to cause the film to be banned from screening in Lebanon and most of the Arab world. But *The Attack* is not a justification, or even an explanation, of suicide bombing. Siham left no "martyr video" or letter of explanation, so a major part of the film follows Amin's return to Palestine in an ultimately futile quest to understand his wife's motivation. He meets clerics who preach hostility to Israel and comes to understand that the nephew he has naively allowed to use a room at his Tel Aviv apartment is an Islamic activist. He sees from the "martyr" photographs of his wife plastered on the walls of the town that her action has wide public support. He also becomes aware that, unknown to him, his wife had, over the years, developed her own political commitments to the Palestinian cause.

But there is never any explanation of why she took the final step to become a suicide bomber, killing herself and a group of innocent children. No motivation was given in the original novel, and Doueiri and his wife, while scripting the film, could not come up with a plausible set of reasons either. As a result, it is hard to disagree with Doueiri when he asserts that, despite its subject matter, *The Attack* is not a political analysis of the Arab-Israeli conflict but is "a love story":

> It's about a man looking for his wife, trying to understand her. You think you understand the person you love and you build an idea of happiness, but that doesn't mean it matches your own idea of happiness. . . . The plot had to revolve around a man seeking the truth and the psychology of when you are so in love. In spite of the fact that your wife commits such a horrendous act, you still love her in the end. I love that idea.[122]

The film also has a more immediate significance for Doueiri, who now lives in the United States, in that "it's about the ambivalence of living in two societies. Like I do. I'm still juggling between the Arabic society and my life in the West."[123]

Samir Habchi was born in 1961 and studied film at the Kiev Higher Film Institute and then at VGIK in Moscow. He initially made a handful of short films, in both the USSR and Lebanon, and much later completed a feature-length documentary, *The Lady of the Palace / La dame du palais / Sayidat el-kasr* (2003). He is best known, however, for his two features, made sixteen years apart.

The Tornado / Le tourbillon / Al-i'sar (1992), the first feature to be completed after the end of the civil war, was a Russian co-production with a Russian crew. Habchi considers cinema to be "above all the art of image and movement,"[124] and this first film is built largely out of panning and tracking shots, marked by the highly fluent camera work of Grigori Boulkot (and his Russian-trained assistant, Miled Taouk), as well as the pulsating musical score provided by Igor Stetsiouk. *The Tornado*'s narrative is highly complex as it shifts, often disconcertingly, between reality and nightmare to capture the atmosphere of Beirut at the height of the civil war. It begins with elements which will recur throughout the film: shots of a bare landscape and clouds, funereal music and Gregorian chant. We move on to follow a driver in the empty landscape, initially uncertain of our location and his identity. In fact, we are in Lebanon and he is a car bomber (who will also return, with a new bomb, later in the film), but we only realize this when the car he has abandoned in the middle of the road explodes. As well as surprising us in this way with its plot twists, *The Tornado* also contains intriguing figures who reappear regularly without contributing in any way to the plot, although each seems potentially to have a story to tell. In these early scenes, there is Shehadeh, a crippled cigarette seller; later in the film, an old man, Brahim, will turn up from time to time, constantly listening to his portable radio.

We cut abruptly from the car explosion to Akram, a student in Russia, watching the report on television. From there we move, without any marked transition, into what we only later discover to be one of the film's numerous nightmare sequences, featuring Akram, black-clad women, dead bodies, and a potential executioner. Back in the real world, Akram flies to Beirut, where the atmosphere is deceptively quiet as he joins the other males living in his block, in watching a beautiful girl rehearsing her dance routine in a neighboring apartment. The first sign of what is to come occurs when Akram is dining out with a friend and sees the bearded Abu Hadid (visually his alter ego) dining at a nearby table. Abu Hadid loudly boasts of his prowess as a sniper and states the film's basic theme: "If you are not a wolf, the wolves will eat you."

As they drive back from the café, Akram has his first taste of Beirut violence, when, at a roadblock manned by masked militants, they witness the savage summary execution of another driver, whose only crime is to look straight back at his assailants. While Akram is driving to the cinema that evening with two other friends, their car is stopped and his friends are mindlessly shot down, merely for getting out of the car. Later, while Akram is showing photographs to other friends, gunfire is heard—just the guys on the demarcation line having fun, he is told. But the incident develops into a full-scale artillery assault, provoking a (stunningly shot) descent to the cellar. Next day, the madness of Beirut is summed up in a couple of shots, when Abu Hadid responds to being caught up in a traffic jam by casually taking out his machine gun and shooting out the red traffic light.

For Akram, things get steadily worse, as the mindless deaths accumulate. He witnesses a drive-by killing, and the dancer's boyfriend, a car thief, foolishly steals a booby-trapped car (left by the bomber from the film's opening sequence) and is blown up on the road out of town. Finally, setting out to make his visit to his parents' village, Akram is blocked, first by a funeral cortège, then by a parked car. He honks the horn at the car incessantly, only to discover too late that it belongs to Abu Hadid, who beats him mercilessly. An intervention from Akram's sole surviving friend, armed with a machine gun, persuades Abu Hadid to move the car. But he is not a man to be humiliated in public, and he quickly returns to shoot Akram's rescuer in the back. The Gregorian chant resumes as he dies, and it continues to mingle with the cries and gunfire at his funeral. Stetsiouk's pulsating music resumes, as Akram sets out to kill Abu Hadid, in a shooting which provokes no response from bystanders.

Having seen his three friends "eaten by the wolves," Akram now becomes a wolf himself, but this solves nothing. Up to this point in the film, the violence has been relentless yet conveyed in realistic fashion. Now, with the breakdown of Akram's life, the sequences become totally nightmarish, and the reality of what we see is increasingly problematic. Music dominates virtually wordless scenes, which obliterate all sense of logic. While Akram miraculously survives the snipers on the demarcation line and reaches the airport, this is transformed into an empty place of nightmare, resembling the set of a Greek tragedy, with motionless black-clad women and the executioner from the first nightmare. Apparently reverting to normality, Akram finds himself at the busy check-in desk, but since he does not have his passport, he steals a car to go back into Beirut. On the way, he finds himself at a fresh checkpoint, from which he drives off under fire, pursued by a armored jeep. Again he miraculously escapes, wounded but still able to run, only to meet again the silent black-clad women and snipers who shoot him down. But this is yet another nightmare, from which he awakens in his room. He is immediately plunged into a new nightmare, featuring first a crate of oranges spilled over the roadway and then a white horse galloping free. There is a sharp cut to a church filled with massacre victims, where a Christlike figure emerges, bathed in light in the doorway, to the chanting of *Kyrie eleison*. Turning, the figure transforms into an armed militant, who shoots the old man Brahim dead. The film cuts to the victims' funeral procession—which Akram attends and which, largely thanks to the music, becomes a farcical dance of the dead—that is shot at by snipers on a neighboring roof. The film ends as Akram climbs to the top of a hill to fire into the clouds. First blood, then rain, drops onto his anguished face, and the film ends with a freeze-frame.

The Tornado is stylistically one of the most audacious of all Lebanese films dealing with the civil war, moving beyond the documentary realistic approach most filmmakers employ and making real demands on the viewers. Lina Khatib quotes Habchi as saying that because of its avant-garde style and subject matter, "this kind of film would not be shown in Arab countries,"[125] but in fact, in Beirut at least, *The Tornado* enjoyed a success rivaling that of Hollywood releases, with 55,000 tickets sold.[126]

Habchi spent many years working in television. One documentary to emerge internationally during those years is *Lady of the Palace / La dame du palais / Sayidat el-kasr* (2003), made for Youssef Chahine's company, Misr International Films. This is a story of a remarkable woman, Nazira Jumblatt, who is unjustly ignored in many accounts of Lebanese history but who, from the ancestral palace at Moukhtara, led the Jumblatt family and a portion of the Druze community for some twenty-five years. This is a unique achievement for a woman in Lebanese society, and the film opens with testimony to her charm, persuasiveness, and intelligence from members of her family and from those who knew her as adults or children. This is of necessity an external account of her achievements, not a truly personal portrait. As Habchi tells us in the opening credits, the filmed scenes of Nazira are all reenactments, as only three images of her exist (presumably the three photographs with which Habchi brings his documentary to a close).

Although the film is full of precise details of alliances, rivalries, and civil wars within Druze society, it offers few wider political judgments. Nazira Jumblatt worked constantly for unity and tolerance, but also to ensure her son Kamal his rightful place (as she saw it) in the Druze community. Aside from her assertion of herself as a leader, despite being a woman, she maintained a belief in essentially feudal values, seeing the marriages of her children, for example, as mere political alliances designed to ensure cohesion and power within the community. When Kamal came of age, she coerced her bookish son into a political career, but to her horror, instead of preserving her values, he founded the Progressive Socialist Party. She could not cope with the son she regarded as a "bey" being addressed as "comrade Kamal" by fellow socialists.

Sixteen years after his feature debut, Habchi followed up with another film in a similar vein, *Beirut Open City / Beyrouth ville ouverte* (2008), set this time in the 1990s. Again the focus is on an outsider, here the young Egyptian filmmaker Khaled, in Beirut to script a fictional feature and to research it through video interviews. When, by chance, he films the violence perpetrated by the men guarding the American ambassador's car as it speeds through the streets, he himself is caught up in the violence. After this, nothing is what it seems. The killing of an innocent bystander by one of the guards, which threatens a blood feud, appears to be resolved by the ambassador kneeling by the graveside to ask forgiveness at a clan gathering. But the guard is subsequently reported to have "fallen down a flight of steps" and the ambassador's car is mysteriously blown up on a lonely road. Khaled himself is arrested, tortured, and jailed as a terrorist, but by this time the narrative has become increasingly fractured. We see Khaled's fantasies as well as his real experiences, and the evidence he has accumulated is seemingly constantly contradicted. Farcical moments are scattered amid the violence (a policeman who allows cars to pass only when the lights are red, and a neighbor who blows himself up in his precious car while trying to protect it). False television reports on the action complicate matters still further. *Beirut Open City* is a powerful and fast-moving mixture of violence and farce, harsh reality, fantasy, and lies, which constantly plays with audience expectations to create a nightmare image of Beirut's continuing self-destruction.

Joana Hadjithomas and **Khalil Joreige**, both born in 1969, have been together and worked as a team since the 1990s. Both are teachers at IESAV in Beirut, where she teaches screenwriting and he aesthetics and experimental video. In the early 1990s they began a joint career, which embraces experimental video works and gallery installations, as well as a range of publications. They have made a number of short films from 1994 onward.

The most substantial of their early documentaries is the fifty-two-minute *Khiam* (2000), which is striking for its absolute austerity and unwavering focus. Six ex-inmates of the Israeli prison of Khiam—Afif Hammoud, Kifah Afifé, Soha Béchara, Rajaé Abou Hamain, Sonia Beydoun, and Neeman Nasrallah—relate their experiences of up to ten years' imprisonment, often with very lengthy spells of solitary confinement. What is especially distinctive about *Khiam* is the manner in which it is shot. Apart from the final sequence, it consists solely of the intercut statements of the six interviewees, all filmed face-on to the camera, seated successively in the same center-screen chair against a blank background, mostly in long or medium shot, with only the occasional close-up. This technique, rigidly adhered to for fifty minutes, gives great power to their words. The experiences they recount are truly remarkable.

At first they talk of their privations: losing their names and becoming just numbers; being isolated, hooded, and subjected to seemingly random beatings with barbed wire and torture with electricity. Their sufferings were enhanced by their indeterminate sentences and the awareness that, in some cases, other members of their family had been arrested and imprisoned because of their resistance activities. Overcrowding, primitive toilet facilities and the refusal to allow access to other prisoners outside their cells added to their problems. Dreams, stories, and conversations with their cellmates became immensely important.

But human beings are immensely resourceful. Despite being deprived of the most basic items, such as a needle or a pencil and paper, they managed to make these from scraps of garbage they found, from such things as the wrappings of the food they were given and by using their bedding and clothing. Since they were locked up for perhaps twenty hours a day, they had the time for the most delicate and painstaking tasks. Although discovery of their primitive tools or the products they devised would mean confiscation and punishment, they persisted against all odds. This life of isolation and concentrated, all-absorbing activity made it difficult for them to adjust when they were eventually released into the world outside. They had new strengths, but they were no longer at home in the everyday world. As one of them says, without a trace of irony, "inside the camp, you have the most wonderful freedom." After this statement, the film is utterly silent for the concluding few minutes, as we are shown a succession of the small objects they were able to make and preserve: toys, strings of beads, combs, drawings and sculptures, a chess game with figures carved from soap, even a Christmas tree. *Khiam* is a moving tribute to both the endurance and the resourcefulness of human beings deprived of virtually everything we all take for granted.

Hadjithomas and Joreige made their first venture into fiction with the twenty-six-minute *Ashes / Cendres / Ramad* (2002), co-written with their favorite actor, Rabih Mroué. It is a simple narrative. Nabil arrives back in Beirut, having smuggled in with him an urn containing the ashes of his father, who has died while undergoing hospital treatment in France. But to his astonishment, the family, led by his mother, insists on going through the full traditional funeral ritual, even though there is no body. One of the family even volunteers to act as the shrouded dead man in the open coffin, and Nabil is given his father's black suit to wear. Afterward, the family behave exactly as if the ceremony had been a real one, even commenting on the expected guests who did not turn up.

On one level, *Ashes* is a farce, a black comedy, played with utter deadpan conviction. On another level, it is an adumbration of themes which recur in the later feature works. The problem for the Lebanese is their inability to live securely in the present because they have failed to come to terms with the reality of the civil war (there has been no "truth and reconciliation" procedure in Lebanon). At the same time, there has been a headlong plunge into the present, with its dream of instant new wealth, typified by the policies of Rafiq Hariri.

The pair's first feature-length fictional film was *Around the Pink House / Autour de la maison rose / Al-beit al-zahr* (1999), a Lebanese-Canadian co-production. It deals with a very topical subject at the time of filming: the disruption of the lives of two families, the Adaimis and the Nawals, caused not by the civil war but by the surge of change and reconstruction which comes after its cessation. For eleven and a half years, the families have been living as refugees in a former Beirut palace, the Pink House. Suddenly, they are given ten days to vacate the building by the new owner, who wishes to redevelop the area. The families try to resist by circulating a petition, hiring a lawyer, and engaging a TV cameraman, but all to no avail. The tension of leaving reveals hidden secrets and animosities within the families and sets them against the shopkeepers living on the opposite side of the street, who hope for fresh prosperity, which they assume the new development will bring (although it turns out later that their shops too may well be destroyed in the development process).

Despite the reputation of Hadjithomas and Joreige as experimental video makers and installation artists, *Around the Pink House* is shaped as a very conventional light comedy. This is a world where young men either shout in the street because they are kept away from the girl they love by her father, or hold back timidly from declaring themselves when encouraged by the girl's mother. The surface humor tends to detract from any serious comment on Beirut the filmmakers may be intending. The families eventually accept the inevitable and take the money on offer, after selling off the house's furnishings and fittings. The two sides of the street are reconciled in time to sit down together and watch the last act of the drama, as the young people in the two families hire a bulldozer and smash down the ornate pink façade of the building. This monument to the past is destroyed without a second thought by those who have grown up within its walls for more than eleven years. In what is essentially an inconsequential work, none of the potential tensions are fully realized, the wider issues involved in the rebuilding of Beirut are ignored, and the question of what happens to the families—now again reduced to the status of refugees—is left unresolved.

A Perfect Day / Un jour parfait / Yawm akhar (2005) is a difficult film, beginning with the heavy irony of its title. This could not conceivably be deemed in any way a perfect day, since it is the day on which Claudia, who has for fifteen years sustained the hope that her husband Riad, kidnapped in 1988, is alive, finally takes the legal steps to have him declared dead. The film opens with a touching scene in which Claudia gently wakens her adult son Malek, who, we later learn, suffers from narcolepsy, which means that he falls asleep without warning several times a day and that any of these incidents could prove fatal. Malek emerges as the key figure. He is remarkably detached at the session with the lawyer and has neglected to bring along the necessary papers. He never asks about his father, and when he fetches the papers, he skims through them and then hides them where his mother will not find them. He also discovers his father's loaded revolver along with the papers, but this is a narrative red herring, which plays no part in the unfolding action.

Despite his very troubling affliction, it is difficult to empathize with Malek. He neglects his mother on this crucial day, and while away, he refuses to respond to her phone calls (although he must realize that she will be terrified that his affliction has taken its toll). His obsession is with his beautiful girlfriend, Zeina, with whom he has what seems to be an on-off relationship. She texts him at one point, asking him to leave her alone but also telling him precisely where she will be that night. He goes to work but falls asleep and cannot cope with the problems there, then drives around Beirut, ending up on a stone bench overlooking the sea. There, inevitably, he falls asleep.

The depiction which follows of the events occurring during the night has the feel of a living nightmare. There is no apparent logic to the sequencing of events and no indication as to why Malek behaves as he does. He returns home where his mother is sleeping, but creeps around and sneaks off as soon as she wakes up. He pursues Zeina to a nightclub but falls asleep while spying on her. Zeina wakens him gently while murmuring "Don't wake up," and they drive off, making love as they do so. She is clearly physically attracted to him (he is a good-looking guy). But at the final moment of commitment, she freezes, and on this far from perfect day, runs off into the darkness. At this point, Malek has the invulnerability of a character in a dream. He is able to drive safely while giving all his attention to making love to Zeina. After she has run off, he puts on her contact lens (why?) but is able to navigate the car across Beirut (even, it seems, through a tunnel) without crashing, although his view is reduced to a psychedelic swirl of lights and colors which gives the film its visual climax. There is a return to dawn and the stone bench and a new awakening. Has the night indeed been just a nightmare? Perhaps. Nothing is unambiguously resolved. Malek's run along the beach is intercut with birds flocking in preparation for migration—the last images of the film.

There is no indication in any of the filmmakers' statements that the description of the film just given corresponds to their intentions: it is only one reading. But they have made clear that they wanted the life rhythms of Claudia and her son to be out of synch: she has come to terms with her mourning, while he pursues the hectic rhythms of nighttime Beirut. The gap between them is emphasized by the casting—Julia Kassar (Claudia) is the only professional actor in the cast—and by Hadjithomas and Joreige's style of directing.

They did not allow any of the players access to the full script, so scenes were played without their knowing how these fitted into the whole narrative. Instead, the actors were, it seems, constantly put into situations they had not been expecting. It is clear that Ziad Saad, for example, had no idea that he would find the father's loaded revolver. This was in fact to play no part in the coming action, but at the time of filming, he had no way of knowing that. The result of this method of filming is that the present is never secure; no one is at home in it. This is in keeping with the view of Lebanese society as being unable to cope with the present, common to earlier film fictions. *A Perfect Day* leaves many questions open. The mother, Claudia, is evidently a representative of the generation which lost everything in the civil war, but how far the deeply troubled Malek and Zeina are truly representative of the new generation is not as clear, although the filmmakers do see them as such.

Hadjithomas and Joreige returned to documentary with the widely shown *I Want to See / Je veux voir* (2007). This docudrama is a film which, though almost as minimalist as *Khiam*, could hardly be more different. It features a trip to Southern Lebanon by the French film star Catherine Deneuve, accompanied by the Lebanese actor Rabih Mroué, with whom the pair have frequently collaborated. Their destination is Mroué's native village, Bint El Jbeil, one of those devastated by the Israeli invasion. Originally planned as a seven-minute short and with a shooting schedule of just seven days, the film eventually emerged as a full-length, seventy-five-minute work. The title—along with Deneuve's repeated opening words—implies that the impetus came from Deneuve, but in fact the work was planned and pre-scripted by the two filmmakers themselves, in response to finding themselves stranded in Paris at the time of the July 2006 Israeli invasion (the 33-Day War). The question they asked themselves then was whether they could find a new way of seeing and telling the horror of this war. A chance meeting with a producer who could offer an introduction to Deneuve (whom they had never met) gave them the focus for a novel approach, shaped by bringing together two seeming opposites: a documentary on the aftermath of the fighting in Southern Lebanon and a film star, Catherine Deneuve, who, for them, "incarnates a certain idea of cinema, a cinema which has a history." They approached the shooting as an adventure whose outcome was uncertain. The film was pre-planned in detail, but when it was acted out in front of them, it surprised them totally.[127]

I Want to See is very much a documentary about making a documentary. The slightly awkward first meeting with Deneuve, at which they introduce themselves and Mroué, was in fact the first time the four had met. The filmmakers themselves appear from time to time, resolving the (presumably) real problems which arise during the shooting. But this is a very minimalist documentary, comprising mostly close shots of the pair driving together, shot from outside through the car windows, or the couple filmed from inside the car, from the back seat. Little emotion is generated between Deneuve and Mroué, and their conversations generate few original insights. Mroué, who says he feels like a tourist in his own country, cannot even locate his grandmother's house in the scene of empty devastation of the outskirts of Beirut. Deneuve remains the elegant outsider, who has little interaction either with the horrors of the war's aftermath, which she encounters, or with the abiding beauties of the Lebanese landscape, which she witnesses. There is a fascinating moment when the screen is blank and Mroué declares his love for her—but this is a quotation from Buñuel's *Belle de jour* (which sounds equally good in Arabic). Deneuve and Mroué are buzzed by Israeli pilots "having fun"; there are encounters with the weird national mix of UN troops (who of course want souvenir photos); and negotiations are undertaken with the Israelis to open up a strip of road. On the way back along the coast road, they see mile after mile of trucks delivering rubble from the suburbs to be dumped into the sea—provoking the only piece of (Arabic language) commentary in the film and one of its few musical sequences. Deneuve smiles radiantly at Mroué as she sits down at the formal gala dinner held to mark her presence in Beirut. But no conclusions are drawn about the trip, and Mroué makes no comment in the film's very last sequence, as he drives through the darkened streets of Beirut to the music of the band Scrambled Eggs. This is an honest look at the contradictions of Lebanon and the difficulties of talking about them, marred only by a few shots involving Deneuve in apparent danger, which seem clumsily contrived.

Hadjithomas and Joreige have since contributed one episode, *Jacques Tati,* to the collective work *Childhood / Enfances* (2008), which re-creates episodes in the childhood of half a dozen great filmmakers (the others are Fritz Lang, Orson Welles, Jean Renoir, Alfred Hitchcock, and Ingmar Bergman). This is the first time the team has filmed outside their native Lebanon.

The Lebanese Rocket Society (2013) contains a commentary which alternates the voices of the two filmmakers and shows both the intensity with which they involve themselves in the research for their documentary projects and the range of media in which they explore their concerns. It begins with their discovery of "a hidden forgotten story" in Lebanese history—the efforts by Manoug Manougian, a professor at the small Armenian University of Haigazian, to involve his students in the worldwide research into space exploration of the 1960s. Although these efforts were commemorated with a postage stamp at the time, they were unknown to people of the filmmakers' generation (both were born in 1969). Having explored the few documentary records available in Lebanon, the filmmakers managed to make contact with Manougian himself, in the United States, where he is now professor of mathematics at the University of South Florida. His archive—tracing the successive stages of rocket development—provides the film with the bulk of its visual material, including a memorable mishap when the assembled body of staff and students of Haigazian University watched a missile go off backwards and narrowly miss a nearby church. The work of Manougian and his students was purely scientific, but it attracted the support of the military (vital for the provision of rocket propellant) and the president of Lebanon before it was closed down, partly, it seems, because of international pressure in the late 1960s.

The documentaries of Hadjithomas and Joreige are never merely simple statements of fact, and *The Lebanese Rocket Society* includes footage of their commissioned reconstruction of the final rocket (Cedar IV) and its transport through the streets of Beirut, from the launch site at Dbayeh to the University of Haigazian, where it was formally installed. The documentary ends with an animated sequence by Ghassan Halwani tracing what might have been, had the Lebanese "space adventure" been allowed to continue. The filmmakers supplemented this feature-length documentary with a number of photographic exhibitions, an audiovisual installation, and even a hand-woven carpet, made in Armenia and reproducing the original 1964 postage stamp.

* * *

Contemporary Lebanese cinema in the 2000s, like Algerian filmmaking, is largely a cinema of exiles. Many of the new generation, born since 1960, have close links with Paris, among them Philippe Aractingi, Michel Kammoun, Chadi Zeneddine, and more recently, Georges Hachem.

Philippe Aractingi, who was born in 1964 in Beirut, studied at the CLCF in Paris. He began his television career in Lebanon, before moving back to Paris, where he worked for twenty years in French television, many of his documentaries dealing with Arab issues. He has subsequently made two feature films in Lebanon.

The Bus / L'autobus / Bosta (2005), described by its author as a musical road movie and a huge popular success in Lebanon, was a very conscious effort on Aractingi's part to get beyond the constant chronicling of deaths and disasters which characterized his documentary output for French television. On the death of his father, Kamal, a composer and choreographer, returns from fifteen years of exile in France to reunite some of his dance-school classmates to present his new "techno" version of the traditional Lebanese dance, the *dabke*. When this is rejected out-of-hand by the authorities overseeing the national festival at Anjar, the group decide to renovate the old school bus and take their dance production on a tour around Lebanon. They are supported by a national television company which broadcasts daily accounts of their progress (but only, as Kamal finally discovers, for sordid commercial reasons).

The film opens with a huge traffic jam, caused when the aged bus, dating from pre–civil war years, breaks down. The bus, which also gives its name to the film, has a particular significance in Lebanese culture, since by some accounts, it was an initial explosion on a bus which triggered the whole fifteen-year Lebanese civil war. Here the jauntily repainted school bus is used as a token of reconciliation. The journey—to Rachaya, Baalbek, and Junieh—reveals the beauty of the Lebanese landscape, for once not torn apart by war, and lays bare the past loves and rivalries of the reunited group as well as their present aspirations. For several of them this journey becomes a personal confrontation with their own families—who demand justification for how they have lived their lives (studying dance rather than medicine, for example) considering the familial hopes that gave them their opportunities.

Even more important, however, is the way in which Aractingi uses the remodeling of a musical tradition and the clash of generations (in particular, fathers and sons) that it represents to look at the future of Lebanon. The young people have an energy and respect for the past that older audiences can appreciate. Their first performance is received hesitantly, but next morning people come out with offerings of food in appreciation of their efforts. A later performance creates difficulties concerning their attitude to Lebanese traditions, but older men can join in the dance. Carried by the energy of the performers and the dynamics of the dance rhythm, the film can conclude with an ecstatic finale involving them all, including the troubled (now self-doubting) Kamal. *The Bus* is a positive affirmation of hope for the future, after the bleak years of the civil war.

But such affirmations did not last, of course. Aractingi's second feature, *Under the Bombs / Sous les bombes / Taht al-qasef* (2007), reflects his disillusionment and remains one of Lebanese cinema's finest explorations of war and its aftermath. *Under the Bombs* is a powerful study of life immediately after the 33-Day War. Again structured as a road movie, it focuses on two very disparate people who undertake a journey to Southern Lebanon together. In doing so, the film fuses the depiction of these two fictional characters with the actual suffering and devastation they encounter, which is filmed with real documentary insight. Tony is a poor Christian taxi driver, undertaking the trip solely for the money it offers. Zeina is a rich Shiite expatriot, seeking her son Karim, lost in the bombing of her native village of Kebet Selm, where he was staying with family members. The film traces sensitively the growing relationship between the pair, as they reveal their very different personal lives. Eventually it is Tony who drives the search forward, but in the end, the project is unsuccessful: Karim has been killed, along with his aunt.

Crucial to the film is the series of glimpses it offers of the impact of the Israeli assault on ordinary Lebanese civilians. The images of human suffering are particularly harrowing because these are real victims, filmed by an experienced documentary filmmaker at the moment of their loss. The human immediacy is what strikes the viewer most: as Philippe Aractingi has said, the experience of *Under the Bombs* was less that of making a film, more that of living the film.

Michel Kammoun was born in 1969 in Sierra Leone; he says that from his earliest childhood he was totally fascinated by cinema and dreamed of becoming a filmmaker. After initial studies of mathematics in Lebanon, he studied filmmaking at ESEC in Paris. He subsequently made a number of short films in France and the United States and has since taught scriptwriting in Beirut. He describes himself as living between Beirut and Paris. Commenting on the problems of making a feature film in Lebanon, Kammoun has aptly noted that it is "not just a matter of building a train, but also of laying the track." He says of his first feature, *Falafel* (2006), that he imagined a world where "falafel would represent a manner of thinking, a way of living, and a new vision of things."[128] The film, in which the music of Toufic Farroukh plays a key role in establishing the tone, is set fifteen years after the end of the civil war and follows a single night in the life of a young man, Toufic, on the verge of manhood.

Toufic's principal desire is to drive around Beirut on a borrowed scooter, party with his friends, and maybe start a relationship with the beautiful Yasmin. But life intervenes, and the evening does not unfold as he imagines. Kammoun builds his narrative out of a succession of tiny scenes which differ markedly in tone. There are, initially, bits of traditional storytelling: Toufic's barber fantasizes about the way in which Lebanon's 200,000 gifted women belly dancers could impact the world, and a shopkeeper tells an unlikely tale of hungry people in Sumatra being fed when a rain of falafel falls on them. Although much of the film is focused on a group of young people lightheartedly partying, disgracing themselves, and spying on their neighbors, there are also hints of the underlying violence of the city, as when Toufic witnesses a violent kidnapping. This realist level is combined with moments of magic, as when Toufic turns a star chosen at random by Yasmin into a shooting star, and when he himself is deluged by a rain of falafel.

The manner in which the narrative will unfold is set by the opening sequence, in which Toufic, on his scooter, is brushed off the road by a verbally abusive driver going the wrong way down a one-way street. A second humiliation comes much later, when he is beaten up after intervening in a dispute about a scratched car. He sets out on a path of revenge, actually buying a pistol and imagining himself as an avenging Hollywood hero. But the violence does not in fact happen and the tone of comedy-drama is sustained. Our last sight of Toufic is of him at home, sleeping like a child, alongside the little brother he loves. *Falafel* offers a fascinating insight into the realities below the surface in Beirut as well as the frustrated hopes of a new generation.

The much younger **Chadi Zeneddine**, who was born in 1979 in Libreville, capital of Gabon, received professional training in filmmaking, video, and communication in Beirut before relocating to Paris to study for a doctorate at the Sorbonne and work in television. He has made dramas and documentaries as well as directing his own short films. His work is of particular interest because, being born abroad in the late 1970s, he is one of the first Lebanese feature filmmakers not to have experienced the civil war at first hand, though he does say, in his statement of intent, that his filming was haunted by the sound of war, "another war," which he experienced when he visited the Lebanese capital. The sound of bombing opens the film, and its dislocated structure was no doubt also influenced by the fact that, because Zeneddine had no secure financing, the film was shot intermittently over a period of three years.

Whatever the circumstances of its production, *Falling from Earth / En attendant Beyrouth / Wa-ala el-ard el-sama'a* (2007) is a film deliberately shaped to be narratively enigmatic. It opens and closes with a shot of an empty rowboat on a canal, which has no obvious relationship with any of the events in the film. The film's tone is set by the opening section, which depicts the film's aging, bearded narrator, Youssef, inexplicably playing soccer with a blue balloon, only to be interrupted by a Roman centurion on horseback (apparently an actor in a film being shot nearby) who proclaims his love for Beirut and for the beauty of its women. Youssef collects photographs of citizens of Beirut in happier times, but no link is made between any of these and the stories encapsulated in the film's narrative.

Each new section of the narrative is introduced by the same static image of a sunlit Beirut landscape and accompanied by a voice-over comment by Youssef. Each episode is also precisely dated, but there is no sense of temporal progression or change within the film. Each of the protagonists is an isolated figure, whose past is barely sketched in and whose present is lacks human contact. The characters wander through empty or alien spaces, where their image is constantly reduplicated (on CCTV, in mirrors, or in presumably imagined self-images) and often subject to voice-over reflections from unknown sources in Arabic or French. Most of the film reflects the waiting implied in its French title. As Zeneddine has stated: "I watch my characters lost and voiceless turning in circles, still searching or waiting for a 'no way' out." At the same time they are, he says, "simple humans *Falling from Earth* and craving to stay in Beirut, where angels are reborn," and, at the end, Youssef is seemingly reborn as a youthful angel, who vanishes in a dazzling blaze of light.[129]

Georges Hachem first studied theatre at university in Lebanon and then filmmaking at the École Louis-Lumière in France. Since his return to Lebanon in 2006, he has run the audiovisual department of Antonine University in Beirut. He has also directed plays and made a first short, twenty-minute film, *Evening Mass / Messe de soir* (2009). His first feature film, *Stray Bullet / Balle perdue* (2011) is set in 1976, during the civil war, but Hachem argues for its contemporary relevance: "My generation has the impression that history repeats itself. . . . A country like Lebanon is condemned by its geography and demography to foster civil war or be a mode of intercultural peace. There is not much margin for a choice." This is an opinion with which his interviewer, Virginia de Marco, agrees: "It was filmed in 2009 before the onset of the Arab Spring. However, those watching *Balle perdue* can get a taste of what will subsequently happen."[130]

Hachem explains that *Stray Bullet* is set in a northern suburb in 1976 at a very precise moment in time during the civil war:

> After the first "events" which lasted 18 months, there was a truce. For the people at that time it was the end of what they called the "events." At this moment, nobody thought that it would rebound and plunge the country into a war which would last a dozen years. This moment of truce, at which *Stray Bullet* is set, corresponds to the unawareness of the people then who did not see the horror which was coming.[131]

In the foreground is the story of Noha, who decides to rebel and to refuse to marry the husband chosen for her by her family, just a fortnight before the ceremony and on the day when her brother has organized a dinner party for her. The film brings together and interrelates two central themes of Lebanese cinema, the war and the condition of women.

In his review of the film, Thomas Messias writes:

> The symbolism could be heavy, but Georges Hachem fortunately shows great finesse in the way he interweaves the destinies of Noha, the other women around her, and the country, which imprisons them but which they would not leave for anything in the world. . . . Neither the heroine nor her country will emerge from this crucial day sure of themselves; but, at the same time, they will have grown up, matured, become aware of their potential and their real aspirations. The simultaneity of these two crises of conscience touches us as much as it stimulates us.[132]

Hachem's skill in constructing a tight narrative focus on a single day, and the powerful performance of Nadine Labaki in the lead role ensured that the film won a number of prizes for best film or best performance at Namur, Dubai, Cairo, and Angoulême.

* * *

There are four other male filmmakers from the 2000s with a diverse range of foreign connections: Josef Fares and Hany Tamba, who both have strong European connections, and Assad Fouladkar and Wajdi Mouawad, who have links to North America.

Josef Fares was born in 1977 in Lebanon but settled with his family in Sweden at the age of ten. From the age of fifteen, he began making amateur films, and in 1998, at twenty-one, he began formal film training. Between 1995 and 2002 he made a number of fictional shorts. His first two features, *The Best Man's Wedding / Jalla! Jalla! / Vite! Vite!* (2000) and *Kopps / Les flics* (2003), were made in Sweden. *Jalla! Jalla!* is a lighthearted Swedish-language comedy which touches peripherally on life in the immigrant Lebanese community in Sweden. Its main focus, however, is on the personal relationship problems of two young men, who work together as municipal gardeners, Mans and Roro. Mans has sexual problems with his live-in girlfriend Jenny, with whom he acts out a number of amusing ploys to restore their relationship. They play-act being just neighbors (an excellent opening for the film), and he tries sex toys and marital aids, flagellation, and oriental medicine, all with embarrassing results and to no avail. Eventually Jenny packs her bags and leaves. The Lebanese-born Roro's problems are rather different. He likewise has a live-in Swedish girlfriend, Lisa, whose family accept him without any problems. But he is reluctant to introduce Lisa to his own family, because they are planning a traditional arranged marriage for him with Yasmin, a girl he has never met. The film contains a lively succession of chases, fights, misunderstandings, awkward moments, and unlikely coincidences, accompanied by a cheerful musical score. All ends happily, of course, when, as the planned wedding ceremony is about to go ahead, Roro plucks up courage to confront his family about his love for Lisa, and Mans and Yasmin declare their love for each other.

Fares returned to Lebanon to shoot part of the semi-autobiographical *Zozo* in 2005, but he remains based in Sweden, where he has since made two more Swedish comedies, *Leo* (2007) and *Balls / Farsan* (2010). These are basically mainstream Swedish films. *Balls,* for example, is a comedy with often farcical overtones about male frailties and self-deceptions. All the characters have aspects of their lives which they cannot face up to or accept (the inability to have children; arrogant patriarchal self-esteem; the refusal to accept that a much-loved old dog is dying). There are gags, chases, and moments of poignancy before the inevitable happy ending, but the national origins or identities of these characters are irrelevant to the impact of the film.

Zozo (2005) is obviously based to some extent on Fares's own experience, since he himself left Beirut for Sweden as a ten-year-old in 1987. The film opens largely in what is a conventional realist fashion, with a Beirut-based family, which is already preparing to emigrate to join the grandparents in Sweden, suddenly caught up in the bombing. Thanks to his brother's efforts, Zozo is the sole survivor, although he can hardly comprehend what is going on when he emerges from his hiding place. At this point the tone of the film changes radically, and it becomes more of a fantasy, often deeply sentimental and overlaid with emotional music (even celestial choirs!). Earlier, there had been a hint of what is to come, when Zozo has an (imaginary) conversation with a day-old chick, which advises him (in a deep masculine voice) about Sweden and the fact that his brother will not return.

The bulk of the film is an attempt to capture with humor and occasional touches of absurdity the subjective world of Zozo, who is still a child but scarred by memories of loss and violence. The childish side of him comes out in his relationship with a girl of his own age, Rita, with whom he can play freely and uninhibitedly. But the field where they play is littered with spent cartridges from the adult shooting of wild birds, and her father intervenes brutally to destroy their dream of running off to Sweden together. Zozo is also abandoned by his chick, which tells him it prefers to hang out with its friends and have a few beers.

Zozo's grandfather in Sweden proves to be yet another adult male macho figure, boasting about the fights he had in his youth and urging Zozo to stand up for himself. Although his grandparents decide not to mourn or talk of the past, Zozo is inevitably haunted by recurrent dreams, nightmares, and visions of his mother, for whom he longs desperately. Zozo always shies away from violence, but it is there everywhere in the adult world. Bullied at school, he eventually finds a friend in Leo, who is also bullied and has a violent father at home. The film ends, however, with the same idyllic golden seaside imagery with which it had begun, showing Zozo and Leo fishing peacefully together. *Zozo* is a film apart from mainstream Lebanese cinema, attempting to deal with the aftermath of war and its effect on children with a unique mixture of nostalgia and sentimentality, humor and absurdity.

Hany Tamba, who was born in 1961 in Beirut, studied graphic design in the United Kingdom and worked on a number of commercials while living there. He followed a number of short films with his first feature, *Melodrama Habibi / Une chanson dans la tête* (2008). This is a lighthearted comedy with music in which Lebanon's very real problems are turned into farce: the Hafouche family's seemingly violent chauffeur-cum-bodyguard did not really take part in the civil war and, when Randa Hafouche is kidnapped, her wealthy husband is more concerned about his missing Mercedes than about his wife. In a similar way, the narrative uses outrageous coincidences to assure that all ends well, and the plot moves easily between supposed reality and moments of dream and wish fulfillment. The narrowly avoided scars of war can be recalled with nostalgia, and the real wounds cured by a brief sexual fling. The story is that of an aging Paris hotel receptionist, Bruno Caprice, who had a single hit song, "Quand tu t'en vas," thirty years before, in the 1970s. Although he hates to be reminded of this brief and transient moment of glory while he is in Paris, he allows himself to accept a profitable invitation to sing in Beyrouth, at the reception offered by the wealthy businessman Hafouche to his wife Randa, for whom his song has a particular poignancy. She was at Bruno's Beyrouth concert when he continued singing after a bomb cut off the electricity. Had the concert not continued, she would have been killed when her own apartment was caught up in the subsequent gunfire.

Bruno's experiences in Beyrouth are chaotic but reinvigorating. He is even able to compose a second song, dedicated to Nadine, whose tragic memories of her father's death, linked in her mind to "Quand tu t'en vas," his favorite song, he has managed to assuage.

Assad Fouladkar was born in 1961 in Beirut, where he studied drama. Subsequently he moved to the United States, where he obtained his master's degree in filmmaking at Boston University. During this period he made a number of short films and documentaries, the best known of which is *Kyrie Eleison* (1989), a twenty-four-minute study of Beirut during the bombing. In the United States he worked for Arab American Television. After his return to Lebanon, he has presented a weekly radio program on film and worked as a film critic and in television production. He has also taught filmmaking at the Kaslik University and at the Lebanese American University (LAU).

As his first feature, he made *When Maryam Spoke Out / Quand Maryam s'est dévoilé / Lamma hikyit Maryam* (2002), which was produced on a tiny budget by LAU. Lina Khateb records Fouladkar's account of the film's production:

> The biggest problem when making the film was that the people working on it did not take the project seriously. Shooting on video, with a small crew, on a low budget, surrounded by my students—to the actors it looked like a university project, not a set. There was little money; I barely paid the actors anything.[133]

The film, one of the rare Lebanese features not to deal with the civil war, tells the story of a young couple, Ziad and Maryam, whose happiness is destroyed when it is discovered that Maryam is infertile.

Wajdi Mouawad was born in Lebanon in 1968 but left with his family to live in France at the age of eight. For some reason he was unable to obtain the papers necessary for residence in France and left for Quebec in 1983 at the age of fifteen. In Quebec, he studied drama at the Canadian national theatre school from 1991 and, on graduating, gradually became a major figure in Canadian French-language theatre. He has published two novels and over a dozen plays. He has also directed various theatre companies in Canada, staging his own plays and numerous classic dramas; his work has won him a number of major theatrical awards. His sole venture into film directing was *Littoral* (2004), adapted from his own play, which was first staged in 1997. The play deals with an adolescent whose father dies unexpectedly and who is angered when his family decide not to follow his father's wishes and arrange for burial in Lebanon. After finding tape recordings made on each birthday by his father, he discovers for the first time the circumstances of his mother's death. He decides to organize his father's burial at Kfar Ryat in Lebanon. Though shown at the 8th Biennale des cinémas arabes in

Paris in 2006, the film does not seem to have made much impact and is not mentioned in either of the standard histories of Lebanese cinema.

* * *

There is a strong representation of women, too, among those born in the 1970s. Nadine Labaki is rare among Lebanese filmmakers in not having studied abroad—she trained in Beirut. Both Danielle Arbid and Dima El-Horr have the more typical foreign links, Arbid having lived all her adult life in Paris, while El-Horr studied in the United States. Lara Saba first studied in Beirut but spent several years working in French television. Sabine El Gemayel studied in Canada and worked in the United States, but her connections with Iran, from childhood onward, mean that her first feature, which began as a Lebanese project, ended up as an Iranian film.

Nadine Labaki, who was born in Lebanon in 1974, lacks a background in foreign film training, but she did receive an award from the Cannes Film Festival, which allowed her to spend six months in Paris, scripting her first feature film. She studied at IESAV in Beirut and has since worked as an actress in a number of Lebanese features, including Philippe Aractingi's *The Bus* (2005) and, more recently, Georges Hachem's *Stray Bullet* (2011). She began her career as a filmmaker while still a student, making an award-winning short, *11 rue Pasteur* (1998). She has since filmed numerous commercials and musical numbers featuring leading Arab female singers. Perhaps because they are largely structured as comedies, her two features—both French co-productions—have enjoyed perhaps the widest international circulation among the films of her generation.

Labaki, who was seventeen when the civil war ended, deliberately turned her back on those years of strife in her first feature, *Caramel* (2007), but within a week of the completion of shooting in 2006, hostilities resumed, with the bombardment of Beirut. The film, which focuses on the lives of women in what seems an optimistic period of peace, is largely set in a Beirut beauty salon—the word "caramel" has not only the Western meaning of burnt sugar but also an additional Arab connotation as the word for a traditional Oriental method of depilation, using boiled sugar and lemon. Labaki herself, who plays the salon owner, is the only professionally trained actress in the group, the others having been chosen largely for their physical resemblance to the characters she had envisaged. In this "typically feminine universe, these women—who suffer from the hypocrisy of a traditional Oriental system face-to-face with Western modernism—help each other in the problems they encounter with men, love, marriage, and sex,"[134] regardless of each individual's own personal place in a Lebanon still divided on sectarian terms.

Their problems are varied. Layale, the character played by Labaki, is a Christian who is the mistress of a married man. Her problems increase when she finds herself giving beauty care to his pleasant, unsuspecting blonde wife. Her close friend Nisrine, a Muslim, is not the virgin her intended husband assumes her to be and has to resort to surgery to create the appropriate impression on her wedding night. Rima, a hairdresser at the salon, perhaps discovers her own sexual orientation for the first time when she is overwhelmed by a beautiful, unnamed woman who comes into the salon on impulse but then returns constantly for further hair care by Rima. The eventual outcome is left open, but the film ends with the woman admiring her own mirrored reflection, after Rima has totally changed her image by trimming her long black hair. This range of characters is supplemented by two contrasting older women. Jamale, who has been left by her husband for a younger woman, continually returns to the salon because she cannot admit her age and give up dreams of becoming an actress. In contrast, Rose, a neighbor, who has devoted her life to her mentally troubled older sister, cannot ultimately face up to the possibility of escape offered by a respectful older man.

The external world which Labaki depicts is not particularly sympathetic to women: a bride is expected to be a virgin; hotels expect people spending the night together to be married; the discovery of an engaged couple sitting and talking in a car at night leads to a police arrest. But the individual men depicted—Nisrine's fiancé Charles, who courts Rose, and the neighborhood policeman attracted to Layale—are all sympathetic (Layale's married lover is never shown). To a large extent, the women's emotional problems are of their own making and would probably cause as many difficulties in any Western society as they do in Lebanon. *Caramel* is essentially an optimistic view of contemporary Arab life which is touching at times but never strays from its basic mode of comedy. In Labaki's view, Lebanese women "are survivors. Like all Arab women they are passionate and temperamental. But they refuse to dramatize themselves or let themselves be carried away with unhappiness."[135]

Whereas *Caramel* is basically a realistic, if sentimental, depiction of Arab women's lives, her second feature, *Where Do We Go Next? / Et maintenant on va où?* (2011), is a more ambitious and, perhaps for that reason, a more uneven work. While it is still essentially a comedy in which music plays a key role, *Where Do We Go Next?* is in essence a fantasy about what women *could* achieve. The new film has the same French co-production backup; and Labaki has worked again with the same two male scriptwriters (Jihad Hojeily and Rodney El Haddad), the same composer (Khaled Mouzanar), and once again plays the lead role herself, while employing a cast made up largely of non-professionals. But here the tone is very different, as the women's concerns are not with their own emotional problems but with the wider issue of the potential for male violence in a fragmented Lebanese society. In *Caramel*, Labaki had tried to turn her back on the civil war, but finding herself pregnant in a Beirut again under siege, she felt impelled to make a film which, while not reflecting upon war, speculated imaginatively on how women might join together to avoid it.[136]

The film, set in an isolated village where Christians and Muslims live harmoniously together, is entirely imaginary, although Labaki did find an actual village in which to shoot part of the film where the church and the mosque are in fact side by side. It begins with a voice-over by Labaki—"I'm going to tell you a story"— and the early scenes have a certain fairy tale air. The first image of the black-clad women in the cemetery shows them advancing in a dance movement; and the flirtation of the Christian heroine, Amale (played by Labaki), and her Muslim housepainter is shown through an imagined duet they sing together (Labaki has said the style of the film was influenced by *Grease* as well as by *Snow White* and *Cinderella,* films she saw as a child).[137] At first the installation of a communal television in the village brings in not only new (unimagined) erotic images but also news of conflict in the outside world, between Christians and Muslims. Subsequently, comparatively small incidents—the accidental damaging of a crucifix and the disappearance of the shoes of worshippers at the mosque—threaten to plunge the community into communal male violence.

The women's response is certainly imaginative—they band together to hire a troupe of belly dancers from town to distract the men from violence. The scene in which they all combine to cook and spike the men's food before the performance certainly merits a new musical number. But the introduction of a real death (that of one of the young men who daily fetch provisions, who is caught in the crossfire of a sectarian battle on his way back from town) strikes a discordant note in an otherwise lighthearted narrative. Despite the women's efforts, there can be no true closure. The final images return to the cemetery seen in the film's opening, but now there is no dance movement. The villagers unite for the funeral of the young man and move along the path between the two cemeteries, Christian on one side, Muslim on the other. But as they pause, they find themselves, quite literally, at a point where the divide between the two communities is obvious. There can be no resolution, only the question which gives the film its title, "Where Do We Go Next?"

Labaki's second film is fascinating and original, and it leaves the outside viewer troubled. Ultimately, it seems evident that there is no way to bring together *Snow White* and the realities of Lebanese sectarian politics. The director desperately wants to find—even through a story line which begins so lightly—a way of demonstrating that women can find the solution to the perpetual strife. But while the film certainly celebrates the vitality and resourcefulness of Lebanese women, in the end Labaki has the honesty to admit that they alone can find no answer.

Danielle Arbid, who was born in 1970, left Lebanon at the age of seventeen to study literature and journalism in Paris, where she is now resident. She worked as a journalist for several years before turning to filmmaking. She made a number of fictional short films before completing two feature-length documentaries. She has also been involved with interactive art and video installations, and contributed to the collective project *Videos under Siege* (2008).

The first of Arbid's two feature-length documentaries, both of which were shot on Beta SP in the early 2000s, is *Alone with the War / Seule avec la guerre / Halat harb* (2000). The film shows clearly her background as a journalist. She is visible, in shot, during most of the informal interviews she does, and she presents herself as working for French television (the documentary is a French co-production). She left Beirut toward the end of the civil war, and *Alone with the War* is her examination of the war's aftermath: "I wanted to film the void which it has left. Its ghostly presence."[138] She describes herself as being totally caught up in her subject matter and wishing to show things as she sees them, subjectively: "I have no distance. I lived through it. . . . My only qualification is being myself, asking questions about things that bother me."[139] The film has no apparent prearranged structure. It begins with a memory, footage of the demonstration to mark the assassination of the Phalangist leader Bachir Gemayel, in which Arbid participated as a twelve-year-old, and it includes a single staged scene, a tribute to her handsome Maronite militiaman cousin Samir, who was her idol when she was seven but was killed during the fighting.

Otherwise the film is a vivid, firsthand piece of reportage, as Arbid moves around Beirut and poses questions no one wants to answer. Her initial supposition is that "officially the war didn't exist, we fantasize it, we invent it, we buy it, we sell it," and nothing in her subsequent investigations calls this into question. She meets a man (Abou Lello) who offers trips to the sites of "massacres, torture or kidnappings" for $400 a day, and seems genuinely outraged when she is unconvinced by the seemingly carefully placed "props" he produces. At the Sabra and Shatila camps, the site of the most notorious massacre, she meets only children who happily play up to the camera; and at Tall Zaatar, no one in the market area admits to knowing anything. At the time of the civil war, images of "martyrs" were plastered everywhere on the walls; now the only photographs to be seen are those held out desperately by the mothers whose children disappeared without a trace in the conflict—and these aging women are not even treated respectfully by the police. Not a single person she meets—not even the minister of the interior (Michel El Murr) or the local member of parliament—shares her sense of the need for a monument to commemorate all the dead of the civil war.

The most revealing testament to the actual cost to a human being of involvement, from adolescence, in the conflict, comes from a series of extracts from interviews with a Maronite militiaman. At first he points out that everyone was given amnesty in 1991, so no one is guilty of anything, and that going to work now is just like going to the demarcation line during the war. But gradually his inner demons are revealed. He is driven to go to Southern Lebanon, just to hear bombs exploding again, and, paradoxically, finds peace only at the sites of massacres in which he participated. In truth, he lives with a sense of evil within himself. After one of those brief autobiographical moments that seem indispensable in 2000s Arab video-shot documentary—a conversation by Arbid with her father, who still keeps a pistol under his pillow—the filmmaker's final conclusion, face to camera, is that "all the evil that was done is still there, within us."

Arbid describes her second documentary, the Franco-Belgian co-production *At the Borders / Aux frontières* (2002), as "a Middle Eastern road movie."[140] The ostensible subject is "a country, which bears two names: Palestine/Israel." But she "never crossed its borders. I looked at it as people from outside look at it, fantasize it, despise or love it. My film follows my wanderings."[141] These take her most of the way along Israel/Palestine's borders with its Arab neighbors: Southern Lebanon, Jordan, Syria, and Egypt. Again there is no sense of a clear, pre-planned structure: the documentary begins with the limited footage of a 1998 holiday visit to a half-abandoned Palestinian refugee camp in Sinai and ends abruptly when she is denied permission to film the last stage of her journey, the trip along the Egyptian border. For Arbid, who grew up a child in Beirut during the civil war, "it's not worth making films unless one puts oneself at risk." She always wants to know what is going on, and for her any documentary idea is constructed out of accidents and chance encounters. To get the footage she wants, she is quite prepared to make use of the fact that she is a woman, wearing a miniskirt, for example, or presenting herself as a bit of an idiot: "I'm a girl. I'm a bit lost."[142]

The people discovered haphazardly in her travels for *At the Borders* often have surprising attitudes, but there is nothing here with the dramatic force of her interviews with former militiamen in the earlier film (one, not included in the film, was apparently so troubling that she was physically sick afterward). There is the man in Hezbollah's propaganda department in Southern Lebanon who believes that if he never uses the word "Israel," then it doesn't exist. Zaki, another Southern Lebanese, accepts with apparent equanimity the fact that he has been imprisoned and fined for working in Israel, even though this was the only way to feed his children. At the Rashidieh refugee camp, Abou Bashar points across the water to his native village, Al Bassa. It is just ten minutes' drive away, and although he comes to look at it every day, he is resigned to the fact that he will never visit. In Syria, a spokesman shows her the martyred city of Quneitra, but otherwise there is little to see except Syrian television. In Jordan, she meets a man who farms right up to the border, growing a profusion of fruit and vegetables in the rich soil. He wears a T-shirt inscribed "I'm not a tourist, I live here" and reports that all his visitors see this spot as paradise. Encounters at the Jordanian border are less involving—there are restrictions on filming and people are less forthcoming, although she does meet a group of young people who gather regularly at the border because on a good day they can see the Dome of the Rock in Jerusalem. *At the Borders* is a film of frustration—permanent for the displaced individuals she encounters and, to some extent, for the filmmaker herself.

In the Battlefields / Dans les champs de bataille / Maarek hob (2004), the first of Arbid's three features, is set during the civil war, in 1983, when she was herself an adolescent in Beirut. The protagonist, Lina, is a moody twelve-year-old, and Arbid has acknowledged that there are autobiographical elements in the film. She is hesitant to specify which elements: "It's cinema. I'm not making a documentary about my life."[143] But she does mention in one interview that her father played poker and that her aunt is a character in the film.[144] One important autobiographical aspect of the film is its exclusive concern with the Christian community—Muslims are unseen and unknown aliens. This is not a matter of prejudice—she is a close friend of Ziad Doueiri, author of *West Beirut,* and these two are, as Lina Khatib notes, the only films which show "the possibility of having fun under difficult circumstances."[145] Rather, it is a question of knowledge: "I grew up in a Christian community where people wore crosses. I write about what I know. . . . I did not know people called Rami and Nawal, I knew George and Georgette."[146]

The film's title has a double resonance. On the one hand, there is, of course, the civil war, with its militia troops (some still teenagers), its roadblocks, and the incessant background of rifle fire, as well as the constant bombardments which make the characters spend their nights cramped in a cellar. But Lina accepts this as a normal part of life, just as Arbid did at this age: "It is very important to show the war not as an exotic thing, but just as one of living life. When I was a kid, I used to think this was normal, that the whole world lived in war. I didn't know what peace was."[147] At the very end of the film there is the obligatory homage to Beirut and the ruins caused by war.

On the other hand, there is the battlefield which does deeply affect Lina—that within her own family. This is a bourgeois Christian family living in East Beirut, given to formal gatherings and family councils and dominated by the cruel and autocratic Aunt Yvonne. Lina's own immediate family is a broken one. Her father Fouad is a failed but compulsive gambler, who has men from the collection agency constantly on his trail. At one point, when she is sent to fetch him, Lina witnesses him being accused of cheating at the card table and beaten up when he tries to leave with his winnings. Lina has to intervene to stop him when he fetches his gun to try to exact vengeance. Her mother Thérèse is pregnant, a defeated, self-pitying woman, who, like Fouad, gives little thought to Lina and starves her of affection. Isolated within her own family, Lisa turns to Siham, her aunt's Syrian maid. The unsparing view of Christian family life that emerges in the film was deliberately intended to be so: "Society in the film is harsher than the war. The Lebanese have good qualities, but at the same time the society is harsh. . . . You can hide from missiles, but not from internal problems."[148]

Just as Arbid's two documentaries have the air of films made up of random events and chance encounters, so too the narrative line of *In the Battlefields* is a loose succession of incidents, not a plot-driven dramatic structure. Siham is an uninhibited young woman, very much in love with her boyfriend Marwan. Still an inexperienced adolescent, Lina is partly fascinated, partly put off, when she witnesses the couple making love in the back of a car or on the stairs. But she is intrigued, and one night, in the cellar where they are huddled close together, she gets Siham to teach her what kissing involves (one of the film's few comic scenes). Lina is very close to Siham, but when Siham reveals that she is planning to run off and demands Lina's help with her luggage, Lina turns against her and denounces her to the aunt. The result is a beating for Siham, who is kept locked up, even during bombardments. When she finally escapes, she quarrels violently with Lina because of her betrayal but finally manages to escape—to an uncertain fate—leaving Lina more isolated than before.

In the Battlefields is a film which holds the attention, but Arbid follows the events rather than probing her characters. We never get inside Lina's head or learn anything about the actual relationship of Siham and Marwan (is he really planning to marry her?). Arbid does not even make clear the circumstances of Fouad's death, which forms the climax to the family drama. For much of the film, the camera is close in but recording, not probing. Where Arbid is truly involved is in her filming of the sex scenes in the car and on the stairway, which have more of an uninhibited French feel to them than an Arab one. This reflects perfectly Arbid's own sentiments: "I love to film sex. Really, I love filming bodies, the skin, the movement of the skin. That's why I take my camera up very close. It's very sensual. I love to film sensual things. It's not provocative. It's just emotional."[149]

A Lost Man / Un homme perdu (2007), a French-language film shot in Jordan and Lebanon, enabled Arbid to pursue this personal interest further, as, on the most superficial level, it consists of an alternation of nude sex scenes in hotel rooms and shots of the male protagonists drinking in nighttime bars or walking through desolate landscapes. As usual with Arbid, the plot is loose and episodic. Things are shown but not explained, and there is a minimum of dialogue. The exact circumstances, at the very beginning of the film, surrounding a stabbing which drives Fouad Saleh into flight through and out of Beirut, are explained only at the end of the film. We merely meet up with him, a wandering vagrant who has blocked out the past, twenty years later. Similarly, at the end of the film, we never learn exactly how the French photographer Thomas has managed to discover the identity and location of Fouad's wife in Beirut. Between these two points we move in a fairly leisurely linear fashion from one chance encounter to another, with no attempt to build up any sort of conventional dramatic suspense.

At the heart of the film is the relationship which grows up, almost by chance, between two men who very different in many ways but are also to some extent mirror images of each other. Thomas is a French photographer with seemingly limitless pockets, who is roaming the Arab world seeking to acquire a portfolio of sexual images, presumably for some future erotic publication (the character is based in part on the real-life French photographer Antoine D'Agata, who it seems led this sort of life and acted as advisor to the film). Thomas's life is an endless repetitive cycle of drinking in bars, watching women gyrate on the dance floor, picking up prostitutes, and photographing himself having sex with them. Although he is, in a sense, an exile, he evidently feels no nostalgia, and the film offers no insight into his past. He shows no personal concern for anyone around him, certainly not the prostitutes whose services he buys. His life changes almost imperceptibly, however, when he encounters Fouad.

Fouad, the lost man of the title (although both men would in some ways qualify for this description), is in more desperate straits. He has no money or ambition and has (or so he claims) lost all memory of the past, even his own nationality. Meeting him, almost inevitably after surreptitiously photographing him kissing a woman, Thomas befriends him and hires him as his interpreter. But what seems on the surface to be a friendship is always fraught because of their differences. Whereas Thomas seeks no more than (graphically interesting) sex from the prostitutes he hires, Fouad is desperately in search of love, from the woman he is photographed with in the early sequence and, much later in the film, from the whore Thomas hires for him (so he can film them together). The relationship (like that between Siham and Lina in the earlier film) soon develops into a power struggle, marked by frequent confrontations and quarrels, with Fouad getting Thomas beaten up in the street at one point. Thomas, personally involved more than is customary in his life, sets out to discover the truth about Fouad's past. He succeeds, but reverts to type, seducing the wife and photographing her in her greatest moment of crisis as she rejects Fouad, who, we now learn, had fled after stabbing her all those years before. The film's ending offers little hope for either protagonist. Fouad is last seen fleeing the family to whom he has been restored, while Thomas is back in Paris, alone with his pile of erotic photographs and cut off from Fouad.

In many ways, given Arbid's penchant for following characters rather than probing them, these two essentially empty characters are ideal for her. Their motives remain opaque to us, but she is able to set them in context with perfect visual precision. Since this inner emptiness is never filled, however, and neither character makes any effort toward this end, it is difficult for the spectator to feel involved with their fate. Arbid's skill in using a minimal crew and lightweight equipment, combined with low levels of lighting and her concern to film intimately and up close, gives the film its distinctive personal style. And the freedom she allows her actors and actresses to choose their own movements and gestures to interpret the hesitations, tensions, and pleasures of the sex scenes makes these scenes the most aesthetically pleasing, as well as most audacious, in Arab cinema up to this date.

When, prior to the screening of the film, journalists heard that Arbid's third feature, *Beirut Hotel/Beyrouth Hotel* (2011), had been banned by the censor in Lebanon, the common assumption was that this must be because of its erotic content. After all, her two previous features had upset the censors because of their treatment of sexuality, and the new film's working title was "Hotel Rooms." Moreover, the plot summaries—echoed by the eventual DVD cover—spoke of a passionate affair between a Lebanese singer, Zaha, who is separating from her husband, and a visiting French business lawyer, Mathieu, who claims to be work-ing on a telecommunications deal. As the DVD cover puts it, "They experience for a few days a love story filled with fears and desires, intrigue and violence."

But in her interviews, Arbid does not talk about sex but about paranoia: "It's the fear I feel when I am in my own country. I hate this certainty that no one can protect me when I'm there and this fear becomes part of me."[150] Indeed, the res-ervations of the Censorship and General Security Committee, a part of the coun-try's internal security services, were in no way related to the film's erotic content. They were troubled by the fact that the film's plot "raised questions about the as-sassination of Rafiq Hariri (the country's former president), which could endan-ger the country's security."[151] From the outside, this seems an absurd criticism of a film in which even the name Hariri is hardly mentioned. Arbid appealed, arguing that her only sources were newspaper reports, which she had read two years earlier and which she thought really lent themselves to fiction: "As dramatic material, it's rather interesting. But I specifically did not name any political par-ties, nor campaign for anyone, nor insult anyone."[152] Yet, at the time of writing, the ban on the film is still in place.

The censorship action may seem totally misguided, but it bears out the film's assumption that Beirut—"a very strange city, a meld of violence and compas-sion"[153]—is a city of fear. The very fact that the ban was instituted shows one of the differences separating *Beirut Hotel* from Arbid's earlier work. Another is the visual style. The new film is much more formally structured and controlled, with the characters observed from a cool distance rather than followed by a handheld camera and locked in intimate close-ups. Arbid has commented that she wanted it "to be glamorous because the main character is a singer. Sexy, but not vulgar, very Lebanese in a way."[154] The narrative has a stronger dramatic shape as well. This is indeed the story of a passionate sexual affair, but erotic scenes of lovemak-ing play a comparatively small part. The essence of the film is about how two people can get to know each other, how far one can trust the other. For Arbid, this is part of the game, what makes it exciting. Finding herself alone in Mathieu's apartment, Zaha's immediate instinct is to search his belongings to find out more about this man she has unexpectedly fallen in love with. Perhaps the finest scenes in the film are those at the very beginning, after the couple have met by chance in a bar. He is both assertive and withdrawn; she is attracted but hesitant, drawn to him but instinctively holding back, until they finally make love.

While Mathieu may now be a business lawyer in Beirut to conclude a deal, what he was doing there three years earlier remains a mystery. It involved the French embassy and got him into trouble, from which he was rescued by his Lebanese colleague, Abbas. Now Abbas is in trouble and reappears to ask for Mathieu's help in getting a French visa. In return, he claims he can offer the French some (unspecified) information about the Hariri assassination. Unfortunately Mathieu cannot come up with his side of the bargain, but his association with Abbas means that he too becomes a suspect. Only after Abbas's death is Mathieu cleared, but he is ordered to leave Beirut immediately. As always in Arbid's films, deaths occur off-screen (it appears that Abbas was shot by the police, who subsequently found him to be innocent), and the ending in fact resolves nothing. Instead, it leaves the characters suspended, Zaha back singing in the restaurant and Mathieu off to an unknown future in France.

This story about a man who may or not be a spy is well suited to Arbid's customary approach to her characters: she observes but never explains them. Here we have a genuinely dramatic plot—not just a succession of events—and the film generates real suspense With five feature-length films in the decade, Arbid has emerged as a major figure: continually inventive, making a sure transition from documentary to fiction, creating a consistent view of life from film to film, and demonstrating an increasing authority in her filmmaking at each step of the way.

Dima El-Horr, who was born in 1972 in Beirut, began her study of filmmaking in 1995 at the Art Institute of Chicago, where she made her first short film, *The Street,* in 1997. She now teaches at the Lebanese American University in Beirut. The best known of her early works is the short fictional piece *Ready to Wear Imm Ali / Prêt à porter Imm Ali* (2003), about a woman who tries in vain to increase sales at her shop.

Every Day Is a Holiday / Chaque jour est une fête (2009) is a self-consciously structured experimental narrative, which begins with a stylized dream sequence, variations of which recur at intervals throughout the film, and to which the narrative returns allusively at the end. The plot as such is simple: a group of women, who have set out on a three-hour bus ride from Beirut to visit their husbands in prison, have their journey ended abruptly when a stray bullet kills the driver, leaving them stranded in a desert landscape. For the three very diverse women on whom the film focuses, this is the entry into a nightmare, in which the realities of war (refugees, fighting, massacres) are transformed into abstract patterns of anonymous figures crossing the landscape, half-heard menacing sounds, and often, mere emptiness and rumor. Death is a column of hearses and seven coffins carried in silhouette across a hilltop. The desert, whose dangers are less than expected, becomes the incongruous backdrop for the measured progression of three elegant women, whose high heels are never broken and whose makeup remains immaculate.

The stories of those they encounter are either self-parodies (the lorry driver who picks them up at one point and then abruptly abandons them) or ridiculed by the main characters (the widower in the hearse). Narrative logic disappears as the three are separated, meet up again, and are then magically translated to the prison, where we are told (but do not see) that all the men are dead. El-Horr has said in an interview, "I wanted essentially to speak about things very deeply buried in me, that constitute who I am. . . . Knowing how to accept confrontation is a path toward understanding."[155] In the film, the central figure, Tamara, tells us that the journey has been to find out about the realities of love and death. But given that the women remain mere ciphers, seemingly unaffected by their inexplicable experiences, these insights remain muted.

Lara Saba graduated in 1994 from the Jesuit University in Beirut with a degree in communications. She subsequently worked as assistant director on films by prominent Lebanese directors, such as Jean-Claude Codsi and the team of Joanna Hadjithomas and Khalil Joreige, and also for foreign directors, including Merzak Allouache and Sally Potter. In 1998 she began making her own documentaries and subsequently moved for a while to France, where she worked for French television and for the Al Jazeera Children's Channel. On her return to Beirut, she made other documentaries and began work on her first feature.

Blind Intersections / Le temps d'une seconde / Ossit sawani (2012) was designed from the start as a non-judgmental study of three levels of Beirut society and, for authenticity, the three stories were shot in three distinct areas of the city: Raouche, Karam al-Zaytoun, and Nabaa. Each level is represented by a particular character: Andia, a rich young woman, who has everything in life except the child she and her husband long for; Nour, a middle-class student, whose life falls apart when the death of her parents leaves her penniless and potentially homeless; and Marwan, a twelve-year-old boy, who runs away from his alcoholic mother who prostitutes herself and leaves him open to sexual abuse. Although their lives intersect in crucial ways, they are in no way aware of each other's existence.

Blind Intersections is a powerful study of a city about which Saba has strong opinions. For her, Beirut is "a city that rubs us, steps on us, tears us apart, while circumstances, destinies and meetings push our lives out of our control. . . . Beirut is a schizophrenic city, full of contrasts."[156] Certainly a forceful picture does emerge of a twenty-first-century Beirut, which is not haunted by memories of the past (the fifteen-year civil war) but shaped by a contemporary slide into prostitution, pedophilia, and drug addiction.

Nibal Arakji, who wrote the script and subsequently produced the film, conceived *Blind Intersections* as three separate stories, and it was Saba's decision to weave the three together in order to give the film greater weight. The film therefore begins with an enigmatic car crash and ends with a repetition of the same images, intended to make the spectator aware of the impact of the unexpected interaction of the three lives. What Saba seems not to have realized is that if the three stories are to be so intimately connected, then the logical protagonist of the third story is not Marwan but rather the mother whose abuse drives him to homelessness and drug addiction. The second problem for the spectator is that of the time frame. As we watch the film unfold, constantly intercutting between three characters, we inevitably assume that these lives are contemporaneous. But, in fact, the scenes of Andia and Marwan show the events leading up to the tragic crash, while those of Nour, whose parents are killed in the crash, depict its subsequent consequences. Despite its narrative difficulties, *Blind Intersections* offers a fresh and vivid depiction of rarely seen aspects of Beirut society in the period preceding the Arab Spring.

Sabine El Gemayel grew up in Lebanon and Iran, moved to Canada in 1987, and graduated in 1993 with a degree in communication studies from Montreal's Concordia University. She made three short films before moving to Los Angeles in 1994. She has worked as an editor, most notably on Hanna Elias's Palestinian film *The Olive Harvest* (2002). She received Fonds Sud funding for her first feature, *Niloofar* (2008), which was inspired by a meeting with a young woman in Lebanon and was intended to be set and shot in Lebanon. The film deals with the controversial issues of arranged marriage and honor killings. The plot concerns a twelve-year-old girl whose dream is to read and write. She finds a woman able and willing to help her, but meanwhile her father arranges her marriage, as a young teenager, to an older man. This is a situation she cannot face, and she runs away with her uncle. Her family considers itself dishonored and sends her stepbrother to track her down.

In the course of its production, the project underwent considerable changes, as El Gemayel has explained:

> Originally, the story was written as a Lebanese story and was taking place
> in the south of Lebanon. Because of the political situation at the time and
> some financial concerns, I chose to make the film in Iran because my family
> lives in Tehran. . . . We made it an Iraqi story because we needed the concept
> of honor to be a strong one and it is in Arab culture more than in Persian
> culture.[157]

Although the notional setting remained Lebanon, the film became a Iranian project, "shot in the Khuzestan province in Iran by the Iraqi border," with Iranian actors, some of whom "were Persian stars." Asked whether living for a good part of her life in Iran helped her with the making of *Niloofar,* El Gemayel replied: "I don't think I would have been able to make the film if it wasn't from this culture. It helped me shape the film as well as interact with my crew."[158]

Palestine

Although her own work since the 1980s, with her husband Jean Chamoun, has dealt almost exclusively with Lebanon, the Palestinian documentarist Maï Masri has provided one of the best definitions of the special role of Palestinian cinema:

> Cinema can create an imaginary Palestine, but it can never replace a real Palestine that consists of land, rights, and freedom for millions of dispossessed Palestinians. In the meantime, our cinematic Palestine can play a powerful role in preserving and developing Palestinian identity and in nurturing the personal and collective dream of a real Palestine.[159]

This is a task which a number of talented filmmakers, women as well as men, have successfully tackled in the 2000s.

The difficulties for Palestinians who are Israeli Arabs and make films with Israeli financing were clearly revealed when *Ajami,* co-directed by the Israeli Palestinian Scandar Copti and the Israeli Jewish filmmaker Yaron Shani, was nominated for an Oscar. In an interview conducted with the two directors in Hollywood, Copti stated: "The film does not represent Israel because 'I cannot represent a country that does not represent me.'" The co-director Shani disagreed: "It's an Israeli film, it represents, it speaks 'Israeli' and deals with Israel-related problems." The response to Copti by the Israeli authorities was swift. Sports and Culture Minister Limor Litvak stated: "In the name of artistic license and pluralism, the movie was given a budget of more than NIS 12 million. It is sad that a director supported by the state ignores those who helped him create and express himself." Michael Ben Ari, a member of the Knesset, demanded that "support for a film should not be granted unless the editors, producers, directors and actors sign a declaration of loyalty to the State of Israel, its symbols and its Jewish-democratic values."[160]

* * *

Just one older Palestinian filmmaker made the breakthrough to feature filmmaking in the 2000s, **Hanna Elias**, who was born in 1957 in Jerusalem but studied at UCLA and now lives in the United States. He followed an award-winning short, *The Mountain / La montagne / Al-jabal* (1992), with his sole feature to date, *The Olive Harvest / La cueillette des olives / Mawsim al-zaytun* (2002). Despite the opening quotation from Mahmoud Darwish, this is essentially a rural melodrama of a conventional kind, played out between a limited range of characters. The patriarch Abu Saleh (played by actor-director Mohamed Bakri) has just two daughters (Raeda and Arren), while the two central male characters, the brothers Mazen and Taher, have lost both their parents. Raeda and Taher, who works for Settlement Watch, an organization trying to prevent further Israeli settlement, are in love, but she refuses to give him even a kiss until their relationship is formally agreed to by her father. Their situation is complicated by the return, after fifteen years in an Israeli prison, of his elder brother, Mazen, once an activist, now devoted solely to poetry and the family olive grove. The naive Raeda finds herself in love with both brothers at the same time (her fate sealed, as in all good melodrama, when her eyes and Mazen's first meet as he enters the village on his return, a village hero, from prison). The dying Abu Saleh tries to find a successor for his olive grove by ordering Raeda to marry Mazen. But in the end Raeda cannot forsake Taher, and the drama concludes fittingly in a thunderstorm, with Raeda, in her wedding dress, writhing disconsolately in the mud, and the two brothers fighting ferociously off-screen.

Although the Israeli threat is always there and the settlements are described by Taher as "a network of cancer cells," *The Olive Harvest* is essentially a hymn to Palestinian rural life. As Abu Saleh proclaims, "the land always comes first," and the landscape of olive groves is filmed lovingly. The two-thousand-year-old olive tree, the "Mother Tree" of the village, is almost a character in its own right, and its destruction by Taher at the height of his despair only strengthens the dramatic climax. But this is a very romanticized rural life, where tradition is respected, not seen as a problem, and the olive harvest involves smiling peasants in colorful clothing singing traditional songs. As Gertz and Khleifi note, the film "is not particularly innovative," although it "revives Michel Khleifi's early cinema in the construction of the landscape and the camera movements."[161]

* * *

Paradoxically, although there is no production infrastructure in Palestine, it was two filmmakers born there, Rashid Masharawi and Elia Suleiman, who were among the first of the Arab generation born after 1960 to be able to establish themselves, first with documentaries and then with feature films, as early as the 1990s. Both were no doubt helped by their strong overseas connections.

Rashid Masharawi was born in 1962 in the Shatila refugee camp in Gaza and moved to Tel Aviv at the age of twelve to help support his family by taking on a succession of menial jobs. He began work in film at eighteen and made his first short films in the 1980s. He followed these with a number of other longer documentaries: *Long Days in Gaza / Longues journées à Gaza / Lyaam tsaawila fi Gaza* (1991), *House, Houses / Une maison, des maisons / Dar wa dûr* (1991), and *The Magician* aka *Enchanting / Le magicien / As-sahr* (1992). In 1993 Masharawi moved to the Netherlands for three years, returning to found a film production center, and since 1994 he has interspersed a dozen documentary films among his fictional features.

Masharawi is both the most prolific and, at the same time, one of the least known of Palestinian filmmakers (compared, for example, with his contemporary Elia Suleiman). He decided to settle in Ramallah, although this meant distancing himself from the production support he needed from Europe. There he set up the Cinema Production Centre (CPC), to both train and foster young local filmmakers and to satisfy some of his personal needs: "I didn't want to be in a desert. I need an environment in order to make films, to have other filmmakers around, to hear music, see exhibitions, and to have a more active relation to cinema and culture."[162]

Masharawi's real impact on the international scene did not come until *Laila's Birthday* in 2008, and his films have had comparatively limited distribution. As Gertz and Khleifi note, his films reflect his birth and background. His cinema "delineates the refugees' here-and-now daily struggle for survival within a space that has been gradually diminishing, from the time Palestinians were driven out from their native villages and gathered in the refugee camps." They also quote Masharawi's interview with Ali Waked: "Jaffa is always present in my subconscious. It is true that I love Jaffa, but I do not have to mourn over it in a blatant and acrimonious way. . . . The tedious repetition of my story as a refugee would only diminish its strength and significance."[163]

Masharawi's first feature, *Curfew / Couvre-feu / Hatta isaar akhar* (1993), deals with a situation with which he is personally familiar, since he himself once experienced a forty-day curfew when visiting the Shatila camp where he was born.[164] The film opens with wide shots of Gaza, but quickly focuses in on the Abu Raji family as they are imprisoned in their home during an Israeli-imposed curfew. Their situation worsens throughout the day: first the confinement, then darkness (as the electricity is cut off), preventing even the reading of a letter from one of the sons, who lives in exile in Germany. Then tear gas seeps in, causing further problems; and finally, the Israeli troops burst in on them and their neighbors, taking away the older son, Raji. Gertz and Khleifi explain the difficult circumstances under which the film was made:

> It was shot in 1993, during the First Intifada. As it was not possible to film openly in Gaza at that time, the director had to shoot the panoramic views of the city from hidden lookouts or rooftops. The streets of the refugee camp were filmed in the Jenin camp in the West Bank, while the interior scenes were filmed in a house in Nazareth, in Israel proper—far from the camp-dwellers' real home, far from the expanses of the town, which not only the protagonists of the film, but its actors as well, could not reach.[165]

In Masharawi's second feature, *Haifa / Haïfa / 'Haifa* (1996), the central figure (played with splendid exuberance by Mohamed Bakri) is a variation on the traditional Arab figure of the wise fool. Haifa, so called because he marches through the streets, dressed in uniform but with a wooden gun, chanting "Haifa, Jaffa, Acre," is a man full of memories, stories, songs, and aspirations. As such, he is an accepted member of the community, constantly invited to sit and eat with the families he visits. At the start, life is as ordinary as it can be in an enclosed refugee camp, from which wide expanses of open land, which once used to be Palestinian but are now totally out of reach, can be viewed. Haifa patrols the streets; adolescents meet up secretly; mothers try to find brides for their sons. Abu Said, having lost his job as a policeman, makes a living selling pink cotton candy to schoolchildren, while his neighbor Abbas awaits the birth of a child (to be called Arafat if it's a boy and Palestine if it's a girl).

The basic subordination of women in this society is unquestioned—wives do not make decisions and young girls do not choose their husbands (although a few are offered the possibility of further education). Haifa's aunt longs for the return of her three sons (mistaking/hoping that Haifa is one of them each time he visits), but she never mentions her daughter Latifa, who is also in exile. Thoughts of revolt are stifled. Although Abu Said's son Said is in an Israeli prison, there is little evidence offered here of Palestinian political organization and resistance. We do not learn the reasons for the strike decreed early on in the film, and the political demonstration, which brings the film to an end, involves dozens of people we have never seen before and comes totally out of the blue.

Masharawi's vision is extremely bleak. The characters in *Haifa* are ordinary people, with whom we can identify. At the beginning, there is a mood of muted optimism: perhaps the Washington talks on the Palestinian/Israeli question will be fruitful. Said is due for release in a few days, and his mother hopes to find him a wife, while Abu Said, still respected in the community, has dreams of getting his old job back. But the seventy-five-minute narrative of *Haifa* smashes all hopes. Obviously, the peace initiative comes to nothing. At the center of the film, Haifa's crazy dream of an extravagant wedding in Haifa comes crashing down when he learns that his childhood sweetheart, his cousin Latifa, is happily married in Beirut. Haifa's aunt dies, without seeing any of her three sons. Abu Said is offered official re-employment as a policeman, but the letter of appointment comes only after he has been paralyzed by a stroke. Said is released from prison but seems lost in the community to which he returns and shatters his mother's dream by rejecting the idea of marriage. The possible upsurge to be obtained from the political demonstration at the end, when the streets are finally teeming with young people, is undermined when it crosses the funeral procession for Haifa's aunt. The film ends with a close-up of the confused face of a man caught in the middle, Haifa, the madman whose dreams have come to be a symbol of Palestinian aspirations.

Masharawi's first feature film of the 2000s, *Ticket to Jerusalem / Un ticket pour Jérusalem / Tathkararaton ila al-Quds* (2002), shot during the Second Intifada, follows the narrative pattern of the earlier features. The protagonist, Jaber, makes a precarious living, operating a mobile film projection unit showing films to children in refugee camps. This involves constantly trying to maneuver his way through Israeli checkpoints. At home, he has problems with his parents, who disapprove of his operations, and with his wife, while his dream of organizing a film show in Jerusalem is deemed a crazy fantasy. *Ticket to Jerusalem* chronicles his seemingly endless series of problems: roadblocks, car breakdowns, electricity failure, a projector that fails to operate when transferred from one car to another in order to get around Israeli restrictions. In the end, as Gertz and Khleifi point out, he achieves a minor success, arranging a screening in a friend's yard recently taken over by Jewish settlers:

> This is indeed a very minor victory, however, since the invaders stay and remain in the yard, the roadblocks are in operation, and the violence in the streets continues. The significance of this victory diminishes even further then we realize that the film screened is, in fact, Masharawi's own previous film, *Haifa,* that ends in utter despair. And yet the final shot of *Ticket to Jerusalem* captures this Palestinian crowd filling the yard, while the protagonist is seen hugging his wife.[166]

The director has pointed out how close this film is to his personal experience:

> The film refers to what I know—in the CPC, we do run the mobile cinema, we have difficulties to get out, the Israeli tanks are next to our office. I have difficulties to travel anywhere outside of Ramallah. . . . It is evident I am speaking about the Palestinian refugees, and the settlements, Jerusalem and the Israeli occupation while making this film now, and in a very complicated situation I try to connect those things in what appears as a simple story.[167]

For anyone familiar with Masharawi's other films, seeing the opening scenes of *Waiting / Attente / Intizar* (2006) can only arouse anxiety for the characters and a grim sense of the inevitable ending. Entering Gaza after a two-hour delay at the airport (for carrying a rock in his luggage), the protagonist Ahmad is persuaded by his friend, the theatre director Abu Jamil, to shoot casting sessions with Palestinian actors exiled in Jordan, Syria, and Lebanon. The European Union has funded an ambitious project to build a Palestinian National Theatre in Gaza, a building with two thousand seats and parking for five hundred cars. Fifty actors are needed in two months' time for the opening performance, which Abu Jamil insists will happen, although the project has already been subject to eight years of delays. Ahmad is a reluctant participant—his career has been blocked for years because he wants the chance to make a comedy or a satire rather than yet another documentary about the occupation (the kind of project he is always offered). To accompany Ahmad, Abu Jamil selects his niece Bassan, a well-known Palestinian television journalist, and she brings along her cameraman Mounir, known to his friends as Lumière. Inevitably, despite their EU paperwork and official government invitations, the trio suffer delays at every border crossing.

Waiting becomes routine for them, as it does for the would-be actors, who line up and wait patiently waiting for the auditions which have been organized for them.

Presumably owing to his personal frustrations, Ahmad has chosen the subject of "waiting" for the performers' individual improvisations. Much of the film comprises a series of cameos of would-be actors struggling desperately with the topic. One young man does a very convincing rendition of his experience at airports, waiting to be strip-searched; and a singer and a dancer give spirited, if hardly relevant, renditions. But most are perplexed by the topic, which is too much a part of daily routine life in a refugee camp to inspire acting. In any case, most of those who attend are not really actors at all. They have assumed that the team are shooting material for Palestinian television and want desperately to send messages to close relatives there or to join the return journey as a way of getting into Palestine. Perhaps the most illuminating presentations to camera are those of Bassan, who participates in the preliminary sound tests for Lumière. She presents, with apparent sincerity, the cliché'd opening half-sentences of the constantly repeated television news items: "The US president proposed today . . ."; "The EU has presented its support . . ."; "The UN is prepared to take serious action if . . ."; "The Israeli PM has proposed conditions . . ."; "The Pope is praying for continued peace . . ."; and so on.

The reactions of the members of the team vary widely. Bassan had been dreaming of the possibility of visiting Lebanon to meet up with her father, whom she has not seen for ten years. She is shattered to learn that he has remarried but plucks up the courage to make her planned visit. She learns that her father has been away in Syria for seven months (his new wife is yet another character in the film who is forced to wait). Preserving her anonymity by presenting herself as just a "family member," Bassan is able to meet up with her stepmother and play for a while with her little half brother. Lumière, for whom this is his first trip outside Palestine, has a brief one-night affair with Anouar, their guide and helper in Syria. He emerges convinced that they will somehow meet up again (although Israeli visa restrictions make this highly unlikely). The major weakness of the film is the conception of the character of Ahmad. Excellently played by the Jordanian-based filmmaker Mahmoud al-Massad (whose own films are discussed in the section on documentaries), Ahmad is understandably frustrated by the way his career has unfolded and by the routine nature of his task here. But he is hard to sympathize with, as (with the exception of just one conversation with Bassan) he is consistently rude and unsympathetic to those he would be expected to try to fill with enthusiasm. He offers no help or guidance to those who audition and is seemingly uninvolved with the Palestinians and their demonstrations. Never is there the slightest indication that he is capable of directing a film comedy.

Abu Jamil has kept in constant touch with Bassan throughout. His final call confirms what they have just learned from television: that the theatre has been destroyed by Israeli bombing, rendering all their efforts meaningless. The political situation also leaves them stranded, unable to return home. The problems faced by the characters at the end of the film are precisely those with which Masharawi himself is personally familiar. When he tried attend the US premiere of *Waiting* at the Chicago Palestine Film Festival in 2006, the Israeli authorities prevented him: "Masharawi was due to be present in person but could not apply for a US visa without getting a new Palestinian Authority passport from Gaza. He could not go to Gaza because he could not guarantee that he would be allowed to leave when he wanted to."[168]

Laila's Birthday / L'anniversaire de Laila / Eid milad Laila (2008) was produced by Masharawi's own company and largely funded by a combination of Maghrebian and Dutch sources. It follows the same basic narrative pattern as the earlier films—the simple chronological account of the daily upsets in the life of a single character, Abu Laila, again played by Mohamed Bakri but this time with complete reticence and control. The day begins badly, when he is woken by shattering glass, and gets worse as he faces his regular humiliation at the Ministry of Justice (where officials and office curtains are changed with equal regularity). Though currently working as a taxi driver for his brother-in-law, Abu Laila has a second identity as Judge Jalal Yakoub, who has worked as such for ten years in a neighboring Arab country and was personally invited back to Ramallah by Yasser Arafat. But the new official in charge, more concerned about his curtains than his legal duties, behaves just like his predecessors, openly mocking Abu Laila for his supposed pretensions, refusing to examine his documents, and telling him to "come back tomorrow."

Abu Laila's journey around Ramallah (which inevitably involves a brief sight of the city's celebrated balletic traffic policeman) offers a vivid insight into the dysfunctional nature of Palestinian life. Not only is the Ministry of Justice personally disrespectful to Abu Laila; the very notion of any sort of operating system of justice in Ramallah is ridiculed by many of those he meets. Rules and regulations—not smoking in a taxi, wearing a seat belt, not carrying a rifle in public—are contemptuously disregarded. A policeman stops him, not for a traffic offense but in order to try to buy the taxi, so that he can moonlight at night. The common destinations for passengers are checkpoints (which Abu Laila refuses to drive to), hospitals, and cemeteries. The sight of a waiting line means that passengers disembark to join it, even if they do not know what people are waiting in line for. At one point, a man deliberately steps out in front of Abu Laila's car and then rebukes him for not running him over and killing him.

Everywhere there are obstacles. When he finds a cell phone in the back of the cab and takes it to the police, it is Abu Laila who is treated as the criminal.

He is unable to complete the purchases of a present and a cake for his daughter, whose birthday this is. When his taxi breaks down and he drinks coffee while it is being repaired, he is bombed by an Israeli helicopter and his taxi used to take a dying man to hospital. While he is shopping, his taxi is assumed to be part of a wedding procession and is garishly decorated. Finally, he breaks down, exploding with rage, taking over a police control vehicle, and, through the loudspeaker, haranguing the Israeli helicopter pilot still overhead and his fellow bystanders. But though the pattern of Abu Laila's day matches the experience of other characters in Masharawi's films, the tone of the film is lightly tragicomic, and Bakri embodies a hero with whom we can genuinely sympathize. *Laila's Birthday* even manages a happy ending, with Abu Laila able to improvise a little birthday celebration for his daughter, with the leftovers of the day: a cake left behind in his car, a candle bought for his garage-owner friend, some of the wedding decorations from his car, and a one-shekel necklace bought from a boy on the street. Out of a tale of misfortune, Masharawi is able to conjure a touching portrayal of the value of the little, personal things in life, which even a hostile environment cannot diminish.

In *Palestine Stereo / Falastine Stereo* (2013), we discover the two protagonists, who are brothers, living in an improvised tent, set up in a neighbor's garden in Jenin. Both are victims—"collateral damage"—of Israel's war on supposed terrorists. The Israeli barrage was aimed at the third floor of the apartment block, and their misfortune was that this implied demolishing the fifth floor as well. The elder brother, nicknamed Stereo, lost his wife in the raid, while Sami, who was there to make electrical repairs, was rendered deaf and mute by the blast.

At the outset of the film, both men are in a state of shock, Stereo unable to continue his career as a wedding singer and Sami feeling that his impairments make the continuation of his relationship with his fiancée Leila impossible (although she is and remains deeply in love with him). They move to Ramallah, where their sister has room for them—a flat she and her husband had set up for their son, who has been in Israeli custody for seven years, with no sign of imminent release.

In Ramallah, Stereo pursues his crazy dream—immigration to Canada, a country about which he knows nothing. Their brother-in-law, who is a lawyer, helps with the Palestinian passports (which, ironically, are obtained only in the hope of promptly exchanging them) and the interview with a Canadian embassy official goes surprisingly well. But in between they have to raise $10,000, which involves Stereo using his sound engineering skills at weddings, funerals, and political rallies. The comic potential of a sound engineer working with a deaf-mute assistant is exploited to the full, and the posturings of pompous Palestinian politicians are treated as farcically as they deserve. But there are also deeply touching moments, as when Stereo, bereft of his equipment, has to improvise a version of the Palestinian national anthem, and involve the crowd, with nothing more than a spoon and a drinking glass to back up his voice.

There is a serious undertone throughout the film as well. All the Palestinian demonstrations, however harmless, are ruthlessly gunned down by trigger-happy Israeli conscripts. When Stereo checks through the list of events he has served to make the $10,000, it is a seemingly endless litany of commemorations of Israeli atrocities. There is constant debate too about the rights and wrongs of emigration. At the end of the film, the brothers have everything in place, but the last image of the film is not of them setting off for the unknown. It is a pan across their apartment, where Leila has scrawled her opinion on their walls: that emigrating means just giving up, accepting defeat.

The Palestinian feature filmmaker who began in the 1990s and has achieved the greatest international acclaim is a filmmaker without formal film training, **Elia Suleiman**. Born in 1960 in Nazareth and raised under the Zionist occupation, he spent many years abroad yet still managed to complete his first feature before 2000. He went into exile at the age of seventeen (after both he and his father had been separately arrested by the Israelis), spending a year in London and Paris. After a brief return to Nazareth, he left for the United States in 1981 and lived there for the next twelve years. On his return to Palestine in 1993 he taught at Bir Zeit University, near Ramallah, where he set up a new film and media course funded by the European Commission. He has subsequently been professor of film at the European Graduate School in Switzerland.

From the start of his career, Suleiman has wanted to correct the widespread misrepresentation of Palestinians in Western media and, at the same time, create an alternative to conventional filmic narrative structures. Lacking formal film training, he began reading avidly the writings and interviews of leading European directors of the 1980s: "I started to read Godard for example and suddenly felt that I was not a lone voice, that I belonged to a sect of people who were rebellious against narrative structure as such. . . . I started to read all the interviews I could get hold of and I started to see that there was another way of telling."[169] But there is a huge distance between the work of the directors he cites—Godard, Bresson, Antonioni—and his own filmmaking style. For one thing, as he told an interviewer, while his own work is essentially comic, "the people I was inspired by are not known for their humour."[170] It was not until 1994, when shooting his first feature, that he discovered the work of the European filmmaker who might have served as the model for his particular brand of comic cinema, Jacques Tati.

In 1990, while still in the United States, Suleiman co-directed his first forty-five-minute video, *Introduction to the End of an Argument / Introduction à la fin de l'histoire / Uqaddimah li-nihayat-jidal* (1990) with the Canadian-Lebanese experimental video artist Jayce Salloum. Aptly described by Hamid Dabashi as a "gem of docu-satirical pastiche" and as a "Tourette's syndrome of visual and

sound clips,"[171] this is a film which defies all notions of formal narrative structure: it opens with three successive titles indicating the beginning of part 1 and
concludes long after the end title. It juxtaposes tiny clips from all kinds of material: Hollywood films (*Exodus, Lawrence of Arabia, Black Sunday,* and *The Little Drummer Girl*), along with Gillo Pontecorvo's *The Battle of Algiers* and old
French colonial features, extracts from television material (newsreader presentations and political interviews), as well as documentaries, ads, and cartoons.
None of the sources is named, and none of the material is identified by place or
time. Sometimes the connections are satirical, at other times merely whimsical.
The pace is hectic, and even the best archival material (such as the clip from an
old documentary on early Jewish settlement, which solemnly proclaims, "They
found a hostile land filled with swamps, snakes and Arabs") flashes by in a moment. The whole mad mixture underlines the caricature and distortion of Arab
life which fills all aspects of Western media, and this meaning is made unambiguously explicit in the film's final statement: "Can't You Leave the Poor Fucking
Arabs Alone?"

Suleiman also contributed one episode, *Homage by Assassination / Hommage par assassinat / Takrim bi al-qalt,* to the collective film *After the Gulf? /
La guerre du Golfe . . . et après? / Harbu al-khalij wa ba'du?* (1992), in which the
Tunisian producer Ahmed Attia brought together episodes by five Arab filmmakers (the other four were Borhan Alawiya, Nouri Bouzid, Mustafa Derkaoui,
and Néjia Ben Mabrouk). This is very much a transitional work. It follows the pattern of *Introduction to the End of an Argument* by including a succession of tiny
(at times almost subliminal) fragments of feature films, ranging (according to
the credits) from works by John Ford and Nicholas Ray, Antonioni, Godard and
Sergio Leone, to clips from works as diverse as a Maï Masri documentary, Monty
Python's *Life of Brian,* and an amateur film about toy monsters. At various points
we also see on-screen a dozen or so Arab proverbs, which have little immediate
connection with the ostensible purpose of the film, namely, to offer reflections on
the US response to the Iraqi invasion of Kuwait and Iraq's use of Scud missiles
against Israeli targets.

What is new and would set the pattern for Suleiman's subsequent features
is the appearance of ES, the filmmaker himself. He adopts what will be his customary role of observer, watching a couple in the street outside his apartment
but from behind half-closed blinds, so there can be no chance of his gaze being
returned. In his apartment, he is surrounded by every conceivable modern communications device, but he remains totally silent in the face of an international
crisis he can in no way influence. The radio commentator who phones him for an
interview cannot get through (so he doesn't need to answer), and his only outgoing call gets no response. When the phone rings, he does not converse with his
friend Samir, but listens on the answering machine to Samir's joke about God

and his angels debating whether Palestinians should go to heaven or hell, with God—caught in the middle—finally deciding: "Build them a camp."

Most of the film consists of static images of ES alone in his apartment, sitting at his computer, going to the toilet, playing with a remote-controlled toy car, and (almost) making coffee. He never speaks, but we see on-screen what he types (he is ostensibly writing the script of a film called *Homage by Assassination*). He photocopies a bunch of roses to send to his Iraqi-born Jewish friend, and the response (read by Ella Shohat) comes through by fax. At the end, his apartment is transformed into a virtual video post-production studio, but we hear only white noise. The last images are of a Hollywood Jesus proclaiming "He among you that is without sin, let him cast the first stone," followed by an image of stone-throwing children participating in the Intifada.

Suleiman followed these first works with three other, lesser-known short films: the documentary *War and Peace in Vesoul / La guerre et la paix à Vesoul* (made with Israeli filmmaker Amos Gitai; 1997); *The Arab Dream / Le rêve arabe / Al-hilm al-'arabi* (1998), an account of another return by Suleiman to Palestine; and *Cyber-Palestine* (2000), a modern-day version of the story of Joseph and Mary, described by Dabashi as "an experimental film with a sardonic sense of humour."[172]

Suleiman began his feature film career with *Chronicle of a Disappearance / Chronique d'une disparition / Sijil 'ikhtifa'* (1996).[173] The tone is set by the opening image, a long-held static shot, beginning in near darkness from which the face of his sleeping father gradually emerges into view. The film is ostensibly an account of Suleiman's return to his birthplace but contains none of the usual features of such a film (effusive welcomes and eager questioning, the exchange of stories about the past, the examination of old photographs, etc.). Everything in the film is laid-back and distanced. In fact, Suleiman (ES) never speaks or communicates directly with his parents. The return of ES involves not an account of his attempt to reintegrate with Palestinian life but the chronicle of the absence, the disappearance, of any Palestinian life into which he could possibly integrate. There is seldom any direct connection between image and sound, between what we see on-screen and what the radio (playing constantly) communicates through its news programs or music. The reporting and the music do not enhance in any way the scenes viewed, instead counterpointing them with echoes of another world.

The film consists of two parts, the first of which is titled "Nazareth—Personal Diary." Here the humor arises from Suleiman's ironic viewpoint on everyday life, its triviality (peeling garlic, cleaning fish) and its repetitions (particularly sleeping). We see recurrent but formally organized, static, and fragmentary images of the Suleiman family home, the local café, the garage, and the souvenir shop ("The Holyland," run by ES's cousin). Particularly significant of the basically fraught atmosphere are two scenes outside the local café, when two characters arrive in a car (first two friends, then a father and son) and have to be physically separated when they start to fight violently. The direct-to-camera comments, all filmed by a fixed camera, are particularly revealing. ES's aunt reveals the dysfunctionality of Palestinian family life, while a priest reveals the impact of Israeli settlement around the Sea of Galilee, where Jesus is reputed to have walked on the water: the lake is now so polluted with the excrement of tourists, he claims, that anyone could walk across it. Never is there a sense of any possibility of freedom, movement, or progression. The father's pets, to which he talks lovingly—his songbird and his dog—are both shown penned up. The writer Taha Mohamed Ali's account of the beauties of Istanbul as told by his grandfather comprises a lifetime of repetitions of the same banal moment. The series of little incidents and statements presented does not constitute a developing narrative—they are separated off, one from the other, by the same recurring title: "The Day After." This is a suffocating, dislocated, and dysfunctional world, and it is fitting that part 1 ends with a replay of the scenes we have seen, now reduced to single, static, frozen images, as ES projects his slides recording the sequence of scenes that we have just seen.

Part 2, "Jerusalem—Political Diary," follows many of the same formal patterns, including the fragmentation of the narrative into disconnected scenes and the continual depiction of ES as a detached observer (here, of repetitive aerobic displays outside his window). But this second part of the film has a very different tone. Part 1 is infused with melancholy and loss, although it contains no overt indication of the actual cause of this: the Israeli occupation of Palestinian territories. Part 2 deals directly with the Israeli presence, but treats this as a pretext for farce and frivolity.

There is a new openness from the very start of part 2, with the journey to Jerusalem (blocked only by a camel) accompanied by an Arab song asking "Why Do We Fight, We Were Once Friends." A stop at the American Colony Hotel records a foreign perspective: a conversation in French about the incomprehensible mess of Palestinian-Israeli relations. ES's friend Adnan (played by director-to-be Ula Tabari) makes no progress in getting a new apartment. The estate agent tells her to get married, and telephone enquiries bring her compliments on the quality of her Hebrew but no offers whatever, even to view, when she reveals she is an Arab. ES's own apartment in Jerusalem, large and empty, is filmed in the same style as his parents' apartment in Nazareth, whereas Adnan's apartment is a more complex and open space, complete with walls covered by a kaleidoscope of juxtaposed images and a tailor's dummy dressed in traditional costume. Nothing is what it seems here: the gun and grenade on her desk are just cigarette lighters, and what seem to be bomb-building terrorists are just making fireworks. In what is perhaps a comment on Arab cultural life, ES is invited to make a presentation of his new film about peace, his narrative technique, and cinematographic language (fascinating topics!), but the microphone doesn't work, his voice can't be heard, and his audience is soon distracted.

The key focus of this second part of the film is on the Israeli forces. They make their choreographed entrance piling out of a van, lining up to pee against a (no doubt Palestinian) wall, returning to the van in line, and reporting back to base "Mission accomplished." They inadvertently leave behind a two-way radio, which for ES becomes the soundtrack for whatever he experiences except for a raid on his apartment, when the police (accompanied by a tango-style musical track) search everywhere while treating him as merely part of the furniture (he is an Arab, after all). A later raid on Adnan's apartment is equally revealing, as the police are happy to carry off her tailor's dummy rather than hold on to her. There is humor here in the language used by the police on their radio ("Sorrel to Crow," etc.), but for the passive ES the sound is merely an Israeli intrusion into his life. Adnan's response to the two-way radio, however, is very different. In a wonderful moment of wit and fantasy, she uses her impeccable Hebrew to give orders to the police cars, rushing them around the city and then ordering them to leave Jerusalem: "Withdraw immediately from Jerusalem. Jerusalem is no longer united. Jerusalem is nothing special." She then changes her tone and sings to them, "for a change," the Israeli national anthem.

A second car journey, accompanied by the song "Let's Return to Peace," is the bridge for a final return to a more relaxed and peaceful Nazareth, where we again see the familiar settings of home and neighborhood. This time, two passengers changing seats outside the café do *not* fight, a little boy amuses himself disturbing passers-by with his wolf whistles, and ES's father wins an arm-wrestling contest in the café. The film may end with the Israeli flag and national anthem on their television, but ES's parents are both sound asleep. Suleiman dedicates his film to them both—"The Last Homeland." *Chronicle of a Disappearance,* which won the prize for first feature film at the Venice Film Festival in 1996, is a remarkable achievement. Totally assured in its presentation and structure, it finds, through its use of humor and fantasy, a totally new tone in which to treat the grim realities of the Israeli occupation of Palestinian land.

Elia Suleiman's second feature-length film, *Divine Intervention / Intervention divine / Yadun 'Ilahiyya* (2002), confirms his place as the most idiosyncratic of Palestinian filmmakers. Subtitled "A Chronicle of Love and Pain," it is both highly personal and totally stylized, with the actions of Israeli soldiers, when they eventually appear, choreographed into balletic movements. Once again, the film has no clear linear narrative but is structured as a succession of often absurd, fantastic, or extravagant incidents. There are only fragmentary titles to indicate key relations and themes: "Nazareth," "Al-Ram Check Point," "Jerusalem," "Father Dies," "I'm Mad Because I Love You." Nothing is spelled out clearly—it is not immediately apparent, for example, that ES's father has lost his business and is falling ill.

The film opens in remarkably enigmatic form with a figure dressed as Santa Claus running uphill, pursued by a seemingly hostile band of adolescents and spilling his sack of presents as he goes. When he reaches the top, he turns to reveal that he has been stabbed with a kitchen knife. According to Ella Shohat, the part is played by George Ibrahim, known for his children's programs on state television, but the actor is not listed in the film's pressbook and the precise implications are obscure. This is our introduction to Nazareth, subsequently presented as a ghetto, where "the humour comes from dealing with a population living in a claustrophobic state of stasis, an impotent inability to change the face of their reality. Unable to dislocate or shift the dominant power ruling, they eventually release their frustrations against each other."[174] These frustrations are immediately apparent in the actions of his father (played by Nayef Fahoum Daher), who, as he drives past, waves affectionately to his smiling neighbors while simultaneously mouthing obscenities at them.

This is a world of ordinary actions reduced to repetitive rituals which turn neighbor against neighbor and may end in aggression or be turned into elaborate gags. In Nazareth, there is no overt sign of the Israeli occupation, but its influence is ever present as the little scenes accumulate: one man waits for a bus that he knows will not come; another collects hundreds of bottles on a roof to throw at the police when they come to speak to him; a ramp into a garage is meticulously built and then immediately destroyed; a car is left to block a garage for no reason; garbage is thrown repeatedly into a neighbor's garden, provoking anger and disbelief when it is promptly thrown back again. Acts of violence occur, half-concealed, in long shot or almost out of sight. These incoherent, fundamentally absurd actions are filmed virtually silent and with a camera that seldom moves. They are watched over by a figure as detached and totally impassive as ES himself, namely, his father, until he suddenly and quite unexpectedly collapses. The subsequent scenes depicting him in the hospital, cut into the later action, offer a new series of seemingly random, absurd actions. On one occasion, driving to the hospital, ES outstares an Israeli settler who has drawn up alongside his car at the traffic light, blaring out a song on the radio by Natacha Atlas, which begins "I put a spell on you, because you're mine" (the singer also provides the title song for Nabil Ayouch's *Whatever Lola Wants*).

The potential violence contained in all the scenes of everyday Palestinian life subsequently finds expression in a series of wonderful gags and fantasies. The tone shifts abruptly from repetitive ritual to utter fantasy with the first appearance of ES himself. Shown driving along without expression and eating a date, he tosses the pit out of the window of the car, causing a tremendous explosion which engulfs an Israeli tank. He drives on as if this were a totally expected event. The explosion had to be shot in France, and in his pressbook interview Suleiman seems quietly pleased that it took place while Ariel Sharon was on a visit to Paris.

The entry into the action of his beautiful, unnamed girlfriend (played by Manal Khader) is equally spectacular. She walks elegantly and totally fearlessly through an Israeli checkpoint, defying the armed guards. Her passing causes the whole checkpoint tower to crumble behind her.

ES lives in Jerusalem, which is introduced to us through shots (which are later repeated with variations) of random violence against a collaborator (played by George Khleifi) and of an Israeli policeman having to haul a manacled prisoner out of the back of his van to give directions to a tourist who has lost her way. Life for ES is very frustrating. Under Israeli rule, since he lives in Jerusalem while his girlfriend is a resident of Ramallah, neither can visit the other. They can only meet in the car park of the Al-Ram Israeli checkpoint. There their passion is expressed through their clasped and caressing hands, as they sit, otherwise motionless, side by side. We return to the checkpoint several times and witness the tedium of the place, broken only by the arrogant and often brutal behavior of the Israeli guards. Suleiman used Israelis who had served in the military to play the border guards and admits to enjoying himself during his casting sessions: "Some of them shied away from telling me the severe acts they had committed because they wanted the role, whilst others exaggerated because they too wanted to act in the film. I became a little sadistic in my questioning of their moral standards."[175] He also amused himself on set by turning some of their actions into synchronized balletic movements.

It is at the checkpoint that ES has his best fantasy, inflating and releasing a red balloon adorned with the face of Yasser Arafat. Much to the consternation of the guards, it flies through and over the checkpoint. They want to shoot it down, but by the time they get their orders, the balloon is sailing triumphantly over Jerusalem, finally brushing against the Al-Aqsa mosque. His girlfriend fails to turn up for their last two planned meetings but reappears in the film's long penultimate fantasy sequence. Here, at a training session for five Israeli snipers being drilled in shooting images of Arab women, she appears as a Palestinian ninja figure. In a supernatural ballet, she emerges from the smoke to confront them, impervious to their bullets and able to fly with extreme grace. Taking on Christ-like poses, she eliminates them and the helicopter that comes to their rescue, using stones, a sword, and the emblems of Palestinian national identity.

The final sequence shows the filmmaker standing outside his parents' house, listening to yet another tale of local violence, then sitting side by side with his mother in the kitchen, where his father always sat. They are watching a boiling pressure cooker, which seems about to explode; the film ends when she says gently, "That's enough."

The best introduction to Suleiman's third feature, *The Time That Remains / Le temps qu'il reste / Al-zaman al-baqi* (2009), is that given by the director at the various festival screenings the film received in 2009:

> *The Time That Remains* is a semi-biographical film, in four historic episodes, about a family—my family—spanning from 1948 until recent times. The film is inspired by my father's diaries of his personal accounts, starting from when he was a resistance fighter in 1948, and by my mother's letters to family members forced to leave the country since then. Combined with my intimate memories of them, the film attempts to portray the daily life of those Palestinians who remained in their land and were labeled "Israeli-Arabs," living as a minority in their own homeland.[176]

The film, subtitled "Chronicle of an Absent-Present," opens with ES's arrival in Israel, but we hardly see him in the darkened rear of his taxi from the airport. The focus instead is on his Israeli taxi driver, for whom the long journey to Nazareth is, literally, a voyage into the void: the rain pours down, his car radio ceases to work, and soon he is utterly lost.

The first major episode of the film is set on July 16, 1948, the day Nazareth surrendered to the invading Hagana forces. Suleiman has said that he wanted to talk about the realities of this moment: "A lot of people don't want to talk about 1948. But some are willing to take the pain of what happened—not just accept some kind of dream sequence of the creation of the Israeli state, which is a nonsensical story."[177] He brings to this most troubling moment in Palestinian history both his characteristic sardonic wit and a new directness. He does not shy away from showing the reality behind the Israeli propaganda that "the hour of liberation has sounded." He shows the brutality of the Israeli invasion; episodes of their shooting, killing, and violence are all depicted unsparingly, although their looting is, in typical Suleiman fashion, mocked by being carried out (almost choreographed) to the sound of a chirpy Arab song, played on a pillaged Palestinian gramophone.

Suleiman is equally unsparing in his view of the negligible Arab resistance, shown, as usual in his work, in a series of satirical vignettes. His ability to move from farce to tragedy in this, his most comprehensive statement about the Nakba, is masterly. Far from putting up a fight, the first Palestinians we see are lounging about, drinking coffee in the local square. The external Arab assistance to the Palestinians is reduced to a single Iraqi soldier, unable even to find the village he has been sent to liberate. The purported Palestinian resistance fighters put up no fight and are shown throwing away their weapons and shedding their *kaffiyehs,* in an attempt to blend back into the populace. The only Palestinian willing to display resistance to the Israelis openly is a poet, who presents himself proudly only to kill himself in a futile gesture. The car journey of Nazareth's mayor, who has been summoned by the Israelis, is shown in farcical terms, but his personal humiliation, as he is made to sign the unconditional surrender of Nazareth and pose for the photograph which will "immortalize this great historical moment," is all too real. So too is the resistance of Suleiman's future father Fuad, at the time a gunmaker for those hoping to defend Palestine. Even he does not get the chance to fire a single bullet, being denounced by his cousin, beaten viciously, and thrown down a cliff. With typical Suleiman counterpoint, his torture takes place not in a cell but in open woodland, overlooking the beautiful hills surrounding Nazareth.

The second episode, set a dozen years later in 1970, the year of Nasser's death, shows Suleiman's childhood—seemingly an ideal subject for the director's style of irony, since he was educated in a largely Jewish mixed school. This is introduced to us at the moment when the girls' choir wins an award for its performance of Hebrew choral works. The official giving the award talks loftily about this mixed Jewish-Arab school being proof of Israeli aims to bring ideas of democracy and equality to Palestinian children. As usual, there is no single dramatic line; instead, Suleiman picks out tiny episodes (such as those depicting the Suleiman family's drunken and suicidal neighbor) whose repetition (usually with small variations) points to the ways in which life for "Israeli-Arabs" is frustrated and distorted. Somewhat surprisingly, the young ES himself is shown at school only when he is being rebuked by his headmaster, first for calling Americans "colonialists" and then for referring to them in class as "imperialists."

The third episode, set ten years later in 1980, deals with serious issues: the health of ES's parents continues to decline, and he himself is given twenty-four hours to leave the country, accused of insulting the Israeli flag. There are sporadic demonstrations, in which the Israelis shoot at unarmed Palestinians. But in characteristic Suleiman fashion, the key vignette is a farcical one. The adolescent ES and his two friends watch the misfortunes of a neighbor, Abou-Adel, who has become obsessed with the idea of screwing one of the female Israeli guards who continually stop his car. As a result, he arranges for his wife to dress up in uniform and stop him as he drives by. But on the night in question, she stops the wrong car and is abducted, leaving Abou-Adel angry, frustrated, and uncomprehending.

The final episode is set in the present, first in Nazareth and then in Ramallah. Suleiman appears in his customary role as ES, the observer of the life around him, who does not say a word, even to his mother, who is now seriously ill and taken to the hospital in Ramallah. Again these personal troubles are set against moments of comic observation, beginning with the traffic cop in Ramallah who directs the traffic with balletic excess. There is a new sense of defiance from ordinary people now. When a Palestinian woman wheeling a baby carriage through a checkpoint is told to go back home, she turns on the Israeli soldiers and tells them, "You go home." A man putting out his trash is confronted on the road by a huge Israeli tank, the gun barrel of which follows his every movement. He ignores it completely, moving to and fro as he answers his cell phone, quite oblivious to the potential danger. The barrel ends up aiming directly at the camera (and the observing ES). Young people dancing in a nightclub, The Stones, ignore repeated orders to observe the curfew from an Israeli soldier, who finds himself caught up in the dance rhythm. Confronted with the Israeli Wall, ES improbably pole-vaults it.

Elia Suleiman brings a very personal and controversial approach to the problems of Palestinian life and has found himself attacked by both Jewish and Arab critics. Rather than constructing conventional narratives, he juxtaposes small episodes that he has observed or imagined. There is no patriotic rhetoric here. Suleiman has a unique ability to shift mood and, through his intercutting of events, to disorient (and illuminate) his viewers. He deals not just with the paradoxes of life under occupation but also its absurdities. Throughout his three feature films, he effortlessly mixes tragedy and humor. His own description of his films is inevitably ironic: "Just an expression of who I am—a little distant, a little alienated, very sad. At the same time, very humorous. Very Jewish really."[178]

* * *

Two younger male directors, both born in Israel and possessing Israeli passports but with a range of foreign connections, have also achieved an international reputation with their work, thanks to their highly individual voices: Hany Abu Assad and Tawfik Abu Wael.

Hany Abu Assad, by far the oldest of the two newcomers, was born in 1961 in Nazareth. He began his involvement with cinema in the Netherlands, like Rashid Masharawi, whose assistant and subsequently producer he became. After a single short, *A Paper House / Une maison en papier / Bayt min waraq* (1992), he made a "false start" to his career by directing a Dutch-language comedy romance, *The Fourteenth Chick / Het veertiende*.[179] He subsequently shot two documentaries in Palestine in the early 2000s: *Nazareth 2000 / Nasseriya 2000* (2001) and *Ford Transit* (2002). The latter caused controversy when it emerged that it contained staged scenes, and Abu Assad subsequently turned, with great success, to feature filmmaking.

Nazareth 2000 is an informal and lighthearted piece accompanied by a catchy little tune, chronicling Abu Assad's return to his place of birth, where he is on first-name terms with just about everyone we meet. It opens with a little girl reading a poem about Nazareth (by Tawfik Zayyad), which, she shyly admits, she does not understand. Toward the end of the film she returns to tell us that what Nazareth needs is an earthquake "like they had in Turkey" to make people get along better with each other. She first claims that this is her idea, before admitting with a smile that it is "what Hany thinks." The film is set largely at a gas station, just around the corner from where Abu Assad grew up and where "his dad sold cement." The main recurring figures are the two gasoline pump attendants, Abu-Arab and Abu-Maria, who serve the customers, chat, drink tea, and bicker.

We also meet members of Abu Assad's family, a local historian, the mayor, and a local doctor. We see the Church of the Annunciation from a distance, but the camera does not even attempt to enter it. This is a very laid-back film in which nothing—neither tensions between Christians and Muslims over the building of a mosque on Christian land nor even a helicopter visit to Nazareth by the pope—is allowed to generate tension or excitement. The dramatic highpoint is Abu-Arab's decision to leave the garage in order to work behind the counter in a nearby food shop. The millennium celebrations, of course, pass without incident.

Ford Transit is a longer and more substantial work. Gertz and Khleifi reveal that controversy was caused when Abu Assad admitted that Rajai, the transit driver, was "actually an Arab news station cameraman who had acted in one of Abu Assad's previous films."[180] The director's explanation was that he "wanted the confusion to be part of the cinematic narrative. I wished the audience to think that it looked like a documentary film, but to feel uncertain about it. . . . I'm not the first to have blended the documentary genre with fiction."[181] Viewed in the light of this revelation, there are plenty of hints that this is a highly structured work. It introduces us to the action with Ennio Morricone–style music—echoes of *The Magnificent Seven* are not the normal lead-in to a documentary. The interactions between the passengers are just too dramatic not to have been pre-organized, if not pre-scripted. Some of the driver's observations, such as "Palestinians are like ants: they find their way around any roadblock," must have been thought out in advance, and there is no possibility whatever that the series of interviewees—politicians Azmi Bishara and Hanan Ashrawi, filmmakers BZ Goldberg and Suha Arraf, together with a sociologist, a psychologist, and an archimandrite—"just happened to join" this particular transit bus. In any case, their discussion is clearly with the director, not with the driver. Though evidently contrived, *Ford Transit* remains a powerful docudrama with great contemporary relevance, not only documenting the constant harassment of ordinary Palestinians going about their everyday business but also debating the issues involved: why do the Israelis behave like this, and what is the best Palestinian response? This is clearly a very accomplished first step toward completely fictional filmmaking.

Abu Assad's first Arab fictional feature, *Rana's Wedding / Le mariage de Rana / Urs Rana* (2002), is about the difficulties for two Palestinians of getting married in a land under Israeli occupation (as the film's publicity says, "in Jerusalem, love has many roadblocks"). The seventeen-year-old Rana starts the day with a problem: either she has to accompany her father back to Cairo, where he now works, or she has to get married to one of the suitable young men on the list her father has given her. Rana decides instead to marry Khalil, the young man she loves, but she only has until four o'clock to accomplish this.

The film, co-scripted by the novelist and documentary filmmaker Liana Badr, cleverly balances the uncertainties of the young couple—in love, but rushed into a marriage they were not anticipating just yet—with the physical difficulties created by the occupation. In a single day, Rana has to find her way from Jerusalem to Ramallah and back to convince Khalil that they should indeed get married immediately; then she must traverse the city to find a registrar to marry them, persuade her father to give his permission, get her grandmother's blessing, and organize the wedding party. Throughout, Rana's movements are obstructed by the constant features of Palestinian life under Israeli rule: roadblocks and checkpoints, of course, but also the ubiquitous armed soldiers, a funeral, the demolition of a Palestinian dwelling, and a confrontation between troops and stone-throwing youths. But Abu Assad's emphasis is less on the oppressions suffered daily than on the ingenuity of the Palestinians in circumventing such hazards. The film ends with the wedding, which has to be celebrated in a bus parked on the open street, and a quotation from Mahmoud Darwish's poem *State of Siege:*

> Here on the slopes before sunset and at the gun-mouth of time
> Near orchards deprived of their shadows,
> We do what prisoners do, what the unemployed do,
> We nurture hope.

Abu Assad's second feature, *Paradise Now / Al-jinna alaam* (2005), deals with the experiences and motivations of two suicide bombers and has won numerous international awards. Drawing on his skills at depicting the details of everyday life and at mixing documentary and fiction, Abu Assad has made a compelling and involving work, particularly for Western audiences used to the demonization of Islamic terrorists. The director's emphasis throughout is less on the physical oppression by the military occupiers than on the psychological effects of occupation and imprisonment on those who endure it.

In a film concerned with murderous violence, the key moments are not those of physical action but the long-held silent close-ups of the protagonists' faces at moments of decision. From the start, the emphasis is on the empty futility of the lives of Saïd and his friend Khaled, which leaves them with no real future. The director's own viewpoint—that there is an alternative to violence—can come only from Sula, the pretty girl who is an outsider to Nablus and to whom Saïd is immediately drawn (as she is to him). There is no attempt in the film to glorify suicide bombing—the camera does not work when Saïd and Khaled record their suicide videos, and both would-be bombers draw back from their first attempt. Saïd was born in a refugee camp and experienced his father's execution as a collaborator when he was just ten. As he finally articulates the hopelessness of his situation, his decision to respond to the humiliation and violence he has undergone, by undertaking a suicide bombing, becomes all too understandable.

Abu Assad's third Arab feature, *Omar* (2013), was shot with full Israeli authorization in Naplouse, Nazareth, and Bisan (Beit She'an). It depicts an unnamed, fictional Palestinian town, cut in two by the Israeli Wall, which the protagonist, Omar, has to scale to meet up with his schoolgirl sweetheart, Nadia, and two friends he has known since his school days, Amjad and Nadia's brother Tarek.

The film deals with major themes—resistance and treachery, love and betrayal—but is firmly focused on the immediate, intimate responses of the central characters, all of whom, apart from the Israeli agent Rami, are played by young non-professionals. The American-born actor Waleed F. Zuaiter, who plays Rami and has a considerable background in US film and television, produced the film through the newly established company Zbros which he set up with his two brothers.

Omar is both involving and frustrating. It furnishes a vivid portrait of the difficulties and humiliations of life under a hostile occupation, where Israeli soldiers constantly appear to harass, pursue, and humiliate unarmed Palestinians. The Palestinian response is shown in all its futility. The trio of Tarek, Omar, and Amjad plot to attack the occupiers, but when they undertake their first mission, they have only one gun among them (and seemingly only one bullet). There are powerfully engaging depictions of Omar's two primary relationships, both of which are realized with complete conviction. The first is Omar's intensely felt but utterly restrained love affair with Nadia (they kiss only once in the course of the narrative). The second, more dramatically complex relationship is the intimacy which develops between Omar and his torturer, Agent Rami, who sets him free on the condition that he betray his friends, beginning with Tarek. Omar is widely regarded by his community as a traitor (how else could he have received so prompt a release?). But he manages not to compromise himself, handing over Tarek's body only after he has been killed in a brawl over Nadia.

The resolution of the complicity between Omar and Rami gives the film its dramatically surprising climax. But the complex, not to say convoluted, twists of the plot leading up to this undermine the film's coherence. There is, it eventually transpires, no need at all for Rami to engage Omar as a spy, since he has already suborned his close friend Amjad. Crucially, there is no explanation within the narrative as to why Omar immediately believes the lies he is told by Amjad about Nadia's infidelity—we have seen at close hand the love that brings the two of them together. The film's ending is a genuine coup de théâtre: Omar persuades Rami to provide him with a revolver, takes a lesson in how to use it, and then turns to shoot Rami dead. In doing so, he undoubtedly condemns himself to death at the hand of the Israelis, while Amjad, the actual traitor in both politics and love, is left to prosper.

Tawfik Abu Wael was born in 1976 in the Palestinian enclave of Um El Fahem in Israel. He studied film at Tel Aviv University, where he later worked for a while. He began his career with three short films in the early 2000s, the best known of which is *Diary of a Male Whore / Journal d'un prostitué mâle / Yaw'miyat a'hir*

(2001), which was inspired by Mohamed Choukri's novel *For Bread Alone* and caused some controversy. The film, which has a first-person voice-over narration, begins with the protagonist sleeping with a whore on his first day in Tel Aviv and then going out onto the streets himself, to get picked up by a man. Many of the scenes of the fourteen-minute film are shot at night, with darkly atmospheric imagery which will be a characteristic of the director's first feature. The bulk of the film traces the stages of his sexual initiation at the age of twelve to thirteen, on the eve of the Israeli invasion. The film opens with the confession that "chickens and goats were my first females," and we see him observing the sexual activities of the sheep on the farm where he grows up. He overhears his father's brutal beating of his mother; spies on Asya, the most beautiful girl in the village; and when the invasion occurs, witnesses his mother's rape. The film offers no moral comment on any of this behavior and ends in dimly lit obscurity and ambiguity.

Abu Wael went on to win the International Critics' Prize at Cannes with his debut feature, *Thirst / La soif / 'Atash* (2004), which is a highly personal film, set in the area where he was born (Um El Fahem). It is also a film full of unexpected omissions and complex ambiguities. There are no physical signs of the presence of any Israelis in the film, although they are always an unseen menace, and the reasons why the family live as they do are never entirely clear. Abu Wael's synopsis and interview in the pressbook prepared for Cannes are often more explicit than the film, which deliberately shrouds itself in mystery. Abu Shukri and his family have, it seems, lived cut off from the world, in an isolated, deserted village, for ten years, making their living from illegal charcoal burning. Abruptly Abu Shukri decides to build a pipeline to supply tap water to the house, which triggers the series of events which the film records. On one level, the film's title refers literally to this, but for Abu Wael it has other connotations: "*Thirst* is not only a title, but also the atmosphere that surrounds the film. I talk about thirst for water, for food, for freedom, for sex, for eroticism, for love, for desire. . . . Thirst for life."[182]

Thirst conforms to all the unities of classically defined drama. Although the past weighs heavily on the film (why are they here? how did they live before?), the action remains locked firmly in the present, with no flashbacks to past events. The nearest the film gets to exploring the past is Abu Shukri's discovery of his daughter Gamila's small collection of old photographs, which he burns in front of her as a punishment. The action never shifts from the deserted village, set amid isolated hills, where the family now lives. This setting has its own ambiguity, since it feels as if no one has ever lived there, and this is literally true, as the director explains: "It's a place where Tsahal (Israeli army) used to train for urban fighting, a fake Palestinian village. . . . The land where this camp was built belonged to the inhabitants of Um El Fahem until 1948, when it was definitively confiscated by the State of Israel."[183] The action too is focused entirely on the family: Abu Shukri, his wife, his son Shukri, and the daughters Gamila and Halima. The key relationships are between father and son, and between father and elder daughter. As Abu Wael puts it: "The conflict is between the characters, in their soul, in the complexity of their relationship, in their conscience."[184]

Abu Shukri is a tyrant in the traditional Arab mode: he listens to no one and imposes his authority on his family, with beatings if necessary. He keeps his daughters totally sequestered. He does not even allow the children access to the shed where he stores the furniture and trappings from their former life (there is a wonderful scene of release and real joy, when the family break in while he is absent). Initially he resists all his wife's pleas not to waste their money on the pipeline and goes ahead to build it anyway. But later, although he maintains a severe exterior, he seems to weaken, to the extent of buying new clothes for the feast of Aïd El Kebir when his wife begs him to do so (another touchingly performed scene).

There is no overt explanation for this new weakness in Abu Shukri, but the reason seems to lie in his troubled relationship with his elder daughter, Gamila. She is seen reading out passages from Mohamed Choukri's novel *Ingenious* at one point, words about the power of women to destroy men. The family's donkey, which Shukri had ridden to school, is stolen and returned with the words "The whore's brother" daubed on it in red. Gamila also taunts her father, calls him pathetic, and challenges him to shoot her. Yet when he finds her after she has tried to run away, he is initially tender and loving with her, only to turn on her and lock her mercilessly in the shed, as soon as they are back home. Even Arab critics have found this father-daughter relationship ambiguous, with Gertz and Khleifi observing that "it is not clear, for example, what happened to one of the daughters."[185] Although Abu Wael is clear in his interview that "Abu Shukri—torn between his moral cultural duty, and his love for her—invents a third possibility: he removes his whole family to nowhere,"[186] this is by no means unambiguous in the film, which contains no trace of introspection on the part of Abu Shukri.

Far more straightforward is the relationship of father and son. Shukri is kept from school, made to work alongside the rest of the family and guard the water pipe at night. When he disobeys his father, he is savagely beaten, but still made to serve him his meal. Abu Shukri is still dominant even in his death, which comes when he provokes his son into killing him by pretending to be an outsider, attacking the pipeline at night. At the end, although the film has shown attempts to escape by both Shukri and Gamila, the son emerges to take on the role vacated by the father. Nothing will change. Abu Wael claims not to be a pessimist, but he is doubtful about our capacity for change, saying of his film: "It's a call for liberation, but one man can't do it."[187] *Thirst* is a remarkable first feature, formally composed and well paced, always intriguing in its ambiguities.

Abu Wael has since directed a second feature, with mixed Israeli and European funding, in 2011. This was originally titled *Tanathor,* but when it was shown at the Locano Festival and given subsequent European screenings, the title had been changed to *Last Days in Jerusalem / Derniers jours à Jérusalem*. The setting and social situation of the characters—wealthy middle-class Palestinians living in East Jerusalem—could hardly be more different in this new film. But it shows the same fundamental pessimism about human beings' capacity to shape their lives. In the pre-credit sequence we see an attractive young woman, Nour, approaching Iyad, a doctor friend of her mother's, to seek his assistance in getting an abortion. Though initially very reluctant, Iyad does eventually agree to help, but while driving her to meet the surgeon who will perform the operation, they encounter an Israeli roadblock. Although Iyad pretends that they do not speak Hebrew and that Nour is his wife, the guards are not impressed and arrest them both. They are eventually released, Nour has her abortion, and when we next see them, Iyad and Nour are a couple who have been married for several years.

The roadblock is the film's only direct evidence of the Israeli forces' presence in Jerusalem, and significantly, we do not see or hear what happens during their interrogation. We are never told why Nour is released despite the fact that she has no identity papers (these were confiscated on her return from visiting her father in the United States). Abu Wael is utterly opposed to any overt political statements in his work, preferring to concentrate on the complex and tortured relationships experienced by his characters, particularly within a family context. These ambiguities stem largely from within the characters themselves and are not shaped by external social or political factors. Here the roadblock, which could be made to figure as a political indicator, is used in the construction of the narrative as the first of the many blockages which the characters will experience as they try to make decisions about their lives.

When we first see Iyad and Nour as a couple, they have already sold their apartment and are preparing to emigrate to France, although Iyad is totally absorbed in his work as a surgeon and Nour has fresh possibilities as an actress. Perhaps it is their shared reluctance to have children which has denied them the possibility of creating a meaningful life together in Jerusalem (there is no indication that either career has been hindered by their being Palestinian). They get as far as boarding a taxi to the airport when Iyad is called back to the hospital for help coping with the terrible aftermath of a bus accident (again there is no hint that this is a terrorist incident). Nour's reaction to the delay in departure is to sleep with her theatre producer lover, Awer, and prepare for a new appearance on stage. But working together does not draw this couple together, and Nour's performance on stage is a disaster. Iyad is similarly challenged in his work, suffering uncontrollable fits of shaking after operating for hours on end and experiencing nightmares about failure in the operating theatre. He seeks comfort from an older woman, his receptionist.

Nour's closest relationship, apart from that with Iyad, is with her mother, an independent, successful artist. But the contact between these two women is unstable. The first time Nour visits, after the trip to the airport has been interrupted, the two women are warm and intimate, totally open to each other. But, on her second visit, she is greeted with hostility and barely allowed in—her mother has a male guest (who is not Iyad). Meanwhile, the relationship of Nour and Iyad is played out in hotel rooms (they no longer have their apartment). At times there are moments of affection—as when Iyad offers a present of earrings, or Nour seeks him out after he has stormed off—but there are also moments of extreme cruelty. Nour announces she is pregnant and Iyad can calculate that the child—if it exists—is not his. He doubts her story and, in one of the film's most violently revealing scenes, pretends to make love to her, only to produce a syringe and take a blood sample, in order to test the truth of her story. Even here, however, ambiguity remains, as he breaks the syringe in a fit of shaking on his way to the hospital.

Although there is no more than a tentative reconciliation on a road overlooking Jerusalem, the film's final scene shows them together in Paris. But doubt about the nature of their relationship remains, when Iyad abruptly disappears from the café where they have been sitting together. Will they reconcile yet again? Is Paris the place where they can create a new life together? The film's open ending offers no answers to such questions. Despite Abu Wael's obvious visual skill—here manifested in the claustrophobic hotel interiors—and his ability to get striking performances from his actors, he is bound to remain a controversial filmmaker. For one thing, he is awkwardly placed, as an Israeli Arab taking part of his funding from official Israeli film funding sources. While there is no necessity for him to show more political commitment than the European filmmakers he admires, such as Ingmar Bergman and Michelangelo Antonioni, his refusal to give any indication of the impact of Israeli government policies on his Palestinian characters (even when the logic of the narrative seems to demand it) is bound to trouble some in the Arab world.

* * *

The range of approaches adopted by three other male newcomers, all of whom were born in the mid-1970s, is even more diverse. For their first features, Shady Srour, Scandar Copti, and Sameh Zoabi produced, respectively, a totally idiosyncratic self-portrait, a film noir–style thriller, and a light comedy.

Shady Srour has strong US connections. Born in 1973 in Nazareth, he studied at the Academy of Art University in San Francisco and in Tel Aviv and has worked extensively in the theatre. Srour's sole feature, *Sense of Need / L'épreuve du besoin* (2004), is a rare example of highly personal experimental cinema (Srour produced, scripted, and directed, as well as playing the lead and providing the voice-over narration). Problems of identity are common in Palestinian cinema, particularly in films written and directed by Israeli Arabs, but never more so than in Srour's film. The tone of this is set in the opening credit: a soulful Christlike image of Srour himself, with the accompanying text "Identity is the relationship between me and everything else." The film was apparently shot over a period of four years, which is borne out by the striking changes to the main character's appearance in different parts of the film.

The main story line concerns Yusuf/Joseph, who is a music student from Jerusalem studying in the United States and who has a breakdown in the week leading up to the performance of his new piano piece. But there is no attempt at narrative coherence. Parts of what seem to be quite different movies, shot (or at least set) in Jerusalem, are included as thoughts, memories, or interruptions to the narrative: two short comedy sequences (which look like initial film school exercises), a drama involving the intrusion of two Israeli soldiers into his mother's apartment, and a set of absurdist variations involving the young Yusuf blocked at a traffic crossing. As the film progresses, Joseph comes more and more to resemble a conventional image of the suffering Christ. More alarming still are Joseph's conversations with God (who speaks English and looks remarkably like a white-bearded Shady Srour).

Characters are not fixed (Joseph's doctor features twice, once as an Arab, once as a Jew, similar in appearance and both from Jerusalem but offering radically different advice based on very different experiences). Some scenes are relatively naturalistic, others theatrically stylized. The one consistent element throughout the film is the improvised piano accompaniment. The cutting is jagged and abrupt, often without any sense of narrative continuity, and the surface texture of the film is marked by all kinds of jarring filmic devices (passages of blank screen; shots going out of focus or being bleached out; repetitions; even reverse action at one point, when Joseph's hair grows longer as it is shaved and cut). *Sense of Need* is a curious, if highly original, film. As the Palestine Film Foundation database observes: "Srour (who describes his film as a 'genius feature') moves between deafening pretensions and self-parody without leaving the viewer knowing quite where the line ought to be drawn."[188]

Scandar Copti was born in 1975 in Jaffa and trained initially as a mechanical engineer before turning to acting and eventually filmmaking. He co-directed his first feature film with the Israeli Jewish filmmaker, Yaron Shani, in 2009. Copti and Shani's co-directed *Ajami* (2009) is technically an Israeli production, and as such, won five of the top Ophir Awards (the Israeli equivalents of the Oscars)— best film, direction, screenplay, music, and editing. Ajami, where most of the action is set, is a neighborhood in the city of Jaffa, where Arabs, Jews, and Christians live side by side, though not without considerable tensions. The origin of the film goes back to Shani's Tel Aviv University film school days, when, he admits,

"Like an everyday Jewish Israeli, I didn't know much about Arab society in Israel. I didn't speak more than a few words of Arabic, as most Israeli Jews don't speak Arabic at all." Scripting had to wait until 2002, when he met Copti, with whom he developed a strong friendship and a close working relationship.

The two co-wrote a detailed script, with a very precise structure and scenes designed to be "exactly how things happen in reality. If they weren't, everything would go wrong in the shoot."[189] The methods used in the preparation and shooting of the film were unusual. They used only non-professional actors, holding a ten-month acting workshop, initially with over three hundred people attending. In the course of these sessions, "the participants 'became' the characters portrayed in *Ajami.*" When the shooting began, the actors were not given copies of the script: "The actors reacted spontaneously, without written text or any awareness of plot. . . . We threw them into real live situations and they reacted spontaneously, like they would in the real world." The film was shot chronologically, scene by scene, and the actors had no prior knowledge of the plot's many surprises: "For example, in the opening scene when young Nasri's neighbor gets shot by unknown assassins, none of the actors knew anything [in advance] about the shooting." They reacted to it as if it were a real event, expressing real emotions of surprise and horror. The filmmakers' concern with reality was paramount: even the Israeli policemen in the film "were played by real former policemen" and reacted to Arab crowds as they would have done in real life.

Shooting with two cameras took about twenty-three days, and normally only one take was made: "We made a second take only when the outcome of the first take did not go with our plans." In all, eighty hours of footage, requiring a year to edit, was produced. In the end, the directors were convinced that they had succeeded in their aim of creating "a fiction film which shows 'real' people acting and feeling 'real' emotions in 'real' situations, although they were never aware how they were secretly being directed according to a pre-written script."

The film is shaped as a thriller; the central thread of the narrative—narrated and commented on by the young boy Nasri (who can to some extent anticipate future events)—is extremely simple. Two teenagers in desperate need of large sums of money for family reasons attempt unsuccessfully to involve themselves in the local drug trade. The opening sequence sets the film's tone of violence: a well-orchestrated drive-by killing of an innocent child, wrongly mistaken for his older cousin. When this is followed by the shooting of the boy's father, it is clear to the nineteen-year-old Omar that his whole family is in danger. There is no doubt about the reason: days before, his uncle had shot a Bedouin running a protection racket, and now the dead man's powerful family, the Abul-Zen, want vengeance or else substantial compensation.

The subsequent action of the film is divided into five chapters, each devoted to one of the characters involved directly or peripherally in the plot. These chapters are not in chronological order, so that sometimes we go back in time to understand previous events better and occasionally we see the same events from different perspectives. This complex patterning is generally well handled, and the effect is to convey the wider context of a violent, crime-ridden society, divided into hostile ethnic groups or clans.

In chapter 1, Omar acquires a gun and receives the help of the Christian restaurant owner and businessman Abu Elias, who gives him a job. With the help of Abu Elias, Omar attends the traditional Bedouin court, which disregards the fact that his uncle was defending himself and his property and orders a payment of 35,000 dinars. Chapter 2 introduces a sixteen-year-old Palestinian illegal immigrant, Malek, who is also employed by Abu Elias. Malek too needs money: $25,000 to pay for his mother's operation. Malek discovers that Binj, the restaurant's cook (played by Copti himself), has a stash of coke (sent for him to hide by his brother Nizar, who is in trouble with the Israeli police). After Binj dies under suspicious circumstances, seemingly killed by three Hebrew-speaking thugs, Omar and Malek steal the coke and try to sell it. But the package is a fake, and the apparent buyers are in fact Israeli policemen. There is a scuffle, in which one policeman, Dando, is shot.

In chapter 3, we go back in time to view the incident in which Nizar kills a Jewish neighbor. Dando and his colleagues have difficulty trying to arrest a drug dealer, who is supported by his local community. Dando also has a more pressing problem, trying to find his brother Yoni, who has gone missing from his military service. Eventually, a body which turns out to be Yoni is found. In chapter 4 we again go back in time, to find out the truth about Binj, who, we discover, has a Jewish girlfriend. After a threatening but fruitless police raid and search, in which we discover that the three Hebrew thugs are in fact Dando and two fellow cops, Binj destroys half the stash of coke, replaces it with flour, and then overdoses (and kills himself) with the rest.

The final chapter is again focused on Omar. We discover that he and Hadir, Abu Elias's daughter, are in love, but her father will not countenance the relationship. We also see Omar and Malek set out once again, as in chapter 2, on their ill-fated attempt to sell what they think is a package of coke. The shooting which was earlier unexplained is now made clear. It was the boy Nasri, who accompanied them in the back of the car, who fired the first shot in order to help them. Nasri wounds Dando and is then shot and killed himself. Malek is held by the police, but in the final images Omar is free—for the time being at least—but on the run.

Co-directed by an Arab and a Jew, employing actors and technicians from both communities and using a mixture of Arabic and Hebrew dialogue, *Ajami* presents a vivid portrait of the troubled city of Jaffa. With its skillful handling of actors and its elaborate (if at times baffling) plotting, the film displays both the filmmakers' knowledge of contemporary Hollywood thrillers and their ability to capture—in a totally fresh location—an authentic film noir tone.

Sameh Zoabi was born in 1975 in Iksal, a village near Nazareth. He subsequently studied film and literature at Tel Aviv University, before completing three years' film study at Columbia University in New York. Zoabi's first short, the internationally shown *Be Quiet / Reste tranquille* (2004), which was made as his graduation film, is focused on a clash between father and child, and the same theme recurs in his debut feature.

Man without a Cell Phone / Téléphone arabe (2011) is shaped as a light comedy with a catchy theme tune, a film from which all real violence, deprivation, and serious oppression are absent. The film's location is made clear in Zoabi's opening voice-over: this is Iksal, where he grew up and still lives, set in land taken over by the Israelis in 1948 but where the descendants of the earlier Palestinian Arab population continue to struggle to live traditional lives. *Man without a Cell Phone* portrays the confrontation between an older father, Salem, and his twenty-year-old son, Jawdat, who does as little work as possible, fails the Hebrew exam necessary for entry to college, and instead constantly uses his cell phone to chat up a succession of girls.

Though an attractive young man, full of self-confidence and with a ready smile, Jawdat is unsuccessful in his search for a girlfriend. Even his best friend calls him a loser. Early in the film, he shocks the parents of one girl, Manal, with his flippant approach to the likely problems of a mixed marriage (they are Christians). Later, he loses Manal, too, when he turns up at college with Rana, his sister's closest friend, who is a forceful young woman who has already ditched three boyfriends because they have failed to stand up to her policeman brother, Sami, who is very possessive. Jawdat also fails to bluff his way into a Jewish Greenpeace social gathering (where he assumes the Jewish girls will be welcoming) and is prevented from meeting up with another girl, Jenine, from Ramallah because his frequent phone calls have been logged by the Israeli secret police.

Meanwhile, his aging father Salem, grumpy, overweight, and entirely involved with his olive grove, becomes obsessed with the cell phone tower planted overnight just next to his land. He accuses his neighbor but learns that the land is in fact state owned. This merely increases his suspicion that the tower is there to poison the Arab villagers and contaminate their produce. He even seems to be disappointed when a close friend, who has to be taken to the hospital, turns out not to be suffering from cancer. His obsession grows to such an extent that his wife eventually "goes on strike" for a while, refusing to prepare his meals. Her eventual resumption, serving delicious fried eggs, is one of the film's many joyous, celebratory moments.

Salem manages to destroy the first tower without getting caught, only to find that it has been replaced almost instantly by a new one, this time equipped with a video camera to film intruders. When he attempts to involve the whole community in a petition against the tower, Jawdat becomes crucial in helping to organize a mass protest of villagers (who, of course, turn up using their cell phones). The protest is dispersed by the Israeli police, but Salem and Jawdat get their revenge by spraying the two policemen left to guard the tower with water. As they seek shelter, the two policemen seem to dance to the rhythm of the film's catchy theme tune.

Although the protest fails, the process of helping to organize it provides Jawdat with a new closeness to his father and a new sense of purpose. At the film's open ending, Jawdat is seen setting off for a more serious life (to attain his Hebrew qualification?), but as soon as he is on the bus, he gets out his new cell phone, this time to chat to the very serious and demanding Rana.

Man without a Cell Phone does touch, lightly, on serious issues: Israeli land expropriation and covert surveillance, the operations of an oppressive Israeli police force, the impact of modern technology on a traditional community, the growing gap between an older Arab generation attached to the soil and a younger one largely indifferent to it (Jawdat is contemptuous of the idea of eventually inheriting the family olive grove). But the real focus is always on the ironic little details of everyday life in the Arab community (such as the protesters still using their cell phones, Salem looking for disasters that will confirm his suspicions about the cell phone tower, and his complaining that his son must be becoming Jewish if he is reluctant to work on Saturday). Such details are consistently treated with a light touch, and the director maintains his chosen tone of gentle humor throughout.

* * *

Another young filmmaker of note, who is difficult to define nationally, is **Yahya Alabdallah**. Though generally described as "Palestinian-Jordanian," he was born in 1978 in Libya and brought up initially in Saudi Arabia. His first feature was co-funded by the Royal Film Commission in Jordan and the Dubai Film Market. After initially studying literature, Alabdallah turned to film, making a number of internationally screened short films and studying for three years in Paris. He established his own production company, ME Films, in Amman, where he is now based and where he set his debut feature, *The Last Friday / Al-juma al-akheira* (2011). This low-budget film bears little trace of its hectic shooting schedule (apparently fifty-five locations in eighteen days),[190] being composed with extreme formal precision, largely in fixed, long-held shots, with an emphasis on small movements and gestures. The sense of distance created by this filming style is enhanced by the very limited amount of dialogue the writer-director includes. The white city of Amman is constantly seen, but always as a background from which the protagonist is detached.

The taciturn forty-year-old Youssef is shown from the beginning of the film as a man who has lost out in life, because, it seems, of his gambling habit. He once tried to make his fortune in the Gulf, only to be cheated out of the money. He used to work as a salesman for a luxury car firm, but now has to make do as a taxi driver. His beautiful wife Dalal has divorced him, and he now lives in a shabby apartment, where he is reduced to stealing electricity from his neighbors. His sorry plight is echoed by that of his teenage son, Imad, with whom he has had little close contact. Imad—presumably neglected by his mother, with whom he lives, as well as by Youssef—has failed all his exams and can barely read. Suddenly, Youssef finds he needs a great deal of money to fund a vital medical operation, and he is driven to reconsider his life, revisiting his ex-wife and trying to establish contact with his son.

All the events in *The Last Friday* are underplayed. There are no violent character interactions or dramatic climaxes. Although Youssef must know Imad has stolen from his wallet, there is no direct confrontation between the two of them. Even when Youssef wins the money he desperately needs, little tension is generated: we cut to the middle of a game, the cards are shown, and the winnings are scooped up, all in a single take. The occasional moments of humor, as when his parking voucher is stolen, are equally underplayed. Even at the end, as he emerges from the hospital, Youssef is granted no moment of elation, merely shown in long shot as he labors up the hill back to his apartment. *The Last Friday* shows the emergence of a talented director, and the film has been very successful on the international festival circuit. But Alabdallah's chosen style generates little warmth for his characters: we follow their actions, but hardly any sense of real involvement is generated.

* * *

In addition, three new female Palestinian feature film directors emerged in the 1970s: Najwa Najjar, Annemarie Jacir, and Cherien Dabis. All were brought up and educated abroad, and each of their debut films has a distinctive focus and frame of reference.

Najwa Najjar was born in 1973 to Jordanian/Palestinian parents in Washington, DC, and studied politics and economics before taking courses in filmmaking. She made around ten short films prior to her feature debut, *Pomegranates and Myrrh / La grenade et la myrrhe / Al-mor wa al-rumman* (2008), which was shot under difficult circumstances in Ramallah. The film opens with an emblematic shot of olive groves stretching into the distance—Palestinian land. The action itself begins with an exuberantly celebrated wedding—despite the guests' difficulty in crossing the checkpoint separating Ramallah from Jerusalem. The couple are clearly in love, and the two families are united in supporting the marriage. The initial focus is on the husband, Zaid, who is extremely concerned with the forthcoming olive harvest. But his hopes for the next crop are abruptly destroyed by the advent of an Israeli army patrol announcing the confiscation of the family's land, on the grounds that "a child has thrown a stone at a passing military vehicle." Zaid is provoked into assaulting an Israeli soldier, which leads inevitably to his arrest. Zaid's family persist in trying to obtain his release, employing an Israeli lawyer (played forcefully by Lea Tsemel, a real-life lawyer known for her support for Palestinian rights). Meanwhile, Zaid, despite brutal treatment in prison, refuses to perform the one act that would secure his release—signing over his land for Jewish settlement.

Zaid encourages his wife, Kamar, to continue her involvement in a troupe devoted to traditional Palestinian dancing. But this causes family friction, particularly after Zaid's mother is refused permission to visit him in prison. Kamar is expected to play the role of "prisoner's wife," but instead she wants and indeed needs to find a personal form of expression. This leads to real complications when a new choreographer, Kais, born locally but brought up in Lebanon, is put in charge. He enables Kamar to find her own identity as a dancer, and he has worthy objectives, such as reopening the children's fairground, which his father had once run. A fascinating role in the action is played here by Umm Habib, an ex–cabaret dancer and now café owner, marvelously portrayed by Hiam Abbass. She helps Zaid's family to market their crop and is totally fearless in confronting the armed Israeli conscripts who threaten her coffee shop, treating them as children. But she is a very ambiguous role model for Kamar, who is unsure how independently she herself can behave. Kamar's uncertainty is quite real and on the film's release was criticized in some Arab circles. But she does reject Kais, and her dance with the troupe is (a little awkwardly) intercut with Zaid's release from prison. The film ends with Kamar and Zaid's exchanged glances.

Pomegranates and Myrrh is both a celebration of Palestinian attachment to the land they see as theirs (symbolized, as so often, by the olive grove) and an indictment of the processes of the Israeli occupation. But like so many films by this new generation of Arab filmmakers, it is also and equally importantly the celebration of a woman's independence in the face of the double threat of Israeli aggression and the weight of Arab society's own outdated traditions. It fulfills the director's stated ambition of deepening "the understanding of the present Palestinian story—transcending the barriers of culture and language."[191]

Annemarie Jacir was born in 1974 in Saudi Arabia, which she left at the age of sixteen for the United States. There she studied filmmaking at Claremont College, worked in various production roles on a number of independent films, and made eight short films from 1994 onward. Her best-known short is the seventeen-minute fictional film *Like Twenty Impossibles / Comme vingt impossibles /*

Ka'inana ashrun mustachii (2003), shot in Palestine in December 2001. Shown at festivals throughout the world and the recipient of numerous prizes, the film opens with a documentary sequence shot at the Kalandia checkpoint, about which Jacir has said, "Narratively and technically it's too long. . . . It makes no sense and shouldn't be there. Which is exactly how I feel about those check-points."[192] The rest of the film traces the disintegration of a Palestinian film crew, led by the United States–based director Anne-Marie, en route to shoot in Jeru-salem. Blocked at Kalandia, she decides they should take a detour. When they are again stopped, by other Israeli soldiers who are checking this road, we see vividly the brutal impact of the Israeli occupation. The actor is arrested "on sus-picion" and the sound recordist is detained because he is an Israeli Arab, banned as such from entering the West Bank. The director, who has brought her crew into this situation, finds that her permission to film is invalid in "Zone B." Her protestations are ignored and she is made to retreat. The film, now deprived of sound, peters out into blackness: filmmaking is impossible. In Jacir's words: "I found cinema was a perfect metaphor for what is happening in Palestine today and has been happening for the last 57 years. By the end of the film, because all the elements have been torn from each other—there is no film. There *cannot* be a film."[193] Jacir was a poet before becoming a filmmaker, and the end credits reveal the significance the film's enigmatic title, a poem titled *We Shall Remain*, by Tawfik Zayyad:

> It is a thousand times easier for you
> To pass an elephant through the needle's eye
> To catch fried fish in the Milky Way
> . . .
> A thousand times easier
> Than smothering with your oppression
> The spark of an idea
> Like twenty impossibles
> We shall remain

Having thus ably demonstrated the impossibility of filming in Palestine, Jacir then succeeded in doing just that in her first feature, *Salt of This Sea / Le sel de la mer* (2008). The film, which was presented at Cannes and had largely European funding, again opens with documentary footage, this time obtained from the military archive in Jerusalem, shot from one of the boats taking Arab refugees away from Haifa in 1948. These images of separation from the land of Palestine set the tone for what is otherwise a very personal film. The family his-tory of the leading actress, Suheir Hammad, is very similar to that of the char-acter she plays, Soraya (although Soraya's response is quite her own). Likewise, Soraya's experience of humiliation at the airport, when she enters Ramallah at the beginning of the film, recalls Jacir's own experiences (she has both a Jordanian and a US passport and was, at the time of filming, resident in Ramallah). Shooting, first in Ramallah and then in Israel, on eighty locations was difficult in ways that tell us a great deal about the Israeli occupation. As an Israeli citizen, Saleh Bakri (son of the great actor / documentary filmmaker Mohamed Bakri) was banned by law from entering Ramallah. Likewise, the Palestinian members of the crew had no right to leave Ramallah (just like the male characters, Emad and Marwan, in the film).

Soraya, who was born in Brooklyn, visits Ramallah with two projects in mind: to recuperate the money her grandfather left in his bank account when he was expelled from Haifa in 1948 and to establish her Palestinian citizenship. Early on, she encounters Emad, a resident of Ramallah, whose ambition is quite the opposite: to escape from the place where he is imprisoned and to take up a scholarship to study in Canada. Together they go into the hills overlooking Ramallah, from which they can see the cities of Jaffa and Tel Aviv—so close yet cut off, for Emad, by the Israelis. On their return, Emad's frustration turns to humiliation. The pair are stopped by Israeli police, and he is made to strip in the headlights of the patrol car.

The ambitions of both Soraya and Emad are thwarted. They are essentially marginalized in occupied Palestine—she is refused both her grandfather's money and a Palestinian passport, and his visa application is denied (for the fourth time). But the bank manager's advice to Soraya when he turns down her request—"no need for stunts or dramatic stories, just take a loan"—seems to act as a provocation. Emad's closest friend is Marwan, a frustrated filmmaker, who shoots documentary footage of the Israeli oppression but would really prefer to film romantic stories of impossible love. Together the three embark on a crazy scheme to rob the bank which holds Soraya's grandfather's money. They succeed (Soraya disguising herself in a burka) and bluff their way through an Israeli checkpoint. From this point on, the film becomes a Palestinian road movie (rooted in the *Bonnie and Clyde* tradition), taking the protagonists through the West Bank and the length of Israel, past Jerusalem and Jaffa, as far as Haifa and the hills beyond. Their success is perhaps a little too easy to be fully credible, but this (entertaining) fictional structure allows real truths about the Palestinian situation to be brought to the fore.

The fugitives are all in an illegal situation (Soraya's two-week visa has run out), but paradoxically, as long as they are able to pass unobserved, Israel becomes a place of liberty for the three of them: no poverty, no restrictions on movement, no checkpoints. They enjoy themselves on the beach and plunge joyously into the sea (which Emad has not been permitted to see for seventeen years, although it is almost in sight, beyond Tel Aviv, from the hills of Ramallah). It is noticeable that, throughout the film, whenever a Palestinian is asked where he or she is from, the reply is not their own place of birth but the place from which their grandparents were expelled in 1948, the Nakba. Thus, Soraya's need is to visit Haifa. She knows the names of the streets, the favorite café, the local cinema, from her grandfather's stories as a child. Now she is able to see the family house which he built.

The present occupant is Irit, an Israeli artist, who welcomes them to explore the house and to stay as long as they wish. But she is fundamentally unable to understand Soraya's anger at the confiscation of the house and her sense of ownership. There is a painful scene between the two women, one of whom sees what happened in the past as having nothing to do with her personally, while the other is devoured by the past, seeking an identity constantly denied her during what she regards as her return home. Thrown out (although Marwan stays behind), Soraya and Emad now seek his place of origin, the village of Dawayma. They manage to find the half-ruined village, where they stay the night and erect a little memorial. They make love and even talk of having a child together ("the first baby to be conceived in Dawayma since 1948"). But in the morning, harsh reality reasserts itself. They are told they cannot camp there by an Israeli schoolteacher, who has brought his pupils to hear his (Jewish) account of the ruins. When they go into town to pick up supplies, they are apprehended by the Israeli police: Emad is arrested, Soraya is expelled. To the police at the airport, she makes a final proud statement of identity: she is from this place; regardless of the details on her passport, she is a Palestinian.

Salt of This Sea is a very impressive first feature. It is full of personal touches. The (real-life) balletic policeman and the small boy carrying the Palestinian flag, which Soraya sees as she enters Ramallah, are the director's memories of her own first visit. At the same time, the film realizes Jacir's sense that cinema can do a great deal for Palestine. As she has said, "There are so many stories, so many things. We have been reduced to invisibility all our lives. . . . Then there is this silence imposed on us, which has lasted and still lasts. Cinema is just a different way for us to express ourselves."[194] *Salt of This Sea* is always understated—only in the end credits are we told that Dawayma was the site of a major Israeli massacre of Palestinians in 1948. The film conveys powerfully the Palestinian attachment to a land which they feel, absolutely, is theirs. With two utterly convincing performances from its leading players (one a Palestinian professional actor, the other a New York–based Palestinian poet), it also captures the essential dignity and pride of a people living deprived of so many of the basic rights and freedoms which are taken for granted in a civilized society.

Jacir's second feature, *When I Saw You / Lamma shoftak* (2012), funded largely by the Dubai Film Festival (with some additional Greek financing) and made after she had settled in Amman, Jordan, has very personal roots. First, it is set in 1967, the year in which (before her birth) her family was expelled from

Bethlehem. Inevitably, this was a key family date, constantly cropping up in conversations when she was growing up: "I wanted to tell a story from this important period, because it is connected to what is happening today."[195] The second impulse for the film came from the personal situation in which she found herself in Amman—forbidden, for the first time, to enter Palestine:

> My whole world collapsed and my heart broke. . . . When I was not allowed to return, and I could only see Palestine across the Jordan Valley, I finally understood something. I felt something I had not experienced before, just like all dispossessed Palestinians. The most difficult thing they have to do is to stand somewhere in the Valley and look at Palestine without being able to go back.[196]

Although she began to write the script at a time when she desperately needed hope in her own life, *When I Saw You* emerges as a positive, idealistic film, unashamedly romanticizing the struggles of the late 1960s: "There is something romantic about that period. They [the fedayeen] were just regular people, they weren't a trained army. In the film, you don't see the violence of what has happened and the violence that the refugee families have escaped from."[197]

The events of the film, beginning in a Palestinian camp in Jordan, are seen through the eyes of eleven-year-old Tarek (played by a non-professional who himself lives in a Jordanian refugee camp). This allows the film to elide most of the tensions, rivalries, antagonisms, and daily humiliations that must be present in such a camp, which keeps filling up after the devastating Arab defeat in the 1967 Six-Day War. Tarek seeks his father daily among the truckload of refugees brought to the camp and demands to know from his mother Ghaydaa why they cannot return home. He has problems with his schooling. Although he is lively, intelligent, and outgoing, he cannot read (for reasons the film does not explain), a fact which leads to his being expelled from school. He is, however, gifted in mathematics, as demonstrated by his farewell sally correcting his teacher.

Frustrated at home, Tarek resolves to walk back home to Palestine. He comes by chance upon a concealed fedayeen training camp, where the fighters adopt him as one of their own. These fighters are depicted as idealized figures, attractive young men and women, living together as equals and without tensions. They play music, sing together, and make the occasional painting, but never discuss the warfare they are planning or express political opinions about the Israelis or the limited support coming to them from their fellow Arabs. They accept without question the brutal training regime to which they are submitted (run by a commander who, Tarek is delighted to find out, is also illiterate). They undertake without debate or discussion the missions to which they are assigned. Similarly, they are happy to welcome among their ranks Ghaydaa, when she arrives seeking

Tarek. The young boy wants to join one of the missions but is not allowed for obvious reasons. So he continues his own personal quest to enter Palestine and be reunited with his father. He is able to calculate in his head the timing of the sole military vehicle patrolling the frontier and thus can lead his mother forward at an appropriate moment. The film ends with a freeze-frame as they come close to the frontier wire.

When I Saw You, which was received enthusiastically by audiences within the Arab world, is an amazingly lyrical account of a period which involved brutal dispossession and violent armed response. Keeping to the viewpoint of its constantly positive and optimistic eleven-year-old protagonist, the film offers us a vision of this period of the Palestinian struggle which contains no hint of the wider issues or subsequent disappointments and failures.

Cherien Dabis was born in 1976 in Omaha, Nebraska, grew up in New York and Jordan, and studied filmmaking at Columbia University. She had already shot a short film in the West Bank when she began shooting her first feature film in Ramallah, for which she received scriptwriting support from a range of international sources. While Jacir's *Salt of This Sea* tells of an American-born woman trying to establish herself in Ramallah, Dabis's *Amreeka / Amerrika* (2009) traces a reverse trajectory. The Palestinian Muna, newly divorced by her husband, unexpectedly receives visas for herself and her teenage son, Fadi, to leave Ramallah to live with her sister in the United States. The early scenes show the familiar daily humiliations undergone by Palestinians at Israeli checkpoints, and Fadi expresses his frustration at the fact that, however hard he studies, there will be no career possibilities for him in the West Bank. The tone changes with their arrival in the United States. Here the examination by customs officers is almost comic, as Muna has to explain that she has no country of origin (the Palestinian Territories are not a state) and, asked about her occupation, replies that they have been occupied by the Israelis for the last forty years.

Although their arrival coincides with the fall of Saddam Hussein in Iraq, no real political concerns are explored. Instead, the film is a domestic comedy of social adaptation: homesickness, Muna's difficulties in getting a job (her ten years' experience working in a bank counts for nothing and she has to get a job in a burger bar), Fadi's problems in fitting into his new school environment, and the bullying he receives. Fadi is ill at ease and provoked into a fight which leads to his arrest; Muna is humiliated by the job forced on her. The pair's social difficulties are paralleled by the domestic pressures within her sister's family, which are due largely to her brother-in-law Nabil's inability to make a proper living as a doctor. The one outsider who shows concern and provides them with real help is Fadi's headmaster, a Polish Jew, who is invited to the Arab celebratory meal with which the film concludes.

There is little specifically Palestinian about the family's problems—they are those likely to be faced by any immigrants. The film's incidents are markedly less dramatic than the reported experiences of Dabis's own family in Ohio, where the family "received death threats" and "the Secret Service even came to her high school to investigate a rumor that her seventeen-year-old sister threatened to kill the president."[198] The film's tone is also uneven, but Dabis explains that this is deliberate: "I have made a movie that is 50 percent English and 50 percent Arabic. People don't know whether it's a comedy or a drama. It sort of escapes definition, kind of like me."[199]

Iraq

Unsurprisingly, there has been very little feature filmmaking in Iraq in the 2000s by new filmmakers and none at all by new women directors (as is the case as well with new Iraqi documentary). Virtually all Iraqi directors are, inevitably, based abroad. Much of the filmmaking is focused on Kurdistan and made by ethnic Kurds (who by definition are not Arabs). In handling this situation, my approach is cultural, not political. When dealing with Palestinian filmmakers, I made no distinction between those who had an Israeli identity (having been born in the areas annexed by Israel after 1948) and those living abroad or in the Palestinian Territories. Here, I do not separate the Arabs and the Kurds of Iraq, viewing them as united in a real, if tentative, Iraqi cultural identity. In this approach, I am following the example of the Iraqi documentary filmmaker Layth Abdulamir, who has said that he set out in his first feature-length documentary to seek "the shared basic common cultural, social and historical elements, which make Kurds, Arabs or Turkamen, Shiites, Sunni or Christians, villagers and city-dwellers, Iraqis as well."[200] The filmmakers themselves seem happy to accept this dual identity: Hussein Hasan Ali and Massoud Arif Salih, for example, allowed their film *Narcissus Blossom* (2005) to be included in competition at the 8th Biennale of Arab Cinema in Paris, 2006.

Of course, Kurdish identity is not constrained by arbitrary national boundaries. There are a number of striking fictional features set in Iraq but directed by Iranian Kurds which have received widespread international screenings and considerable audience approval. Among these films, which fall outside the scope of this volume, are *Whisper with the Wind / Les murmures du vent / Sirta la gal ba* (2009), directed by Shahram Ailidi (who was born in 1971 and received his training at Tehran University), and *The Flowers of Kirkuk / Les fleurs de Kirkuk / Golakani Kirkuk,* which has a cast of actors from no fewer than nine countries (but no Iranians) and was directed by Fariborz Kamkari (who was also born in Iran in 1981 and studied in Tehran but who now lives and works in Italy). Above all, there is the work of Bahman Ghobadi (who was born in 1969 in Baneh in Iranian

Kurdistan). He has set all or part of his first three Iranian-produced features in Iraqi Kurdistan: *A Time for Drunken Horses* (2000), *Marooned in Iraq* (2002), and *Turtles Can Fly* (2004).

* * *

Among the slightly older Iraqi filmmakers, all born in the late 1950s and turning to feature filmmaking after 2000, are Amer Alwan, Ravin Asaf, Koutaïba al-Janabi, and Abbas Fahdel. All four have lived for many years in Europe, Alwan and Fahdel in France, Asaf in Germany, and al-Janabi in the United Kingdom. They are all foreign trained and have backgrounds in journalism and/or documentary, but their approaches are distinctive. While three of them—Alwan, Asaf, and al-Janabi—draw directly on their documentary experience in the shaping of their first fictional works, Fahdel adopts a very different strategy.

Amer Alwan, who was born in 1957 in Babylon, began his studies of drama and film in Baghdad. He was subsequently forced into exile in 1980 to France, where he continued his film studies and established himself as a documentary filmmaker in Paris. His sole feature, *Zaman, the Man from the Reeds / Zaman, l'homme aux roseaux* (2003), was produced by Arte and shot digitally, because of the embargo banning the import of 35mm film into Iraq. Five videocassettes (four hours of rushes) were confiscated by the Saddam Hussein government's censors. Subsequently, there were further difficulties with the censorship system set up by the US administration, which initially banned the screening of the film in Iraq unless certain cuts were made.

Zaman, one of the few feature films shot in Iraq during the last months of Saddam's rule, is a tribute to a passing way of life—that of the Madan or Marsh Arabs. It is, however, a strictly non-political film, making no reference to the dictator's vindictive draining of the marshes (which he viewed as a refuge for opponents of his regime) after the First Gulf War of 1991. Nor is any comment made on the background images of Saddam, seen on television or on billboards. Yet by the time the film was shot, the population of the marshland area, with its distinctive way of life, had been reduced from 500,000 to under 2,000. The film avoids all wider issues; its focus is fully and unwaveringly on the simple human story it recounts.

The film begins with a pre-credit sequence in documentary style, with black-and-white images of the marshland situated between the Tigris and Euphrates Rivers, accompanied by voice-over comments by the filmmaker, who reveals his own fascination with an area he first visited as a teenager. This is an area with a history going back three thousand years B.C., as well as a mythical status as the legendary location of the Garden of Eden. There is, however, no attempt to endow the characters with mythical status. Zaman and Najma are simple people, an aging couple with no children who have taken in five-year-old Yasin after his parents were killed in a bombing raid. Zaman tries to cheer the child up while reminding him of the simple precepts which should rule his life: patience, prayer, optimism, and faith in Allah. He points to a nearby palm tree to reinforce his point. The slow rhythms of the action and a pleasing but barely audible musical score convey a sense of people in tune with the natural environment in which they live.

The family's problem is that Najma is ill, suffering from a disease for which, the doctor tells Zaman, there is no remedy available locally. He therefore sets out on the long trip to Baghdad, where the rhythms of life and the urban environment are quite alien. Nevertheless, he eventually finds the medicine at the St. Raphael Hospital and, despite the indifference of the corrupt hospital director, obtains what he needs, thanks to a sweet and sympathetic nurse. He returns home with presents for Najma, Yasin, and the neighbor, Om Abbas, who has been looking after his wife. The next morning, however, he finds his wife has died, before she could start her cure. Now it is for Yasin to comfort the old man and to utter the words of advice with which Zaman had comforted him at the film's opening.

Zaman, the Man from the Reeds is a simple tale of human endurance and suffering which never becomes self-indulgent. Its combination of neorealist attention to the details of gestures and daily rituals with a sensitive handling of its setting makes this a moving and thoroughly satisfying piece of work.

Ravin Asaf was born in 1957 in Iraqi Kurdistan but began his film studies in Baghdad. Nine years after graduation, he emigrated to Germany, where he studied visual communication at the University of Fine Arts in Hamburg. Since 1994 he has worked as a producer and journalist for various European television channels, focusing on Iraq and Kurdistan. His first feature film, *The Smell of Apples / Le parfum des pommes* (2008), was produced by the Kurdish cultural authorities and marks the twentieth anniversary of Saddam Hussein's poison gas attack on the town of Halabja on March 16, 1988, in which five thousand people were killed. The film opens with a personal statement by Asaf about memories: "Memories won't bring change, even if I, like many others, keep talking about it." The pre-credit sequence is a dream evoking the choking gas attack, which, because of its coincidence with harvest time, became forever associated with the smell of apples.

The Smell of Apples offers a broad (perhaps too broad) panorama of life in Halabja twenty years later. At its center is Yusuf, a Kurdish pharmacist who, having spent twenty years in Germany, has returned to help the people injured in the gas attack, to which German companies contributed (by being among those who sold the weapons to Saddam Hussein). He is immediately regarded as an alien by the community, and the mutual attraction between him and the schoolteacher Sara—although both keep their distance—ruins her reputation in this small and very conservative community. Sara's brother Omar works with Yusuf and supports him but has his own domestic problems, as his wife desperately wants children, despite the fear that they might be damaged or deformed. In the course of the narrative, the situations of these four characters undergo a transformation. Omar lands the secure job with the aid agency that he longs for, and his wife gets pregnant. Yusuf decides to return to Germany and has to confess to Sara that he already has a wife there. Sara, as an abandoned woman, has to leave Halabja and seek a new life elsewhere.

Life is much more problematic for the fifteen-year-old Rizgar, who is highly intelligent but was born crippled because of the gas attack, which led to the eventual deaths of both his parents. Understandably bitter at his own fate, he is emotionally unstable, blaming Yusuf for all the German wrongdoing while insulting Sara, the teacher he secretly adores. He launches a personal vendetta against Yusuf, luring him to a secluded, very deep (and conveniently located) hole in the ground. There he torments the imprisoned Yusuf, sentencing him to death in the name of Kurdistan, and releasing him only when he thinks he may be able to save Sara, who has fallen ill. After this, his attitude is transformed: he reconciles himself with Yusuf and even starts learning German ("to go abroad to seek reparations for the village").

Despite its many virtues and insights, *The Smell of Apples* does not have a strong and convincing narrative. It is full of random incidents presumably included to capture the sense of the time (an assault on a checkpoint in Baghdad, a discussion of the US occupation of the South, the regular appearance of a pair of thuggish, xenophobic unemployed men). Curiously, Rizgar is the only member of his generation to be shown as physically and mentally scarred. His responses are purely individual, and they seem inadequate to represent a balanced picture of Halabja twenty years after the atrocity.

Koutaïba al-Janabi was born in 1959 in Baghdad but has lived since 1989 in London, where he has worked for MBC television. After studying filmmaking at the Budapest University of Film and Theatre Arts in the 1980s, he first made fictional shorts: *Still Life / Nature morte* (1998), *The Train / Le train* (1999), and *Transient* (2003); and then documentaries: *My Friend Nassir* (2003) and *Against the Light* (2007). While most of the Iraqi expatriates have filmed tentative attempts at a return to Baghdad, such as Fahdel's *Return to Babylon* and *We Iraqis,* or from an older generation, Pachachi's *Return to the Land of Wonders,* al-Janabi's debut feature traces a journey in the opposite direction.

Leaving Baghdad / Al-raheel min Baghdad (2011) is a low-budget variant of the road movie, scripted, directed, and photographed by al-Janabi and drawing directly on his documentary experience. The film contains several interwoven threads. First, it traces the desperate attempt by Abu Samir, once Saddam Hussein's personal cameraman and a respected member of his presidential entourage, to flee from Baghdad to London, where his wife already lives. Parallel to this are recurrent shots of the secret service man dispatched to find and kill him. The clear competence of this security operative and the fact that he's always close behind Abu Samir make one aspect of the film's denouement increasingly clear. With this, the film intercuts live-action dramatic footage, material from television archives recording the complexity of Saddam's character: riding triumphant on a horse through Beirut but stumbling awkwardly when called upon to perform a traditional dance;, a family man happy in the context of family parties (such as a child's birthday), but also, in the latter parts of the film, shown to be responsible for the vicious torture and murder of Iraqi citizens, which his own cameras are set up to record. The fourth strand of material comprises the letters to Abu Samir's missing son, Samir, one of the many Iraqi dissidents who have disappeared without a trace, which take on added significance as the action unfolds.

At the start of the film, Abu Samir is not an immediately sympathetic character. He is abrasive to his wife on the phone, and his first mental letter to his missing son blames him for what has happened while dwelling on the glory reflected on the family of living so close to the great national leader. But al-Janabi's close-in, handheld camera style, and Abu Samir's situation as someone trying in every possible way to make his escape, lead us to empathize with him. The classic late-night knock on the door causes him to flee, and he tries to organize convincing paperwork and travel documents. As he embarks on the seemingly endless succession of bus and train rides, which eventually take him as far as Budapest, he composes a second letter to his son, detailing his progress.

But Abu Samir is increasingly lost. His phone calls to London bring no financial support, and he is steadily running out of money. His life consists of cheap empty bedrooms, nightmares of Saddam's cruelty, and daytime encounters with people who offer help but whom he cannot trust. His third letter to his son is strident in its accusations: all the family problems, the loss of status and privilege, are his fault. His decision to join the Communist Party was the cause of all the family's problems. He follows advice from a fellow Iraqi to go to the border, but his appearance in a traditional Hungarian farming community naturally draws attention. As his pursuer finally catches up with him, he composes his fourth letter to his son, and now the horrendous truth is revealed. It was Abu Samir who was forced to reveal the whereabouts of his son—and to accept a reward for doing so. He hoped that his personal closeness to Saddam would result in leniency. But no. As his last act before being expelled from his position and the party, Abu Samir was compelled to film the beheading of his own son.

Leaving Baghdad is a soft-spoken but hugely powerful film. The sparse narrative is totally convincing; we are caught up with the fate of the protagonist, whose final confession could not be more powerfully handled. This is perhaps Iraqi cinema's most powerful indictment of the rule of Saddam Hussein, the "family man" who knew just how to force those most concerned to protect their own families to compromise themselves totally and fatally.

Abbas Fahdel, who was born in Babylon in 1959, moved to Paris at the age of eighteen to study at the Sorbonne (where he eventually received his doctorate in film). He now lives in France, where he works as a journalist and film critic; he is a French citizen. Fahdel made two 50-minute video documentaries, which are accounts of visits to Iraq before and then after the 2003 war.

Back to Babylon / Retour à Babylone (2002) is a very personal account—with a voice-over by Fahdel himself—of the director's return to Baghdad and to his birthplace, Babylon, after an absence of twenty-five years. It is the complete antithesis of the work of Kamal Aljafari in Palestine, full of joyful (if brief) re-unions, exchanges of old photographs, and reminiscences about how things were then and what has happened in the intervening years. His first stop is in Baghdad to meet his brother (who has hung a photograph of Fahdel as a child in Babylon on the bedroom wall), and he has contact with other relatives, sharing a family celebration of the festival of Aïd El Kebir.

But Fahdel's main focus is on his schoolboy friends, since the impulse behind this trip is the question of what would have become of him if he had stayed in Iraq. Inevitably, despite the warmth of the greetings and the assistance of his brother, he remains an outsider, a prosperous-looking man with a big, glossy car, a white jacket, and French passport who is passing through. What strikes him most, looking at the streets and buildings of his childhood, is that everything is as he remembers it, except that, at the same time, nothing is as he remembers it—everything is now exceedingly run-down. The lives of his friends are also modest. His close friend Mohamed, for example, now runs the local cinema where they shared their youthful passion for movies. Others live in poverty, and some suffered long years of imprisonment (as many as eighteen years) because of the Iran-Iraq War. Fahdel wonders at the moral strength of the Iraqis, able to accept such hardships without becoming bitter. Among his friends, only Sami Kaftan, now a popular television actor, has really been successful, and the film ends with one of his songs, proclaiming that there is "no peace in exile," that "only your homeland will be a haven." Although life in Baghdad and Babylon is overshadowed by the aftereffects of the First Gulf War, there is no attention given to the current political situation or the rule of Saddam Hussein.

In *We Iraqis / Nous, les Irakiens* (2004), the first part of which was shot just a year later, politics plays a much larger role. The sight of anti-war demonstrations on French television in 2003 prompts Fahdel to make a fresh return, and this time it is his family which forms the focus of his concern. He finds the older members of the family calm and resourceful despite the menacing atmosphere and the near certainty of war. A water pump is being built for emergencies, and food and medicine are being stockpiled. The family even have a tiny bit more freedom, now able to celebrate the opening of a Shiite festival that includes the whole family and the neighbors. The children play happily, and it seems almost as if there is no threat. Fahdel returns to Paris, but in four days he sees US president George W. Bush on television, announcing the beginning of the invasion.

After two months of anxious waiting, and with no news of his family, Fahdel decides to go back to Baghdad, but this time the only way is by crossing the border with Jordan. In Baghdad, he finds the family safely returned from sheltering in the country and trying to resume a normal life. But much has changed. Officials such as his brother-in-law, who drives him around, have been dismissed from their posts, and, although schools have reopened, the teachers are unpaid and demoralized. The national museum and the university attended by his niece have been plundered, and the former television station is in ruins. Some still speak up for the former dictator, but most are already impatient for an end to the occupation. Painful for Fahdel, if ignored by most, is the destruction of Baghdad Cinema Studios, which housed the Iraqi national film archive. The film ends with the reported deaths of Saddam's two sons and a note of hope for the future: the birth of his brother's child—the first in the family to be born in freedom.

The strength of Fahdel's two documentaries lies not in any analysis of broader events but in the direct and immediate capturing of the feel of a people under extreme pressure. It is the little details of how people survive and keep up their spirits that give the films their power and allow Fahdel to maintain a positive outlook on the resilience of the Iraqis.

Fahdel's first feature, for which he received Fonds Sud funding, is *Dawn of the World / L'aube du monde* (2007). This is very different in tone and visual texture from his two documentaries. Whereas they were informally shot, often comprising improvised responses to immediate events, *Dawn of the World* uses long takes and a static camera to create a formal (perhaps too formal) texture for the film. Indeed, the Tigris and Euphrates delta, the home of the Marsh Arabs (Madan), is presented as a Garden of Eden (hence the film's title). The editing, using a static camera, which intersperses the action with stunning images of dusk, dawn, and water, is backed up by the music of the German Jürgen Knieper (who has worked with Wim Wenders), so that a powerful and poetic sense of place is conveyed. The sense of solemnity is enhanced by the fact that the wise ferryman of the village, Hadji Noh, is an explicit tribute to the mythical figure of Noah, and the film's central couple are seen by the director as "the Adam and Eve of a post-apocalyptic world," on whose love and survival "the survival of humanity, or at least of the Marshes, will depend."[201] What is surprising to the uninformed viewer is that, because of the destruction caused when Saddam Hussein drained and destroyed the marshes (driving the inhabitants into exile) and owing to current military restrictions, the film was not shot in southern Iraq but in Egypt, at

Lake Manzala, near Port Said, with its Iraqi-style Madan village dwellings carefully reconstructed.

In some ways the beauty of the setting in *Dawn of the World* overwhelms the villagers of Hufaidh, as they are reduced to largely immobile figures set against a resplendent backdrop, speaking slowly in composed tones, like characters on a stage. Dialogue is reduced to a minimum—partly, it seems, because most of the actors are not native Iraqi speakers. Because of the film's formality, we lose the sense that these Marsh Arabs are poverty-stricken peasants, despised in Baghdad and persecuted by Saddam. *Dawn of the World* is also a film which shies away from the direct depiction of violence. The real circumstances of Saddam Hussein's wars against Iran and against his own people are never shown explicitly.

There are no bombs or shellfire in the sequence depicting the conflict with Iran, just two defeated Iraqi soldiers making their way through the desert and stumbling to cross a minefield. The aircraft submerged cockpit-down in the mud, which dominates the entrance to the village, is not a specific warplane (Iraqi or American) but is intended as "an object that is more poetic than realistic," according to the director.[202] Similarly, we do not see the final helicopter attack on Hufaidh, which kills some of the villagers and drives most of the others into exile in Iran—we merely witness the aftermath.

In *The Dawn of the World*, Fahdel attempts to combine beauty and a recoil from screen violence with a tribute to the culture of the Marsh Arabs. The narrative of the film is stripped of dramatic crises and reversals, and even the inevitable cultural gap between a townsman from Baghdad and a Marsh Arab girl is masked. The film offers a simple and uplifting tale of love and compassion. Mastour and Zahra are cousins, so they know at the age of ten that, in this traditional community, they are destined to marry. They are close as children and, seven years later, the marriage does indeed go ahead. But on their wedding night, Zahra becomes scared and runs off, and the next morning Mastour is conscripted into the army. While serving together in the Iran-Iraq War, Mastour and Riad, who comes from Baghdad, become very close friends, and when he is dying from the mine explosion, Mastour makes Riad promise to take care of Zahra and marry her. There are the usual problems and barriers, but although he is in an alien environment, Riad's love grows ever stronger, even after Zahra admits she was assaulted by one of the soldiers in the helicopter attack.

Dawn of the World is a thoughtful and sincere tribute to a centuries-old way of life, imbued with the optimism with which Fahdel, who lived through the Iraqi wars, albeit in exile, fills all his films.

*   *   *

There are two Iraqi feature film directors, both of Kurdish origin, born in the 1960s, Hiner Saleem and Jano Rosebiani.

Hiner Saleem made his first features in the late 1990s but only established himself as an international figure in the 2000s. He has since proved himself one of the most prolific of the 2000s Kurdish filmmakers but has increasingly been drawn into mainstream French filmmaking. One example of this is his slow-moving and touching (if rather sentimental) study of old age, *Beneath the Roofs of Paris / Sous les toits de Paris* (2007), starring Michel Piccoli. Saleem, who was born in 1964 in Aqrah in Iraqi Kurdistan, fled the Saddam Hussein regime at the age of sixteen, living first in Italy and then in France. There he published his first French-language novel, *My Father's Rifle,* and established himself as a filmmaker. He began with two features dealing with the Kurdish community in Europe, *Long Live the Bride . . . and the Liberation of Kurdistan / Vive la mariée . . . et la libération du Kurdistan* (1997) and *Beyond Our Dreams / Passeurs de rêve* (1999).

Saleem subsequently made his international reputation with *Vodka Lemon / Vodka Leymûn* (2003), a wry comedy shot in a Kurdish village in Armenia, where the (locally lamented) collapse of the USSR has left poverty and economic ruin. Although the film opens and closes with surreal images, the emphasis throughout is on the total lack of resources within this snow-engulfed community, which drives the young to exile, prostitution, and violence. Even the letters from the young people abroad, in France, contain not money but pleas for financial help. The ceremonies of burial and marriage are acted out in the traditional manner, but these formalized rituals are observed coldly, from afar, by Saleem's camera. There are some good jokes (Question: "If this is vodka lemon, why does it taste of almonds?" Answer: "We're in Armenia"), but no attempt is made to gloss over the dire situation of the characters. The protagonist, the newly widowed Hamo, wins the love of the widow tending a nearby grave; but during the course of their muted courtship, he has to sell off all his possessions, and she loses the bar she runs, the Vodka Lemon. They are left united, but in total poverty.

Saleem followed this with *Kilometer Zero / Kilomètre zéro* (2005), set in 1988 during the Iran-Iraq War and a few weeks after Saddam Hussein launched his poison-gas attack on the Kurdish village of Halabja. The film's protagonist, Ako, finds himself conscripted into the army to fight for a cause that is not his. War is depicted as a tragic farce, its boredom interrupted by sudden deadly bombardments, endured by men who dream of a Europe symbolized for them by Anita Ekberg emerging from the Trevi Fountain in Federico Fellini's *La dolce vita.* Ako is given the task of returning the corpse of a fellow Kurdish "martyr" to his home village, and the core of the film is Ako's uneasy relationship with his Iraqi Arab taxi driver as they drive through an empty desert landscape. Like the war sequences, the journey mixes moments of horror (the sheer number of "martyrs" being returned home) and farce (the constant reappearance of trucks bearing a statue of Saddam Hussein in heroic mode). In the end Ako is miraculously transported to Paris at the joyous moment of the fall of Baghdad, but not before the film has revealed with clarity and humor both the defiant spirit of the Kurdish people and the gulf that separates them from the Arabs who rule them (and with whom they have otherwise so much in common). Both *Vodka Lemon* and *Kilometer Zero* are shot as sequences of formally controlled long takes, setting the characters in a broad landscape (whether of snow or sand) and edited with a slow, meditative rhythm which matches perfectly the temperaments of the two thoughtful, somewhat passive protagonists.

Saleem has since made *Dol or The Valley of Drums / Dol ou la vallée des tambours* (2007), *After the Downfall / Après la chute* (2009), and *If You Die, I'll Kill You / Si tu meurs, je te tue* (2010).

If You Die, I'll Kill You looks again at the Kurds in France, but this time from a detached, quizzical perspective, the principal representatives of their community being seven brothers who operate as one, even to the extent of synchronizing their drinking at the bar. The film's protagonist, however, is a Frenchman, Philippe, recently emerged from prison, who makes friends with a young Kurd he meets while drinking. Avdal is awaiting the arrival of his fiancée, Siba, but he dies unexpectedly while riding on a bus to meet Philippe (the unlikelihood of such an event is underlined by a Kurdish shopkeeper, who states that Kurds do not die of natural causes, only because of chemical weapon attacks, cancer, or exile). Philippe is left with Avdal's possessions (including a gun and a large sum of money) and with responsibility for the body, which he arranges to have cremated. When Avdal's fundamentalist father arrives, Philippe discovers that cremation is abhorrent to all Kurds. Meanwhile Siba has arrived in Paris and is distraught at not being met at the airport, but eventually she is able to meet up with Philippe through their mutual contacts in the Kurdish community. Her prospective father-in-law, who also arrives in Paris, sees the only honorable solution for Siba as marriage with Avdal's younger brother, but Siba manages to hold on to the freedom she has found in Paris and the possibility (lightly sketched) of a new relationship with Philippe. The tone of light comedy is preserved throughout, and Saleem manages to remain true in tone to the definition of Kurdish life given him by his grandfather: "We Kurds have a sad history, our present is catastrophic, but luckily we do not have a future."[203]

Jano Rosebiani was born in 1961 in Zakho in southern Kurdistan and, at the age of fourteen, was caught up in the uprising against Saddam Hussein. He emigrated to the United States while still a teenager and attended Northern Virginia Community College, where he studied English literature. He later became involved in theatre management and public access television. In 1988 he moved to Los Angeles, where, seven years later, he made a 16mm feature film, *Dance of the Pendulum* (1995). He returned to Kurdistan in 2002, to make *Life / Jiyan,* a fictional feature set in the Kurdish city of Halabja, the scene of one of Saddam's worst massacres, a 1988 chemical attack which killed 5,000 people. Inevitably, there were numerous production difficulties: he had to "smuggle the filmmaking equipment into the region through Turkey and later smuggled the footage out to Belgium, where he did the postproduction."[204]

David Lipfert sets out the basic plot of *Life:*

> The action takes place in Halabja about five years after Saddam's infamous poison gas attack. Diyari (Kurdo Galali) has come from his new homeland, America, with enough cash to put up a badly needed new orphanage. As construction proceeds, he gradually becomes acquainted with the tragic individual stories of the survivors. Prime among these is orphan girl Jiyan (Pesheng Berzinji) whose one-side-beautiful, one-side-disfigured face epitomizes the people's plight.[205]

For Lipfert, "Rosebiani makes his strongest points when emphasizing the Kurds' pre-Islamic roots," while a review by Jaap Mees draws attention to the contribution, as director of photography, of the future Iraqi feature director Koutaïba al-Janabi, "who excels in creating sublime images, his shots of the flute player on the roof at night, the capturing of a sandstorm, his sense of time and place are unforgettable."[206]

Rosebiani stayed on in Kurdistan after completing the film, making two documentaries, *Saddam's Mass Graves* (2004) and *Chemical Ali* (2005), and hoping to help develop filmmaking in his native country. But in 2007 he returned to the United States to settle in California, whence he produced a further feature, *Chaplin of the Mountains* (2009), an English-language film shot in Kurdistan with a mixed cast of Americans and Kurds.

* * *

Among the younger directors, born in the 1970s and making their debuts in the 2000s, are Mohamed al-Daradji, Oday Rasheed, and the Kurds Shawkat Amin Korki and the team of Hussein Hasan Ali and Massoud Arif Salih.

Mohamed al-Daradji was born in 1978 in Baghdad, where he studied at the Institute of Fine Arts before moving abroad to study filmmaking at the Hilversum Media Academy in the Netherlands and Leeds Metropolitan University in the United Kingdom. He worked as a cameraman and directed two short films before making his first feature. He shot *Dreams / Rêves / Ahlaam* (2005) with funding from Dutch and UK sources.

Dreams has a complex time structure, beginning with the Americans' "shock and awe" bombing of Baghdad and ending with the appearance of US troops on the streets of the city. The central figures are a doctor, Mehdi, and two patients, Ali and Ahlaam, at a psychiatric hospital destroyed by the bombing. The early parts of the film trace the previous lives and suffering of the three under Saddam Hussein's regime: Mehdi as the son of a dissident; Ali as a conscript, first bombed by the United States and then tortured as a deserter by his own side; and Ahlaam as a bride whose husband is shot dead before her eyes on her wedding day. Although *Ahlaam* is not without hope—Ali recovers sufficiently to help some of his fellow patients—the movement toward tragedy is reflected in the camera work, as the brightness of some of the earlier sequences are replaced with a somber and all-pervading gray tone. The abiding image is that of Ahlaam (whose name means "dreams" in Arabic). Clearly the symbol of a tortured Iraq, she is left to wander in her wedding dress through the empty streets of a nightmarish Baghdad, where she is raped and abandoned.

The very difficult circumstances under which this film was made in Iraq in 2004—with an Iraqi crew and cast—are chronicled in al-Daradji's feature-length diary of the filmmaking, *War, Love, God, Madness / Guerre, amour, dieu, folie* (2009). As well as facing logistical and casting problems, al-Daradji was arrested by the Iraqi police, shot at by insurgents, kidnapped and beaten by militants, and then subjected to five days of ill treatment by the American military. What enabled him to survive was his Dutch passport. He recounts elsewhere that, after the filming, the two leading members of the cast, the actors playing Mehdi and Ahlaam, both had to move from the areas where they lived.[207] Al-Daradji's personal experiences find their reflection in the film, but its focus is always on the sufferings of the people rather than on political issues; his stated aim was to tell the human story of the Iraqi people.

Al-Daradji's second fictional feature, *Son of Babylon / Fils de Babylone / Ibn Babil* (2009), is based on a family experience, that of his aunt who never found her son after the Iran-Iraq War, although in the film her experiences are transposed to a Kurdish grandmother. For al-Daradji, the basic idea behind the film was to "bind two generations, the older steeped in suffering, the younger bearing hope for the future": "a mother's search for her lost son; a boy's journey to find himself and his father, each in the abyss I felt against the backdrop of war and occupation, as I struggled to comprehend the tragedy."[208] *Son of Babylon* is set in April 2003, three weeks after the fall of Saddam Hussein, an event which has prompted Um Ibrahim to act on the last news she received about her son, a letter dating from 1991 telling her he was in the Nasiriyah prison. Despite the distance from Kurdistan, her own age, and her inability to speak Arabic, she sets off with her grandson Ahmad to seek out the son she is convinced is still alive.

The film opens with stunning shots of Um Ibrahim making her way through the desert. Although Ahmad is twelve, he is still a child, hopping and skipping behind his grandmother and occasionally playing what we later discover is his father's flute. Although the outcome of their journey is inevitable, al-Daradji's narrative holds one's attention throughout. They have various encounters along the way, the first with a cynical driver who curses both Saddam and the American occupiers and refers to having a pee as "speaking to Saddam on the phone."

Initially he cheats Um Ibrahim over the cost of the ride, but he then has a change of heart and returns the money when they eventually reach Baghdad.

There Ahmad and his grandmother are almost separated when she is left behind by the bus driver, but Ahmad's new friend Qasim manages to stop the bus. Although she dresses Ahmad up in his best clothes to meet his father, the vast prison of Nasiriyah is empty and her son's name is not on any list of survivors or identified dead. The mood of the film darkens, and they travel from one newly opened mass grave to the next. Ahmad, who has to act as his grandmother's interpreter, gradually matures under the impact of his experiences, a change symbolized by his grandmother's allowing him to wear his father's jacket, which she had brought with her to give to her son. When Musa, an Arab who can speak Kurdish and befriends them, turns out to have served in Saddam's army in the North, it is Ahmad who now reminds his grandmother of her own lesson to him about the need to show forgiveness. Despite Musa's help, the quest is hopeless, and as they travel at last through Babylon, Um Ibrahim dies. Ahmad is left alone, but the many instances of personal kindness the couple have experienced leave one optimistic about his future. Although the strength of the film lies in its depiction of the small gestures of human contact in adversity, it does convey the wider message about Iraq, spelled out in the film's final titles: "Over the last 40 years over a million men, women and children have gone missing in Iraq. By April 2009, 300 mass graves had been discovered, containing between 150,000 and 250,000 bodies. The majority are still missing or unidentified."

Both of al-Daradji's features paint vivid and moving pictures of the aftermath of Saddam's rule and the difficulties of the American takeover. Both move slowly but seemingly inevitably toward disaster, and there is no possibility of a happy outcome for the characters his films depict. But whereas *Ahlaam* was irremediably bleak, there is, in *Son of Babylon* at least, a figure of hope for a better future: Ahmad.

Oday Rasheed, who was born in Baghdad in 1973, was one of the few Iraqi directors not to go into exile. He began and interrupted his studies at several higher educational institutions, dissatisfied by the quality of the student experience under Saddam's rule. He worked as a writer and journalist, made a few short films, and was part of an artistic collective known as Najeen (The Survivors).[209] The shooting of his first feature, *Underexposure / Sous-exposition / Ghair salih* (2004), which began in November 2003, was self-financed by Rasheed and his crew, using outdated film stock apparently recovered from looters. It is a mixture of drama and documentary about a film director, overwhelmed by the devastation he finds on the streets of Baghdad and uncertain of how to create a coherent drama out of what he experiences.

In his presentation of the film, Rasheed explains that *Underexposure* "blends reality and fiction to create a lyrical and textured work that captures the dizzying atmosphere of life after war and fiercely illuminates a part of the world long left in the dark": "Friends, lovers, strangers and family members are woven together by the complexities of their new reality. The past is only a moment behind them, with the presence of death a constant companion into the future." His statement of intent is couched as a series of questions:

> What is happening in Baghdad these days? Where is Baghdad between the moments of real nightmares and soft dreams? What are the feelings of someone who was burnt by the war without dying?[210]

After *Underexposure,* Rasheed left Iraq for Berlin to study film and to develop the script of his second feature. On his return to Iraq in 2008, he set up the Iraqi Independent Film Center, together with Mohamed al-Daradji, and shot *Qarantina* (2010), a study of contemporary Baghdad. According to the official synopsis, the film deals with a broken family living uneasily within the gated courtyard of a dilapidated house in Bagdad. There are tensions within the family, which is headed by the patriarch Salih, and new problems threaten with the arrival of their boarder, a man who works as a hired killer. It was this enigmatic figure who was the starting point for Rasheed when he began his script.

Rasheed has spoken interestingly about the differences between his two features: "My first feature was based on voice-over and dialogue, voice-over and dialogue. I tried this. That was my situation in 2003." After his years of study in Berlin, Rasheed had a new perspective in 2008: "I started to see life differently—the relationship between film and life. Andrei Tarkovsky talks about how you 'fix the time' in a shot. For me, fixing the time is connected with what's been said and what you are waiting to say—there's a space in between. This space of silence, I think it's full of energy, and economic too in terms of the beauty of narration."[211] A first response to the film came from Ned Parker, a journalist and friend of Rasheed's: "In *Qarantina,* Oday made a movie that is incredibly personal. That's the beauty of the film. You don't need to know anything about the Iraq War to appreciate *Qarantina*. The film shows people making choices and reflecting on their pasts—Baghdad, with all its troubles, serves as a backdrop and character in their searching, but the story is about the people first."[212]

Shawkat Amin Korki was born in 1973 in Kakko in Iraqi Kurdistan but had to flee in his teens to Iran, where he lived until 1999. Since his return, he has made a number of short films and subsequently completed two features in the late 2000s. He began with a low-budget road movie, *Crossing the Dust / À travers la poussière / Parinawa la ghobar* (2006), featuring two Kurdish peshmerga fighters, Azad and Rashid, who are charged with driving a truckload of food supplies to their colleagues on the front line. The setting is 2003, in the immediate aftermath of the US invasion, and the film opens with a group of Kurds cheering as they watch the fall of Saddam's statue in Baghdad on television. The pair's mission is basically a simple one, but it becomes more complicated when Azad insists on picking up a five-year-old Arab boy they see crying by the roadside. Their problem now becomes what to do with the boy. Azad, who doesn't speak Arabic, tries to cheer the boy up with a little wooden pipe he carries with him. His more morose comrade Rashid, who does speak some Arabic, remains hostile to the boy, particularly when he learns his name is Saddam. He wants to ditch him so that they can get on with their real mission. Azad, however, will not simply abandon the boy and tries to find him shelter, first with an American tank column, then with the imam of an empty mosque. He meets only with refusals.

The two peshmerga now begin to drive around in circles, getting lost and even losing their car temporarily, when it is used to take a wounded man for medical care. Their confused journeys bring them face to face with the realities of the moment—the looting of Saddam's party offices and the initial attempts to uncover bodies in one of Saddam's mass graves. Ironically, their path repeatedly almost crosses that of the boy Saddam's parents, who are urgently seeking their son and arguing about which of them it was who decided to take the money offered by the old regime to all parents who called their sons "Saddam." All the while, the ongoing war is in the background, with helicopters circling overhead and explosions heard in the background. In the end, Azak and Rashid come face to face with some of those still supporting the former regime, when they are hunted down by a pair of snipers—disguised as a husband and his burka-clad wife—who coldly shoot them down and abduct the boy. Azad is killed in the encounter, but Rashid survives to carry on their mission and even pick up the boy again, finding him once more weeping at the roadside. Nothing is resolved; the film's last image is of little Saddam looking out of the truck's rear window and imagining the dead Azad reviving to play his pipe again.

The plot of *Crossing the Dust* is full of chance encounters, failed opportunities, and coincidences, but these allow it to capture vividly the sheer chaos that followed the US invasion of Iraq. It is a humane film about war, showing the caring response of some individuals in the midst of a situation of horror, but honest enough to reveal as well that humane actions may, in these circumstances, have no positive outcome.

Korki has subsequently completed a second feature, *Kick Off* (2009), produced, curiously enough, by a Japanese company, which deals with the potential of soccer to bring together groups of Kurdish, Turkish, and Arab refugee children. The film is set in a neglected, run-down soccer stadium in Kirkuk, where families from various communities are squatting, each with its own clearly defined domestic space. We seldom leave this space: the world around it seems hostile. Helicopters circle constantly, and from time to time the silence is shattered by a nearby explosion. The families are all homeless and impoverished, and even their security in the stadium is threatened by a property developer who wants to evict them.

The success of an improvised group television screening of Iraq beating Saudi Arabia at soccer to win the Asian Cup prompts Aso to get together with his friend Sato to organize a soccer match aiming to bring the families together in friendly competition. Aso is a typical Arab protagonist, energetic enough to plan a community project, but too diffident to approach Helin, the girl he loves. When, against all the odds, the game does go ahead, it is plagued with problems: arguments over refereeing, a horse galloping around the field of play, a truck arriving to deliver gasoline, injury to the Kurdish goalkeeper, and a ball which ends up in a minefield. It is while buying a new ball in the nearby market that Aso is killed (off-screen) in a totally unanticipated bombing. *Kick Off* is clearly a low-budget production, shot in a mixture of black-and-white and color. Its sentiments are admirable, and the players give spirited performances, but the script has not been worked through sufficiently to give real dramatic impact either to Aso's death or the very real difficulties of his younger brother Diyar, who cannot cope with the loss of his leg in a separate, earlier mine explosion.

Hussein Hasan Ali and **Massoud Arif Salih** were both born in Duhok in Kurdish Iraq, in 1974 and 1973, respectively. Each had considerable experience in Iraqi television when they came together to make their first feature for cinema release, Ali having directed extensively, while Salih had worked as an actor. Salih also had considerable theatre experience. For *Narcissus Blossom / Le temps des narcisses / U nergiz biskvin* (2005), which received French production backing, they served as co-directors and co-scriptwriters, and each played a major acting role in the film. *Narcissus Blossom* is a tale of the struggle of a militant peshmerga group to counteract Saddam Hussein's oppression of the Kurds. Almost all accounts of the film speak of the situation of the fighters rather than the specific action of the film. The synopsis provided at the screening of the film at the 2005 Berlin Film Festival, for example, begins:

> Peshmerga, or "those who face death," is the term used by Kurds for the armed Kurdih forces struggling for an autonomous Kurdistan on the border between Iran and Iraq. The militia was founded in 1976 after the Shah and Saddam Hussein redivided up Kurd territory between them.[213]

Similarly, the filmmakers' most quoted statement describes the situation, not the action of the film:

> While fighting Saddam's dictatorship the peshmerga never lost their hope of attaining freedom. During their struggle, which is their only hope of surviving, they never once deserted their deep-seated conviction that war is no

solution and that the future can only be found through peace and democracy.[214]

Devrim Kilic, however, does make clear the nature of the action:

> Based on a story by Mihemed Mihsan, the film is a political drama, shot from the perspective of a university student, Jeger, who later joins the peshmerga forces due to the increase of state oppression on students in Duhok. Though Jeger joins the peshmerga, his mind is obsessed with his family and his university friends. In reality, he is a person who is against the use of weapons and force. That's why he is deeply affected by the peshmerga life. It is a humanist film that reflects the desire for freedom and peace of Kurds and it idealizes the Kurds' struggle.[215]

Syria

Lack of material, especially access to the films, means that only an outline of developments in Syrian filmmaking can be given here. In the early 2000s, Syria saw the emergence of two young filmmakers with quite varied backgrounds, born in the very early 1960s.

Nidal al-Dibs, who was born in 1960, studied architecture in Damascus before leaving to study film at the VGIK in Moscow. On his return, he worked as assistant to Oussama Mohammad and Abdellatif Abdelhamid and made a number of short films. His sole feature film to date is *Under the Ceiling / Sous le toit / Tahta al-saqf* (2005), produced by the Syrian State Film Organization. The ceiling is that of Marwan's room, in which he has to work out how to proceed when his best friend dies. The widow, Lina, and he were once in love, and now they must decide how they will deal with this new situation.

Khatib El Bassel was born in exile in 1962 in Holland, but followed the Syrian tradition of studying film at the VGIK in Moscow, where he graduated in 1987. Since his return to Syria, he has published a novel, *Dreams of the Sacred Plant,* and translated the autobiographies of Andrei Tarkovsky and Ingmar Bergman. He has also made short films and worked in television. He completed his first feature film, *The Last Message / Le dernier message,* in 2000.

* * *

There was also a small upsurge of filmmaking in 2009, with the release of feature films by two new directors, Hatem Ali and Joud Saeed. These two newcomers—from very different backgrounds—lacked the Moscow film school training that gave such a distinctive feel to earlier Syrian cinema.

Hatem Ali, who was born in 1962, studied theatre in Syria and has published collections of short stories and plays. He has also worked for many years as an actor and director in Syrian television and teaches acting at the Higher Institute of Dramatic Arts in Damascus. His first feature, *The Long Night / La longue nuit / Al-layl al-taweel* (2009), received wide international screenings but was banned in Syria. It was scripted and produced by the television writer-director Haitham Hakki. He has explained that the film is a reflection of a brief moment of hope in Syrian society, when Bashar al-Assad succeeded his father as president in 2000. Bashar began a (short-lived) program of reform, which included the release of a number of political dissidents, some of whom had been imprisoned for twenty years or more. His father Hafez al-Assad's period of rule is one connotation of the title *The Long Night*.

The film has a double focus. First, it considers the prisoners themselves, as Hakki explains:

> There were a lot of promises of reforms when Bashar al-Assad took power. But the program of reforms failed and the Damascus Spring was brought to an end. In this movie, I wanted to show this breaking point, the release of political prisoners after the Damascus Spring.[216]

The second, and perhaps more important, focus of the film is on the families the prisoners left behind. The careers of some of their children have suffered because of their activities—an inability to obtain official recognition or to work on government contracts. Others, in order to survive, have had to make their own compromises with the regime:

> The inspiration of the movie came from the children of prisoners (*awlad al-sujana*) who developed strong ties with members of the regime who had jailed their parents. Because these regime members jailed their former friends and comrades, they felt a form of guilt, so they took care of the prisoners' children, by giving them job opportunities, for instance. . . . Because they had to live, the children of prisoners participated, in one way or another, [in] the corruption, despite the high price their parents had paid in jail.[217]

The film opens with one of Hassan's nightmares (a memory, perhaps?)—he is playing Lear in the storm sequence—and he awakens, confused, in the cell he shares with three other detainees: Kamal, Maje, and Karim (also known as Abu Nidal), their erstwhile leader. The four men talk, prepare breakfast, and read their only source of "news" (the official Baathist newspaper), as on any other day. Then the authorities intervene arbitrarily and in a way the detainees cannot understand. Three are to be released at hourly intervals, restored to their identity as respectable, besuited middle-class citizens. Only the dissident actor Hassan is excluded and left behind. No explanation is offered to the prisoners (or to us, the audience) as to the reasons behind either the timing or the choices made—this is authoritarian rule in operation. The prisoners who emerge are stunned by the world outside—the lights, the traffic, the market, television, and later, for Abu Nidal, the rain.

Meanwhile, for their children, many of whom are now married and have children of their own, the releases come as a total surprise. One response is, of course, simple joy. But there are other sorts of feelings and emotions provoked by this unexpected event as well. Some have concerns about the way they themselves have lived since their parents were imprisoned: a daughter who has married into the ruling elite; a son who has taken over his father's house, not expecting him ever to be released; another son who now lives in exile in Paris with his wife and child and who is troubled at not being there to meet his father.

All are disturbed, as memories of the past resurface and they are brought to question their own actions. Old resentments (but also lost intimacies) come back to the fore. This is particularly true for Abu Nidal's family, since he seems to have vanished after his release. During the long wait, even his chief adversary (once his closest friend) becomes troubled by the past. This night of waiting, of uncertainty, of reawakened tensions, of preparing meals that are not eaten, is the second connotation of the title. It is also a long night for Hassan, who remains in custody, alone now in the cell, and for Kamal, who still awaits release, having refused to sign the papers put before him.

In fact, as his son Kifah eventually realizes, Abu Nidal is not planning to return to Damascus. He has gone back to his roots, to Umm Bdour, and it is there that Kifah finds his body, propped against a tree, next morning. Abu Nidal's funeral not only brings the family together but also allows Kamal, now finally at liberty, to meet for the first time his Parisian granddaughter. The film, however, does not stop at this moment of hope for a new beginning. It ends as it began, with images of Hassan, now alone and delirious with fever, still reciting some of Shakespeare's bleakest verses. *The Long Night* is an utterly assured first feature, showing the depth of Ali's prior professional experience in its pacing, the quality of the acting, and the acuteness of its observations. Though focused on a moment of hope, it rightly emphasizes the difficulties of transition after a long period of single-party authoritarian rule and is as relevant after the 2011 Arab Spring as it was when it was released.

Joud Saeed, who was born in 1980, began by studying engineering, then switched to filmmaking, which he studied at the Université Louis-Lumière in Lyon. He made two short films before completing his first feature. In presenting his first feature at the JCC in 2010, Saeed proclaimed: "I have two languages: Arabic I grew up in, French I learned filmmaking in." Unfortunately, this first feature film, *Once More / Encore une fois / Kara okhra* (2009), is far from being an assured work, since the two halves of the narrative fail to cohere meaningfully. After a brief documentary opening dealing with the Syrian occupation of Lebanon, the film's action begins in 1980, with Syrian troops responding to Israeli pressure.

A general's wife is killed in an assassination attempt aimed at him, and his young son Majed is largely brought up on the military base. There, as a child, he suffers a self-inflicted gunshot wound, which causes him to lose his memory. After his father's death, Majed is adopted and given a foreign education by an ex-colleague of his father, now a wealthy businessman. At this point, the action shifts abruptly to 2006. Majed now has a post as IT manager in a Syrian bank, which appoints its first Lebanese manager, an attractive young woman, Joyce. The two are drawn together, but the relationship ends abruptly when Joyce discovers (from Majed's badly treated ex-girlfriend) that he has been using his computer skills to spy on her private conversations with her family. But when Joyce's mother and daughter are trapped amid renewed violence in Beirut, Majed—with his social and military connections—is the only person to whom she can turn. He duly facilitates a successful border crossing. *Once More* is a curiously flawed work. Though produced by the state organization, its early scenes do not depict the Syrian army in a positive light and the later ones show wealthy Syrians enjoying an exceedingly affluent lifestyle in a context in which the most modern information technology is ready to hand for them, while so many others are living in poverty.

* * *

An outsider to Syrian cinema is **Ruba Nadda**, who was born in 1972 in Montreal to a Syrian father and Palestinian mother. She studied literature at York University in Toronto and film at New York University. She made numerous short films in the late 1990s and turned to feature filmmaking with *I Always Come to You* (2000) and *Unsettled* (2001). She first received international attention in 2005 with *Sabah,* which deals with a partially assimilated Syrian family, settled in Canada. After the death of his father, Majid tries to maintain a totally traditional Muslim family. His sisters all wear the *hijab,* Arabic continues to be one of the languages spoken at home, and Canadians are referred to as "foreigners." It is assumed that the oldest daughter, forty-year-old Sabah, will have no life of her own but will simply care for her mother. During illicit visits to a swimming pool, however, she meets and falls in love with a native Canadian, Stephen, who is not only divorced but an atheist. The hesitancies in the blossoming relationship are well realized, the key moment of commitment being, of course, when she first removes the *hijab* to uncover her hair.

The revelation of the affair—seen as altogether shameful by Majid—initially threatens the unity of the family. But the tone of light romantic comedy is maintained. Mutual respect and tolerance prevail, and so the film can end with the women—mother, daughters, niece, and daughter-in-law—dancing together. Perhaps the best scenes are those involving the niece Souheire, whose response to an arranged marriage shows how far she has put her traditional Muslim past behind her: "I don't care if he's Prince Fucking Charming. I want to have a choice!" At the formal first family meeting of the betrothed couple, she appears in a burka, refuses to shake hands or listen to music, announces she wants eight children, and leaves the gathering ostensibly to pray. Later, she discovers that actually he is an attractive guy, who shares her taste for disco partying.

Nadda's subsequent feature, *Cairo Time* (2009), traces a parallel trajectory, the discovery of Egypt—and the unexpected possibility of romance—by a Canadian wife intending to rejoin her husband, a UN official working in Gaza. He is detained there, and she is introduced to Cairo by his former colleague, Tareq. Nadda's continued exploration of the emotions of mature women and her tracing of the tentative gestures of cross-cultural relationships are admirable, but *Cairo Time* cannot be considered as in any way an Arab film. It rightly won the award for Best Canadian Feature Film at the 2009 Toronto International Film Festival.

The Gulf

Apart from the trio of pioneering Kuwaiti films made by Khalid al-Siddick in the 1970s and early 1980s, his compatriot Hashim Muhammad's sole feature, *The Silence* (1979), and Bassam al-Thawadi's isolated Bahraini feature, *The Obstacle* (1988), virtually all the Gulf's three dozen or so feature films have been made since the mid-2000s. Most are debut works, some showing, it would seem, real promise. Many of these filmmakers have been educated abroad, and several of them belong by age to the generation with which this study is concerned. But their work is largely unavailable in the West, and there seems to be no distribution point in the Gulf itself. Two filmmakers who do show possible paths for the future development of Gulf feature filmmaking are the Yemeni director Bader Ben Hirsi and the Saudi female filmmaker Haifaa al-Mansour.

Bader Ben Hirsi was born in London in 1968 to exiled Yemeni parents. He studied media production at Goldsmiths, University of London, and continues to live and work in England. His first feature-length work is a video documentary, *The English Sheikh and the Yemeni Gentleman / Le cheikh anglais et le gentleman yéménite* (2000), an engaging chronicle of his exploration of his country of origin in the company of the eccentric English traveler Tim Mackintosh-Smith, who admits that his own book, *Yemen: Travels in Dictionary Land,* "treads the fine line between seriousness and frivolity."[218] Beautifully shot by the cinematographer-turned–film director Koutaïba al-Janabi, the film begins with a quotation from the Yemeni writer and poet Abdullah al-Baradouni in 1995: "Our land is the dictionary of our people—this land of far horizons where the graves of our ancestors sleep, this earth trodden by processions of sons and sons of sons." The theme of tradition is continually stressed in the film, with a retreat from modernity seen as integral to Yemeni identity.

At the opening of the film, Ben Hirsi introduces the very different backgrounds of the two key figures. He himself was born in London, son of an exiled

Yemeni general and the youngest of fourteen children. He still lives in London and has previously made one rather disappointing visit to Yemen. He wants to use the present opportunity to counter the media image of Yemen as a place of violence and terrorism. Indeed, there is no mention of politics in the film, and Aden is depicted not in terms of its colonial past but as an example of the impact of modern life on Yemen. Mackintosh-Smith is the perfect companion for Ben Hirsi. He too has no interest in politics but is totally involved in everyday life in Sana'a, where he has lived since leaving the university fifteen years ago. Although he remains a Christian, he speaks fluent Arabic and relishes the local food and the habit of constantly chewing qat.

The film's narrative is simple, following the pair's explorations of the capital, Sana'a, and their journey across the country, including visits to the birthplaces (a hundred miles apart) of each of Ben Hirsi's parents. This trajectory is loosely structured by a succession of titles describing certain Arab concepts: al-Muhajir (the immigrant), al-Baraka (blessing), al-Dhia (light), al-Atal (ruins), and al-Howas (madness or possession). The contrast between the two men adds to the liveliness of the film. Mackintosh-Smith is open, outgoing, and at ease through-out, whereas Ben Hirsi is more hesitant, even though this is *his* country. He re-fuses to chew qat, declines to taste the national dish, and distances himself from local parties and dance ceremonies by hiding behind his own little video camera. By the end of the film, however, he has been totally won over by Yemen (though more entranced by the mountains than by Sana'a) and even appears in traditional dress, complete with curved sword, for the film's final images. The film itself is a perfect introduction to the country once known (appropriately, it seems) as Ara-bia Felix and to the Yemeni people, described as being like watermelons, tough-skinned on the outside "but soft and melting when you get inside."

After work for British television, Ben Hirsi made his first fictional feature, *A New Day in Old Sana'a / Un jour nouveau dans le vieux Sana'a* (2005). This is a tale of everyday Yemeni life, written by Ben Hirsi himself and told obliquely, using an Italian photographer, Federico, as its (English-speaking) narrator. Set in the picturesque old capital of Sana'a, it is a tale of passion and misunderstand-ing, setting the power of love against the force of tradition. Federico's assistant Tariq falls passionately in love with his upper-class fiancée Bliquis (whom he has never met) when he sees her—unbelievably—wearing the dress he has bought her and dancing bareheaded in the street after dark. He is quite unable to cope with the unexpected impact of love, but to make things worse, he is mistaken. The woman who has captured his heart is in fact Inès, a humble girl without a family who works as a *managasher,* applying the local variant of henna to other women, especially to brides. Tariq's carefully chosen dress, which Inès is briefly accused of stealing, has in fact been thrown out of the window by Bliquis, as "only fit for a Bedouin."

The film captures well both the women's world of gossip and emotion, jealousy and intrigue, and the emotional immaturity of a young man like Tariq. Ben Hirsi constructs a deftly shaped, lighthearted narrative, broken up by snatches of questioning voice-over by a narrator intrigued by his discoveries of an unknown culture and enlivened by musical interludes. Inevitably, tradition wins out at the end, as Tariq listens to reason and returns to his chosen fiancée. The disappointed Inès, we are told, returns every night to wait at the bridge which was to have been their rendezvous for the start of a new life together.

Much of the joy of Ben Hirsi's films lies in the way he conveys his own sense of the pleasurable discovery of his roots. He is an outsider to this society yet totally involved in exploring it, since it is so meaningful to him.

By contrast, **Haifaa al-Mansour**, the first Saudi woman to direct a feature film in Saudi Arabia, is very much an insider, born and raised near Riyadh, in a family comprising twelve children. At the same time, however, she too, as a woman, is in many ways an outsider in this patriarchal society in which women are not allowed to drive a car and certainly not expected to direct a film using a largely male German crew. While shooting the location scenes, al-Mansour was not allowed to mix with her crew on the streets but had to direct from the back of a van. Her father, who has supported her film ambitions from the start, is the poet Abdul Rahman Mansour. She also received encouragement (and some financial support) from the Saudi prince Al-Waleed bin Talal, so this was far from a guerrilla production, although its making provoked real hostility. Born in 1974, al-Mansour began by completing a BA in comparative literature at the American University in Cairo, followed by a master's degree in filmmaking at the University of Sydney. She started making her own films in the early 2000s, with three prize-winning shorts and then a forty-five-minute documentary on the situation of women in the Gulf, *Women without Shadows / Femmes sans ombre* (2005).

Wadjda (2012), which is set in Riyadh, tells parallel stories, foregrounding that of a feisty little eleven-year-old girl, Wadjda, and using that of her mother as a constant backdrop. In a society in which male heirs are crucial to a man's self-esteem, the mother's fate is sealed. She cannot bear additional children, and so her husband is set on marrying a second, younger wife, who may be able to give him the son he desires. The mother initially dreams of thwarting her husband's move, even planning to buy a glamorous, expensive red dress in hopes of winning him back. Wadjda—the only girl to go to her class wearing sneakers, though otherwise clad, like the rest, from head to toe in her black *abaya*—one day sees a green bicycle. It's a magical sight, as it seems to be flying through the air (it's on top of a truck that's hidden by an intervening wall). The bicycle becomes her obsession, even though she is told that little girls don't ride bikes and that if they did they wouldn't be able to have children.

Although she tries various little schemes to raise the 800 rials, which the bicycle costs, she has no hope until the school announces a Koran reading competition for which the prize is 1,000 rials. Wadjda devotes herself wholly to this unexpected challenge, but when she wins and proclaims to her classmates that she will now be able to buy her bicycle, she is abruptly told that this is impossible: the money will go to the Palestinian cause. But all is not lost. Realizing that there is no hope of winning back her husband and that Wadjda is now all that she has in the world, the mother spends her money on the bicycle instead of the red dress. The film has its second magical moment when she unveils this to Wadjda, who is now able to achieve her other ambition, that of racing against her friend Abdallah and actually beating him.

Although the film is never stridently assertive or political, it paints a disturbing picture of the position of women in Saudi society. Powerless, they are excluded from family gatherings at home, and when they emerge outside, they are hampered by their long black robes and bullied by the chauffeurs they have to employ. They are constantly fearful that their daughters will "get into trouble" (which might involve no more than talking to a boy). Worse still, perhaps, this regime is reinforced by other women, such as Wadjda's teacher, who schools the girls in submission and denies them any sort of freedom or self-expression. Yet the overall message of the film is positive, thanks to the drive of its young heroine, whose ambition matches that of the director herself in making the film. Both look to the future. This is filmmaking at the highest level, full of nice visual touches, drawing striking performances from its two lead players, and offering a well-structured narrative line. It places Haifaa al-Mansour firmly alongside her female contemporaries in the Maghreb and Lebanon who, thanks to their time spent abroad and the freedoms offered by foreign co-production, tell stories and display attitudes inconceivable to an earlier generation.

Notes

Introduction

1. Wissam Mouawad, "Petite réflexion sur le néo-orientalisme," *Cahiers de l'Orient* 106 (2012): 99–104.
2. Moussa Sene Abso, cited in Roy Armes, *African Filmmaking: North and South of the Sahara* (Edinburgh: Edinburgh University Press; Bloomington: Indiana University Press, 2006), p. 143.
3. Danielle Arbid, interview with Ali Jaafar, www.bidoun.org (n.d.).
4. Annemarie Jacir, interview with Geoffrey Macnab, *The Independent* (London), April 2, 2013, p. 39.
5. Elia Suleiman, interview with Sabah Haider, www.electronicintifada.net.
6. Djamila Sahraoui, interview with Marion Pasquier, www.critikat.com (March 23, 2013).

1. Characteristics of the New Cinema

1. For a chronology of all Egyptian films between 1923 and 2007, see Roy Armes, *Dictionary of African Filmmakers* (Bloomington: Indiana University Press, 2008), pp. 151–211.
2. Denise Brahimi, *50 ans de cinéma maghrébin* (Paris: Minerve, 2009), p. 11.
3. Hélé Béji, *Le désenchantement national: Essai sur la décolonisation* (Paris: François Maspero / Cahiers Libres, 1982).
4. Dalia Fathallah, statement of intent for *Beirut Cowboy*.
5. Kevin Dwyer, "Un pays, une décennie, deux comédies," in Michel Serceau, ed., *Cinémas du Maghreb*, special issue, *CinémAction* 111 (2004): 86–91.
6. Brahimi, *50 ans de cinéma maghrébin*, pp. 18–19.
7. Ibid., p. 15.
8. Patricia Kubala, "The Music Video and Muslim Piety: Satellite Television and Islamic Pop Culture in Egypt," in Samir and Roseanne Saad Khalaf, eds., *Arab Society and Culture* (London: Saqi, 2009), p. 471.
9. Ibid.
10. Martin Dale, *The Movie Game* (London: Cassell, 1997), p. 187.

2. The Filmmakers

1. Nouri Bouzid, "New Realism in Arab Cinema: The Defeat-Conscious Cinema," *Alif* 15 (1995): 242–250.
2. Nadia El Fani, interview, in Rebecca Hillauer, *Encyclopedia of Arab Women Filmmakers* (Cairo: American University in Cairo Press, 2005), p. 292.
3. See Roy Armes, "Women Pioneers of Arab Cinema," *Screen* 48, no. 4 (Winter 2007): 517–520.

4. Omar al-Qattan, "The Challenges of Palestinian Filmmaking (1990–2003)," in Hamid Dabashi, ed., *Dreams of a Nation: On Palestinian Cinema* (London: Verso, 2006), pp. 110–111.

5. Ibid., p. 111.

6. Elia Suleiman, "Filming Notes," in the pressbook for *Divine Intervention*.

7. Hélène Schoumann, *Dictionnaire du cinéma israélien* (Paris: Cosmopole, 2012), p. 165.

8. Raphaël Nadjari, *Une histoire du cinéma israélien* (ARTE Éditions, 2009).

9. Nizar Hassan, "A Letter from the Rest of the World to 'The Afghan Arabs,'" in Dabashi, *Dreams of a Nation*, pp. 104–109.

10. Ella Shohat, *Israeli Cinema: East/West and the Politics of Representation*, 2nd ed. (London: I. B. Tauris, 2010), p. 273.

11. Nabil Ayouch, in the pressbook for *Whatever Lola Wants*.

12. For an account of how this package was put together, see the account by the producers, Jacques Bidou and Marianne Dumoulin, "Sur les routes de Palestine" (April 2008), in the pressbook for *Le sel de la mer* prepared for the Cannes Festival.

13. Dima El-Horr, interview, www.indiewire.com (September 1, 2009).

14. Nadia El Fani, interview, in Hillauer, *Encyclopedia of Arab Women Filmmakers*, p. 391.

15. Malek Bensmaïl, interview with Baptiste Etchegaray, in the pressbook for *La Chine est encore loin*.

16. Jilani Saadi, interview, www.africine.ora (October 30, 2007).

17. Ibrahim El Batout, interview with Vincenzo Mattei, "Another Way of Shooting," www.vicenzomattei.com.

18. Cited in www.ahmadabdalla.net.

19. Ibid.

20. Laïla Marrakchi, comments, in the pressbook for *Marock*.

3. Documentary

1. Jim Lane, *The Autobiographical Documentary in America* (Madison: University of Wisconsin Press, 2002), p. 23.

2. Ibid.

3. Nurith Gertz and George Khleifi, *Palestinian Cinema: Landscape, Trauma and Memory* (Edinburgh: Edinburgh University Press, 2008), p. 196.

4. Quoted in *The Guardian* (London), April 5, 2011, p. 14.

5. Maryse Gargour, interview, www.menassett.com (July 17, 2008).

6. On this point, see Shlomo Sand, *The Invention of the Jewish People* (London: Verso, 2009).

7. Gertz and Khleifi, *Palestinian Cinema*, p. 49.

8. Ibid., p. 50.

9. Ibid., p. 51.

10. Dahna Abourahme, interview with Almany al-Sayyed, http://electronicintifada.net (November 25, 2010).

11. Rania Jawad, "Narrating the Past, Confronting the Present," www.jadaliyya.com (March 28, 2011).

12. Jeremy Hardy, in the pressbook for *Jeremy Hardy versus the Israeli Army*.

13. Leila Sansour, in ibid.

14. Sobhi al-Zobaïdi, quoted in Gertz and Khleifi, *Palestinian Cinema*, p. 135.

15. Khaled Jarrar, interview with Alistair George, www.palsolidarity.org (November 21, 2011).

16. Ibid.

17. Raed Andoni, interview, in the pressbook for *Fix Me*.

18. Ibid.

19. Ibid.

20. See, for example, Laila Hotait, "Itinéraire des cinéastes libanais de l'après-guerre: Le parcours d'une reconstruction," in Nicolas Puig and Franck Mermier, eds., *Itinéraires esthétiques et scènes culturelles au Proche Orient* (Beirut: Presses de l'Ifpo, 2007), pp. 204–219.

21. Dalia Fathallah, comment, in the publicity material for *Beirut Cowboy* (echoing her commentary in the film).

22. Simon El Habre, "The Making Of," included on the film's DVD.

23. Akram Zaatari, interview with Laura Ghaninejad and Jérémy Gravayat, www.derives .tv (Summer 2009).

24. Ibid.

25. "Akram Zaatari: *This Day*," www.saic.edu/cate (October 19, 2006).

26. "New York Premiere—*This Day* Akram Zaatari," www.veralistcenter.org (January 22, 2005).

27. Akram Zaatari, interview with Nina Siegal, www.nytimes.com (June 19, 2013).

28. Akram Zaatari, *A Conversation with an Imagined Israeli Filmmaker Named Avi Mograbi* (Aubervilliers: Laboratoires d'Aubervilliers; Paris: Kadist Art Foundation; Berlin: Sternberg Press, 2012).

29. Ella Shohat, *Israeli Cinema: East/West and the Politics of Representation*, 2nd ed. (London: I. B. Tauris, 2010), p. 285.

30. Review of *We Were Communists*, www.labiennale.org (September 2010).

31. Maher Abi Samra, interview with Laila Hotait Salas, www.nisimazine.eu (n.d.).

32. Ibid.

33. Nadia Kamel, "Director's Statement," www.wmm.com.

34. The calculation is by Joseph Massad, www.ahram.org.eg.

35. Hanan Abdalla, interview, www.unwomen.org (United Nations Entity for Gender Equality and the Empowerment of Women).

36. Gérard Collas, notes accompanying the DVD set of Bensmaïl's documentaries.

37. Malek Bensmaïl, statement of intent, in the pressbook for *La Chine est encore loin*.

38. Malek Bensmaïl, interview with Baptiste Etchegaray, in the pressbook for *La Chine est encore loin*.

39. "Z'har (Un)Lucky," www.dubaifilmfest.com (2009).

40. Beti Ellerson, "Fatma-Zohra Zamoun: Z'har/(Un)Lucky," www.africanwomenin cinema.blogspot.co.yuk (April 26, 2011).

41. Fadwa Miadi, "Morocco: An Interview with a Very Independent Director," www .babelmed.net (July 5, 2010).

42. Ibid.

43. All quotations in the discussion of *Iraq: The Song of the Missing Men* are from Layth Abdulamir, pressbook for *Irak, le chant des absents*.

44. Synopsis, www.idfa.niL (November 2010).

45. Hala al-Abdallah, pressbook for *Hey! Don't Forget the Cumin*.

46. Sarah Kane, cited in http://en.wikipedia.org.

4. Feature Filmmaking

1. Hamid Naficy, *An Accented Cinema: Exilic and Diasporic Filmmaking* (Princeton, NJ: Princeton University Press, 2001).

2. René Prédal, *Le jeune cinéma français* (Paris: Nathan, 2002), p. 136.

3. Ibid., pp. 116–117.

4. Ibid., pp. 138–139.

5. www.abusdecine.com (n.d.).

6. Nadir Moknèche, interview with Bernard Stora, in the pressbook for *Viva Laldjérie,* p. 12.

7. For a detailed analysis of *Madame Osmane's Harem* and *Viva Laldjérie,* see Hakim Abderrezak, "The Modern Harem in Moknèche's *Le Harem de Mme Ousmane* and *Viva Laldjérie,*" in Andrea Khalil, ed., *North African Cinema in a Global Context: Through the Lens of the Diaspora* (London: Routledge, 2008), pp. 71–92.

8. Moknèche, Stora interview.

9. Karin Albou, "Note d'intention," included with the DVD of *La petite Jérusalem.*

10. Ibid.

11. Karin Albou, interview, in www.aviva (April 2011).

12. Yamina Bachir-Chouikh, interview included with the DVD of *Rachida.*

13. Djamila Sahraoui, interview with Marion Pasquier, www.critikat.com (March 23, 2013).

14. Ibid.

15. Nadia Cherabi-Labidi, interview with Gudula Meinzolt, in Rebecca Hillauer, *Encyclopedia of Arab Women Filmmakers* (Cairo: American University in Cairo Press, 2005), p. 301.

16. Nadia Cherabi-Labidi, interview with Raffaele Cattedra and Christiane Passevant, www.divergences.be (July 13, 2008).

17. Ibid.

18. Christiane Passevant, "Le cinéma algérien des femmes," www.chroniques-rebelles.info (September 11, 2008).

19. Kamal Dehane, interview with Jean-Michel Vlaeminckx, "Kamal Dehane à propos du film *Les suspects,*" www.cinergie.be (January 1, 2005).

20. Ibid.

21. Ibid.

22. "*Les suspects,*" www.clapnoir.org (2005).

23. Olivier Barlet, "*Les suspects* de Kamal Dehane," www.africultures.com (November 19, 2004).

24. Rabah Ameur-Zaïmèche, in the pressbook for *Wesh Wesh.*

25. Ibid.

26. All quotations in this paragraph are from an interview with Rabah Ameur-Zaïmèche by Audrey Jeamart, www.critikat.com (June 7, 2006).

27. All quotations in this paragraph from an interview with Rabah Ameur-Zaïmèche by Marion Pasquier, www.critikat.com (October 21, 2008).

28. Ibid.

29. Rabah Ameur-Zaïmèche, interview with Raphaël Clairefond, www.vodkaster.com (January 2012).

30. Lyes Salem, quoted by Jordan Elgrably, "Lyes Salem's Debut, *Masquerades,* Gently Ribs Algeria," www.levantinecenter.org (2001–2002).

31. Abdelhaï Laraki, www.africultures.com (February 9, 2007).

32. For a detailed analysis of the film, see Roy Armes, *Postcolonial Images: Studies in North African Film* (Bloomington: Indiana University Press, 2005), pp. 169–177.

33. Nabil Ayouch, "Notes de production," in the pressbook for *Whatever Lola Wants.*

34. Nabil Ayouch, interview with Frédéric Strauss, www.télérama.fr (March 2013).

35. Nabil Ayouch, interview with François Aubel, www.lefigaro.fr (February 2013).

36. Ayouch, Strauss interview.

37. Nabil Ben Yadir, interview, in the pressbook for *La marche.*

38. Toumi Djaidja, interview, in the pressbook for *La marche.*

39. Nour-Eddine Lakhmari, interview with Mahmoud Jemni, www.africine.org (February 2, 2010).

40. www.premiere.fr.

41. Ismaïl Ferroukhi, interview, www.monstersandcritics.com (September 22, 2005).

42. Ibid.

43. Benjamin Stora, interview, in the pressbook for *Les hommes libres.*

44. Ismaïl Ferroukhi, interview, in the pressbook for *Les hommes libres.*

45. Faouzi Bensaïdi, unsourced interview, quoted in the National Film Theatre program, London, July 2004.

46. Faouzi Bensaïdi, interview, www.africultures.com (May 2003).

47. For a detailed analysis of Bensaïdi's *A Thousand Months,* see Armes, *Postcolonial Images,* pp. 183–190.

48. Faouzi Bensaïdi, interview, in the pressbook for *WWW.*

49. Faouzi Bensaïdi, interview, www.filmlinc.com. (n.d.).

50. Faouzi Bensaïdi, interview, "J'ai toujours eu cette noirceur en moi," www.telquel-online.com (February 28, 2012).

51. Bensaïdi, filmlinc interview.

52. Ibid.

53. Denise Brahimi, *50 ans de cinéma maghrébin* (Paris: Minerve, 2009), p. 50.

54. Laïla Marrakchi, comments, in the pressbook for *Marock.*

55. Ibid.

56. Brian T. Edwards, "*Marock* in Morocco: Reading Moroccan Films in the Age of Circulation," in Khalil, *North African Cinema,* p. 22.

57. Marrakchi, in the pressbook for *Marock.*

58. Edwards, "*Marock* in Morocco," pp. 12–13.

59. Ibid., p. 28.

60. Leila Kilani, interview with Clarisse Fabre, *Le Monde,* January 31, 2012.

61. Leila Kilani, interview with Olivier Barlet, www.africultures.com (August 2003).

62. Leila Kilani, interview with Noura Borsali, www.africine.org (April 4, 2009).

63. Olivier Barlet, "Nos lieux interdits," www.africultures.com (November 26, 2008).

64. Kilani, Fabre interview.

65. Kilani, Barlet interview.

66. Khalid Ghorbal, statement of intent, in the pressbook for *Fatma.*

67. Ferid Boughedir, "Les principales tendances du cinéma tunisien," in Mouny Berrah, Victor Bachy, Mohand Ben Salah, and Ferid Boughedir, eds., *Cinémas du Maghreb,* special issue, *CinémAction* 14 (1981): 160.

68. Nawfel Saheb-Ettaba, statement of intent, in the pressbook for *The Bookstore.*

69. Olivier Barlet, review of *Par-delà les rivières,* www.africultures.com (August 15, 2007).

70. Ibrahim Letaief, "Note du réalisateur," www.africiine.org (n.d.).

71. Nicolas Krief, review of *L'esquive,* www.panorama-cinema.com (n.d.).

72. Abdellatif Kechiche, interview with Auréliano Tonet, in the booklet accompanying the DVD of *Vénus noire.*

73. Abdellatif Kechiche, interview, in the pressbook for *La vie d'Adèle chapitres 1 et 2.*

74. Mehdi Ben Attia, interview with Cécile Guthleben and Florence Lemaire, www.123people.fr (n.d.).

75. Ibid.

76. Mehdi Ben Attia, interview with Marie-Elizabeth Rouchy, in the pressbook for *Je ne suis pas mort.*

77. Ibid.

78. *"Hiya wa howa,"* www.tunisia-today (April 29, 2004).

79. Synopsis of *Wailing Wall,* published by the International Film Festival Madrid, May 2011.

80. For a detailed analysis of Amari's *Red Satin,* see Armes, *Postcolonial Images,* pp. 176–182.

81. Raja Amari, interview, www.indiewire (2004).

82. Raja Amari, interview, in the pressbook for *Satin rouge.*

83. Annette Koback, *Isabelle: The Life of Isabelle Eberhardt* (London: Chatto and Windus, 1988), p. 245.

84. For a fuller analysis of the film, see Josef Gugler, *"Bedwin Hacker* (Nadia El Fani): A Hacker Challenges Western Domination of the Global Media," in Josef Gugler, ed., *Film in the Middle East and North Africa* (Austin: University of Texas Press, 2011), pp. 284–293.

85. Quoted by Christiane Passevant, www.divergences2 (March 21, 2013).

86. For a chronological listing of all Egyptian features from 1923 to 2007, see Roy Armes, *Dictionary of African Filmmakers* (Bloomington: Indiana University Press, 2008), pp. 151–212.

87. Ferid Boughedir, quoted in Alberto Elena, ed., *Las mil y una imágenes de cine marroqui* (Las Palmas: Festival Internacional de Cine de las Palmas de Gran Canaria; Madrid: T&B Editores, 2007), p. 326.

88. Khaled El Hagar, interview with Omar Kholeif, www.filmint.nu.

89. Khaled El Hagar, "Note d'intention," in the pressbook for *Room to Rent.*

90. Ibid.

91. Ogova Ondego, "New York Diaspora Film Festival Honours Egyptian Film Director Khaled El Hagar," www.artmatters.info (November 22, 2009).

92. Ibid.

93. See Wael Eskandar, "Kill the Director," www.theatrereviewmagazine.blogspot.co.uk (June 15, 2012).

94. Khaled El Hagar, interview, www.doharfilminstitute.com (October 11, 2011).

95. Atef Hetata, interview with Olivier Barlet, www.spot.pcc.edu (July 2000).

96. Aaron Mushengyezi, "Problematizing a 'Fundamentalist' Ideology: A Close Analysis of Atef Hetata's *The Closed Doors* and Phil Mullally's *The Martyrs of Uganda," Journal of African Cinemas* 1, no. 2 (2009): 187.

97. Chale Nafus, *"Closed Doors (Al-abwab al-moghlaka),"* www.austinfilm.org (n.d.).

98. All quotations from Ibrahim El Batout are from the interview with Olivier Barlet, "Je ne vois aucun changement en Égypte," in Patricia Caillé and Florence Martin, eds., *Les cinémas du Maghreb et leurs publics,* Africultures 89–90 (Paris: L'Harmattan, 2012), pp. 288–289.

99. Ibrahim El Batout, www.wikipedia.org.

100. Ibid.

101. Plot summary, www.euromedincultue.org.

102. Ahmad Abdalla, interview with Olivier Barlet, "Le chemin devant nous est bien long," in Caillé and Martin, *Les cinémas du Maghreb,* p. 305.

103. Ibid.

104. Plot summary, described in www.en.wikipedia.org.

105. Abdalla, Barlet interview, p. 307.

106. Ahmad Abdalla, unsourced interview contained in program material at the November 2013 screenings at the NFT in London.

107. Ibid.

108. Ibid.

109. Mohammad Mirbashiri, review of *Microphone*, www.arabbritish centre.org.uk.

110. Ahmed Rashwan, www.dreamprodeg.com.

111. Maggie Morgan, cited in www.africultures.com.

112. Lina Khatib, *Lebanese Cinema: Imagining the Civil War and Beyond* (London: I. B. Tauris, 2008), p. 31.

113. Bahij Hojeij, quoted in Khatib, *Lebanese Cinema*, p. xxii.

114. Philippe Aractingi, quoted in Khatib, *Lebanese Cinema*, p. xxii.

115. Jean-Claude Codsi, quoted in Khatib, *Lebanese Cinema*, p. xxiii.

116. Randa Chahal, quoted in Khatib, *Lebanese Cinema*, p. xxiii.

117. Bahij Hojeij, quoted in Khatib, *Lebanese Cinema*, p. 173.

118. Ibid.

119. Ibid.

120. For a detailed analysis of the film, see Mona Deeley, "*Beyrouth al gharbiyya / West Beirut*," in Gönül Dönmetz-Colin, ed., *The Cinema of North Africa and the Middle East* (London: Wallflower Press, 2007), pp. 191–210.

121. Khatib, *Lebanese Cinema*, p. xv.

122. Ziad Doueiri, interview with Christine Spines, www.wordandfilm.com (June 19, 2013).

123. Ibid.

124. Samir Habchi, quoted in Hady Zaccak, *Le cinéma libanais* (Beirut: Dar al-Mashreq, 1997), p. 162.

125. Khatib, *Lebanese Cinema*, p. 44.

126. Zaccak, *Le cinéma libanais*, p. 161.

127. Information derived from an interview with Claire Vassé, included on the French DVD.

128. Michel Kammoun, interview with Gaillac-Morgue, in the pressbook for *Falafel*.

129. All quotations from Chadi Zeneddine, www.fallingfromearth.com.

130. Georges Hachem, interview with Virginia Di Marco, "Lebanon Can Generate Peace or War," www.ansamed.info (March 19, 2013).

131. Georges Hachem, interview with Rsassa Taycheh, www.cinemovies.fr (November 23, 2011).

132. Thomas Messiah, review of *Balle perdue*, www.artistikrezo.com (November 23, 2011).

133. Assad Foulakar, interview with Lina Khatib, in Khatib, *Lebanese Cinema*, p. 38.

134. Nadine Labaki, interview, in the pressbook for *Caramel*.

135. Ibid.

136. Nadine Labaki, interview, in the pressbook for *Et maintenant on va où?*

137. Ibid.

138. Danielle Arbid, cover notes to the DVD of her two features.

139. Danielle Arbid, interview with Thierry Méranger, included on the DVD of the two documentaries.

140. Ibid.

141. Arbid, cover notes.

142. Arbid, Méranger interview.

143. Danielle Arbid, interview with Ali Jaafar, www.bidoun.org (n.d.).

144. Danielle Arbid, interview, www.universcine.com (n.d.).

145. Khatib, *Lebanese Cinema*, p. xx.

146. Danielle Arbid, quoted in Khatib, *Lebanese Cinema*, p. xx.

147. Ibid.

148. Ibid.

149. Ibid.

150. Danielle Arbid, interview with Natalie Shorter, www.timeoutbeirut.com (January 12, 2012).

151. Ibid.

152. Danielle Arbid, interview with Sabine Lange and Laure Siegel, www.mondearabe.arte.tv (January 20, 2012).

153. Arbid, Shorter interview.

154. Ibid.

155. Dima El-Horr, interview, www.indie.com (March 23, 2010).

156. Lara Saba, interview with Nohad Topalian, www.al-shorfa.com (October 13, 2012).

157. Sabine El Gemayel, interview with Bijan Tehrani, "*Niloofar*, a Different Look at Honor Killing," www.cinemawithoutborders.com (January 23, 2009).

158. Ibid.

159. Maï Masri, "Transcending Boundaries," www.thisweekinpalestine.com.

160. All quotes from www.jpost.com/ArtsandCulture (October 3, 2010).

161. Nurith Gertz and George Khleifi, *Palestinian Cinema: Landscape, Trauma and Memory* (Edinburgh: Edinburgh University Press, 2008), p. 197.

162. Rashid Masharawi, interview with Fareed Armaly, www.fareedarmaly.net (April 2002).

163. Gertz and Khleifi, *Palestinian Cinema*, p. 101.

164. Jenny Gheith, "*Curfew*," www.electronic intifada.net (May 1, 2005).

165. Gertz and Khleifi, *Palestinian Cinema*, p. 104

166. Ibid., p. 116.

167. Masharawi, Armaly interview.

168. Ali Abunimah, review of *Waiting*, www.electronicintifada.net (May 8, 2006).

169. Elia Suleiman, interview, quoted in Hamid Dabashi, ed., *Dreams of a Nation: On Palestinian Cinema* (London: Verso, 2006), p. 149.

170. Elia Suleiman, interview with Jason Wood, www.kamera.co.uk (2004).

171. Suleiman, Dabashi interview, pp. 149–150.

172. Ibid., p. 156.

173. For a detailed, Freudian-inspired analysis of the film, see Haim Bresheeth, "*Segell Ikhtifa / Chronicle of a Disappearance*," in *The Cinema of North Africa and the Middle East*, ed. Gönül Dönmez-Colin (London: Wallflower Press, 2007), pp. 169–178.

174. Suleiman, Wood interview.

175. Ibid.

176. Elia Suleiman, presentation of the film at the BFI 53rd London Film Festival in 2009.

177. Elia Suleiman, interview with Steve Rose, www.guardian.co.uk (June 15, 2010).

178. Elia Suleiman, quoted in Kamal Abdel-Malik, *The Rhetoric of Violence: Arab-Jewish Encounters in Contemporary Palestinian Literature and Film* (New York: Palgrave Macmillan, 2005), p. 134.

179. Einat Fischbein, quoted in Gertz and Khleifi, *Palestinian Cinema*, p. 48.

180. Gertz and Khleifi, *Palestinian Cinema*, p. 49.

181. Hany Abu Assad, quoted in Gertz and Khleifi, *Palestinian Cinema*, p. 49.

182. Abu Wael, interview, in the pressbook for *Thirst*.

183. Ibid.

184. Ibid.

185. Gertz & Khleifi, *Palestinian Cinema*, p. 198.

186. Wael, pressbook interview.

187. Ibid.

188. www.palestinefilm.org/resources.

189. All quotations in the following three paragraphs are taken from the joint interview in the pressbook for *Ajami*.

190. Alissa Simon, www.variety.com (December 15, 2011).

191. Najwa Najjar, www.palestinefilm.org.

192. Annemarie Jacir, director's note, www.mecfilm.de.

193. Ibid.

194. Annemarie Jacir, interview with Alain Gresh, in the pressbook for *Le sel de la mer*.

195. Annemarie Jacir, "Romancing the Naksa Narrative," interview with Rasha Hilwi, www.al-akhbar.com (October 10, 2012).

196. Ibid.

197. Annemarie Jacir, interview with Geoffrey Macnab, *The Independent*, April 2, 2013, p. 39.

198. Michael Archer, interview with Cherien Dabis, www.guernicamag.com (September 2009).

199. Cherien Dabis, ibid.

200. Layth Abdulamir, in the pressbook for *Irak, le chant des absents*.

201. Abbas Fahdel, interview, in the pressbook for *L'aube du monde*.

202. Ibid.

203. Hiner Saleem, interview, included on the DVD of *Si tu meurs, je te tue*.

204. See "Jano Rosebiani," www.en.wikipedia.org.

205. David Lipfert, "The Walking Wounded," www.offoffoff.com (June 13, 2003).

206. Jaap Mees, "*Life (Jiyan)*," www.talkingpix.co.uk (June 18, 2010).

207. Mohamed al-Daradji, interview with Amber Wilkinson, www.eyefor film.co.uk (n.d.).

208. Mohamed al-Daradji, statement in the pressbook for *Son of Babylon*.

209. See "Oday Rasheed," www.en.wikipedia.org (n.d.).

210. Oday Rasheed, in the pressbook for *Underexposure,* www.art-action.org (n.d.).

211. Oday Rasheed, interview on the making of *Qarantina*, www.blog.globalfilm.org (January 23, 2012).

212. Ted Parker, ibid.

213. Short synopsis of *Narcissus Blossom*, www.berlinale.de (n.d.).

214. Ibid.

215. Devrim Kilic, "Narcissus Should Blossom," www.kurdishcinema.com (June 8, 2006).

216. Haitham Hakki, interview with Line Zouhour Adi, www.blogs.commons.georgetown .edu/alqawl (April 16, 2012).

217. Ibid.

218. Tim Mackintosh-Smith, *Yemen: Travels in Dictionary Land* (London: John Murray, 1997), p. xi.

Bibliography

World Cinema, Colonialism, Immigration

Béji, Hélé. *Le désenchantement national: Essai sur la décolonisation.* Paris: François Maspero / Cahiers Libres, 1982.
Benguigui, Yamina. *Mémoires d'immigrés: L'héritage maghrébin.* Paris: Albin Michel, 1997.
Bernstein, Matthew, and Gaylyn Studlar. *Visions of the East: Orientalism in Film.* London: I. B. Tauris, 1997.
Bossaerts, Marc, and Catherine Van Geel, eds. *Cinéma d'en francophonie.* Brussels: Solibel, 1995.
Chaudhuri, Shohini. *Contemporary World Cinema.* Edinburgh: Edinburgh University Press, 2005.
Codell, Julie F., ed. *Genre, Gender, Race and World Cinema.* Malden, MA: Blackwell, 2007.
Dale, Martin. *The Movie Game.* London: Cassell, 1997.
Dönmez-Colin, Gönül. *Women, Islam and Cinema.* London: Reaktion Books, 2004.
Elad-Bouskila, Ami. *Modern Palestinian Literature and Culture.* London: Frank Cass, 1999.
Elena, Alberto. *"Romancero marroquí": El cine africanista durante la guerra civil.* Madrid: Filmoteca Española, 2005.
Ezra, Elisabeth, and Terry Rowden, eds. *Transnational Cinema: The Film Reader.* London: Routledge, 2006.
Frodon, Jean-Pierre, ed. *Au sud du cinéma.* Paris: Cahiers du Cinéma / ARTE Éditions, 2004.
Gugler, Josef. *"Bedwin Hacker* (Nadia El Fani): A Hacker Challenges Western Domination of the Global Media." In *Film in the Middle East and North Africa,* edited by Josef Gugler, pp. 284–293. Austin: University of Texas Press, 2011.
———, ed. *Film in the Middle East and North Africa.* Austin: University of Texas Press, 2011.
Guneratne, Anthony R., and Wimal Disanayake. *Rethinking Third Cinema.* New York: Routledge, 2003.
Gutmann, Marie-Pierre, ed. *Le partenariat euro-méditerranéen dans le domaine de l'image.* Morocco: Service de Coopération d'Action Culturelle de l'Ambassade de France au Maroc, 1999.
Hafez, Kai. *The Myth of Media Globalization.* Cambridge: Polity Press, 2007.
Hennebelle, Guy. *Les cinémas nationaux contre Hollywood.* Paris: Éditions du Cerf / Éditions Corlet, 2004.
Hjort, Mette, and Scott Mackenzie, eds. *Cinema and Nation.* London: Routledge, 2000.
Iorndanova, Dina, David Martin-Jones, and Belén Vidal, eds. *Cinema at the Periphery.* Detroit: Wayne State University Press, 2010.

Kassir, Samir. *Being Arab*. London: Verso, 2006.

Khalaf, Samir, and Roseanne Saad, eds. *Arab Society and Culture: An Essential Reader*. London: Saqi, 2009.

Koback, Annette. *Isabelle: The Life of Isabelle Eberhardt*. London: Chatto and Windus, 1988.

Lane, Jim. *The Autobiographical Documentary in America*. Madison: University of Wisconsin Press, 2002.

Lazare, Pascal, and Jean-Daniel Simon, eds. *Guide du cinéma africain (1989–1999)*. Paris: Écrans Nord-Sud, 2000.

Leaman, Oliver, ed. *Companion Encyclopedia of Middle Eastern and North African Film*. London: Routledge, 2001.

Mackey, Sandra, *Lebanon: A House Divided*. New York: W. W. Norton, 2006.

Mowitt, John. *Re-takes: Postcoloniality and Foreign Film Languages*. Minneapolis: University of Minnesota Press, 2005.

Naficy, Hamid. *An Accented Cinema: Exilic and Diasporic Filmmaking*. Princeton, NJ: Princeton University Press, 2001.

———, ed. *Home, Exile, Homeland: Film, Media, and the Politics of Place*. New York: Routledge, 1999.

Naudillon, Françoise, and Jean Ouédraogo, eds. *Images et mirages des migrations dans les littératures et les cinémas d'Afrique francophone*. Montreal: Mémoire d'Encrier, 2011.

N'Zelomona, Berthin. *La francophonie*. Paris: L'Harmattan, 2001.

Prédal, René. *Le cinéma d'auteur, une vielle lune?* Paris: Éditions du Cerf, 2001.

———. *Le jeune cinéma français*. Paris: Nathan, 2002, p. 136.

Salibi, Kamal. *A House of Many Mansions: The History of Lebanon Reconsidered*. London: I. B. Tauris, 2005.

Salt, Jeremy. *The Unmaking of the Middle East: A History of Western Disorder in Arab Lands*. Berkeley: University of California Press, 2008.

Sand, Shlomo. *The Invention of the Jewish People*. London: Verso, 2009.

Spagnoletti, Giovanni, ed. *Il cinema europeo del métissage*. Milan: Editrice il Castoro, 2000.

Spass, Lieve. *The Francophone Film: A Struggle for Identity*. Manchester, UK: Manchester University Press, 2000.

Tarr, Carrie. *Reframing Difference: Beur and Banlieue Filmmaking in France*. Manchester, UK: Manchester University Press, 2005.

Trabulsi, Fawwa. *A History of Modern Lebanon*. London: Pluto Press, 2007.

Tshimanga, Charles, Didier Gondala, and Peter J. Bloom, eds. *Frenchness and the African Diaspora*. Bloomington: Indiana University Press, 2009.

Vitali, Valentina, and Paul Willemen, eds. *Theorising National Cinema*. London: BFI, 2006.

Wayne, Mike. *Political Film: The Dialectics of Third Cinema*. London: Pluto Press, 2001.

Studies of Arab Cinema

Abdel-Malek, Kamal. *The Rhetoric of Violence: Arab-Jewish Encounters in Contemporary Palestinian Literature and Film*. New York: Palgrave Macmillan, 2005.

Abderrezak, Hakim. "The Modern Harem in Moknèche's *Le Harem de Mme Ousmane* and *Viva Laldjérie*." In *North African Cinema in a Global Context: Through the Lens of the Diaspora*, edited by Andrea Khalil, pp. 71–92. London: Routledge.

"African Cinema." *Sight and Sound*, February 2007, pp. 26–35.

Ahmad, Ali Nobil, ed. *Cinema in Muslim Countries*. Special issue, *Third Text* 24, no. 3 (2010).

Al-Janabi, Koutaïba. *Far from Baghdad*. Delft: Aqwaas, 2007.

Al-Qattan, Omar. "The Challenges of Palestinian Filmmaking (1990–2003)." In *Dreams of a Nation: On Palestinian Cinema*, edited by Hamid Dabashi, pp. 110–111. London: Verso, 2006.

Al-Roumi, Mayyar [Meyar], and Dorothée Schmid. "Le cinéma syrien: Du militantisme au mutisme."In *Cinéma et monde musulman: Cultures et interdits*. Special issue, *EuroOrient* 10 (2001): 4–25.

Amar Rodriguez, Victor Manuel, ed. *El cine marroqui: Secuencias para su conocimiento*. Cadiz: Servicio de Publicaciones de la Universidad de Cadiz, 2006.

Armbrust, Walter, ed. *Mass Mediations: New Approaches to Popular Culture in the Middle East and Beyond*. Berkeley: University of California Press, 2000.

Armes, Roy. *African Filmmaking: North and South of the Sahara*. Edinburgh: Edinburgh University Press; Bloomington: Indiana University Press, 2006.

———. *Arab Filmmakers of the Middle East: A Dictionary*. Bloomington: Indiana University Press, 2010.

———. "Cinemas of the Maghreb." *Black Camera*, n.s. 1, no. 1 (2009): 5–29.

———. *Dictionary of African Filmmakers*. Bloomington: Indiana University Press, 2008.

———. "Imag(in)ing Europe: The Theme of Emigration in North African Cinema." In *Mediating the Other: Jews, Christians, Muslims and the Media*, edited by Tudor Parfitt and Yulia Egorova, pp. 68–77. London: RoutledgeCurzon 2004.

———. *Postcolonial Images: Studies in North African Film*. Bloomington: Indiana University Press, 2005.

———. "Women Pioneers of Arab Cinema." *Screen* 48, no. 4 (Winter 2007): 517–520.

Austin, Guy. "Against Amnesia: Representation of Memory in Algerian Cinema." *Journal of African Cinemas* 2, no. 1 (2001): 27–35.

Barlet, Olivier. *Les cinémas d'Afrique des années 2000: Perspectives critiques*. Paris: L'Harmattan, 2012.

Bax, Dominique, ed. *Youssef Chahine*. Bobigny: Le Magic Cinéma, 2010.

Bensalah, Mohamed. *Cinéma en Méditerranée, une passerelle entre les cultures*. Aix-en-Provence: Édisud, 2005.

Berrah, Mouny, Victor Bachy, Mohand Ben Salah, and Ferid Boughedir, eds. *Cinémas du Maghreb*. Special issue, *CinémAction* 14 (1981).

Boughedir, Ferid. "Les principales tendances du cinéma tunisien." In *Cinémas du Maghreb*, edited by Mouny Berrah, Victor Bachy, Mohand Ben Salah, and Ferid Boughedir. Special issue, *CinémAction* 14 (1981): 153–160.

Bouzid, Nouri. "New Realism in Arab Cinema: The Defeat-Conscious Cinema." *Alif* 15 (1995): 242–250.

Brahimi, Denise. *50 ans de cinéma maghrébin*. Paris: Minerve, 2009.

Bresheeth, Haim. "The Continuity of Trauma and Struggle: Recent Cinematic Representations of the Nakba." In *Nakba: Palestine, 1948, and the Claims of Memory*, edited by Ahmed H. Sa'di and Lila Abu-Lughod, pp. 161–187. New York: Columbia University Press, 2007.

———. *"Segell Ikhtifa / Chronicle of a Disappearance."* In *The Cinema of North Africa and the Middle East,* edited by Gönül Dönmez-Colin, pp. 168–178. London: Wall-flower Press, 2007.

Caillé, Patricia, and Florence Martin, eds. *Les cinémas du Maghreb et leurs publics.* Africultures 89–90. Paris: L'Harmattan, 2012.

Carter, Sandra Gayle. *What Moroccan Cinema? A Historical and Critical Study, 1956–2006.* Lanham, MD: Lexington Books, 2009.

Challouf, Mohamed, Giuseppe Gariazzo, and Alessandra Speciale, eds. *Un posto sulla terra: Cinema per (r)esistere.* Milan: Editrice il Castoro, 2002.

Chamkhi, Sonia. *Le cinéma tunisien 1996–2006 à la lumière de la modernité.* Manouba, Tunisia: Centre de Publication Universitaire, 2009.

———. *Cinéma tunisien nouveau.* Tunis: Sud Éditions, 2005.

Chikaoui, Tahar. 'Le cinéma tunisien des années 90: Permanences et spécifités." *Horizons maghrébins* 46 (2002): 113–119.

Choukroun, Jacques, and François de La Bretèche, eds. *Algérie d'hier et d'aujourd'hui.* Perpignan: Institut Jean Vigo; *Cahiers de la Cinémathèque* 76, 2004.

Cinéma marocain, filmographie générale longs métrages, 1958–2005. Rabat: Centre Cinématographique Marocain, 2006.

Les cinémas d'Afrique: Dictionnaire. Paris: Éditions Karthala and Éditions ATM, 2000.

Coletti, Maria. *Di diaspro e di corallo: L'immagine della donna nel cinema dell'Africa francofono.* Rome: Fondazione Scuola Nazionale di Cinema, 2001.

Dabashi, Hamid, ed. *Dreams of a Nation: On Palestinian Cinema.* London: Verso, 2006.

———. "Paradise Delayed: With Hany Abu-Assad in Palestine." *Third Text* 24, no. 1 (2010): 11–24.

De Fransceschi, Leonardo. *Hudud! Un viaggio nel cinema maghrebino.* Rome: Bulzoni Editore, 2005.

Deeley, Mona. *"Beyrouth al-Gharbiyya / West Beirut."* In *The Cinema of North Africa and the Middle East,* edited by Gönül Dönmez-Colin, pp. 190–198. London: Wallflower Press, 2007.

Devictor, Agnès, ed. *Cinémas arabes du XXIe siècle: Nouveaux territoires, nouveaux enjeux.* Special issue, *Revue des mondes musulmans et de la Méditerranée* 134 (2013).

Dönmez-Colin, Gönül. *The Cinema of North Africa and the Middle East.* London: Wallflower Press, 2007.

Du fonds d'aide . . . à l'avance sur recettes. Rabat: Centre Cinématographique Marocain, 2006.

Dwyer, Kevin. "Moroccan Filmmaking: A Long Voyage through the Straits of Paradox." In *Everyday Life in the Muslim Middle East,* edited by Donna Lee Bowen and Evelyn A Early, pp. 349–59. Bloomington: Indiana University Press, 2002.

———. "Un pays, une décennie, deux comédies." In *Cinémas du Maghreb,* edited by Michel Serceau. Special issue, *CinémAction* 111 (2004): 86–91.

Edwards, Brian T. *"Marock* in Morocco: Reading Moroccan Films in the Age of Circulation." In *North African Cinema in a Global Context: Through the Lens of the Diaspora,* edited by Andrea Khalil, pp. 11–32. London: Routledge, 2008.

Elena, Alberto, ed. *Las mil y una imágenes de cine marroqui.* Las Palmas: Festival Internacional de Cine de las Palmas de Gran Canaria; Madrid: T&B Editores, 2007.

Friedman, Yael. "Palestinian Filmmaking in Israel: Negotiating Conflicting Discourses." PhD dissertation, Westminster University, London, 2010.

Gertz, Nurith, and George Khleifi. *Palestinian Cinema: Landscape, Trauma and Memory.* Edinburgh: Edinburgh University Press, 2008.

Gugler, Josef. *African Film: Re-imagining a Continent.* London: James Currey, 2003.

——, ed. *Film in the Middle East and North Africa: Creative Dissidence.* Austin: University of Texas Press, 2011.

Hafez, Sabry. "The Quest for / Obsession with the National in Arabic Cinema." In *Theorising National Cinema,* edited by Valentina Vitali and Paul Willemen, pp. 226–253. London: BFI, 2006.

Halbreich-Euvrard, Janine. *Israéliens, Palestiniens: Que peut le cinema? Carnets de route.* Paris: Éditions Michalon, 2005.

Hassan, Nizar. "A Letter from the Rest of the World to 'The Afghan Arabs.'" In *Dreams of a Nation: On Palestinian Cinema,* edited by Hamid Dabashi, pp. 104–109. London: Verso, 2006.

Hawal, Kassem. "Regard sur le cinéma irakien." In *Septième biennale des cinémas arabes,* pp. 99–113. Paris: Institut du Monde Arabe, 2004.

Hellal, Abderrazak. *Histoire du cinéma: "Le refus d'une mise en images"—L'algérien sur les écrans français.* Algiers: Editions Rafar, 2011.

Hillauer, Rebecca. *Freiräume—Lebensträume: Arabische Filmemacherinnen.* Unkel am Rhein: Arte-Edition, 2001. English translation: *Encyclopedia of Arab Women Filmmakers.* Cairo: American University in Cairo Press, 2005.

Hotait, Laila. "Itinéraire des cinéastes libanais de l'après-guerre: Le parcours d'une reconstruction." In *Itinéraires esthétiques et scènes culturelles au Proche Orient,* edited by Nicolas Puig and Franck Mermier, pp. 204–219. Beirut: Presses de l'Ifpo, 2007.

Ismaël. *Cinéma en Tunisie.* Tunis: Arts Distribution, 2008.

Jaïdi, Moulay Driss. *Cinéma et société.* Rabat: Almajal, 2010.

Jemni, Mahmoud. *Quarante ans de cinéma tunisien.* Tunis: Jemni, 2007.

Jibril, Mohamed. "Cinéma marocain, l'improbable image de soi." In *Le Maroc en mouvement: Créations contemporaines,* edited by Nicole de Pontcharra and Maati Kabbal, pp. 179–184. Paris: Maisonneuve et Larose, 2000.

Joyard, Olivier. "La Palestine dans l'oeil d'Elia Suleiman le nomade." *Cahiers du cinéma* 572 (2002): 12–19.

Kchir-Bendana, Kmar. "Ideologies of the Nation in Tunisian Cinema." In *Nation, Society and Culture in North Africa,* edited by James McDougall, pp. 35–42. London: Frank Cass, 2003.

Kennedy-Day, Kiki. "Cinema in Lebanon, Syria, Iraq and Kuwait." In *Companion Encyclopedia of Middle Eastern and North African Film,* edited by Oliver Leaman, pp. 364–419. London: Routledge, 2001.

Khalil, Andrea, ed. *North African Cinema in a Global Context: Through the Lens of the Diaspora.* London: Routledge, 2008.

Khatib, Lina. *Filming the Modern Middle East: Politics in the Cinemas of Hollywood and the Arab World.* London: I. B. Tauris, 2006.

——. "*Kan ya ma kan Beirut / Once upon a Time in Beirut.*" In *The Cinema of North Africa and the Middle East,* edited by Gönül Dönmez-Colin, pp. 156–166. London: Wallflower Press, 2007.

———. *Lebanese Cinema: Imagining the Civil War and Beyond.* London: I. B. Tauris, 2008.

Khayati, Khémais. *En désespoir d'image: Chroniques de cinéma et de télévision.* Tunis: Éditions Sahar, 2000.

Khélil, Hédi. *Abécédaire du cinéma tunisien.* Tunis: Hédi Khélil, 2007.

———. *Le parcours et la trace: Témoignages et documents sur le cinéma tunisien.* Salammbô, Tunisia: MediaCon, 2002.

———. "Representations de la femme dans le cinéma tunisien." In *L'image de la femme au Maghreb,* edited by Khadija Mohsen-Finan, pp. 47–70. Le Méjan, Algeria: Actes Sud; Algiers: Éditions Barzakh, 2008.

Krifat, Michel. "Gros plan sur le cinéma palestinien." In *6e Biennale des cinémas arabes à Paris,* pp. 93–127. Paris: Institut du Monde Arabe, 2002.

Kubala, Patricia. "The Music Video and Muslim Piety: Satellite Television and Islamic Pop Culture in Egypt." In *Arab Society and Culture,* edited by Samir and Rose-anne Saad Khalaf. London: Saqi, 2009.

Kummer, Ida, ed. *Cinéma Maghrébin.* Special issue, *CELAAN* 1, nos. 1–2 (2002).

Leaman, Oliver, ed. *Companion Encyclopedia of Middle Eastern and North African Film.* London: Routledge, 2001.

Lequeret, Elisabeth. *Le cinéma africain: Un continent à la recherche de son propre regard.* Paris: Cahiers du Cinéma / Scérén / CNDP, 2003.

Lledo, Jean-Pierre. "Le cinéma documentaire et la révolution." In *Art et engagement: Actes du colloque en hommage à Abdelhamid Benzine.* Algiers, 2008.

Mackintosh-Smith, Tim. *Yemen: Travels in Dictionary Land.* London: John Murray, 1997.

Mahajar, Jaffar. "The Transformation of the Act of Narration: Strategies of Adaptation of *Al-Qamar w'al-Aswar.*" *Alif: Journal of Comparative Politics* (Cairo) 28 (2008): 165–187.

Mandelbaum, Jacques. "Au Moyen-Orient, tous les cinéastes sont des Palestiniens." In *Au sud du cinéma,* edited by Jean-Michel Frodon, pp. 60–73. Paris: Cahiers du Cinéma / ARTE Éditions, 2004.

Mansouri, Hassouna. *De l'identité, ou Pour une certaine tendance du cinéma africain.* Tunis: Éditions Sahar, 2000.

Martin, Florence. *Screens and Veils: Maghrebi Women's Cinema.* Bloomington: Indiana University Press, 2011.

———. "Tunisia." In *The Cinema of Small Nations,* edited by Mette Hjort and Duncan Petrie, pp. 213–228. Edinburgh: Edinburgh University Press, 2007.

Mével, Quentin, ed. *Le cinéma de Joana Hadjithomas et Khalil Joreige: Entretiens.* Paris: Independencia Editions, 2013.

Miduni, Hamid. *Ahmed Baha Eddine Attia: Une vie comme au cinéma.* Tunis: Editions Rives Productions, 2008.

Millet, Raphaël. *Cinémas de la Méditerranée, cinémas de la mélancolie.* Paris: L'Harmattan, 2002.

Mondolini, Dominique, ed. *Cinémas d'Afrique.* Notre librairie 149. Paris: ADPF, 2002.

Mouawad, Wissam. "Petite réflexion sur le néo-orientalisme." *Cahiers de l'Orient* 106 (2012): 99–104.

Mushengyezi, Aaron. "Problematizing a 'Fundamentalist' Ideology: A Close Analysis of Atef Hetata's *The Closed Doors* and Phil Mullally's *The Martyrs of Uganda.*" *Journal of African Cinemas* 1, no. 2 (2009): 173–188.

Naudillon, Françoise, Janusz Przychodzen, and Sathya Rao, eds. *L'Afrique fait son cinéma: Regards et perspectives sur le cinéma africain francophone.* Montreal: Mémoire d'Encrier, 2006.

N'Zelomona, Berthin. *La francophonie.* Paris: L'Harmattan, 2001.

Orlando, Valérie K. *Francophone Voices of the "New" Morocco in Film and Print: (Re)presenting a Society in Transition.* New York: Palgrave Macmillan, 2009.

———. *Screening Morocco: Contemporary Film in a Changing Society.* Athens: Ohio University Press, 2011.

Où va le cinéma algérien? Special issue, *Cahiers du Cinéma,* hors-série (February–March 2003).

Oudjedi, Larbi. *Rupture et changement dans "La colline oubliée."* Tizi-Ouzou, Algeria: Éditions Achab, 2009.

Pallister, Janis L., and Ruth A. Hottell. *Francophone Women Film Directors: A Guide.* Madison, NJ: Fairleigh Dickinson University Press, 2005.

Petiot, Pierre. *Méditerranée: Le génie du cinéma.* Montpellier: Indigène Éditions, 2009.

Quarante ans de cinéma algérien. Algiers: Dar Raïs Hamidou, 2002.

Salhab, Sabine, ed. *Cinéma: Le Moyen Orient sous les projecteurs.* Special issue, *Cahiers de l'Orient* 106 (2012).

Salti, Rasha. "From Resistance and Bearing Witness to the Power of the Fantastical: Icons and Symbols in Palestinian Poetry and Cinema." *Third Text* 24, no. 1 (2010): 39–52.

———, ed. *Insights into Syrian Cinema: Essays and Conversations with Contemporary Filmmakers.* New York: Rattapallax Press / Arte East, 2006.

———. *"Nujum al-Nahar / Stars in Broad Daylight."* In *The Cinema of North Africa and the Middle East,* edited by Gönül Dönmez-Colin, pp. 101–110. London: Wallflower Press, 2007.

Schoumann, Hélène. *Dictionnaire du cinéma israélien.* Paris: Cosmopole, 2012.

Seigneurie, Ken. *Standing by the Ruins: Elegiac Humanism in Wartime and Postwar Lebanon.* New York: Fordham University Press, 2011.

Serceau, Michel, ed. *Cinémas du Maghreb.* Special issue, *CinémAction* 111 (2004).

Shohat, Ella. *Israeli Cinema: East/West and the Politics of Representation.* 2nd ed. London: I. B. Tauris, 2010.

Smihi, Moumen. *Écrire sur le cinéma: Idées clandestines 1.* Tangiers: Slaïki Frères, 2006.

Soil, Daniel, ed. *Parcours de cinéma.* Tunis: Cérès Éditions, 2010.

Stollery, Martin. "Masculinities, Generations, and Cultural Transformation in Contemporary Tunisian Cinema." *Screen* 42, no. 1 (2001): 49–73.

Thoraval, Yves. *Les écrans du croissant fertile: Irak–Liban–Palestine–Syrie.* Paris: Atlantica-Séguier, 2002.

Thouard, Sylvie, ed. "Palestine-Israel—Territoires cinématographiques." *Revue documentaire* 19–29 (2005): 5–124.

Tsoffar, Ruth. "Forget Baghdad: Jews and Arabs—The Iraqi Connection." In *The Cinema of North Africa and the Middle East,* edited by Gönül Dönmez-Colin, pp. 256–265. London: Wallflower Press, 2007.

Westmoreland, Mark. "Cinematic Dreaming: On Phantom Poetics and the Longing for a Lebanese National Cinema." *Text, Practice, Performance* 4 (2002): 33–50.

White, Jerry. "Children, Narrative and Third Cinema in Iran and Syria." *Canadian Journal of Film Studies* 11, no. 1 (2002): 78–97.

Yahi, Naima, ed. *Images et representations des Maghrébins dans le cinéma en France.* Special issue, *Migrance* 37 (2011).

Yazbek, Elie. *Regards sur le cinéma libanais (1990–2010).* Paris: L'Harmattan, 2012.

Zaatari, Akram. *A Conversation with an Imagined Israeli Filmmaker Named Avi Mograbi.* Aubervilliers: Laboratoires d'Aubervilliers; Paris: Kadist Art Foundation; Berlin: Sternberg Press, 2012.

Zaccak, Hady. *Le cinéma libanais: Itinéraire d'un cinéma vers l'inconnu (1929–1996).* Beirut: Dar al-Mashreq, 1997.

Index

·

Roy Armes is emeritus professor of film at Middlesex University in the United Kingdom. He has published widely on world cinema for the past forty-five years, with 20 books, contributions to some 60 collectively authored volumes, and 180 journal articles and shorter pieces. His initial concern was with European film history (France, Italy, the United Kingdom) and aspects of cinematic modernism. More recently, his research—beginning with the widely distributed *Third World Film Making and the West* in 1987—has focused on third-world issues and, especially, on African and Arab cinemas: *Arab and African Film Making* (with Lizbeth Malkmus, 1991), *Dictionary of North African Film Makers / Dictionnaire des cinéastes du Maghreb* (1996), *Omar Gatlato* (1998), *Postcolonial Images: Studies in North African Film* (2005), *African Filmmaking: North and South of the Sahara* (2006), *Dictionary of African Filmmakers* (2008), and *Arab Filmmakers of the Middle East: A Dictionary* (2010). His work has been translated into fourteen languages, with books published in French, Spanish, (Brazilian) Portuguese, Hebrew, Arabic, Japanese, and Chinese.